Religious Approaches to Death

Edited by
David Gordon White

KENDALL/HUNT PUBLISHING COMPANY
4050 Westmark Drive Dubuque, Iowa 52002

ISBN 0-7575-2887-2

Printed in the United States of America

10 9 8 7 6 5 4 3 2

Contents

Chapter 1

The Epic of GILGAMESH

Translated by Maureen Gallery Kovacs

A DREAM OF THE DEAD

152 Enkidu's innards were churning,
lying there so alone.
He spoke everything he felt, saying to his friend:
"Listen, my friend, to the dream that I had last night.
The heavens cried out and the earth replied,
and I was standing between them.
There appeared a man of dark visage—
his face resembled the Anzu,[1]
his hands were the paws of a lion,
his nails the talons of an eagle!—
he seized me by my hair and overpowered me.
I struck him a blow, but he skipped about like a jump rope,
and then he struck me and capsized me like a *raft*,
and trampled on me like a wild bull.
He encircled my whole body in a clamp.
167 'Help me, my friend!' (I cried),
but you did not rescue me, you were afraid and did not . . ."
[4 lines are missing here.]
173 "Then he . . . and turned me into a dove,
so that my arms *were feathered* like a bird.
Seizing me, he led me down to the House of Darkness, the dwelling of Irkalla,
to the House where those who enter do not come out,
along the road of no return,

to the House where those who dwell do without light,
where dirt is their drink, their food is of clay,
where, like a bird, they wear garments of feathers,
and light cannot be seen, they dwell in the dark,
and upon the door and bolt lies dust.
On entering the House of Dust,
everywhere I looked there were royal crowns gathered in heaps,
everywhere I listened, it was the bearers of crowns who in the past had ruled the land,
but who now served Anu and Enlil cooked meats,
served confections, and poured cool water from waterskins.
188 In the House of Dust that I entered
there sat the high priest and acolyte,
there sat the purification priest and ecstatic,
there sat the anointed priests of the Great Gods.
There sat Etana, there sat Sumukan,
there sat Ereshkigal, the Queen of the Netherworld.
Beletseri, the Scribe of the Netherworld, knelt before her,
she was holding the tablet[2] and was reading it out to her (Ereshkigal).
She raised her head and when she saw me—
197 '*Who* has taken this *man*?'"

[Only the last word of a few of the next 50 lines remain: grave, Ereshkigal, ecstatic priest, flood, Egalmah. The text resumes apparently with Enkidu speaking to Gilgamesh:]

248 " . . . I (?) who went through every difficulty,
remember *me and forget (?) not* all that I went through (with you)."

[Gilgamesh speaks:]

"My friend has had a dream that *bodes ill(?).*"

The day he had the dream . . . came to an end.

THE DEATH OF ENKIDU

252 Enkidu lies down a first day, a second day,
that Enkidu . . . in his bed;
a third day and fourth day, that *Enkidu . . . in his bed;*
a fifth, a sixth, and seventh, *that Enkdu . . . in his bed;*
an eighth, a ninth, a tenth, *that Enkidu . . . in his bed.*
Enkidu's illness *grew ever worse.*
The eleventh and twelfth day *his illness grew ever worse.*
Enkidu *drew up* from his bed,
and called out to Gilgamesh . . . :[3]

261 "My friend hates me . . .
(Once), while he *talked with me* in *Uruk*
as I was afraid of the battle (with Humbaba), he encouraged me.
My friend who *saved* me in battle *has now abandoned me!*
I and *you* . . ."

[About 20 lines are missing here to the end of the tablet, telling of Enkidu's death. A passage from the Megiddo tablet may belong here.]

At his noises (death rattle) *Gilgamesh* was roused . . .
Like a dove he moaned . . .
"May he not be held, in death . . .
O preeminent among *men* . . ."
To his friend . . .
"I will mourn him (?) . . .
I at *his side* . . ."

Watching by Enkidu's deathbed, Gilgamesh pours out a torrent of memories about their experiences together, and in disbelief touches the stilled heart. He then casts off his regal finery and puts on the rough skins of a wanderer of the wilderness. He has a rich memorial statue crafted, dedicated to "My Friend," as promised, and has the city go into mourning. Following a long break which probably involves funerary rituals, Gilgamesh makes an offering to Shamash, and then probably sets out on a journey. An earlier Sumerian work known as "The Lamentation over Enkidu" is too poorly preserved to compare to Tablet VIII. The Neo-Assyrian composition purporting to be a letter of Gilgamesh (discussed in the last section of the Introduction) draws on the material of this tablet.

Tablet VIII is very poorly preserved, missing more than 175 lines, and one of the principal texts is a school copy full of errors.

LAMENTATION OVER ENKIDU

1 Just as day began to dawn
Gilgamesh addressed his friend, saying:
"Enkidu, your mother, the gazelle,
and your father, the wild donkey, engendered you,
four wild asses raised you on their milk,
and the herds taught you all the grazing lands.
May the Roads of Enkidu to the Cedar Forest mourn you
and not fall silent night or day.
May the Elders of the broad city of Uruk-Haven mourn you.
May the peoples who gave their blessing after us mourn you.
May the men of the mountains and hills mourn you.
May the . . .

May the pasture lands shriek in mourning as if it were your mother.
May the . . . , the cypress, and the cedar which we destroyed(?) in our anger mourn you.
May the bear, hyena, panther, tiger, water buffalo (?), jackal, lion, wild bull, stag, ibex, all the creatures of the plains mourn you.
May the holy River Ulaja, along whose banks we grandly used to stroll, mourn you.
May the pure Euphrates, to which we would libate water from our water skins, mourn you.
May the men of Uruk-Haven, whom we saw in our battle when we killed the Bull of Heaven, mourn you.
May the farmer . . . , who extols your name in his sweet work song, mourn you.
May the . . . of the broad city, who . . . exalted your name, mourn you.
May the herder . . . , who prepared butter and light beer for your mouth, mourn you.
May . . . , who put ointments on your back, mourn you.
May . . . , who prepared fine beer for your mouth, mourn you.
May the harlot, . . . you rubbed yourself with oil and felt good, mourn you.
May . . . , . . . of the wife placed(?) a ring on you . . . , mourn you.
. . .
May the brothers go into mourning over you like sisters;
. . . the lamentation priests, may their hair be shorn off on your behalf.
Enkidu, your mother and your father are in the wastelands,
I mourn you . . ."
"Hear me, O Elders of Uruk, hear me, O men!
I mourn for Enkidu, my friend,
I shriek in anguish like a mourner.
You, axe at my side, so trusty at my hand—
you, sword at my waist, shield in front of me,
you, my festal garment, a sash over my loins—
an *evil demon*(?) appeared and took him away from me!
My friend, the swift mule, fleet wild ass of the mountain, panther of the wilderness,
Enkidu, my friend, the swift mule, fleet wild ass of the mountain, panther of the wilderness,
after we joined together and went up into the mountain,
fought the Bull of Heaven and killed it,
and overwhelmed Humbaba, who lived in the Cedar Forest,
now what is this sleep which has seized you?
You have turned dark and do not hear me!"

45 But his (Enkidu's) eyes do not move,
he touched his heart, but it beat no longer.
He covered his friend's face like a bride,
swooping down over him like an eagle,
and like a lioness deprived of her cubs
he keeps pacing to and fro.
He shears off his curls and heaps them onto the ground,
ripping off his finery and casting it away as an abomination.

THE MONUMENT TO "MY FRIEND"

53 Just as day began to dawn, Gilgamesh . . .
and issued a call to the land:
"You, blacksmith! You, lapidary! You, coppersmith!
You, goldsmith! You, jeweler!
Create 'My Friend,' *fashion a statue of him.*
. . . he fashioned a statue of his friend.
His features . . .
. . . , your chest will be of lapis lazuli, your skin will be of gold."
[20 lines are missing here[4]]
81 "I had you recline on the great couch,
indeed, on the couch of honor I let you recline,
I had you sit in the position of ease, the seat at the left, so the princes of the world kissed your feet.
I had the people of Uruk mourn and moan for you,
I filled happy people with woe over you,
and after you (died) I let a filthy mat of hair grow over my body,
and donned the skin of a lion and roamed the wilderness."
Just as day began to dawn,
he undid his straps . . .
91 . . . carnelian,
[85 lines are missing here.[5]]
177 " . . . to my friend.
. . . your dagger
. . .
to Bibbi . . ."
[40 lines are missing here.]
221 " . . . the judge of the Anunnaki."
When Gilgamesh heard this
the *zikru* of the river(?) he created . . .
Just as day began to dawn Gilgamesh opened(?) . . .

and brought out a big table of sissoo wood.
A carnelian bowl he filled with honey,
a lapis lazuli bowl he filled with butter.
228 He provided . . . and displayed it before Shamash.
[All of the last column, some 40–50 lines, is missing.]

Gilgamesh is grief-stricken by the loss of his friend, and becomes acutely aware that such will one day be his own fate. Rebelling, he determines to find the secret of eternal life from the only mortal man known to have attained it. This is Utanapishtim, a king who in ancient times survived the great Flood, and now lives at the Mouth of the Rivers, at the end of the earth. In spite of what the surviving fragments suggest is an ominous dream, Gilgamesh sets out. On the first stage of his quest he meets a scorpion-being and its mate, who guard the passage through the mountain of the rising sun. They try to dissuade him from this treacherous and ultimately futile journey, but Gilgamesh insists and they allow him on. Through ten leagues of pitch darkness (the hours of deep night) he walks, until at dawn, the twelfth hour, he finds himself in a fabulous jeweled garden. He continues on to the edge of the sea, where he sees the house of Siduri.

This is the worst-preserved tablet of the entire Standard Version, and may have been composed relatively late in the development of the Epic. A Hittite fragment of the Middle Babylonian period has a parallel to the curious episode of the attack by two lions at night and the appeal to the Moon God Sin (IX, 7–9), followed immediately (3 lines later) by the departure of Gilgamesh and his reaching the sea where Siduri lived.

THE QUEST

1 Over his friend, Enkidu, Gilgamesh cried bitterly, roaming the wilderness.
"I am going to die!—am I not like Enkidu?!
Deep sadness penetrates my core,
I fear death, and now roam the wilderness—
I will set out to the region of Utanapishtim, son of Ubartutu, and will go with utmost dispatch!
When I arrived at mountain passes at nightfall,[6]
I saw lions, and I was terrified!
I raised my head in prayer to Sin,
To . . . *the Great Lady* of the gods my supplications poured forth, 'Save me from . . . !'"
He was sleeping *in the night*, but awoke with a start with a dream:

11 *A warrior*(?) enjoyed his life—,
he raised his axe in his hand,
drew the dagger from his sheath,
and fell into their midst like an arrow.
He struck . . . and he scattered *them*,
. . .
. . .
. . .
The name of the former . . .
The name of the second . . .
[26 lines are missing here, telling of the beginning of his quest.]

UTANAPISHTIM

179 Utanapishtim was gazing off into the distance,
puzzling to himself he said, wondering to himself:
"Why are 'the stone things' of the boat smashed to pieces?
And why is someone not its master sailing on it?
The one who is coming is not a man of mine, . . .
I keep looking but not . . .
I keep looking but not . . .
I keep looking . . ."
[20 lines are missing here.]
207 Utanapishtim said to Gilgamesh:
"Why are your cheeks emaciated, your expression desolate?
Why is your heart so wretched, your features so haggard?
Why is there such sadness deep within you?
Why do you look like one who has been traveling a long distance
so that ice and heat have seared your face?
. . . you roam the wilderness?"
214 Gilgamesh spoke to Utanapishtim saying:
"Should not my cheeks be emaciated, my expression desolate?
Should my heart not be wretched, my features not haggard?
Should there not be sadness deep within me?
Should I not look like one who has been traveling a long distance,
and should ice and heat not have seared my face?
. . . should I not roam the wilderness?
My friend who chased wild asses in the mountain, the panther of the wilderness,
Enkidu, my friend, who chased wild asses in the mountain, the panther of the wilderness,

we joined together, and went up into the mountain.
We grappled with and killed the Bull of Heaven,
we destroyed Humbaba who dwelled in the Cedar Forest,
we slew lions in the mountain passes!
227 My friend, whom I love deeply, who went through every hardship with me,
Enkidu, my friend, whom I love deeply, who went through
every hardship with me,
the fate of mankind has overtaken him.
Six days and seven nights I mourned over him
and would not allow him to be buried
until a maggot fell out of his nose.
I was terrified *by his appearance*(?),
I began to fear death, and so roam the wilderness.
The issue of my friend oppresses me,
so I have been roaming long trails through the wilderness.
The issue of Enkidu, my friend, oppresses me,
so I have been roaming long roads through the wilderness.
How can I stay silent, how can I be still?
My friend whom I love has turned to clay;
Enkidu, my friend whom I love, has turned to clay!
Am I not like him? Will I lie down never to get up again?"
243 Gilgamesh spoke to Utanapishtim, saying:
"That is why (?) I must go on, to see Utanapishtim whom they call
'The Faraway.'[7]
I went circling through all the mountains,
I traversed treacherous mountains, and crossed all the seas—
that is why (?) sweet sleep has not mellowed my face,
through sleepless striving I am strained,
my muscles are filled with pain.
I had not yet reached the tavern-keeper's area before my clothing gave out.
I killed bear, hyena, lion, panther, tiger, stag, red-stag, and beasts of
the wilderness;
I ate their meat and wrapped their skins around me.[8]
The gate of grief must be bolted shut, *sealed* with pitch and bitumen!
As for me, dancing . . .
For me unfortunate(?) it(?) will root out . . ."
256 Utanapishtim spoke to Gilgamesh, saying:[9]
"Why, Gilgamesh, do you . . . sadness?
You who *were created* (?) from the flesh of gods and mankind
who made . . . like your father and mother?
Have you ever . . . Gilgamesh . . . to the fool . . .
They placed a chair in the Assembly, . . .

But to the fool they gave beer dregs instead of butter,
bran and cheap flour which like . . .
Clothed with a loincloth (?) like . . .
And . . . in place of a sash,
because he does not have . . .
does not have words of counsel . . .
268 Take care about it, Gilgamesh,
. . . their master . . .
. . . Sin . . .
. . . eclipse of the moon . . .
The gods are sleepless . . .
They are troubled, restless(?) . . .
Long ago it has been established . . .
You trouble yourself . . .
. . . your help . . .
If Gilgamesh . . . the temple of the gods,
. . . the temple of the holy gods,
. . . the gods . . .
. . .
. . . mankind,
they took . . . for his fate.
You have toiled without cease, and what have you got?
Through toil you wear yourself out,
you fill your body with grief,
your long lifetime you are bringing near (to a premature end)!
Mankind, whose offshoot is snapped off like a reed in a canebreak,
the fine youth and lovely girl
. . . death.
290 No one can see death,
no one can see the face of death,
no one can hear the voice of death,
yet there is savage death that snaps off mankind.
For how long do we build a household?
For how long do we seal a document?
For how long do brothers share the inheritance?
For how long is there to be jealousy in the land(?)?
298 For how long has the river risen and brought the overflowing waters,
so that dragonflies drift down the river?[10]
The face that could gaze upon the face of the Sun
has never existed ever.
How alike are the sleeping(?) and the dead.
The image of Death cannot be depicted.
(Yes, you are a) human being, a man (?)!

305 After Enlil had pronounced the blessing,[11]
the Anunnaki, the Great Gods, assembled.
Mammetum, she who fashions destiny, determined destiny with them.
They established Death and Life,
309 but they did not make known 'the days of death.'"[12]

A CHANCE AT IMMORTALITY

[The Story of the Flood ends. Utanapishtim now addresses Gilgamesh again.]

204 "Now then, who will convene the gods on your behalf,
that you may find the life that you are seeking?
Wait! You must not lie down for six days and seven nights."
As soon as he sat down (with his head) between his legs
sleep, like a fog, blew upon him.
Utanapishtim said to his wife:
"Look there! The man, the youth who wanted (eternal) life!
Sleep, like a fog, blew over him."
His wife said to Utanapishtim the Faraway:
"Touch him, let the man awaken.
Let him return safely by the way he came.
Let him return to his land by the gate through which he left."
216 Utanapishtim said to his wife:
"Mankind is deceptive, and will deceive you.
Come, bake loaves for him and keep setting them by his head
and draw on the wall each day that he lay down."
She baked his loaves and placed them by his head
and marked on the wall the day that he lay down.
The first loaf was dessicated,
the second stale, the third moist(?), the fourth turned white, its . . . ,
the fifth sprouted gray (mold), the sixth is still fresh.
The seventh—suddenly he touched him and the man awoke.
226 Gilgamesh said to Utanapishtim:
"The very moment sleep was pouring over me
you touched me and alerted me!"
Utanapishtim spoke to Gilgamesh, saying:
"*Look over here,* Gilgamesh, count your loaves!
You should be aware of what is *marked on the wall!*
Your first loaf is dessicated,
the second stale, the third moist, your fourth turned white, its . . .
the fifth sprouted gray (mold), the sixth is still fresh.
The seventh—at that instant you awoke!"

Gilgamesh said to Utanapishtim the Faraway:
"O woe! What shall I do, Utanapishtim, where shall I go?
The Snatcher has taken hold of my flesh,
in my bedroom Death dwells,
and wherever I set foot there too is Death!"

HOME EMPTY-HANDED

241 Utanapishtim said to Urshanabi, the ferryman:
"May the harbor reject you, may the ferry landing reject you!
May you who used to walk its shores be denied its shores!
The man in front of whom you walk, matted hair chains his body,
animal skins have ruined his beautiful skin.
Take him away, Urshanabi, bring him to the washing place.
Let him wash his matted hair in water like *ellu*.
Let him cast away his animal skin and have the sea carry it off,
let his body be moistened with fine oil,
let the wrap around his head be made new,
let him wear royal robes worthy of him!
Until he goes off to his city,
until he sets off on his way,
let his royal robe not become spotted, let it be perfectly new!"
255 Urshanabi took him away and brought him to the washing place.
He washed his matted hair with water like *ellu*.
He cast off his animal skin and the sea carried it off.
He moistened his body with fine oil,
and made a new wrap for his head.
He put on a royal robe worthy of him.
Until he went away to his city,
until he set off on his way,
his royal robe remained unspotted, it was perfectly clean.
Gilgamesh and Urshanabi boarded the boat,
they cast off the *magillu*-boat, and sailed away.

A SECOND CHANCE AT LIFE

266 The wife of Utanapishtim the Faraway said to him:
"Gilgamesh came here exhausted and worn out.
What can you give him so that he can return to his land (with honor)?"
Then Gilgamesh raised a punting pole
and drew the boat to shore.

Utanapishtim spoke to Gilgamesh, saying:
"Gilgamesh, you came here exhausted and worn out.
What can I give you so you can return to your land?
I will disclose to you a thing that is hidden, Gilgamesh,
a . . . I will tell you.
There is a plant . . . like a boxthorn,
whose thorns will prick your hand like a rose.
If your hands reach that plant *you will become a young man again.*"
266 Hearing this, Gilgamesh opened a conduit(?) (to the Apsu)
and attached heavy stones to his feet.
They dragged him down, to the Apsu they pulled him.
He took the plant, though it pricked his hand,
and cut the heavy stones from his feet,
letting the *waves*(?) throw him onto its shores.
Gilgamesh spoke to Urshanabi, the ferryman, saying:
"Urshanabi, this plant is a plant against decay(?)
by which a man can attain his survival(?).
I will bring it to Uruk-Haven,
and have an old man eat the plant to test it.
The plant's name is 'The Old Man Becomes a Young Man.'[13]
Then I will eat it and return to the condition of my youth."
At twenty leagues they broke for some food,
at thirty leagues they stopped for the night.
294 Seeing a spring and how cool its waters were,
Gilgamesh went down and was bathing in the water.
A snake smelled the fragrance of the plant,
silently came up and carried off the plant.
While going back it sloughed off its casing.[14]
At that point Gilgamesh sat down, weeping,
his tears streaming over the side of his nose.
"*Counsel me,* O ferryman Urshanabi!
For whom have my arms labored, Urshanabi?
For whom has my heart's blood roiled?
I have not secured any good deed for myself,
but done a good deed for the 'lion of the ground'!"[15]
Now the high waters are coursing twenty leagues distant,[16]
as I was opening the conduit(?) I turned my equipment over into it (?).
What can I find (to serve) as a marker(?) for me?
I will turn back (from the journey by sea) and leave the boat by the shore!"

DEEDS OVER DEATH

310 At twenty leagues they broke for some food,
at thirty leagues they stopped for the night.
They arrived in Uruk-Haven.
Gilgamesh said to Urshanabi, the ferryman:
"Go up, Urshanabi, onto the wall of Uruk and walk around.
Examine its foundation, inspect its brickwork thoroughly—
is not (even the core of) the brick structure of kiln-fired brick,
and did not the Seven Sages themselves layout its plan?
One league city, one league palm gardens, one league lowlands, the open area(?) of the Ishtar Temple,
319 three leagues and the open area(?) of Uruk it (the wall) encloses."

ENDNOTES

1. The lion-headed eagle of mythology.
2. "The tablet" refers to the "Tablet of Destinies," inscribed with the fates of the dead.
3. Only the first half of the following lines are preserved, for which a totally different restoration and interpretation are found in A. Schott and Wolfram von Soden, *Das Gilgamesch-Epos* (Stuttgart: Philipp Reclam, 1958, rev. ed. 1982.), p. 70:
   "I have been cursed, my friend, *with a great curse,*
   I do not die like one who *falls in fighting.*
   I was afraid of battle *so I die without peace.*
   My friend, he who dies in battle *is fortunate.*
   But I *suffer disgrace in death* (?)."
4. In the break was probably a description of Gilgamesh sitting in ritual mourning for six days and seven nights, since this is mentioned in Tablet X.
5. Another tablet fragment with the ends of some twenty lines on each side may belong here in the Epic of Gilgamesh or may be a related text. It mentions jewels, precious stones, gold "for his friend," gold overlays, followed by some offerings of "*mashaltappu* of the earth/Netherworld" to Shamash, and the phrases "may he go by his side," "whose forehead is of lapis lazuli," "inlaid with carnelian."
6. The tenses in the next lines are difficult, and have been "adjusted" for sense. This enigmatic episode with the killing of two lions is referred to again in Tablet X, 57, and parallels. The Hittite fragment reads: "The heroic god Sin *said:* 'These two lions which you have killed, go take the two of them into the city, take them into the temple of Sin.'" Both the lion and the following dream episode seem garbled.
7. Apparently Gilgamesh has not yet realized that he is already talking with Utanapishtim, whom he expected to look very different from an ordinary human being. (See beginning of Tablet XI). It is only after Utanapishtim's soliloquy on death that Gilgamesh realizes whom he is speaking to.
8. The following three lines are fragmentary, and what is preserved is still obscure. These lines may be related to the equally obscure two lines in the Old Babylonian version which follow "He put on their skins and ate their meat" (clearly an echo of the present line): "*In* the wells, Gilgamesh, that which has never been, . . . my wind will lead on the waters (?)."

9. The following speech, only partly intelligible, may be derived from traditional Mesopotamian wisdom literature. The gist of Utanapishtim's remarks in lines 260–67 may be that "the village idiot . . . wears wretched clothes and eats bad food, but no one accords him merit for that—he is just a fool." (Interpretation of Foster, "Gilgamesh: Sex, Love and the Ascent of Knowledge," p. 41.)
10. This and the next five lines are much disputed, and open to sharply different interpretation. W. G. Lambert, who edited the entire speech of Utanapishtim in "The Theology of Death," in B. Alster, ed., *Death in Mesopotamia* (vol. 8 of *Mesopotamia;* Copenhagen, 1980), p. 56, proposes:

X vi 22 = 299	So that dragonflies drift on the river,
23	Their faces staring into the face of the sun god?
24	Suddenly there is nothing.
25	The prisoner and the dead are alike,
26	Death itself cannot be depicted.
27 = 304	But Lullu—man—is incarcerated.

11. Finishing his soliloquy on life and death, Utanapishtim here reveals how death came to be the fate of mankind, and implicitly how Utanapishtim himself was spared. This is apparently the "secret of the gods" that Gilgamesh has been seeking. These last five lines refer to the "Myth of Atrahasis" (Atrahasis = Utanapishtim), in which Enlil grudgingly allows the pious Atrahasis who escaped the Flood to live for eternity, but Enlil and the other gods then establish death for all other humans as a necessary means of population control. The Flood Story is retold at length in Tablet XI.
12. The "days of death" probably means the day on which an individual's death will occur, although some interpret the line to mean "they did not fix a limit to death."
13. The same as the apparent meaning of the name "Gilgamesh."
14. This scene is an etiological story of how the snake came to shed its old skin—after eating a "plant of rejuvenation."
15. "Lion of the ground" is a very rare phrase occurring only here and in scribal word lists. A translation "chameleon" has been proposed because the "chameleon" in Greek appeared to be composed of the same elements, "lion of the ground." "Chameleon" is now believed, however, to be not a native Greek compound, but itself a loan translation from Semitic.
16. This line and those following are fragmentary, and the sense is not at all certain. The verbal tenses in line 309 are normally understood as "Would that I had turned back and left the boat by the shore." A past conditional could reflect Gilgamesh's regret at his failed journey. On the other hand, the adjacent lines suggest that Gilgamesh and Urshanahi now abandon the sea voyage for lack of certain equipment (l. 307) and continue overland to Uruk. The present translation reflects this understanding.

Chapter 2

Gilgamesh in Quest of Immortality

Mircea Eliade

The *Epic of Gilgamesh* is certainly the best known and most popular of Babylonian creations. Its hero, Gilgamesh, king of Uruk, was already famous in the archaic period, and the Sumerian version of several episodes from his legendary life has been found. Despite these antecedents, however, the *Epic of Gilgamesh* is a product of the Semitic genius. It is in the Akkadian version in which it was composed on the basis of various isolated episodes that we may read one of the most moving tales of the quest for immortality, or more precisely, of the final failure of an undertaking that seemed to have every possibility of succeeding. This saga, which begins with the erotic excesses of a hero who is at the same time a tyrant, reveals, in the last analysis, the inability of purely "heroic" virtues radically to transcend the human condition.

And yet Gilgamesh was two-thirds a divine being, son of the goddess Ninsun and a mortal.[1] At the outset the text praises his omniscience and the grandiose works of construction that he had undertaken. But immediately afterward we are presented with a tyrant who violates women and girls and wears men out in forced labor. The inhabitants pray to the gods, and the gods decide to create a being of gigantic size who can confront Gilgamesh. This half-savage creature, who receives the name of Enkidu, lives in peace with the wild beasts; they all drink together at the same springs. Gilgamesh obtains knowledge of his existence first in a dream and then from a hunter who had come upon him. He sends a courtesan to bewitch him by her charms and lead him to Uruk. As the gods had foreseen, the two champions compete as soon as they meet each other. Gilgamesh emerges victorious, but he conceives an affection for Enkidu and makes him his companion. In the last analysis, the gods' plan was not foiled; henceforth Gilgamesh will expend his strength on heroic adventures.

Accompanied by Enkidu, he sets out for the distant and fabulous forest of cedars, which is guarded by a monstrous and all-powerful being, Huwawa. After cutting down his sacred cedar, the two heroes kill him. On his way back to Uruk, Ishtar sees Gilgamesh. The goddess invites him to marry her, but he returns an insolent refusal. Humiliated, Ishtar begs her father, Anu, to create the Bull of Heaven to destroy Gilgamesh and his city. Anu at first refuses, but he gives in when Ishtar threatens to bring the dead back from the underworld. The Bull of Heaven charges at Uruk, and its bellowings make the king's men drop dead by hundreds. However, Enkidu succeeds in catching it by the tail, and Gilgamesh thrusts his sword into its neck. Furious, Ishtar mounts the city walls and curses the king. Intoxicated by their victory, Enkidu tears a thigh from the Bull of Heaven and throws it at the goddess's feet, at the same time assailing her with insults. This is the culminating moment in the career of the two heroes, but it is also the prologue to a tragedy. That same night Enkidu dreams that he has been condemned by the gods. The next day he falls ill, and, twelve days later, he dies.

An unexpected change makes Gilgamesh unrecognizable. For seven days and seven nights, he mourns for his friend and refuses to let him be buried. He hopes that his laments will finally bring him back to life. It is not until the body shows the first signs of decomposition that Gilgamesh yields, and Enkidu is given a magnificent funeral. The king leaves the city and wanders through the desert, complaining: "Shall not I, too, die like Enkidu?" (tablet 9, column 1, line 4).[2] He is terrified by the thought of death. Heroic exploits do not console him. Henceforth his only purpose is to escape from the human condition, to gain immortality. He knows that the famous Utnapishtim, survivor of the flood, is still alive, and he decides to search for him.

His journey is full of ordeals of the initiatory type. He comes to the mountains of Mashu and finds the gate through which the Sun passes daily. The gate is guarded by a scorpion-man and his wife, "whose glance is death" (9. 2. 7). The invincible hero is paralyzed by fear and prostrates himself humbly. But the scorpion-man and his wife recognize the divine part of Gilgamesh and allow him to enter the tunnel. After walking for twelve hours in darkness, Gilgamesh comes to a marvelous garden on the other side of the mountains. Some distance away, by the seaside, he meets the nymph Siduri and asks her where he can find Utnapishtim. Siduri tries to make him change his mind: "When the gods made men, they saw death for men; they kept life for themselves. Thou, Gilgamesh, fill thy belly and make merry by day and night. On each day make a feast, and dance and play, day and night."[3]

But Gilgamesh holds to his decision, and then Siduri sends him to Urshanabi, Utnapishtim's boatman, who happened to be nearby. They cross the Waters of Death and reach the shore on which Utnapishtim lived. Gilgamesh asks him how he had gained immortality. He thus learns the story of the flood and the gods' decision to make Utnapishtim and his wife their "kin," establishing them "at the mouths of the rivers." "But," Utnapishtim asks Gilgamesh, "as for thee, which of the gods will unite thee to their assembly, that thou mayest obtain the life that thou seekest?" (11. 198). However, what he goes on to say is unexpected: "Up, try not to sleep for six days and seven nights!" (199). What we have here is, undoubtedly, the most difficult of initiatory ordeals: conquering sleep, remaining "awake," is equivalent to a transmutation of the human condition.[4] Are we to take it that Utnapishtim, knowing that the gods will not grant Gilgamesh immortality, suggests that he conquer it by means of an initiation? The hero has already successfully gone through several ordeals: the journey through the tunnel, the "temptation" by Siduri, crossing the Waters of Death. These were in some sense ordeals of the heroic type. This time, however, the ordeal is "spiritual," for only an unusual power of concentration can enable a human being to remain awake for six days and seven nights. But Gilgamesh at once falls asleep, and Utnapishtim exclaims sarcastically: "Look at the strong man who desires immortality: sleep has come over him like a violent wind!" (203–4). He sleeps without a break for six days and seven nights; and, when Utnapishtim wakes him, Gilgamesh reproaches him for waking him when he had only just fallen asleep. However, he has to accept the evidence, and he falls to lamenting again: "What shall I do, Utnapishtim, where shall I go? a demon has taken possession of my body; in the room in which I sleep, death lives, and wherever I go, death is there!" (230–34).

Gilgamesh now makes ready to leave, but at the last moment Utnapishtim, at his wife's suggestion, reveals a "secret of the gods" to him: the place where he can find the plant that brings back youth.

Gilgamesh goes down to the bottom of the sea, gathers it,[5] and starts back rejoicing. After traveling for a few days, he sees a spring of fresh water and hurries to bathe. Attracted by the odor of the plant, a snake comes out of the spring, carries off the plant, and sheds its skin.[6] Sobbing, Gilgamesh complains to Urshanabi of his bad fortune. This episode may be read as a failure in another initiatory ordeal: the hero failed to profit from an unexpected gift; in short, he was lacking in wisdom. The text ends abruptly: arrived at Uruk, Gilgamesh invites Urshanabi to go up on the city walls and admire its foundations.[7]

The *Epic of Gilgamesh* has been seen as a dramatized illustration of the human condition, defined by the inevitability of death. Yet this first masterpiece of universal literature can also be understood as illustrating the belief that certain beings are capable, even without help from the gods, of obtaining immortality, on the condition that they successfully pass through a series of initiatory ordeals. Seen from this point of view, the story of Gilgamesh would prove to be the dramatized account of a failed initiation.

ENDNOTES

1. A high priest of the city of Uruk, according to Sumerian tradition; see A. Heidel, *The Gilgamesh Epic,* p. 4.
2. Except as otherwise indicated, we follow the translation by Contenau, *L'épopée de Gilgamesh.*
3. Tablet X, column III, lines 6–9; after the translation by Jean Nougayrol, *Histoire des religions,* vol. 1, p. 222.
4. See Eliade, *Birth and Rebirth,* pp. 14 ff.
5. We may wonder why Gilgamesh did not eat it as soon as he had gathered it, but he was saving it for later; see Heidel, *The Gilgamesh Epic,* p. 62, n. 211.
6. This is a well-known folklore theme: by shedding its old skin, the snake renews its life.
7. Tablet XII, composed in Sumerian, was added later; the incidents narrated in it have no direct relation to the narrative we have summarized.

Chapter 3

Koran: The Heights

Translated by N.J. Dawood

In the Name of Allah, the Compassionate, the Merciful

Alif *lam mim sad.* This Book is revealed to you: let your heart not be troubled about it. It is revealed to you that you may thereby warn the unbelievers and admonish the faithful.

Observe that which is brought down to you[1] from your Lord and do not follow other masters besides Him. But you seldom take warning.

How many cities have We laid in ruin! In the night Our scourge fell upon them, or at midday, when they were drowsing.

And when Our scourge fell upon them, their only cry was: 'We have indeed been wicked men.'

We will question those to whom Our message was sent, as We shall question Our messengers. With knowledge We will recount to them what they have done, for We are watching over all their actions.

On that day their deeds shall be weighed with justice. Those whose scales are heavy shall triumph, but those whose scales are light shall lose their souls, because they have denied Our revelations.

We have given you power on earth and provided you with a livelihood: yet you are seldom thankful.

We created you and gave you form. Then We said to the angels: 'Prostrate yourselves before Adam.' They all prostrated themselves except Satan, who refused.

'Why did you not prostrate yourself?' Allah asked.

'I am nobler than Adam,' he replied. 'You created me of fire and him of clay.'

He said: 'Begone from Paradise! This is no place for your contemptuous pride. Away with you! Henceforth you shall be humble.'

Satan replied: 'Reprieve me till the Day of Resurrection.'

'You are reprieved,' said He.

'Because You have led me into sin,' said Satan, 'I will way-lay Your servants as they walk on Your straight path, and spring upon them from the front and from the rear, from their right and from their left. Then you shall find the greater part of them ungrateful.'

'Begone!' said Allah. 'A despicable outcast you shall henceforth be. With those that follow you I shall fill the pit of Hell.'

To Adam He said: 'Dwell with your wife in Paradise, and eat of any fruit you please; but never approach this tree or you shall both become transgressors.'

But Satan tempted them, so that he might reveal to them their nakedness, which they had never seen before. He said: 'Your Lord has forbidden you to approach this tree only to prevent you from becoming angels or immortals.' Then he swore to them that he would give them friendly counsel.

Thus he cunningly seduced them. And when they had eaten of the tree, their shame became visible to them, and they both covered themselves with the leaves of the garden.

Their Lord called out to them, saying: 'Did I not forbid you to approach that tree, and did I not warn you that Satan was your sworn enemy?'

They replied: 'Lord, we have wronged our souls. Pardon us and have mercy on us, or we shall surely be among the lost.'

He said: 'Go hence, and may your descendants be enemies to each other. The earth will for a while provide your sustenance and dwelling-place. There you shall live and there you shall die, and thence you shall be raised to life.'

Children of Adam! We have given you clothing with which to cover your nakedness, and garments pleasing to the eye; but the finest of all these is the robe of piety.

That is one of Allah's revelations. Perchance they will take heed.

Children of Adam! Let Satan not deceive you, as he deceived your parents out of Paradise. He stripped them of their garments to reveal to them their nakedness. He and his minions see you whence you cannot see them. We have made the devils guardians over the unbelievers.

When they commit an indecent act, they say: 'This is what our fathers used to do before us. Allah Himself enjoined it.'

Say: 'Allah does not enjoin what is indecent. Would you tell of Allah what you do not know?'

Say: 'My Lord has ordered you to act justly. Turn to Him wherever you kneel in prayer and call on Him with true devotion. You shall return to Him as He created you.'

Some He has guided and some He has justly led astray; for they had chosen the devils for their guardians instead of Allah and deemed themselves on the right path.

Children of Adam, dress well when you attend your mosques. Eat and drink, but avoid excess. He does not love the intemperate.

Say: 'Who has forbidden you to wear the decent clothes or to eat the good things which Allah has bestowed upon His servants?'

Say: 'These are for the enjoyment of the faithful in the life of this world, though shared by others; but they shall be theirs alone on the Day of Resurrection.'

Thus We make plain Our revelations to men of understanding.

Say: 'My Lord has forbidden all indecent acts, whether overt or disguised, sin, and wrongful oppression; He has forbidden you to worship that which is not sanctioned by Him, or to tell of Allah what you do not know.'

A space of time is fixed for every nation; when their hour is come, not for one moment shall they hold back, nor can they go before it.

Children of Adam, when apostles of your own come to proclaim to you My revelations, those that take warning and mend their ways will have nothing to fear or to regret; but those that deny and scorn Our revelations shall be the heirs of Hell, and there they shall remain for ever.

Who is more wicked than the man who invents a falsehood about Allah or denies His revelations? Such men shall have their destined share, and when Our angels come to carry off their souls they shall say to them: 'Where are your idols now, those whom you invoked besides Allah?' 'They have forsaken us,' they will answer, and will admit that they were unbelievers.

Allah will say: 'Enter the fire of Hell and join the nations of jinn and men that have gone before you.'

As it enters every nation will curse the one that went before it, and when all are gathered there, the last of them will say of the first: 'These, Lord, are the men who led us astray. Let their punishment be doubled in Hell-fire.'

He will answer: 'You shall all be doubly punished, although you may not know it.'

Then the first will say to the last: 'You were no better than we. Taste the penalty of your misdeeds.'

The gates of heaven shall not be opened for those that have denied and scorned Our revelations; nor shall they enter the gardens of Paradise until a camel shall pass through the eye of a needle. Thus shall the guilty be rewarded.

Hell shall be their couch, and sheets of fire shall cover them. Thus shall the wicked be rewarded.

As for those that have faith and do good works—We never charge a soul with more than it can bear—they are the heirs of Paradise, and there they shall abide for ever.

We shall take away all hatred from their hearts. Rivers shall roll at their feet and they shall say: 'Praise be to Allah who has guided us hither. Had He not given us guidance we should have strayed from the right path. His apostles have surely preached the truth.' And a voice will cry out to them, saying: 'This is the Paradise which you have earned with your labours.'

Then the blessed will cry out to the damned: 'What our Lord promised we have found to be true. Have you, too, found the promise of your Lord to be true?'

'Yes,' they shall answer, and a herald will cry out among them: 'Cursed are the evil-doers who have debarred others from the path of Allah and sought to make it crooked, and who had no faith in the life to come.'

A barrier shall divide the blessed from the damned, and on the Heights there shall stand men who will know each of them by his look. To the blessed they shall say: 'Peace be upon you!' But they shall not yet join them, though they long to do so.

And when they turn their eyes towards the damned they will cry: 'Lord, do not cast us among these wicked people!' Then they shall say to the men whom they recognize: 'Nothing have your riches or your pride availed you. Yet you swore that Allah would not show mercy to the faithful.'

And again turning to the blessed they shall say: 'Dwell in Paradise. You have nothing to fear or to regret.'

The damned will cry out to the blessed: 'Give us some water, or some of that which Allah has given you.' But the blessed shall reply: 'Allah has forbidden both to the unbelievers, who made their religion a pastime and an idle sport, and who were seduced by their earthly life.'

On that day We will forget them as they forgot that day: for they denied Our revelations.

We have bestowed on them a Book which We have imbued with knowledge, a guide and a blessing to true believers. Are they waiting for its fulfilment? On the day when it is fulfilled, those that have forgotten it will say: 'Our Lord's apostles have surely preached the truth. Will no one plead on our behalf? Could we but live our lives again, we would not do as we have done.' They shall forfeit their souls, and that which they devised will fail them.

Your Lord is Allah, who in six days created the heavens and the earth and then ascended His throne. He throws the veil of night over the day. Swiftly they follow one another.

It was He who created the sun, the moon, and the stars, and forced them into His service. His is the creation, His the command. Blessed be Allah, the Lord of all creatures!

Pray to your Lord with humility and in secret. He does not love the transgressors.

Do not corrupt the earth after it has been purged of evil. Pray to Him with fear and hope; His mercy is within reach of the righteous.

He sends forth the winds as harbingers of His mercy, and when they have gathered up a heavy cloud, He drives it on to some dead land and lets water fall upon it, bringing forth all manner of fruit. Thus He will raise the dead to life. Perchance you will take heed.

Good soil yields fruit by Allah's will. But poor and scant are the fruits which spring from barren soil. Thus We make plain Our revelations to those who render thanks.

Long ago We sent forth Noah to His people. He said: 'Serve Allah, my people, for you have no god but Him. Beware of the torment of a fateful day.'

But the elders of his people said: 'We can see that you are in palpable error.'

'I am not in error, my people,' he replied. 'I am sent forth by the Lord of the Creation to make known to you His will and to give you friendly counsel, for I know of Allah what you do not know. Do you think it strange that a warning should come to you from your Lord through a mortal like yourselves, and that He should exhort you to guard yourselves against evil so that Allah may show you mercy?'

They did not believe him. So We saved Noah and all who were with him and drowned those that denied Our revelations. Surely they were blind men.

And to the tribe of Aad We sent their compatriot Houd. He said: 'Serve Allah, my people, for you have no god but Him. Will you not be warned?'

The unbelievers among the elders of his tribe said: 'We can see you are a foolish man, and what is more, we think that you are lying.'

'I am not foolish, my people,' he replied. 'I am sent forth by the Lord of the Creation to make known to you His will and to give you honest counsel. Do you think it strange that an admonition should come to you from your Lord through a mortal like yourselves and that he should warn you? Remember that He has made you the heirs of Noah's people and endowed you with greater power than He has given to other men. Remember the favours of Allah, so that you may prosper.'

They said: 'Would you have us serve Allah only and renounce the gods which our fathers worshipped? Bring down the scourge with which you threaten us, if what you say be true.'

He answered: 'Your Lord's punishment and wrath have already visited you. Would you dispute with me about names which you and your fathers have invented and for which no sanction has been revealed from Allah? Wait if you will; I too am waiting.'

We delivered Houd and all who were with him through Our mercy, and annihilated those that disbelieved Our revelations. They were unbelievers all.

And to Thamoud We sent their compatriot Saleh. He said: 'Serve Allah, my people, for you have no god but Him. A veritable proof has come to you from your Lord. Here is Allah's she-camel: a sign for you. Leave her to graze at will in Allah's land and do not molest her, lest you incur a woeful punishment. Remember that He has made you the heirs of Aad, and provided you with dwellings in this land. You have built mansions on its plains and hewed out houses among its mountains. Remember Allah's favours and do not corrupt the earth with wickedness.'

The haughty elders of his people said to the believers whom they oppressed: 'Do you really believe that Saleh is sent forth from his Lord?'

They answered: 'We believe in the message with which he has been sent.'

Those who were scornful said: 'We deny all that you believe in.' They slaughtered the she-camel and defied the commandment of their Lord, saying to Saleh: 'Bring down the scourge with which you threaten us if you truly are an apostle.'

Thereupon an earthquake felled them, and when morning came they were prostrate in their dwellings. Saleh left them, saying: 'I conveyed to you, my people, the message of my Lord and gave you counsel; but you had no love for those who sought to guide you.'

Remember the words of Lot, who said to his people: 'Will you persist in these indecent acts which no other nation has committed before you? You lust after men instead of women. Truly, you are a degenerate people.'

Their only answer was: 'Banish him from your city, him and all his followers. They are men who would keep chaste.'

We delivered Lot and all his kinsfolk, except his wife, who stayed behind, and let loose a shower upon them. Consider the fate of the evil-doers.

And to Midian We sent their compatriot Shoaib. He said: 'Serve Allah, my people, for you have no god but Him. A veritable sign has come to you from your Lord. Give just weight and measure and do not defraud others of their possessions. Do not corrupt the land after it has been purged of evil. That is best for you, if you are true believers.

'Do not squat in every road, threatening believers and debarring them from the path of Allah, nor seek to make that path crooked. Remember how He multiplied you when you were few in number. Consider the fate of the evil-doers.

'If there are some among you who believe in my message and others who disbelieve it, be patient until Allah shall judge between us. He is the best of judges.'

The haughty elders of his tribe said: 'Return to our fold, Shoaib, or we will banish you from our city, you and all your followers.'

Even though we abhor your creed?' he replied. 'If we returned to the faith from which Allah has delivered us, we should be false to our Lord; nor can we turn to it again except by the will of Allah, our Lord. He has knowledge of all things, and in Him we have put our trust. Lord, judge rightly between us and our people; You are the best of judges.'

But the infidel chiefs said to their people: 'If you follow Shoaib, you shall assuredly be lost.'

Thereupon an earthquake felled them, and when morning came they were prostrate in their dwellings. Those that spurned Shoaib might never have lived there. Lost were those who disbelieved him.

Shoaib left them, saying: 'I conveyed to you, my people, the message of my Lord and gave you good counsel. How can I grieve for the unbelievers?'

Whenever We sent a prophet to a city We afflicted its people with calamities and misfortunes to humble them. Then We changed adversity to good fortune, so that in the hour of prosperity they said: 'Our fathers also had their joys and sorrows.' And in their heedlessness Our vengeance smote them.

Had the people of those cities believed and kept from evil, We would have showered upon them the riches of heaven and earth. But they denied their apostles, and We punished them for their misdeeds.

Were the people of those cities secure from Our vengeance when it overtook them in the night whilst they were sleeping?

Were they secure from Our wrath when it overtook them in the morning at their play?

Did they feel themselves secure from Allah's profound machinations? None feels secure from them except those who shall be lost.

Is it not plain to the present generation that if We pleased, We could punish them for their sins and set a seal upon their hearts, leaving them bereft of hearing?

We have recounted to you the history of those peoples. Their apostles came to them with veritable proofs, yet they persisted in their unbelief. Thus Allah seals up the hearts of the unbelievers.

We found the larger part of them untrue to their covenants; indeed, We found most of them evil-doers.

After those We sent forth Moses with Our signs to Pharaoh and his nobles, but they too disbelieved them.

Consider the fate of the evil-doers.

Moses said: 'Pharaoh, I am an apostle from the Lord of the Creation, and may tell nothing of Allah but what is true. I bring you an undoubted sign from your Lord. Let the Children of Israel depart with me.'

Pharaoh answered: 'Show us your sign, if what you say be true.'

Moses threw down his staff, and thereupon it changed to a veritable serpent. Then he drew out his hand and it appeared white to all who saw it.

The elders of Pharaoh's people said: 'This man is a skilled enchanter who seeks to drive you from your kingdom. What would you have us do?'

Others said: 'Put them off awhile, him and his brother, and send forth heralds to your cities to summon every skilled magician to your presence.'

The magicians came to Pharaoh. They said: 'Shall we be rewarded if we win?'

'Yes,' he answered. 'And you shall become my closest friends.'

They said: 'Moses, will you first throw down your staff, or shall we?'

'Throw down yours,' he replied.

And when the magicians threw down their staffs, they bewitched the people's eyes and terrified them by a display of great wonders.

Then We said to Moses: 'Now throw down your staff.' And thereupon his staff swallowed up their false devices.

Thus the truth prevailed and their doings proved vain. Pharaoh and his men were defeated and put to shame, and the enchanters prostrated themselves in adoration, saying: 'We believe in the Lord of the Creation, the Lord of Moses and Aaron.'

Pharaoh said: 'Do you dare believe in Him without my consent? This is a plot which you have contrived in order to turn my people out of their city. But you shall see. I will cut off your hands and feet on alternate sides and then crucify you all!'

They replied: 'We shall surely return to our Lord. You would punish us only because we believed in His signs when they were shown to us. Lord, give us patience and let us die in submission.'

The elders of Pharaoh's nation said: 'Will you allow Moses and his people to commit evil in the land and to forsake you and your gods?'

He replied: 'We will put their sons to death and spare their daughters. We shall yet triumph over them.'

Moses said to his people: 'Seek help in Allah and be patient. The earth is Allah's; He gives it to those of His servants whom He chooses. Happy shall be the lot of the righteous.'

They replied: 'We were oppressed before you came to us, and oppressed we still remain.'

He said: 'Your Lord will perchance destroy your enemies and make you rulers in the land. Then He will see how you conduct yourselves.'

We afflicted Pharaoh's people with dearth and famine so that they might take heed. When good things came their way, they said: 'It is our due,' but when evil befell them they ascribed it to Moses and his people. Yet it was Allah who had ordained their ill fortune, though most of them did not know it.

They said to Moses: 'Whatever miracles you may work to confound us, we will not believe in you.'

So We plagued them with floods and locusts, with lice and frogs, and with blood. All these were clear miracles, yet they scorned them, for they were a wicked people.

And when each plague smote them, they said: 'Moses, pray to your Lord for us: invoke the promise He has made you. If you lift the plague from us, we will believe in you and let the Israelites go with you.'

But when We had lifted the plague from them and the appointed time had come, they broke their promise. So We took vengeance on them and drowned them in the sea, for they had denied Our signs and gave no heed to them.

We gave the persecuted people dominion over the eastern and western lands which We had blessed. Thus your Lord's gracious word was fulfilled for the Israelites, because they had endured with fortitude; and We destroyed the edifices and towers of Pharaoh and his people.

We led the Israelites across the sea, and they came upon a people zealously devoted to idols which they had. They said to Moses: 'Make us a god like their gods.'

Moses replied: ' You are indeed an ignorant people. The religion which these idolaters follow is doomed and all their works are vain. Should I seek any god for you but Allah? He has exalted you above the nations and delivered you from Pharaoh's people, who had oppressed you cruelly, putting your sons to death and sparing your daughters. Surely that was a great trial from your Lord.'

We promised Moses that We would speak with him after thirty nights, to which We added ten nights more: so that the meeting with his Lord took place after forty nights.

Moses said to Aaron his brother: 'Take my place among my people. Do what is right and do not follow the path of the wrongdoers.

And when Moses came at the appointed time and His Lord communed with him, he said: 'Lord, reveal Yourself to me, that I may look upon You.'

He replied: 'You shall not see Me. But look upon the Mountain; if it remains firm upon its base, then only shall you see Me.'

And when his Lord revealed Himself to the Mountain, He crushed it to fine dust. Moses fell down senseless, and when he came to himself said: 'Glory be to You! Accept my repentance. I am the first of believers.'

He said: 'I have chosen you of all mankind to make known My messages and My commandments. Take therefore what I have given you, and be thankful.'

We inscribed for him upon the Tablets all manner of precepts, and instructions concerning all things, and said to him: 'Observe these steadfastly, and enjoin your people to observe what is best in them. I shall show you the home of the wicked. I will turn away from My signs the arrogant and the unjust, so that even if they witness each and every sign they shall deny them. If they see the right path, they shall not walk upon it: but if they see the path of error, they shall choose it for their path; because they disbelieved Our signs and gave no heed to them.

'Vain are the deeds of those who disbelieve in Our signs and in the life to come. Shall they not be rewarded according to their deeds?'

In his absence the people of Moses made a calf from their ornaments, an image with a hollow sound. Did they not see that it could neither speak to them nor give them guidance? Yet they worshipped it and thus committed evil.

But when they repented and realized that they had sinned, they said: 'If our Lord does not have mercy on us and pardon us, we shall be lost.'

And when Moses returned to his people, angry and sorrowful, he said: 'Evil is the thing you have done in my absence! Would you hasten the retribution of your Lord?'

He threw down the Tablets and, seizing his brother by the hair, dragged him towards him.

'Son of my mother,' cried Aaron, 'the people over-powered me and almost did me to death. Do not let my enemies gloat over me; do not number me among the wrongdoers.'

'Lord,' said Moses, 'forgive me and forgive my brother. Admit us to your mercy, for You are most merciful.'

Those that worshipped the calf incurred the wrath of their Lord and disgrace in this life. Thus shall the faithless be rewarded. As for those that do evil and later repent and have faith, they shall find your Lord forgiving and merciful.

When his anger was allayed, Moses took up the Tablets, upon which was inscribed a pledge of guidance and of mercy to those that fear their Lord. He chose from among his people seventy men for Our meeting, and when the earth shook beneath their feet, Moses said: 'Had it been Your will, Lord, You could have destroyed us long ago. But would You destroy us for that which the fools amongst us did? That trial was ordained by You, to mislead whom You willed and to guide whom You pleased. You alone are our guardian. Forgive us and have mercy on us: You are the noblest of those who forgive. Bestow on us what is good, both in this life and in the hereafter. To You alone we turn.'

He replied: 'I will visit My scourge upon whom I please: yet My mercy encompasses all things. I will show mercy to those that keep from evil, give alms, and believe in Our signs; and to those that shall follow the Apostle—the Unlettered Prophet[2]—whom they shall find described in the Torah and the Gospel. He will enjoin righteousness upon them and forbid them to do evil. He will make good things lawful to them and prohibit all that is foul. He will relieve them of their burdens and of the shackles that weigh upon them. Those that believe in him and honour him, those that aid him and follow the light to be sent forth with him, shall surely triumph.'

Say to your people:[3] 'I am sent forth to you all by Allah. His is the kingdom of the heavens and the earth. There is no god but Him. He ordains life and death. Therefore have faith in Allah and His apostle, the Unlettered Prophet, who believes in Allah and His Word. Follow him so that you may be rightly guided.'

Yet among the people of Moses there were some who preached the truth and acted justly. We divided them into twelve tribes, each a nation. And when his people demanded drink of him, We said to Moses: 'Strike the rock with your staff.' Thereupon twelve springs gushed from the rock and each tribe knew its drinking-place.

We caused the clouds to draw their shadow over them and sent down for them manna and quails, saying: 'Eat of the good things We have given you.' Indeed, they did Us no wrong, but they wronged themselves.

When it was said to them: 'Dwell in this city, and eat of whatever you please; pray for forgiveness and enter the gates adoring: We will forgive you your sins and give abundance to the righteous,'—the wicked amongst them altered these words. Therefore We let loose upon them a scourge from heaven as a punishment for their misdeeds.

Ask them about the city[4] which overlooked the sea and what befell its people when they broke the Sabbath. Each Sabbath the fish used to appear before them floating on the water, but on week-days they never came near them. Thus We tempted the people because they had done wrong.

When some asked: 'Why do you admonish men whom Allah will destroy or sternly punish?' they replied: 'We admonish them so that we may be free from blame in the sight of your Lord, and that they may guard themselves against evil.' Therefore, when they forgot the warning they had been given, We delivered those who had admonished them, and sternly punished the wrongdoers for their misdeeds. And when they had scornfully persisted in what they had been forbidden, We changed them into detested apes.

Then your Lord declared that He would raise against them others who would oppress them cruelly till the Day of Resurrection. Swift is the retribution of your Lord, yet He is forgiving and merciful.

We dispersed them through the earth in multitudes—some were righteous men, others were not—and tested them with blessings and misfortunes so that they might desist from sin. Then others succeeded them who inherited the Scriptures and availed themselves of the good things of this nether life. 'We shall be forgiven our sins,' they said—and persisted in their evil ways.

Are they not committed in the Scriptures, which they have studied well, to tell nothing of Allah but what is true? Surely the world to come is a better prize for those that guard themselves against evil. Have you no sense?

As for those that strictly observe the Scriptures and are steadfast in prayer, their reward shall not be lost.

We suspended the Mountain over them as though it were a shadow (they feared that it was falling down on them) and said: 'Hold fast to that which We have given you and bear in mind what it contains, so that you may keep from evil.'

Your Lord brought forth descendants from the loins of Adam's children, and made them testify against themselves. He said: 'Am I not your Lord?' They replied: 'We bear witness that you are.' This He did, lest you[5] should say on the Day of Resurrection: 'We had no knowledge of that,' or: 'Our forefathers were, indeed, idolaters; but will You destroy us, their descendants, on account of what the followers of falsehood did?'

Thus We make plain Our revelations so that they may return to the right path.

Tell them of the man to whom We vouchsafed Our signs and who turned away from them: how Satan overtook him as he was led astray. Had it been Our will, We would have exalted him through Our signs: but he clung to this earthly life and succumbed to his desires. He was like the dog which lolls out its tongue whether you chase it away or let it alone. Such are those that deny Our revelations. Recount to them these parables, so that they may take thought.

Dismal is the tale of those that denied Our revelations; they were unjust to their own souls.

The man whom Allah guides is rightly guided, but he who is led astray by Allah shall surely be lost.

We have predestined for Hell many jinn and many men. They have hearts, yet they cannot understand; eyes, yet they do not see; and ears, yet they do not hear. They are like beasts—indeed, they are less enlightened. Such are the heedless.

Most excellent are the names of Allah. Call on Him by His names and keep away from those that pervert them. They shall be punished for their misdeeds.

Among those whom We created there are some who give true guidance and act justly. As for those that deny Our revelations, We will lead them step by step to ruin, whence they cannot tell; for though I bear with them, My stratagem is sure.

Has it never occurred to them that their compatriot[6] is no madman, but one who gives plain warning? Will they not ponder upon the kingdom of the heavens and the earth, and all that Allah created, to see whether their hour is not drawing near? And in what other revelation will they believe, those that deny this?

None can guide the people whom Allah leads astray. He leaves them blundering about in their wickedness.

They ask you about the Hour of Doom and when it is to come. Say: 'None knows except my Lord. He alone will reveal it at the appointed time. A fateful hour it shall be, both in the heavens and on earth. It will come without warning.'

They will put questions to you as though you had full knowledge of it. Say: 'None knows about it save Allah, though most men are unaware of this.'

Say: 'I have not the power to acquire benefits or to avert evil from myself, except by the will of Allah. Had I possessed knowledge of what is hidden, I would have availed myself of much that is good and no harm would have touched me. But I am no more than one who gives warning and good news to true believers.'

It was He who created you from a single being. From that being He created his mate, so that he might find comfort in her. And when he had lain with her, she conceived, and for a time her burden was light. She carried it with ease, but when it grew heavy, they both cried to Allah their Lord: 'Grant us a goodly child and we will be truly thankful.'

Yet when He had granted them a goodly child, they set up other gods besides Him in return for what He had given them. Exalted be He above their idols!

Will they worship that which can create nothing, but is itself created? They cannot help them, nor can they help themselves.

If you call them to the right path they will not follow you. It is the same whether you call to them or hold your peace.

Those whom you invoke besides Allah are, like yourselves, His servants. Call on them, and let them answer you, if what you say be true!

Have they feet to walk with? Have they hands to hold with? Have they eyes to see with? Have they ears to hear with?

Say: 'Call on your false gods and scheme against me. Give me no respite. My guardian is Allah, who has revealed this Book. He is the guardian of the righteous. Those to whom you pray besides Him cannot help you, nor can they help themselves.'

If you call them to the right path, they will not hear you. You find them looking towards you, but they cannot see you.

Show forgiveness, speak for justice, and avoid the ignorant. If Satan tempts you, seek refuge in Allah; He hears all and knows all.

If those that guard themselves against evil are tempted by Satan, they have but to recall Allah's precepts and they shall see the light. As for their brothers, they shall be kept long in error, nor shall they ever desist.

When you do not recite to them a revelation they say: 'Have you not yet invented one?' Say: 'I follow only what is revealed to me by my Lord. This Book is a veritable proof from your Lord, a guide and a blessing to true believers.'

When the Koran is recited, listen to it in silence so that Allah may show you mercy. Remember your Lord deep in your soul with humility and reverence, and without ostentation: remember Him morning and evening, and do not be negligent.

Those who dwell with your Lord do not disdain His service. They give glory to Him and prostrate themselves before Him.

THE ELEPHANT

In the Name of Allah, the Compassionate, the Merciful have you not considered how Allah dealt with the Army of the Elephant?[7]

Did He not foil their stratagem and send against them flocks of birds which pelted them with clay-stones, so that they became like plants cropped by cattle?

QURAYSH[8]

In the Name of Allah, the Compassionate, the Merciful for the protection of Quraysh: their protection in their summer and winter journeyings.

Therefore let them worship the Lord of this House, who fed them in the days of famine and shielded them from all perils.

ENDNOTES

1. The Meccans.
2. Mohammed.
3. These words are addressed to Mohammed.
4. Eylat, on the Red Sea.
5. Mankind.
6. Mohammed.
7. The allusion is to the expedition of Abraha, the Christian King of Ethiopia, against Mecca, said to have taken place in the year of Mohammed's birth.
8. Mohammed's own clan. Some commentators connect this chapter with the preceding one.

Chapter 4

Myths from Oceania

Mircea Eliade

THE CAST SKIN: A MELANESIAN MYTH

At first men never died, but when they advanced in life they cast their skins like snakes and crabs, and came out with youth renewed. After a time a woman growing old went to a stream to change her skin. She threw off her old skin in the water, and observed that as it floated down it caught against a stick. Then she went home, where she had left her child. The child, however, refused to recognize her, crying that its mother was an old woman not like this young stranger; and to pacify the child she went after her cast integument and put it on. From that time mankind ceased to cast their skins and died.

R. H. Codrington, *The Melanesians* (Oxford, 1891), p. 265

THE STONE AND THE BANANA: AN INDONESIAN MYTH

Thus the natives of Poso, a district of Central Celebes, say that in the beginning the sky was very near the earth, and that the Creator, who lived in it, used to let down his gifts to men at the end of a rope. One day he thus lowered a stone; but our first father and mother would have none of it and they called out to their Maker, 'What have we to do with this stone? Give us something else.' The Creator complied and hauled away at the rope; the stone mounted up and up till it vanished from sight. Presently the rope was seen coming down from heaven again, and this time there was a banana at the end of it instead of a stone. Our first parents ran at the banana and took it. Then there came a voice from heaven saying: 'Because ye have chosen the banana," your life shall be like its life. When the banana-tree has offspring, the parent stem dies; so shall ye die and your children shall step into your place. Had ye chosen the stone, your life would have been like the life of the stone changeless and immortal.' The man and his wife mourned over their fatal choice, but it was too late; that is how through the eating of a banana death came into the world.

J. G. Frazer, *The Belief in Immortality,* I (London, 1913), pp. 74–5, quoting A. C. Kruijt

THE MOON AND RESURRECTION: AN AUSTRALIAN MYTH

In one of the Wotjobaluk legends it is said that at the time when all animals were men and women, some died, and the moon used to say, 'You up-again,' and they came to life again. There was at that time an old man who said, 'Let them remain dead.' Then none ever came to life again, except the moon, which still continued to do so.

A. W. Howitt, *The Native Tribes of South-East Australia* (London, 1904), p. 429

MAUI AND HINE-NUI-TE-PO: A POLYNESIAN MYTH

Maui now felt it necessary to leave the village where Irawaru had lived, so he returned to his parents. When he had been with them for some time, his father said to him one day, 'Oh, my son, I have heard from your mother and others that you are very valiant, and that you have succeeded in all feats that you have undertaken in your own country, whether they were small or great. But now that you have arrived in your father's country, you will, perhaps, at last be overcome.'

Then Maui asked him, 'What do you mean? What things are there that I can be vanquished by?' His father answered him, 'By your great ancestress, by Hine-nui-te-po, who, if you look, you may see flashing, and, as it were, opening and shutting there, where the horizon meets the sky.' Maui replied, 'Lay aside such idle thoughts, and let us both fearlessly seek whether men are to die or live for ever.' His father said, 'My child, there has been an ill omen for us. When I was baptizing you, I omitted a portion of the fitting prayer, and that I know will be the cause of your perishing.'

Then Maui asked his father, 'What is my ancestress Hine-nui-te-po like?' He answered, 'What you see yonder shining so brightly red are her eyes. And her teeth are as sharp and hard as pieces of volcanic glass. Her body is like that of a man. And as for the pupils of her eyes, they are jasper. And her hair is like the tangles of long seaweed. And her mouth is like that of a barracouta.' Then his son answered him: 'Do you think her strength is as great as that of Tama-nui-te-Ra, who consumes man, and the earth, and the very waters, by the fierceness of his heat? Was not the world formerly saved alive by the speed with which he travelled? If he had then, in the days of his full strength and power, gone as slowly as he does now, not a remnant of mankind would have been left living upon the earth, nor, indeed, would anything else have survived. But I laid hold of Tama-nui-te-Ra, and now he goes slowly, for I smote him again and again, so that he is now feeble, and long in travelling his course, and he now gives but very little heat, having been weakened by the blows of my enchanted weapon. I then, too, split him open in many places, and from the wounds so made, many rays now issue forth and spread in all directions. So, also, I found the sea much larger than the earth, but by the power of the last born of your children, part of the earth was drawn up again, and dry land came forth.' And his father answered him, 'That is all very true, O, my last born, and the strength of my old age.

Well, then, be bold, go and visit your great ancestress, who flashes so fiercely there, where the edge of the horizon meets the sky.'

Hardly was this conversation concluded with his father, when the young hero went forth to look for companions to accompany him upon this enterprise. There came to him for companions, the small robin, and the large robin, and the thrush, and the yellow-hammer, and every kind of little bird, and the water-wagtail. These all assembled together, and they all started with Maui in the evening, and arrived at the dwelling of Hine-nui-te-po, and found her fast asleep.

Then Maui addressed them all, 'My little friends, now if you see me creep into this old chieftainess, do not laugh at what you see. Nay, nay, do not, I pray you, but when I have got altogether inside her, and just as I am coming out of her mouth, then you may shout with laughter if you please.' His little friends, who were frightened at what they saw, replied, 'Oh, sir, you will certainly be killed.' He answered them, 'If you burst out laughing at me as soon as I get inside her, you will wake her up, and she will certainly kill me at once, but if you do not laugh until I am quite inside her, and am on the point of coming out of her mouth, I shall live, and Hine-nui-te-po will die.' His little friends answered, 'Go on then, brave sir, but pray take good care of yourself.'

Then the young hero started off. He twisted the strings of his weapon tight round his wrist, and went into the house. He stripped off his clothes, and the skin on his hips looked mottled and beautiful as that of a mackerel, from the tattoo marks, cut on it with the chisel of Uetonga [grandson of Ru, god of earthquakes; Uetonga taught tattooing to Mataora who taught it to man], and he entered the old chieftainess.

The little birds now screwed up their tiny cheeks, trying to suppress their laughter. At last the little Tiwakawaka could no longer keep it in, and laughed out loud, with its merry, cheerful note. This woke the old woman up. She opened her eyes, started up, and killed Maui.

Thus died this Maui we have spoken of. But before he died he had children, and sons were born to him. Some of his descendants yet live in Hawaiki, some in Aotearoa (or in these islands). The greater part of his descendants remained in Hawaiki, but a few of them came here to Aotearoa. According to the traditions of the Maori, this was the cause of the introduction of death into the world (Hine-nui-te-po was the goddess of death. If Maui had passed safely through her, then no more human beings would have died, but death itself would have been destroyed.) We express it by saying, 'The water-wagtail laughing at Maui-tiki-tiki-o Taranga made Hine-nui-te-po squeeze him to death.' And we have this proverb, 'Men make heirs, but death carries them off.'

Sir George Grey, *Polynesian Mythology* (London, 1855), pp. 56–8

Chapter 5

Creation in the Book of Genesis: Genesis 1–3. New Oxford Annotated Bible

Edited by Herbert G. May and Bruce M. Metzger

Genesis, meaning "beginning," covers the times from the creation (i.e. the beginning of history) to the Israelite sojourn in Egypt. The book falls naturally into two main sections: chs. 1–11 deal with primeval history; chs. 12–50 treat the history of the "fathers" of Israel. The latter section tells the stories of Abraham (chs. 12–25), of Isaac and his twin sons Esau and Jacob (chs. 26–36), and of Jacob's family, the chief member of which was Joseph (chs. 37–50).

Unlike the stories of primeval history, those of the patriarchs can be read against the background of the history of the Near East in the early part of the second millennium B.C. (2000–1500), as documented from extra-Biblical sources (see "Survey of . . . Bible Lands," § 6). The primary purpose of the whole book, however, is to narrate God's dealings with men and, in particular, to interpret Israel's special role in his historical plan. Thus the call of Abraham (12.1–3) is the great turning point. God's creation had been marred by man's persistent wickedness which not even the flood erased. Out of this fallible human material, however, God gradually separated one family line and eventually chose one man, Abraham, promising that he and his people would have a great historical destiny and would be instrumental in bringing divine blessing upon all the dispersed families of mankind.

The book is composed of three main literary traditions (Judean, Ephraimite, and Priestly; see Introduction to Pentateuch) and these, in turn, often preserve ancient oral tradition. Thus the voices of many generations unite in the affirmation that the only true God is the God of Abraham, Isaac, and Jacob, whose redemptive purpose, like the rainbow of his promise, spans the course of human history from its remote beginning to its unrealized future.

In the beginning God created[a] the heavens and the earth. 2 The earth was without form and void, and darkness was upon the face of the deep; and the Spirit[b] of God was moving over the face of the waters.

3 And God said, "Let there be light"; and there was light. 4 And God saw that the light was good; and God separated the light from the darkness. 5 God called the light Day, and the darkness he called Night. And there was evening and there was morning, one day.

6 And God said, "Let there be a firmament in the midst of the waters, and let it separate the waters from the waters." 7 And God made the firmament and separated the waters which were under the firmament from the waters which were above the firmament. And it was so. 8 And God called the firmament Heaven. And there was evening and there was morning, a second day.

9 And God said, "Let the waters under the heavens be gathered together into one place, and let the dry land appear." And it was so. 10 God called the dry land Earth, and the waters that were gathered together he called Seas. And God saw that it was good. 11 And God said, "Let the earth put forth vegetation, plants yielding seed, and fruit trees bearing fruit in which is their seed, each according to its kind, upon the earth." And it was so. 12 The earth brought forth vegetation, plants yielding seed according to their own kinds, and trees bearing fruit in which is their seed, each according to its kind. And God saw that it was good. 13 And there was evening and there was morning, a third day.

14 And God said, "Let there be lights in the firmament of the heavens to separate the day from the night; and let them be for signs and for seasons and for days and years, 15 and let them be lights in the firmament of the heavens to give light upon the earth." And it was so. 16 And God made the two great lights, the greater light to rule the day, and the lesser light to rule the night; he made the stars also. 17 And God set them in the firmament of the heavens to give light upon the earth, 18 to rule over the day and over the night, and to separate the light from the darkness. And God saw that it was good. 19 And there was evening and there was morning, a fourth day.

20 And God said, "Let the waters bring forth swarms of living creatures, and let birds fly above the earth across the firmament of the heavens." 21 So God created the great sea monsters and every living creature that moves, with which the waters swarm, according to their kinds, and every winged bird according to its kind. And God saw that it was good. 22 And God blessed them, saying, "Be fruitful and multiply and fill the waters in the seas, and let birds multiply on the earth." 23 And there was evening and there was morning, a fifth day.

24 And God said, "Let the earth bring forth living creatures according to their kinds: cattle and creeping things and beasts of the earth according to their kinds." And it was so. 25 And God made the beasts of the earth according to their kinds and the cattle according to their kinds, and everything that creeps upon the ground according to its kind. And God saw that it was good.

[26]Then God said, "Let us make man in our image, after our likeness; and let them
have dominion over the fish of the sea, and over the birds of the air, and over the cattle, and over all the earth, and over every creeping thing that creeps upon the earth."
[27] So God created man in his own image, in the image of God he created him; male
and female he created them. [28] And God blessed them, and God said to them, "Be
fruitful and multiply, and fill the earth and subdue it; and have dominion over the fish
of the sea and over the birds of the air and over every living thing that moves upon
the earth." [29] And God said. "Behold, I have given you every plant yielding seed
which is upon the face of all the earth, and every tree with seed in its fruit; you shall
have them for food. [30] And to every beast of the earth, and to every bird of the air,
and to everything that creeps on the earth, everything that has the breath of life, I
have given every green plant for food." And it was so.[3 1] And God saw everything
that he had made, and behold, it was very good. And there was evening and there
was morning, a sixth day.

2 Thus the heavens and the earth were finished, and all the host of them. [2] And on
the seventh day God finished his work which he had done, and he rested on the seventh day from all his work which he had done. [3] So God blessed the seventh day and
hallowed it, because on it God rested from all his work which he had done in creation.
[4] These are the generations of the heavens and the earth when they were created.
In the day that the LORD God made the earth and the heavens,[5] when no plant of
the field was yet in the earth and no herb of the field had yet sprung up—for the LORD
God had not caused it to rain upon the earth, and there was no man to till the
ground;[6] but a mist[c] went up from the earth and watered the whole face of the
ground—[7] then the LORD God formed man of dust from the ground, and breathed
into his nostrils the breath of life; and man became a living being.[8] And the LORD God
planted a garden in Eden, in the east; and there he put the man whom he had
formed.[9] And out of the ground the LORD God made to grow every tree that is pleasant to the sight and good for food, the tree of life also in the midst of the garden, and
the tree of the knowledge of good and evil.

[10]A river flowed out of Eden to water the garden, and there it divided and became
four rivers.[11] The name of the first is Pishon; it is the one which flows around the
whole land of Hav′-ilah; where there is gold;[12] and the gold of that land is good; bdel-
lium and onyx stone are there.[13] The name of the second river is Gihon; it is the one
which flows around the whole land of Cush. [4] And the name of the third river is
Tigris, which flows east of Assyria. And the fourth river is the Euphra′tes.

[15]The LORD God took the man and put him in the garden of Eden to till it and
keep it.[16] And the LORD God commanded the man, saying, "You may freely eat of
every tree of the garden;[17] but of the tree of the knowledge of good and evil you shall
not eat, for in the day that you eat of it you shall die."

[18]Then the LORD God said, "It is not good that the man should be alone; I will
make him a helper fit for him."[19] So out of the ground the LORD God formed every

beast of the field and every bird of the air, and brought them to the man to see what he would call them; and whatever the man called every living creature, that was its name.[20] The man gave names to all cattle, and to the birds of the air, and to every beast of the field; but for the man there was not found a helper fit for him.[21] So the LORD God caused a deep sleep to fall upon the man, and while he slept took one of his ribs and closed up its place with flesh; [22] and the rib which the LORD God had taken from the man he made into a woman and brought her to the man.[23] Then the man said,

"This at last is bone of my bones
and flesh of my flesh;
she shall be called Woman,[d]
because she was taken out of
Man."[e]

[24]Therefore a man leaves his father and his mother and cleaves to his wife, and they become one flesh. [25] And the man and his wife were both naked, and were not ashamed.

3 Now the serpent was more subtle than any other wild creature that the LORD God had made. He said to the woman, "Did God say, 'You shall not eat of any tree of the garden'?" [2] And the woman said to the serpent, "We may eat of the fruit of the trees of the garden; [3] but God said, 'You shall not eat of the fruit of the tree which is in the midst of the garden, neither shall you touch it, lest you die.'" [4] But the serpent said to the woman, "You will not die. [5] For God knows that when you eat of it your eyes will be opened, and you will be like God, knowing good and evil." [6] So when the woman saw that the tree was good for food, and that it was a delight to the eyes, and that the tree was to be desired to make one wise, she took of its fruit and ate; and she also gave some to her husband, and he ate. [7] Then the eyes of both were opened, and they knew that they were naked; and they sewed fig leaves together and made themselves aprons.

[8]And they heard the sound of the LORD God walking in the garden in the cool of the day, and the man and his wife hid themselves from the presence of the LORD God among the trees of the garden. [9] But the LORD God called to the man, and said to him, "Where are you?" [10] And he said, "I heard the sound of thee in the garden, and I was afraid, because I was naked; and I hid myself." [11] He said, "Who told you that you were naked? Have you eaten of the tree of which I commanded you not to eat?" [12] The man said, "The woman whom thou gavest to be with me, she gave me fruit of the tree, and I ate." [13] Then the LORD God said to the woman, "What is this that you have done?" The woman said, "The serpent beguiled me, and I ate." [14] The LORD God said to the serpent,

"Because you have done this, cursed are you above all cattle,
and above all wild animals; upon your belly you shall go, and dust you shall eat all the days of your life.
15I will put emnity between you and the woman, and between your seed and her seed; he shall bruise your head, and you shall bruise his heel."
16To the woman he said,"I will greatly multiply your pain in childbearing; in pain you shall bring forth children, yet your desire shall be for your husband, and he shall rule over you."
17And to Adam he said, "Because you have listened to the voice
of your wife, and have eaten of the tree of which I commanded you, 'You shall not eat of it,' cursed is the ground because of you; in toil you shall eat of it all the days of your life;
18thorns and thistles it shall bring forth to you; and you shall eat the plants of the field.
19In the sweat of your face you shall eat bread till you return to the ground,
for out of it you were taken; you are dust, and to dust you shall return."

20The man called his wife's name Eve,[f] because she was the mother of all living.
21 And the LORD God made for Adam and for his wife garments of skins, and clothed them.
22Then the LORD God said, "Behold, the man has become like one of us, knowing good and evil; and now, lest he put forth his hand and take also of the tree of life,
and eat, and live for ever"— 23 therefore the LORD God sent him forth from the garden of Eden, to till the ground from which he was taken.24 He drove out the man; and at the east of the garden of Eden he placed the cherubim, and a flaming sword which turned every way, to guard the way to the tree of life.

ENDNOTES

a Or *When God began to create*
b Or *wind*
c Or *flood*
d Heb *ishshah*
e Heb *ish*
f The name in Hebrew resembles the word for *living*
g Heb *qanah*, get
z Greek *he*
a Other ancient authorities read *let us*

1.1–2.4a: The Priestly story of creation. Out of original chaos God created an orderly world in which he assigned a preeminent place to man. **1:** Probably a preface to the whole story, though possibly introductory to v. 3: *When God began to create* (note *a*) . . . *God said* (compare 2.4b–7). The ancients believed the world originated from and was founded upon a watery chaos (*the deep;* compare Ps.24.1,2), portrayed as a dragon in various myths (Is.51.9). **3–5:** Creation by the word of God (Ps.33.6–9) expresses God's absolute Lordship and prepares for the doctrine of creation out of nothing (2 Macc.7.28). Light was created first (2 Cor.4.6), even before the sun, and was *separated* from *night,* a remnant of uncreated darkness (v. 2). Since the Jewish day began with sundown, the order is *evening* and *morning.* **6–8:** A *firmament,* or solid dome (Job 37.18), separated the upper from the lower waters (Ex.20.4; Ps.148.4). See 7.11 n. **9–10:** The *seas,* a portion of the watery chaos, were assigned boundaries at the edge of the earth (Ps.139.9; Pr.8.29), where they continue to menace God's creation (Jer.5.22; Ps. 104.7–9). **11–13:** *Vegetation* was created only indirectly by God; his creative command was directed to *the earth.* **14–19:** The sun, moon, and stars are not divine powers that control man's destiny, as was believed in antiquity, but are only *lights.* Implicitly worship of the heavenly host is forbidden (Dt.4.19; Zeph.1.5). **20–23:** The creation of birds and fishes. *Sea monsters,* see Pss.74.13; 104.25–26. **24–25:** God's command for the earth to *bring forth* (compare v. 11) suggests that the animals are immediately bound to *the ground* and only indirectly related to God, in contrast with man. **26–27:** The solemn divine decision emphasizes man's supreme place at the climax of God's creative work. **26:** The plural *us, our* (3.22; 11.7; Is.6.8) probably refers to the divine beings who compose God's heavenly court (1 Kg.22.19; Job 1.6). Made in *the image of God,* man is the creature through whom God manifests his rule on earth. The language reflects "royal theology" in which, as in Egypt, the king was the "image of God." **27:** *Him, them:* man was not created to be alone but is *male and female* (2.18–24). *Man,* the Hebrew word is "adam," a collective, referring to mankind. **28:** As God's representative, man is given *dominion (Ps.8.6–8).* **29–30:** His dominion is limited, as shown by the vegetarian requirement, modified in Noah's time (9.2-3); it is to be benevolent and peaceful (compare Is.11.6–8). **31:** *Very good* (vv. 4,10,12. etc.), corresponding perfectly to God's purpose. **2.1–3:** The verb *rested* (Hebrew "*shabat*") is the basis of the noun sabbath (Ex.31.12–17).

2.4b-3.24: The creation and the fall of man. This is a different tradition from that in 1.1-2.4a, as evidenced by the flowing style and the different order of events, e.g. man is created before vegetation, animals, and woman. **6:** *A mist* (or *flood*) probably refers to the water which surged up from the subterranean ocean, the source of fertility (49.25). **7:** The word-play on *man* (adham) and *ground* (adhamah) introduces a motif characteristic of this early tradition: man's relation to the ground from which he was *formed,* like a potter molds clay (Jer.18.6). Man is not body and soul (a Greek distinction) but is dust animated by the LORD God's *breath* or "spirit" which constitutes him *a living being* or psycho-physical self (Ps.104.29-30; Job 34.14–15). **8-9:** *Eden,* meaning "delight," is a "garden of God" (Is.51.3; Ezek.31.8–9; Jl.2.3) or divine park. **9:** The *tree of life* was believed to confer eternal life (3.22; see Pr.3.18 n.; Rev.22.2,14,19), as the *tree of the knowledge of good and evil* confers wisdom (see 2 Sam.14.17; Is.7.15). **10–14:** The rivers, springing from the subterranean ocean (v. 6), flowed out to the four corners of the known historical world. **15–17:** Man is given a task: to *till* and *keep* the garden. The prohibition against eating the forbidden fruit (3.3) stresses God's LORDship and man's obedience. **18:** *To be alone* is not good, for man is social by nature (see 1.27 n.). *A helper fit for him* means a partner who is suitable for him, who completes his being. **19:** Naming the animals signifies man's dominion over them (compare 1.28). **21–23:** The deep affinity between man and woman is portrayed in the statement that God made the woman from the man's *rib.* **24–25:** Sex is not regarded as evil but as a God-given impulse which draws man and woman together so that *they become one flesh.* **25:** The two were unashamedly *naked,* a symbol of their guiltless relation to God and to one another. **3.1–7:** The temptation begins with the insinuation of doubt (vv. 1–3), increases as suspicion is cast upon God's motive (vv. 4–5), and becomes irresistible when the couple sense the possibilities of freedom (v. 6). **1:** *The serpent,* one of the wild creatures, distinguished by uncanny wisdom (Mt.10.16); there is a hint of a seductive power in man's environment, hostile to God. **5:** *Like God:* perhaps "like gods" (Septuagint), the divine beings of the heavenly court (v. 22; 1.26 n.). *Knowing good and evil,* see 2.9 n. **7:** Bodily shame (2.25) symbolizes anxiety about broken relationship with God. **8-13:** Anxiety leads to a guilty attempt to hide from God (Ps.139.7–12), described anthropomorphically as strolling in his garden. **14–15:** The curse contains an old explanation of why the serpent crawls rather than walks and why men are instinctively hostile to it. **16:** This divine judgment contains an old explanation of woman's pain in childbirth, her sexual *desire* for her husband (i.e. her motherly impulse, compare 30.1), and her subordinate position to man in ancient society. **17–19:** An explanation of man's struggle to eke an existence from the soil. Work is not essentially evil (2.15) but it becomes *toil* as a result of man's broken relationship with his Creator. **17:** The Hebrew word *Adam* is usually translated "man" in this story (see 1.27 n.). Note that the curse is upon the ground, not man. **19:** *Till you return to the ground:* The mortal nature of man was implicit in the circumstances of his origin (2.7); because of man's disobedience, God now makes death an inevitable fate that haunts man throughout life. **21:** *Garments of skins,* a sign of God's protective care even in the time of judgment (4.15). **22:** *Like one of us,* see 3.5 n. *The tree of life* (2.9) does not figure in the temptation story, which explicitly speaks of only one tree in the center of the garden (3.3–6, 11–12, 17). **24:** *The cherubim,* guardians of sacred areas (1 Kg.8.6–7), were represented as winged creatures like the Sphynx of Egypt, half human and half lion (Ezek.41.l8–19). *A flaming sword* (compare Jer.47.6) was placed near the cherubim to remind banished man of the impossibility of overstepping his creaturely bounds (compare Ezek.28.13–16).

Chapter 6

The Resurrection of Christ: 1st Corinthians 15. New Oxford Annotated Bible

Edited by Herbert G. May and Bruce M. Metzger

15 Now I would remind you, brethren, in what terms I preached to you the gospel, which you received, in which you stand, [2] by which you are saved, if you hold it fast–unless you believed in vain.

[3]For I delivered to you as of first importance what I also received, that Christ died for our sins in accordance with the scriptures, [4] that he was buried, that he was raised on the third day in accordance with the scriptures, [5] and that he appeared to Cephas, then to the twelve. [6] Then he appeared to more than five hundred brethren at one time, most of whom are still alive, though some have fallen asleep. [7]Then he appeared to James, then to all the apostles. [8] Last of all, as to one untimely born, he appeared also to me. [9] For I am the least of the apostles, unfit to be called an apostle, because I persecuted the church of God. [10] But by the grace of God I am what I am, and his grace toward me was not in vain. On the contrary, I worked harder than any of them, though it was not I, but the grace of God which is with me. [11] Whether then it was I or they, so we preach and so you believed.

[12]Now if Christ is preached as raised from the dead, how can some of you say that there is no resurrection of the dead? [13] But if there is no resurrection of the dead, then Christ has not been raised; [14] if Christ has not been raised, then our preaching is in vain and your faith is in vain. [15] We are even found to be misrepresenting God, because we testified of God that he raised Christ, whom he did not raise if it is true that the dead are not raised. [16] For if the dead are not raised, then Christ has not been raised. [17] If Christ has not been raised, your faith is futile and you are still in your sins. [18] Then those also who have fallen asleep in Christ have perished. [19] If for this life only we have hoped in Christ, we are of all men most to be pitied.

[20]But in fact Christ has been raised from the dead, the first fruits of those who have fallen asleep. [21] For as by a man came death, by a man has come also the resurrection of the dead. [22] For as in Adam all die, so also in Christ shall all be made alive. [23] But each in his own order: Christ the first fruits, then at his coming those who belong to Christ. [24] Then comes the end, when he delivers the kingdom to God the Father after destroying every rule and every authority and power. [25] For he must reign until he has put all his enemies under his feet. [26] The last enemy to be destroyed is death. [27] "For God[z] has put all things in subjection under his feet." But when it says, "All things are put in subjection under him," it is plain that he is excepted who put all things under him. [28] When all things are subjected to him, then the Son himself will also be subjected to him who put all things under him, that God may be everything to everyone.

[29]Otherwise, what do people mean by being baptized on behalf of the dead? If the dead are not raised at all, why are people baptized on their behalf? [30] Why am I in peril every hour? [31] I protest, brethren, by my pride in you which I have in Christ Jesus our LORD, I die every day! [32] What do I gain if, humanly speaking, I fought with beasts at Ephesus? If the dead are not raised, "Let us eat and drink, for tomorrow we die." [33] Do not be deceived: "Bad company ruins good morals." [34] Come to your right mind, and sin no more. For some have no knowledge of God. I say this to your shame.

[35]But some one will ask, "How are the dead raised? With what kind of body do they come?" [36] You foolish man! What you sow does not come to life unless it dies. [37] And what you sow is not the body which is to be, but a bare kernel, perhaps of wheat or of some other grain. [38] But God gives it a body as he has chosen, and to each kind of seed its own body. [39] For not all flesh is alike, but there is one kind for men, another for animals, another for birds, and another for fish. [40] There are celestial bodies and there are terrestrial bodies; but the glory of the celestial is one, and the glory of the terrestrial is another. [41] There is one glory of the sun, and another glory of the moon, and another glory of the stars; for star differs from star in glory.

[42] So is it with the resurrection of the dead. What is sown is perishable, what is raised is imperishable. [43] It is sown in dishonor, it is raised in glory. It is sown in weakness, it is raised in power. [44] It is sown a physical body, it is raised a spiritual body. If there is a physical body, there is also a spiritual body. [45] Thus it is written, "The first man Adam became a living being"; the last Adam became a life-giving spirit. [46] But it is not the spiritual which is first but the physical, and then the spiritual. [47] The first man was from the earth, a man of dust; the second man is from heaven. [48] As was the man of dust, so are those who are of the dust; and as is the man of heaven, so are those who are of heaven. [49] Just as we have borne the image of the man of dust, we shall[a] also bear the image of the man of heaven. [50] I tell you this, brethren: flesh and blood cannot inherit the kingdom of God, nor does the perishable inherit the imperishable.

[51]Lo! I tell you a mystery. We shall not all sleep, but we shall all be changed, [52] in a moment, in the twinkling of an eye, at the last trumpet. For the trumpet will sound,

and the dead will be raised imperishable, and we shall be changed. [53] For this perishable nature must put on the imperishable, and this mortal nature must put on immortality. [54] When the perishable puts on the imperishable, and the mortal puts on immortality, then shall come to pass the saying that is written:

> "Death is swallowed up in victory." [55] "O death, where is thy victory? O death, where is thy sting?"

[56]The sting of death is sin, and the power of sin is the law. [57] But thanks be to God, who gives us the victory through our LORD Jesus Christ.

[58]Therefore, my beloved brethren, be steadfast, immovable, always abounding in the work of the LORD, knowing that in the LORD your labor is not in vain.

ENDNOTES

15.1–11: Paul's gospel. A restatement against the background of reports that some at Corinth deny the resurrection. **3:** *Scriptures*, Is.53.5–12. **4:** *Scriptures*, Ps.16.10 (compare Acts 2.31). **7:** *James*, "the Lord's brother" of Gal.1.19. **8:** *One untimely born*, the meaning is obscure; Paul perhaps is referring to the separation in time between his own experience and those of the others. For other accounts of Paul's encounter with the risen Christ, see 9.1; Gal.1.16; Acts 9.3–6

15.12–34: The significance of the resurrection. 18: 1 Th.4.16. **21–22:** Rom.5,12–18. **23:** *Coming*, the glorious return of Christ at the end of the age (1 Th.2.19; 4.13–17). **24–27:** *His enemies* are the demonic powers dominating the present age; one of these is *death*. **27:** Ps.8.6. *His feet*, Christ's. **29:** A practice otherwise unknown. Presumably Christians accepted baptism in the names of their loved ones who had died without being baptized in order that the latter might share in the final resurrection. Without advocating this practice, Paul makes it a point in his argument. **31:** *I die*, i.e. I risk death, *every day*. **32:** One cannot say with assurance whether the fighting *with beasts* is to be taken literally or is merely a strong metaphor (compare 4.9) In any case, Paul had bitter and dangerous enemies. The quotation is from Is.22.13. **33:** Paul quotes a Greek proverb (attributed to the Attic poet Menander), warning the Corinthians not to associate with those who deny the resurrection.

15.35–58: The nature of the resurrection. 35–44: Greeks had no trouble in conceiving of the immortality of the soul, but the idea of the raised body was difficult. Paul's point is that there are many kinds of "bodies"; the resurrection body will be a new body (not *perishable*, v. 42, or *physical*, v. 44), which God will provide. **45–47:** Gen.2.7. **50:** Jn.3.6. **51–52:** Mystery, a secret made known in Christ. *We shall not all sleep*, we shall not all die before the Lord's coming (1 Th.4.13–17). **54–55:** Is.25.8; Hos.13.14. **57:** *God gives us the victory* over sin now (Rom. 8.1–2) and hereafter over death (Rom.8.11). **58:** *Immovable*, not shaken by false teaching.

Chapter 7

Death and Resurrection, Time and Eternity

Bruce Lincoln

If the process of aging is seen as a form of erosion whereby life and the body are gradually worn away, there is an inevitable end to such a process. For even if erosion is slowed and the threats posed by time, illness, and accidents are countered with proper nutrition and healing practices, still the end to human existence may only be postponed a bit, never avoided altogether.

All life ends in death, just as all erosion ends in total collapse or pulverization. And just as the PIE verb **ĝer-* straddles the meanings "to age" and "to fall apart," so also the verb **mer-* combines the senses "to die" (thus: Skt *marate* and *mriyate* [the latter with a reduced grade vocalism]; Av *miryeite;* Arm *meṙanim* [first person singular]; Lt *morior;* Lith *mìrštu, mir̃ti;* OCS *mrěti;* Hitt *me-ir-ta* [third person singular preterite]) and "to reduce to small pieces" (thus: Skt *mr̥ṇāti* "to crush, grind"; Gk *marainō* "to rub away, grind down"; Lt *mortārium* "mortar"; ON *merja* "to strike, pound"; Serb *mȑva* "crumbs"; ORuss *moromradi* "to gnaw, erode, crumble"; Hitt *marriattari* "to be shattered, crushed").

Such semantics have strong implications for the understanding of death common among the Indo-European peoples, which—as we shall see—cast death as the dissolution of a complex entity, which was reduced to its constituent parts after a long process of erosion. One of the most obvious ways this dissolution was envisioned was as the separation of body and soul—a falling apart of sorts—that is the hallmark of death in countless texts; other analyses go further and consider the ways in which the body itself crumbles into smaller pieces after death.

A convenient starting point for consideration of these ideas is one of the earliest Greek inscriptions in which the post mortem fate of the soul is discussed: that placed at the burial spot of the Athenian soldiers who died at the Battle of Potidaea in 432 B.C. It states, simply, of the dead, "Aither received their souls, and earth their bodies. Here it is important that the term used to denote souls, Gk *psykhē,* most literally means "life-breath, being derived from the verb *psykhō, psykhein* "to breathe, to blow." The "soul" is thus most fundamentally the air that temporarily resides within a human organism. When it is present, the organism is alive. When it departs once and for all, the organism is dead. And—what is most significant to the present inquiry—when that lifebreath leaves the body, it enters the air, its macrocosmic alloform, from which it first came and to which it returns. Similarly, in many Greek anthropogonic accounts the human body is said to be created from earth, and this inscription informs us that at death the body returns to the earth once more. This point is made explicit in Euripides, *Suppliants,* ll. 531–534:

> Let the corpses now be covered with the earth,
> From which each of them came forth to the light
> Only to go back thither: breath *(pneuma)* to the aither,
> And body to earth.

Something similar is found in two closely related passages from the oldest Russian epic that has come down to us, the *Slovo o P"lku Igorevě* ("The Song of Igor's Campaign"), written shortly after 1185. In both passages the fate of those fallen in battle is metaphorically compared to the treatment of cereal grains. The first, ll. 157–158, reads:

> On the Nemiga (river-banks), sheaves
> Are spread out with heads on them;
> They are threshed with flails of Frankish steel (i.e., enemy swords).
> They lay life down on the threshing floor,
> And winnow soul from body.
> The bloody banks of the Nemiga
> Were unhappily sown—
> Sown with the bones of Russian sons.

Here, as in the two Greek texts cited above, the separation of body and soul is correlated with the return of the body—more specifically, the bones—to the earth. To this is added complex agricultural symbolism. First the corpses are compared to grain that is threshed and winnowed, the souls presumably being associated to grain and the bodies to chaff that is let fall to earth. In line 158, however, the bones—the most solid and enduring part of the body—are further compared to seed, which is sown in the earth in order to produce a rebirth of the grain. In another passage of the *Slovo* (l. 67), this anticipated rebirth is made explicit and given a brilliant poetic twist.

> The black earth underneath (the horses') hooves
> Was sown with bones
> And watered with blood:
> These sprouted as grief
> On the Russian soil.

The power of this image derives primarily from the fact that the reader—or better, the audience, since this work began in an oral tradition and drew on conventions from even older oral traditions—is led to expect a very different type of resurrection. Seed that is planted and watered ordinarily comes to birth as grain of the same sort that produced the seed in the first place. Grain comes from the earth and returns to the earth, only to spring forth again in a neverending cycle. And if the body is compared to grain, we anticipate a similar cycle of bodily death and rebirth. Yet in this decidedly somber description, all that is born is grief.

Another point must be made regarding these lines from the *Slovo*. Whereas lines 157–58, like the Potidaea inscription and the verses from the *Suppliants*, propounded a single fate for the body—return to earth—line 67 describes a differentiated transformation of bodily matter: the bones enter the earth while the blood becomes water, and it is the reunion of bones/seeds-in-the-earth and blood/water that provokes expectations of rebirth. Here, the traditional homology of blood/water has been faithfully preserved, while those of flesh/earth and bones/stones seem to have fallen together.

The Greek sources, being less specific—only the undifferentiated "body" *(sōma)* returns to the earth—avoid this issue entirely, but a similar conflation of homologies that are more often held separate is evident in an Iranian text, *Zad Spram* 34.7, which gives a detailed description of the body's fate. This verse occurs within a broader discussion in which the Wise Lord, Ohrmazd, answers Zarathuštra's question (*ZS* 34.1): "Concerning the corporeal ones who have passed away into the earth—at the Renovation, do they become corporeal again, or are they like shadows?" To this Ohrmazd answers immediately (*ZS* 34.2): "They become corporeal again. They rise up." Concerning the details of their reincorporation, as presented in *ZS* 34.8–19 and elsewhere, I shall have more to say later. But before Ohrmazd passes to that topic, he first describes the corporeal effects of death.

> There are five collectors, receptacles of the corporeal substance of those who have died. One is the earth, which is the keeper of flesh and bone and sinew (or: fat) of men. The second is water, which is the keeper of blood. The third is the plants, preservers of bodily hair and hair of the head. The fourth is light, recipient of fire. Last is the wind, which is the life-breath of my own creatures at the time of the Renovation.

Here three traditional and broadly attested homologies are presented quite straightforwardly: blood/water, breath/wind, and hair/plants. The first two of these we have already encountered in Greek and Slavic descriptions of the effects of death. To these, a fourth homology specific to Iran is added: fire/light, the fire in all likelihood being the internal digestive fire that converts food into bodily warmth. In all of these instances, death effects the transfer of material substance from microcosm to macrocosm: blood entering into water—its homologic "collector" or "receptacle"—

breath into wind, and so forth. Yet the final cosmic element—earth—is said to be the receptacle not only of the body's flesh (the normal alloform of earth, as we repeatedly have seen) but of its bone and sinew (or fat, if the reading *pīh* is preferred to *pay*) as well, which is to say that in Iran—as in Greece and Russia—the earth was treated as the residual category, to which all bodily matter not assigned other cosmic resting places was allocated. Presumably, this formulation derives from burial practices, either primary or secondary, in which bodily remains of varied sorts were, quite literally, consigned to the earth.

Indic sources present much the same analysis of the body's fate as does *ZS* 34.7, although they go into still greater homologic detail. At death, the body is seen to break down into numerous constituent parts, which then become part of ("enter into") those elements which are their macrocosmic alloforms. One famous treatment of this theme is *Bṛhadāraṇyaka Upaniṣad* 3.2.13, in which the same homologies appear as in *ZS* 34.7 (breath/wind, flesh/earth, hair/plants, blood/water), along with certain other traditional alloformic pairs (eye/sun, mind/moon) and others found only in India, drawn from the *Puruṣasūkta* and elsewhere (voice/fire, ears/cardinal directions, self/atmosphere, semen/water). Like *ZS* 34, this Upaniṣadic passage takes the form of a dialogue on matters of ultimate concern. Here, the great sage Ārtabhāga interrogates the even greater sage, Yājñvalkya.

> "Yājñavalkya," he said, "when the voice of a dead man enters the fire, his breath the wind, his eye the sun, his mind the moon, his ear the cardinal directions, his flesh the earth, his self (*ātman*) the atmosphere, his bodily hair the herbs, the hair of his head the trees, and his blood and semen are deposited in the waters, what then does this man become?"
>
> "Take my hand, dear Ārtabhāga. Only we two will know of this. It is not (to be spoken of) by us here in the presence of others."

What Ārtabhāga presents here is an ancient, authoritative teaching on the nature of death and the body's fate, which is preserved in many other IE sources and given in slightly different form elsewhere in the same Upaniṣad (*BṛhadUp* 1.3.11–16). Yet, in what follows, Yājñvalkya adds new ideas to this old theme, for we are told that once the two sages had gone off in private, "They spoke: karma was what they spoke about. Then they praised: karma was what they praised." *Karma*—the theory of cyclical rebirths that depend on deeds performed in previous lives—is a new tenet in the early Upaniṣads, absent from earlier sources, that quickly became a dominant concern of Indian religion and philosophy. In *BṛhadUp* 3.2.13 it is presented as a sacred secret, a mystery reserved for the private conversations of the most elevated sages. The ideas it replaced, however—those presented by Ārtabhāga, in which death is treated as a form of sacrifice, as signaled by his consistent use of *puruṣa,* the name of the first sacrificial victim, to denote "man" in general—are much older, and are found in earlier Indic texts, as for instance *SB* 10.3.3.8, which begins by asking what happens to the fire when it is extinguished, and then considers as a parallel process the fate of the body when life is extinguished:

> When the fire goes out, it is dispersed into the wind. Therefore, they say "It is finished," for truly it is dispersed into the wind. When the sun sets, it enters the wind. The moon and the cardinal directions are established in the wind, and they are born again from the wind .
>
> He who knows thus—he goes forth from this world. He enters the fire with his voice, the sun with his eye, the moon with his mind, the cardinal directions with his ear, the wind with his breath. He, having become one who is made thus, having become whichever of the deities he desires—he is at rest.

When the fire is said to be finished, it is not really finished, it has merely entered the wind; similarly, the sun does not die at sunset but also enters the wind. And just as the sun reappears each morning, so too fire can reappear from its temporary residence in the wind, as is seen when the wind blows on hot coals and causes flame to leap up. Similarly, human death is only an apparent end, for the body enters the cosmos, and there is a strong implication that the body will be reborn from the cosmos, like fire and sun from the wind. After his dispersion to the elements, the dead man is said to be resting (Skt *ilayati*), a verb usually used for the state of sleep or temporary quiescence, from which there is inevitably a reawakening.

The earliest attestation of this view of death is found in an extremely important hymn of the *Ṛg Veda* devoted to the funerary fire, dating perhaps as early as 1200 B.C. In *RV* 10.16.3, the attending priest instructs the deceased:

> Your eye must go to the sun, and your self (must go) to the wind.
> You must go to heaven and earth, according to what is right—
> Or you must go the the waters, if that is fated for you; you must
> stand in the plants with your flesh.

This brief text is among the most fascinating we have seen, for it presents two alternative destinations for the corpse. In the first, articulated in *RV* 10.16.3ab, parts of the body disperse to the three vertical strata of the cosmos: the eye goes to the sun in the highest heavens; the self (*ātman*), understood here as the life-breath, passes to the intermediate wind; and the rest of the body goes to the residual category, the earth. This dispersal, like those in *BṛhadUp* 3.2.13 and *SB* 10.3.3.8, is on the cosmogonic model, whereby pieces of the body join their macrocosmic alloforms at death, just as the same bodily pieces of the first human victim established those elements upon the performance of the first, cosmogonic sacrifice. Whereas the other Indo-Iranian texts develop this theme in some detail, however, *RV* 10.16.3ab presents it in rather abbreviated, almost shorthand fashion, as do the Greek and Russian sources I have considered: soul to wind or air, body to earth being the minimal, irreducible form that the idea may take, as in the Potidaea inscription.

In addition to this analysis of death, *RV* 10.16.3cd offers a second possible fate for the body, introducing this alternative with the contrastive particle *vā* "or". According to this hemistich, the body may enter the waters and plants instead of the three cosmic levels; an adaptation of the sitiogonic pattern to the theme of the body's fate. Should, for some reason, the corpse not replenish the entire cosmos with its material substance, as did the first man at the dawn of time, another possibility exists: it may follow the model of the primordial bovine, and become food in the form of fluids and plants. The same sitiogonic transformation of the corpse is attested in Iran; in *Vīdēvdāt* 5.18–20 the Wise Lord answers two related questions: how does he dispose of corpses, and how do the cosmic seas work:

> I, Ahura Mazdā, carry away the corpse. I, Ahura Mazdā, carry away the afterbirth. I, Ahura Mazdā, cause bones to be sent away. I, Ahura Mazdā, wash off that which is impure. I wash these together to the Pūitika ("Purifying") Sea.
>
> These (contents) stream into the sea. By virtue of their purification (there), the waters run from the Pūitika Sea to the Vouru.kaša Sea (the cosmic ocean), to the tree of the good waters. There all my plants grow, all growing by the hundreds, the thousands, the myriads of myriads.
>
> I cause all these to rain down together,
> I, who am Ahura Mazdā,
> As food for the Right-possessing man,
> As pasture for the beneficent cow.
>
> My grain—man shall eat (that); the pasture is for the beneficent cow.

As in *RV* 10.16.3cd, the deceased here enters the waters and the plants, and we are explicitly told that these are to be understood as food, which will be consumed by men and cattle alike and from which their bodies will be rebuilt. To the best of my knowledge, only these Indo-Iranian sources preserve mention of the sitiogonic alternative, and we also lack any discussion whatsoever of the fate of animals at death. Yet perhaps it is not too much to assume that animals at death repeated the fate of the first animal, from whose body food was created. If this is so, then we might speculate further and suggest that just as an animal victim might do service for a human victim in sacrifice, its body becoming the cosmos instead of just food, so too a human corpse might assume the fate ordinarily reserved for animals, becoming food instead of the cosmos.

Whether these last suggestions hold true or not—and they should be considered no more than suggestions in the absence of further data—the contents of *RV* 10.16.3 may no longer be lightly dismissed as a feeble reworking of themes drawn directly from *RV* 10.90, as some authorities have claimed, for nowhere in the latter does the sitiogonic alternative appear.

Having come to the earliest attestation of this set of ideas, I must also consider one of the most recent: the Fourth Meditation of John Donne's *Devotions upon Emergent Occasions.* The *Devotions,* written in 1624, are a set of reflections on the "Variable, and therefore miserable condition of Man" (First Meditation), and purport to have been written during a grave illness, from which Donne expected to die. They follow the course of the illness and its treatment to Donne's final cure, which he compares to a rebirth like that of Lazarus. The Fourth Meditation occurs at the point where Donne recognizes the full seriousness of the disease, along with the strong possibility of death, and accordingly sends for the Physician. While thus contemplating death and disease, he muses:

> It is too little to call *Man a little World;* Except *God,* Man is a *diminutive* to nothing. Man consists of more pieces, more parts, then the world; then the world doeth, nay then the world is. And if those pieces were extended, and stretched out in Man, as they are in the world, Man would bee the *Gyant,* and the world the *Dwarfe,* the world but the *Map,* and the Man the *World.* If all the *Veines* in our bodies, were extended to *Rivers,* and all the *Sinewes,* to *vaines of Mines,* and all the *Muscles,* that lye upon one another, to Hilles, and all the *Bones to Quarries* of stones, and all the other pieces, to the proportion of those which correspond to them in the *world,* the *aire* would be too little for this *Orbe* of Man to move in, the firmament would bee but enough for this *star;* for, as the whole world hath nothing, to which something in man doth not answere, so hath man many pieces, of which the whol world hath no representation.

To be sure, few of these ideas are original with Donne. The theme of microcosm and macrocosm appears frequently in his writings, and it has been shown that in large measure he took it from the works of Paracelsus, who in turn drew on a variety of Neoplantonic and Hippokratic sources, behind which lay the full Indo-European heritage. In some measure, these ancient ideas still seemed valid and acceptable to a high-ranking Anglican clergyman and prominent intellectual of the seventeenth century. Yet at other points Donne pits himself against the system, as when his powerful humanism requires him to make the self-consciously audacious assertion that the human organism is grander than the universe, having in it parts—one assumes he means the "soul" in a Christian sense—for which there are no macrocosmic alloforms. Donne's Meditation is particularly precious for us no matter how late its date or idiosyncratic its final conclusions, for it reveals the enduring power of the traditional IE view of death to provide some measure of solace to an individual at death's door. The other sources I have examined—funerary inscriptions, tragic choruses, epic laments, and ritual or theological texts—view death from the stand point of an observer, an outsider. Yet countless human beings—and Donne was not the last of them—have drawn comfort from the expectation that when dead they would not disappear but would merge with the cosmos.

Donne's Meditation is a relatively recent variant on a traditional theme—the nature of death—on which the Greek, Slavic, Indic, and Iranian materials offer us more ancient testimony. Within this tradition, death was understood to be a process whereby matter was transmuted from a bodily to a cosmic form, along the lines of well-established homologies. At a bare minimum, the lifebreath became or "entered into" the wind, while the body "entered" or became the earth. Beyond this, other homologies might be added: blood/water appears fairly frequently, as do bones/stones (or some variant thereof) and hair/plants.

Further, this material translation from microcosm to macrocosm was seen as a form of sacrifice, indeed, as the last sacrifice that all human beings perform, in which their very bodies are offered up to ensure the continued existence of the universe. In *Atharva Veda* 12.3, a hymn in which cremation is treated as a form of sacrifice, the priest repeatedly addresses the deceased in terms such as these: "I cause you, who are earth, to dwell in the earth; this body of yours, which was whole, is (now) cut apart" (*AV* 12.3.22ab); "I unite you, who are earth, with the earth" (*AV* 12.3.23b). In the most grandiose statement of all, the corpse about to be consumed by flames is told that it will sustain the world: "Preserver, preserve yourself in the preservation of the earth; the deities must cause you to move on, you who have not yet moved on" (*AV* 12.3.35ab).

Like all sacrifice, death is a repetitive, ritual act. Each death repeats every other death and every other sacrifice: above all the first death, which was also the first sacrifice and, most important, effected the creation of the universe. For while death is the fate of all human beings, death is also a cosmogonic act. Whenever people die, their bodies replenish, sustain, or even re-create the universe at large.

As always, there is more. For by now it should be apparent that within the common IE system of cosmological speculation there is no movement without a countermovement, no cosmogony without an answering anthropogony, no shift of matter that is not balanced by a shift in the opposite direction. It is thus no surprise that there are numerous texts that describe the body's resurrection at the end of time—or, to put it more precisely, at the end of each cosmic cycle.

Iranian sources provide several detailed descriptions of the resurrection of the dead (Pahl *ristāxez*), which is already mentioned in earlier Avestan passages. Consistently, the resurrection is presented as a culminating act in the Renovation or "Making-Wonderful" (Pahl *frašagird*) of the cosmos, which takes place at the end of the twelve thousand years Zoroastrian theology assigns to the history of the material world. A fairly straightforward account is given in the *Pahlavi Rivayat accompanying the Dādestān I Dēnīg* 48.54–55:

> He who is the chief—Sošyans [the eschatological hero], the accomplisher of the Renovation—and those who are his assistants, set out on the resurrection of the body. And Ohrmazd summons bone from the earth, blood from the water, hair from the plants, and life-breath from the wind. He mixes one with the other, and he keeps creating the form proper to each.

The process described here is the reverse of death's effects as described in *ZS* 34.7, for the "receptacles" into which bodily parts fall at death now return them in response to the Wise Lord's call. From this bodily matter, each individual human being is restored. *ZS* 34.8–19, the passage immediately following the discussion of death, presents this same picture of the resurrection, with the added—almost comic—motif that when Ohrmazd issues his summons, the "receptacles" balk at first, saying that they have received the bones or blood or whatever of so many dead bodies that they cannot possibly tell them all apart. It is thus left to the omniscience (*wisp dānišnīh*) of the Wise Lord to distinguish them all and to reassemble each individual as she or he was in life. The process begins with Gayōmard, the first man, from whose body the cosmos was created. The eschaton thus reverses the cosmogony, as the man from whom the cosmos was made is now made from the cosmos. Nor is the point valid for Gayōmard alone: it applies with equal force to each individual. When their bodies are de-created at death, they create the cosmos, and when the cosmos is de-created at the Renovation, their bodies are recreated from it.

Ideas of resurrection are also preserved in numerous Russian folk songs and formal laments, although these are not placed within any grander world-eschatological scheme. Also, just as the Russian discussions of the body's dispersal at death that I considered earlier made use of a very limited set or homologies, so also these texts in which resurrection is suggested make use of only the same few items. Given the late date of these lamentations (eighteenth and nineteenth centuries A.D.), this may be due to gradual attrition of an originally fuller ideology. Two examples may be cited: the first a lament for the Czar, collected at Simbirsk; the second a north Russian lament for one's mother.

> Flow, flow, threatening cloud,
> Pour out, strong dense rain,
> Soak up, damp mother earth!
> Open yourself, damp mother earth
> In all four directions!
> Open, you coffin boards,
> Fling yourself open, thin white shroud,
> Get up, get up, you righteous Czar!

> Roll from the mountains, springtime streams:
> Soak the yellow sands.
> Lift up the coffin lid,
> Open the shrouds.
> Grant to me—I who am stooped with sorrow—to glance once more
> At my parent, my little mother!

In both examples the call is made to the same elements: water, in the form of either rain or rivulets, and earth, in the form of soil or sand. These are to flow to the grave of the deceased, where they will unite and restore life to him or her; recall that in the *Slovo,* 1. 67, the bones of the dead entered the earth and their blood became water, which—when poured on the earth—called forth hopes of a resurrection. Yet in the lament for the Czar there is still a hint that the full cosmos must combine to effect his resurrection, for the water is to flow from all four cardinal directions, which is to say, from the totality of space.

It is doubtful that the speakers in these laments truly expected such a resurrection to take place. Rather, such phrases seem to have been part of the standard expressions of grief: the proper things to say at the death of a loved one. The very similarity of these laments with each other and with others like them shows their stereotyped nature. Yet behind them stands a long tradition, only part of which we can trace. A similar lament is found in the twelfth-century Russian *Slovo,* ll. 168–183, where the princess Jaroslavna, believing her husband, Igor, to be dead, calls on the wind, the river Dnepr, and the sun (which Roman Jakobson has shown to represent the cosmic realms of heaven, sky, and earth) to return him to her. The request is granted, for immediately after her lament—and so it is explicitly called—Igor returns, having miraculously escaped from captivity. Already in the *Slovo* this theme has been rationalized, and limited to an exceptional individual case, but the idea that the elements of the macrocosm may restore the life and substance of the dead is apparent nonetheless.

Certain texts hint at a belief in resurrection among some of the Thracian peoples and also the Celts, but the evidence is too scant to afford certainty. That both Thracians and Celts had elaborate views of an existence beyond physical death is quite certain, but whether this was an immortality of the soul, a metempsychosis, a resurrection, or some other mode of continuity is not clear from the vaguely worded testimonies that have come down to us. Most suggestive, perhaps, is Lucan, who addresses the Druids directly in *Pharsalia* 1.454–458:

According to you as authorities, the shades
Do not travel to the silent abodes of Erebus and the pallid dominions
Of Dis in the deep. The same spirit rules over bodily members (*artus*)
In the other world: death is the midpoint of a long life,
If you sing things which are rightly known.

In contrast to the usual bland assertion that the Druids taught the immortality of the soul, Lucan here ignores the soul and discusses the fate of the body. Moreover, he strongly implies that the material components of the body—*artus* "limbs" is a very striking term in such a context—are reconstituted after death, death being only a moment of transition between different loci of existence. In some ways, this is most similar to the ideas I have been considering, and it is maddening not to know more.

Germanic sources are a bit fuller, but once again there is less than one might like. For while we have several lengthy accounts of Germanic eschatology, as well as some pieces of iconographic evidence, the bulk of it deals with the world catastrophe of the

Ragnarǫk ("Fate of the gods"), with only brief hints of the resurrection that followed the destruction of the cosmos.

Most scholars now accept that the Old Norse Ragnarǫk mythology represents an independent variant of broader and more ancient eschatological traditions, although earlier researchers who noted the striking similarities to certain Indo-Iranian data were more inclined to argue that motifs or even full scenarios diffused from east to west. Similarly, the portions of the myth that tell of the world's restoration after its near-total destruction are now usually considered to be part of the pagan Germanic system, and not (as some had argued) the result of Christian influence. The most authoritative source for these is *Vǫluspá* 59–63, in which the sibyl (ON *vǫlva*) prophesies to Óðinn. The passage follows immediately upon the description of the collapse of the earth and the heavens, and the death of gods and monsters alike.

I see it come up   another time—
The earth from the sea,   green again.
Waterfalls flow,   an eagle flies over,
Who hunts for fish   on the fells.

The Aesir meet   at Íðavǫllr
And talk of the mighty   earth-encircler (ie., the Midgard Serpent),
And there recall   the mighty dooms
And Fimbultyr's (Óðinn's?)   ancient mysteries.

Then afterward   they will find
The wondrous gold gaming-pieces   in the grass,
Which in olden days   they had possessed.

Unsown fields   will grow,
All misfortune will heal.   Baldr will come;
Hǫðr and Baldr dwell there   in Hropt's (i.e., Óðinn's) battlefield,
The temple of the gods of the slain.   Would you know more, or what?

Then Hœnir is able   to work the sacrificial wands,
And the sons of the brothers   of Tveggi dwell
In wide Wind-home.   Would you know more, or what?

This passage systematically presents the period immediately after the cataclysm as a repetition of the paradisal age following cosmogony, and also as a reversal of the eschaton. Thus, the earth rises up from the sea, into which it has sunk as a culminating act of the world's end (*Vsp* 57). The gods meet at Íðavǫllr ("Shining Meadow"), where first they gathered (*Vsp* 7), and there recover the gaming pieces with which they amused themselves before any strife broke into the world (*Vsp* 8). In fact, world history seems to be nothing more than the working out of the gods' game, one round of which was concluded with the Ragnarǫk, and now the game begins again.

Of greatest interest to us, however, is the resurrection of Baldr and Hǫðr, the two slain sons of Oðinn. That this is a literal resurrection of the dead there can be no doubt: Snorri, in his version of the same events (*Gylf* 53), states "they came from Hel," the subterranean realm of the dead, from which Baldr could not be released until after the cosmos was destroyed. Regrettably, we are told nothing of the precise way their resurrection is accomplished, nor whether others will be resurrected after them.

Other features of the *Vǫluspá* account are of considerable interest for the ways in which the end of the world recalls its beginnings. Thus, sacrifice resumes once more with Hoenir's working of the "sacrificial wands" (*hlautviðo*), and the mysterious Tveggi appears (*Vsp* 63), a figure who is barely known elsewhere, but whose name means nothing other than "Twin," being derived from the genitive form (*tveggja*) of the numeral "two" (ON *tveir*). Tveggi, who appears at the end of time, thus recalls those primordial figures whose names also mean "Twin": Tuisco and Ymir.

In many ways, the Germanic eschatological tradition shares important features with Iranian accounts of the Renovation. In both, a resurrection is one of the culminating acts of cosmic restoration after the cataclysm, and new men appear—or, perhaps better yet, new versions of the first men reappear—immediately after the world has been destroyed. This same coalescence of themes is evident in at least three different Greek traditions.

To begin, there is the myth of Deukalion and Pyrrha. Mentioned earliest in Hesiod and Pindar, it is given most fully in Apollodoros, *Bibliotheka* 1.7.2, and Ovid, *Metamorphoses* 1.245–415. Throughout Greco-Roman lore, Deukalion and Pyrrha are honored as the sole survivors of the flood with which Zeus put an end to the Race of Bronze, and they are thus the first humans of our own age. Moreover, they are the first man and woman in another fashion, for they are the first mortal children born of immortal titans—Deukalion being the son of Prometheus and Pyrrha the daughter of Epimetheus by Pandora—whereas all other humans of their age were created by Prometheus out of water and earth.

With the flood, one world age ends, and with the emergence of Deukalion and Pyrrha from their ark, another age begins. The two survivors face a problem: how to repopulate the earth. Piously, they seek an oracle from the goddess Themis to guide them in this endeavor. Ovid (*Met* 1.381–413) tells what happened:

> The goddess was moved and gave an oracle: "Depart from the temple,
> Cover your head, unbind your girded garments,
> And throw the bones of your dear mother behind you."
> For a long time they stood amazed, and Pyrrha first broke
> The silence with her voice. She refused to obey the goddess's commands.
> Trembling, she asked forgiveness for herself, (for) she feared
> To offend her mother's shade by tossing her bones about.
> Meanwhile, they repeated in their dark hiding places the obscure

Words of the oracle given, each considering them separately.
Then Prometheus's son soothed Epimetheus's daughter
With tranquil words. "Either our ingenuity is deceitful," he said,
"Or nothing is pious and the oracles advise a sinful deed.
Our dear mother is the earth; I believe the stones in the earth's body
Are what we called bones. We are ordered to throw *them* behind us!"
Although (Pyrrha) was moved by her husband's interpretation,
Still her hope was in doubt. What is more, both of them distrusted
The heavenly prophecies. But what could it hurt to try?
They separated, covered their heads, ungirded their tunics,
And threw the stones behind their own footsteps.
The rocks—who would believe this, if antiquity did not testify to it?—
Began to give up their hardness and their rigidity,
And gradually to attain a softer, more pliable form.
Soon, when they had been born, a milder nature was reached
By them, and it seemed like a human form:
Not plainly, but more like a statue as it is in the beginning.
Of these rocks, that part which was damp with moisture somewhere
And earthy—that turned into the flesh of the body,
That which was solid and unable to bend changed to bone,
And that which was the veins remained under the same name.
And in brief time, according to the will of the gods, the rocks
Thrown by the man's hands assumed the figure of men,
And from (each) female throw, a woman was remade.

Here is the very same scenario encountered in Scandinavia and Iran: the resurrection of humanity, starting with figures of the first-man type, immediately after the destruction of the world. The only difference is that the cataclysm is somewhat more limited in this myth, affecting only the surface of the earth, not the entire cosmos. Moreover, the myth of Deukalion and Pyrrha goes beyond the Germanic accounts in its detailed description of how humanity was re-created, in this resembling the Iranian and Slavic materials. For the new people who are brought into being by Deukalion and Pyrrha are constructed out of the material remnants of the macrocosm, particularly the elements earth and water, and are built up on the basis of homologic alloforms. Thus, their flesh is made out of the soft earth, their bones out of the hard stones, and their blood vessels from rock striations, this last homology resulting from the fact that one word, Latin *vena,* denotes both, as does its English cognate, vein. These are essentially the same homologies that inform the Russian laments; they also resemble closely the earliest homologies explicitly attested in any Greek source, those in the fragment from Khoirlos considered briefly in Chapter 1: "Stones are the bones of the earth; rivers are earth's veins."

What Deukalion and Pyrrha ask of the goddess after the flood is essentially the same question posed by Zarathuštra to Ohrmazd in *GBd* 34.4 (TD MS. 221.12–14): "Whence is the body remade, which the wind leads off and the water carries away, and how does the resurrection come to be?" What they seek is nothing less than a reversal of the world's end and a reversal of death, or, to put it differently, a re-creation of humanity and a repetition of the anthropogony. In *Metamorphoses* 1.413, which reads *Et de femineo reparata est femina jactu* "And from (each) female throw, a woman was remade," the verb used is *re-parō* "to make or prepare again." With some metrical adjustment, such verbs as *creō*, *faciō*, or *formō* could easily have been used, as could *parō* without the *re-* prefix. Yet Ovid chose a verb that would emphasize the repetitive nature of this anthropogony. It is not just that men and women were created thus by Deukalion and Pyrrha. He makes a stronger point: they were created thus *before*. Recall *Metamorphoses* 1.363–364, where Deukalion wishes he could create people out of earth as did his father, Prometheus. When we consider how it is that human bodies can be built out of these elements, we must also bear in mind the Greek and other IE sources, in which at death the body passes into the earth and the blood into water, from which they can be recalled when the cosmos is de-created at the end of a world age.

Similar ideas are found in the great myth of Plato's *Politikos* 269C–274E, the most elaborate of Plato's discussions on the topics of death and rebirth and cosmic cyclicity. Here, Plato describes the cosmos as a sphere, the motion of which alternates between two phases. In the first of these, the sphere is guided by God's hand, which spins it in one rotational direction (presumably clockwise). The motion is steady and secure, and the world partakes of both moral and physical well-being, this being the paradisal Age of Kronos when animals and humans lived peacefully, the earth produced abundant fruit of itself, and the climate was so mild as to make clothing and shelter unnecessary. But at a certain moment, God releases his hand from the cosmos, and it begins to spin in the opposite direction. The following period is the Age of Zeus, our own age, in which moral and physical conditions gradually deteriorate as the world spins ever more disastrously out of control, ultimately threatening to destroy all. In the face of this threat, God intervenes once more and starts the world rotating again in the same direction it had during the Age of Kronos.

The moments of transition from one rotational direction to another—or from one world age to another—are moments of catastrophe, when "beginning and end rush in opposite directions" (273A). The change of cosmic spin is said to be "the greatest and most complete change" that ever takes place (270B), altering all things. When God lets go of the universe, setting it into the Age of Zeus, earthquakes destroy almost all living creatures (273A), and when he takes control once more there is again a tremendous jolt and great loss of life (270D). Only a very few humans survive, and those survivors experience a total reversal of their lives. Consistent with the reversal of cosmic rotation, the course of life turns backward, and

> all mortal beings stopped coming to seem older; changing back, as it were, they grew younger and softer of skin. The white hairs of the older people turned black, and the cheeks of those with beards became smooth again, restoring the bygone prime of youth to each one. And the bodies of those made young became smoother and smaller every day and night, returning to the state of a newborn child, being made like (such a child) in soul and in body. Thereafter, they faded away altogether and wholly disappeared. (270D–E)

In the Age of Kronos, human beings do not age, but rather grow younger, until they pass beyond infancy and disappear. The mechanism whereby this disappearance is accomplished is spelled out later in the dialogue (272E), where we are told that people in the Age of Kronos "fall into the earth as seeds." It comes as no surprise, then, when we are told that the process of birth is also reversed in the Age of Kronos, people being born at a full old age, from which they grow younger thereafter. Moreover, they come to birth from the soil itself. The Eleatic Stranger, who recounts the *Politikos* myth, explains how this is accomplished:

> When the transition of the old people to the nature of a child is completed, it follows that those lying (dead) in the earth are put back together there and brought back to life, the process of birth being reversed with the reversal of the world's rotation (271B).

What is described is nothing other than a resurrection of the dead: a reversal of the process of death, whereby bodies are "put back together" (*palin . . . xunistamenous*) and spring forth alive from the ground, into which ordinarily bodies are buried or "enter" when dead. Further, this takes place immediately following an eschatological upheaval, the end of a world age, and marks the beginning of a new cycle.

So similar is this mythic scenario to Iranian descriptions of the Renovation that some scholars have argued for direct diffusion of the *Politikos* myth from Iran, specifying Eudoxos of Kyzikos as a possible intermediary, who entered the Academy around 367 B.C. and could have acquainted Plato with Iranian ideas. But while the similarities are undeniable, the Greek sources Plato himself specifies or implies are fully sufficient to have permitted him to construct his myth, and given the evidence of the Deukalion myth and the texts from Empedokles and Anaxagoras I will consider shortly, there is no reason to assume foreign origin for a myth involving resurrection of the dead and cosmic cycles. Rather, Plato—like the Iranian accounts, the Slavic laments, and the *Vǫluspá*—seems here to be drawing on traditional ideas that had come clown to him, in which the end of the world is seen to produce the re-creation of mankind from the material substance of the de-created macrocosm. The same theme is apparent in Plato's great predecessor Empedokles.

As we have seen, Empedokles—following Parmenides in this—rejected any idea of absolute cosmic creation or destruction, holding that the universe is eternal in its fundamental nature. Attempting to restore a sense of dynamism to the static cosmos that Parmenides envisioned, however, Empedokles argued that the universe was not totally without change but was best described as being "motionless in its cycle" (*akinētoi kata kyklon;* fragment B17.14), which is to say, ever changing, but always in the same repetitive (and thus changeless) pattern. This cosmic cycle he described as involving an alternation between two opposite states: a unified sphere, in which the four cosmic elements—which together comprise all the material substance of the universe—are unified; and a fragmented state, in which the elements stand separate from one another. Two forces produce the oscillation between these two states: Love, which draws all matter together, and Strife, which tears it apart (Chapter 1).

The history of the cosmos is thus an infinite repetition of this cycle: from unity to separation to unity again. And what is more, individual lives follow the same pattern, for each living organism is nothing more than a mixture in which the four elements are temporarily combined, and these elements separate out at death, only to be recombined again when the soul enters a new body. Four existing fragments spell out Empedokles' views on this topic:

> I will tell you another thing. There is no "origin" of all
> Mortals, nor is there any end in accursed death.
> But there is only mixture and interchange of the things mixed,
> And this is called "origin" with reference to humans. (B8)
>
> And when (the elements) are mixed into man—
> Or into the race of wild animals, or into bushes,
> Or into birds—then people call that "birth."
> And when they separate out, that is "the evil-spirited destiny" (i.e., death).
> That which is correct, they do not call by name, and customarily I myself speak in similar fashion. (B9)
>
> Infants! For their thoughts are not far-reaching.
> Truly, they suppose that that which did not exist formerly has been born,
> Or that anything dies out and is annihilated everywhere. (B11)
>
> For it is impossible that things are born from that which never existed,
> And (it is) unheard of and incapable of fulfillment that that which is perished utterly.
> For things will always be, eternally, wherever anyone pushes them. (B12)

Empedokles' contemporary Anaxagoras shares this view, perhaps having been influenced by Empedokles, or perhaps having drawn on a common tradition. One of the few surviving fragments of Anaxagoras's own writings (B17) lays out his opinions:

> The Greeks do not believe rightly concerning birth and annihilation. For nothing is born and nothing is annihilated, but (everything) is mixed together out of existing things, and separates (back into those things). Thus, they rightly ought to call birth "mixture," and annihilation "separation."

The picture could not be clearer. At death, a body dissolves into its constituent elements, which rejoin the cosmic totality, and at birth those elements are drawn out of the cosmos and recombined into a human (or animal or plant) organism. Never is there any birth for the first time: every birth is a rebirth, or better yet, a reconstitution of organic shape, a shifting of matter from the macrocosm to the microcosm, and a resurrection. Death, conversely, is never final. It is merely the temporary separation of elements, a shifting of matter from the microcosm to the macrocosm. In this analysis, as in so many others, Empedokles and Anaxagoras are heirs to an extremely ancient tradition, which they adapt in fascinating and novel ways, but which they also preserve with great fidelity.

The outlines of that system are fairly clear by now, although not all details are preserved with equal clarity in every text. Still, it is apparent that traditional IE thought on the topic of death and resurrection rests upon the same premise that informed creation mythology, healing practices, sacrificial ritual, and nutritional theories: the conviction that the material cosmos and the human body are complementary opposites, intimately interrelated and infinitely interchangeable along homological lines. When the world is created, it is created out of man—whether in cosmogony, sacrifice, or death. And when mankind is created—whether in anthropogony, nutrition, healing, or resurrection—it is created from the cosmos. The creation of one always implies the destruction or de-creation of the other. Alternatively, one might also say that the same matter always has existed and always will exist, forever alternating between human and cosmic forms. The processes we "infants" (as Empedokles put it) are accustomed to call "birth" and "death" are nothing other than moments of transition between temporary macrocosmic and microcosmic incarnations of matter. "Cosmogony" and "eschatology" are also such moments of transition, albeit on a larger scale.

What we see is that death and resurrection are reciprocal processes, in which matter passes from microcosm to macrocosm and back again. Death, moreover, is a form of sacrifice, a repetition of the cosmogony—which was simultaneously the first sacrifice, the first death, and the creation of the universe. And just as cosmogony and sacrifice are reversals of anthropogony and nutrition, so also death reverses the last two processes. Similarly it may be said that resurrection repeats the anthropogony and the action of nutrition, while reversing the effects of death, sacrifice, and cosmogony.

I have now reached the point where I can pick up a thread left hanging since the end of Chapter 3. There, after analyzing theories of nutrition, I offered figure 12 as a summary of cosmic processes, including cosmogony, anthropogony, sitiogony, sacrifice, and nutrition. Since then, I have shown that healing, like nutrition, is a form of anthropogony, whereby the body is rebuilt out of matter appropriated from the cosmos, and also that death and resurrection are varieties of cosmogony and anthropogony respectively, matter flowing from microcosm to macrocosm at death, and the flow being reversed with resurrection. Finally, I have shown that eschatology—the destruction of the cosmos at the end of a world age—is not only a destruction but also a creation, for human beings are (re)-created from the matter that is supplied when the cosmos is de-created. These processes can now be added to those described in figure 12, and the result is a broader, more complex, more inclusive, and also more neatly symmetrical account of cosmic processes, as can be seen in figure 14.

Figure 14 represents the various ways matter flows between people, animals, and the universe, with food—a complex and highly important component of the universe—also figuring prominently. In this diagram there is no starting point and no termination. Matter is always in flux, although a dynamic equilibrium prevails: perhaps Empedokles' description is best and all things are "motionless in the cycle." If we arbitrarily start with the matter incarnated in cattle, however, we can follow a turn of the cycle conveniently. Thus, when matter leaves its animal form, either through animal sacrifice or through the natural death of an animal, it becomes food, following the pattern established in the sitiogonic myth. From food, matter passes back into animals when animals eat and drink, or into human form when humans do the same. Matter moves from man to the cosmos, via human sacrifice or natural death, repeating the model established in the cosmogonic portion of creation myth. From the cosmos, matter may shift back to a human locus in healing—as portions of earth, for instance, are appropriated to restore damaged flesh—and also through the

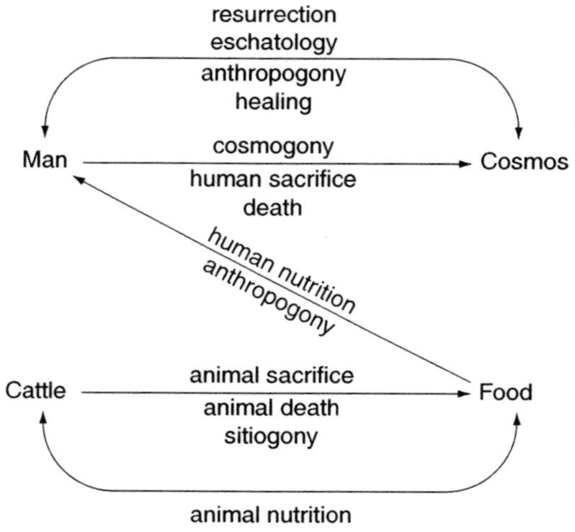

Figure 14. Cosmic processes: cosmogony, sitiogony, anthropogony, sacrifice, nutrition, healing, death, resurrection, and eschatology.

resurrection that takes place at the end of a (not *the*) world. Such shifts from the cosmos to man follow the pattern of the anthropogony. Finally, this constant and varied motion of matter from one entity to another may easily occur, for at the most fundamental level people, animals, and the universe are all the same, their apparent differences being only superficial distinctions of form. Each one is merely an alloform—an alternative shape—of all the others.

The circle is now complete. The myths of cosmic creation lead inevitably to those of cosmic destruction, creation and destruction being perfectly, symmetrically balanced processes. In truth, there appears to be no such thing as "creation" or "destruction" *tout court*. Rather, every act of creation entails a destruction, and every destruction a creation—for whenever something is created, its alloform must be de-created.

The myths I have discussed are concerned primarily with the nature of man and the cosmos, not with gods and the "supernatural." The analysis of material existence set out in these myths is enormously rich and complex, as we have seen, incorporating scores, if not hundreds or thousands, of homologic details and welding them into a coherent, cohesive system. The fundamental premises of this system might be summarized in four points:

1. Man and the cosmos are alloforms of each other.
2. Matter is eternal in its existence, but subject to infinite recombination.
3. Time is infinite.
4. Change is constant, but the same processes cyclically recur.

One who fully understands such points—who comprehends the nature of matter, the various forms it takes, and the interrelations of those forms—can manipulate all things in the universe. Cosmological knowledge is not theoretical only, but emphatically, even radically, instrumental, as seen from the fact that the "requests" in the Vedic hymns are set in the imperative mood, not the subjunctive. They are not requests at all, but commands, commands whereby a fully knowledgeable priest bends the cosmos to his will. Vedic priests, like their Druidic counterparts, regularly claimed that they possessed the ability to create and de-create the universe through the performance of sacrifice, and Empedokles claimed that he could teach how to bring rain, heal disease, and raise the dead (fragment B111). Such confident and audacious claims follow logically from the myths, in which were coded ideas considered nothing less than the secrets of the universe.

Chapter 8

Plato, Pythagoras, and Orphism

Mircea Eliade

According to A. N. Whitehead's celebrated formulation, the history of Western philosophy is only a series of glosses on the philosophy of Plato. Plato's importance in the history of religious ideas is also considerable: late antiquity, Christian theology, especially from the fourth century on, Ismaelitic gnosis, the Italian Renaissance, all were profoundly, if differently, marked by the Platonic religious vision. The fact is all the more significant because Plato's first and most tenacious vocation was not religious but political. In fact, Plato aspired to build the ideal city, organized in accordance with the laws of justice and harmony, a city in which each inhabitant was to perform a definite and specific function. For some time Athens and the other Greek cities had been undermined by a series of political, religious, and moral crises that threatened the very foundations of the social edifice. Socrates had identified the prime source of the disintegration in the relativism of the Sophists and the spread of skepticism. By denying the existence of an absolute and immutable principle, the Sophists implicitly denied the possibility of objective knowledge. In order to show the faultiness of their reasoning, Socrates had concentrated on maieutics, a method of arriving at self-knowledge and the discipline of the soul's faculties. Investigation of the natural world did not interest him. But Plato attempted to complete his master's teaching; and, to provide a scientific basis for the validity of knowledge, he studied mathematics. He was fascinated by the Pythagorean conception of universal unity, of the immutable order of the cosmos, and of the harmony that governs both the course of the planets and the musical scale.[1] In elaborating the theory of Ideas—extraterrestrial and immutable archetypes of terrestrial realities—Plato replied to the Sophists and the skeptics: objective knowledge is, then, possible, since it is based on preexisting and eternal models.

For our purpose it does not matter that Plato sometimes speaks of the world of Ideas as the model of our world—in which material objects "imitate" the Ideas to the extent of their ability—and sometimes affirms that the world of sensible realities "participates" in the world of the Ideas.[2] Still, once this universe of eternal models was duly postulated, it was necessary to explain when, and how, men are able to know the Ideas. It is to solve this problem that Plato took over certain "Orphic" and Pythagorean doctrines concerning the soul's destiny. To be sure, Socrates had already insisted on the inestimable value of the soul, for it *alone* was the source of knowledge. Taking his stand against the traditional opinion, sanctioned by Homer, that the soul was "like smoke," Socrates had emphasized the need to "take care of one's soul." Plato went much further: for him, the soul—*and not life!*—was the most precious thing, for it belonged to the ideal and eternal world. So he borrowed from the "Orphico"—Pythagorean tradition, at the same time adapting it to his own system, the doctrine of the transmigration of the soul and of "recollecting" (*anamnēsis*).

For Plato, in the last analysis, knowing amounts to recollecting (see esp, *Meno* 81 c–d). Between two terrestrial existences the soul contemplates the Ideas: it enjoys pure and perfect knowledge. But in the course of being reincarnated, the soul drinks from the spring of Lethe and forgets the knowledge it had acquired by direct contemplation of the Ideas. However, this knowledge is latent in incarnate man, and, by virtue of the work of philosophy, it can be recalled. Physical objects help the soul to withdraw into itself, and, by a kind of "backward return," to find again and recover the original knowledge that it possessed in its extraterrestrial condition. Death is therefore the return to a primordial and perfect state, periodically lost during the soul's reincarnation.[3]

Philosophy is a "preparation for death" in the sense that it teaches the soul, once delivered from the body, how to maintain itself in the world of the Ideas continually and therefore to avoid a new reincarnation. In short, not only valid knowledge but the only policy that could save the Greek cities from impending ruin was based on a philosophy that postulated an ideal and eternal universe and the transmigration of the soul.[4]

Eschatological speculations were highly fashionable. To be sure, the doctrines of the soul's immortality and of transmigration and metempsychosis were not novelties. In the sixth century Pherecydes of Syros had been the first to maintain that the soul is immortal and that it returns to earth in successive reincarnations.[5] It is difficult to identify the possible source of this belief. In Pherecydes' day it was clearly formulated only in India. The Egyptians considered the soul to be immortal and capable of assuming different animal forms, but we find no trace of a general theory of transmigration. The Getae also believed in the possibility of "making oneself immortal," but they knew nothing of metempsychosis and transmigration.[6]

In any case, Pherecydes' eschatology had no echo in the Greek world. It is "Orphism," and especially Pythagoras, his disciples, and his contemporary, Empedocles, who popularized, and at the same time systematized, the doctrine of transmigration and metempsychosis. But the cosmological speculations of Leucippus and Democritus, recent astronomical discoveries, and, above all, Pythagoras' teaching had radically changed the conception of the survival of the soul and hence of the structures of the beyond. Since it was now known that the Earth was a sphere, neither Homer's underground Hades nor the Isles of the Blessed, supposed to lie in the farthest West, could any longer be localized in a terrestrial mythogeography. A Pythagorean maxim proclaimed that the Isles of the Blessed were "the Sun and the Moon."[7] Gradually a new eschatology and a different funerary geography became dominant: the beyond is now localized in the region of the stars; the soul is declared to be of celestial origin (according to Leucippus and Democritus, it is "of fire," like the sun and the moon), and it will end by returning to the heavens. To this eschatology Plato brought a decisive contribution. He elaborated a new and more consistent "mythology of the soul," drawing from the "Orphico"—Pythagorean tradition and using certain Oriental sources but integrating all these elements into a personal vision. He does not draw at all on the "classical" mythology, based on Homer and Hesiod. A long process of erosion had ended by emptying the Homeric myths and gods of their original meaning.[8] In any case, the "mythology of the soul" could have found no support in the Homeric tradition. On the other hand, in his youthful dialogues Plato himself had opposed *mythos to logos;* at best, myth is a mixture of fiction and truth. However, in his early masterpiece, the *Symposium,* Plato does not hesitate to discourse at length on two mythological motifs, the cosmogonic Eros and, above all, the primitive man, imagined as a bisexual being, spherical in form (*Symp.* 189e and 193d). But these are myths that are archaic in structure. The androgyny of the First Man is documented in several ancient traditions (for example, among the Indo-Europeans).[9] The message of the myth of the androgyne is obvious: human perfection is conceived of as an unbroken unity. However, Plato adds new meaning to it: the spherical form and the movements of the anthromorph resemble the heavenly bodies, from which this primordial being was descended.

What most needed to be explained was man's celestial origin, since it was the basis for Plato's "mythology of the soul." In the *Gorgias* (493) we come for the first time upon an eschatological myth: the body is the tomb of the soul. Socrates defends this eschatology, citing Euripides and the "Orphico"—Pythagorean tradition. Transmigration is here only implied, but this theme, which is of capital importance for the Platonic eschatology, is, as we have just seen, analyzed in the *Meno* (81a–e). In the *Phaedo* (107e) it is further stated that the soul returns to earth after a long time. The *Republic* uses the old symbolism of macrocosm/microcosm but develops it in a specifically Platonic way by showing the homology among the soul, the state, and the cosmos. But it is above all the myth of the Cave (*Rep.,* bk. 7) that bears witness to Plato's powerful mythological creativity.

The eschatological vision attains its high point in the *Phaedrus;* there, for the first time, the soul's destiny is declared to be bound up with the motions of the heavens (246b ff.). The first principle of the cosmos is found to be identical with the first principle of the soul. It is significant that the same dialogue employs two exotic symbolisms: that of the soul as a charioteer driving his chariot, and that of the "wings of the soul." The first is found in the *Katha Upaniṣad* (1. 3. 3–6), but with the difference that, in Plato, the soul's difficulty in controlling the two horses is due to the antagonism between them. As for the "wings of the soul," they "begin to grow" when man "beholds the beauty of this world [and] is reminded of true Beauty" (249e). The growth of wings as the result of an initiation is documented in China, among the Taoists, and in the secret traditions of the Australian medicine men.[10] The image is bound up with the conception of the soul as a volatile spiritual substance, comparable to the bird or the butterfly. "Flight" symbolizes intelligence, comprehension of secret things or metaphysical truths.[11] There is nothing surprising in the use of this immemorial symbolism. Plato "rediscovers" and develops what may be called the archaic ontology: *the theory of Ideas carries on the doctrine of exemplary models that is characteristic of traditional spirituality.*

The cosmogonic myth of the *Timaeus* elaborates certain suggestions contained in the *Protagoras* and the *Symposium,* but it is a new creation. And it is significant that it is a Pythagorean, Timaeus, who, in this supreme cosmogonic vision of Plato's, affirms that the Demiurge created just as many souls as there are stars (*Tim.* 41d ff.). Plato's disciples later arrive at the doctrine of "astral immortality." Now it is by virtue of this grandiose Platonic synthesis that the "Orphic" and Pythagorean elements it had incorporated will achieve their widest dissemination. This doctrine, in which a Babylonian contribution is also discernible (the divinity of the stars), will become dominant from the Hellenistic period on.[12]

The political reform of which Plato dreamed never became more than a project. A generation after his death the Greek city-states were collapsing before Philip of Macedon's dizzying advance. It is one of the rare moments in universal history when the end of a world is almost indistinguishable from the beginning of a new type of civilization: the civilization that is to flower in the Hellenistic period. It is significant that Orpheus, Pythagoras, and Plato are among the sources of inspiration for the new religiosity.

ENDNOTES

1. Aristotle writes, not without malice, that the only difference between Plato and Pythagoras is terminological (*Metaphysics* 987b10 ff.). But, as Burkert rightly observes (*Lore and Science,* p. 44), for Pythagoras things *are* numbers.
2. See Guthrie, *The Greeks and Their Gods,* p. 345, and his *A History of Greek Philosophy,* vol. 4, pp. 329 ff.
3. Eliade, *Myth and Reality,* pp. 121–22. See ibid., pp. 122 ff., for some observations on the analogies between the theory of Ideas and Platonic *anamnēsis* and the behavior of man in archaic societies; see also *The Myth of the Eternal Return,* pp. 34 ff.
4. It may be recalled that Indian metaphysics laboriously developed the doctrine of transmigration *(samsāra)* but did not relate it to the theory of knowledge, to say nothing of politics (§ 80).
5. Cicero, *Tuscul.* 1. 38 (= Diels A 5). See other references in M. L. West, *Early Greek Philosophy and the Orient,* p. 25, nn. 1–2. According to another tradition, Pherecydes had used "the secret books of the Phoenicians"; but this is a cliché without documentary value (West, p, 3), though Oriental influences on Pherecydes' thought appear to be considerable (West, pp. 34 ff.).

6. Herodotus, 4. 93 ff. (cf. § 179, above).
7. But another tradition, describing Pythagoras' *katabasis,* implied belief in an underground Hades.
8. Xenophanes (born ca. 565) already did not hesitate openly to attack the Homeric pantheon, especially the anthropomorphism of the gods. He maintained the existence of "a god above all the gods and all men; neither his form nor his thought has anything in common with that of mortals" (frag. 23). Even so profoundly religious an author as Pindar objects to "unbelievable" myths (*Olymp.* 1. 28 ff.).
9. This conception will be persistently revived, from Neo-Platonism and Christian Gnosticism to German romanticism. See Eliade, *The Two and the One,* pp. 101 ff.
10. The Taoists believe that, when a seeker obtains the *tao,* feathers begin to sprout from his body. On Australian medicine men, see Eliade, *Australian Religions,* pp. 134 ff. These images will be revived and developed by the Neo-Platonists, the Church Fathers, and the Gnostics.
11. "Intelligence (*manas*) is the swiftest of birds" says the *Ṛg Veda* (6. 9. 5). "He who comprehends has wings" (*Pancavimca Brāhmaṇa* 4. 1. 13).
12. See Burkert, *Lore and Science,* p. 360. The belief that the soul is related to the heavens and the stars—and even that it comes from the heavens and returns there—is held by the Ionian philosophers, beginning at least with Heraclitus and Anaxagoras (Burkert, p. 362).

Chapter 9

The Myth of Er

Translated by H. D. P. Lee

The Good Man's rewards in the life after death. The responsibility of the individual and the doctrine of transmigration. This concluding section of the dialogue is cast in the form of a myth, as is Plato's habit when he wishes to convey religious or moral truths for which plain prose is inadequate. Much of the detail is borrowed from contemporary sources, probably Orphic.

614 'These, then,' said I, 'are the prizes and rewards which the just man receives from gods and men while he is still alive, over and above the reward of his own virtue.'

'And very sure and splendid they are,' he replied.

'Yet they are nothing in number and quality when compared to the things that await the just man and unjust man after death; you must hear about these too, so that our discussion may pay them both off in full.'

'There are few things I would hear more gladly.'

'It's no Alcinous' tale I have to tell,' I continued, 'but the story of a brave man, Er, son of Armenius, a native of Pamphylia. He was killed in battle, and when the dead were taken up on the tenth day the rest were already decomposing, but he was still quite sound; he was taken home and was to be buried on the twelfth day, and was already lying on the funeral pyre, when he came to life again and told the story of what he had seen in the other world. He said that when his soul left his body it travelled in company with many others till they came to a wonderfully strange place, where there were, close to each other, two gaping chasms in the earth, and opposite and above them two other chasms in the sky. Between the chasms sat Judges, who, having delivered judgement, ordered the just to take the right-hand road that led up through the sky, and fastened the badge of their judgement in front of them, while they ordered the unjust, who carried the badges of all that they had done behind them, to take the left-hand road that led downwards. When Er came before them,

they said that he was to be a messenger to men about the other world, and ordered him to listen to and watch all that went on in that place. He then saw the souls, when judgement had been passed on them, departing some by one of the heavenly and some by one of the earthly chasms; while by the other two chasms some souls rose out of the earth, stained with the dust of travel, and others descended from heaven, pure and clean. And the throng of souls arriving seemed to have come from a long jouney, and turned aside gladly into the meadow and encamped there as for a festival; acquaintances exchanged greetings, and those from earth and those from heaven
615 inquired each other's experiences. And those from earth told theirs with sorrow and tears as they recalled all they had suffered and seen on their journey, which lasted a thousand years; while the others told of the delights of heaven and of the wonderful beauty of what they had seen. It would take a long time to tell you the whole story, Glaucon, but the sum of it is this. For every wrong he has committed a man must pay the penalty in turn, ten times, for each, that is to say, once every hundred years, this being reckoned as the span of a man's life. He pays, therefore, ten-fold retribution for each crime, and so for instance those who have been responsible for many deaths, or have betrayed state or army, or have cast others into slavery, or had a hand in any other crime, must pay tenfold in suffering for each offence. And those who have done good and been just and god-fearing are rewarded in the same proportion. He told me too about infants who died as soon as they were born or who lived only a short time, but what he said is not worth recalling. And he described the even greater penalties and rewards of those who had honoured or dishonoured gods or parents or committed murder. For he said that he heard one soul ask another where Ardiaeus the Great was. (This Ardiaeus was the tyrant of a city in Pamphylia some thousand years ago, who had killed his old father and elder brother and done many other wicked things, according to the story.) "He has not come, and he never will," was the reply. "For this was one of the terrible things we saw. We were near the mouth of the chasm and about to go up through it after all our sufferings when we suddenly saw him and others, most of them tyrants, though there were a few who had behaved very wickedly in private life, whom the mouth would not receive when they thought they were going to pass through; for whenever anyone incurably wicked like this, or anyone who had not paid the full penalty, tried to pass, it bellowed. There were some fierce and fiery-looking men standing by, who understood the sound, and thereupon seized some and led them away, while others like Ardiaeus they bound hand and foot and neck, flung them down and flayed them, and then impaled them on thorns by the roadside; and they told the passers-by the reason why this was done and said they were to be flung into Tartarus." And Er said that the fear that the voice would sound for them as they went up was the worst of all the many fears they experienced; and when they were allowed to pass in silence their joy was great.

'These, then, are the punishments and penalties and the corresponding rewards of the other world.'

The paragraph which follows gives, in brief and allusive form, a picture of the structure of the universe, in which the rings on the spindle-whorl are the orbits of the planets and the sphere of the fixed stars.

'After seven days spent in the meadow the souls set out again and came on the fourth day to a place from which they could see a shaft of light running straight through earth and heaven, like a pillar, in colour most nearly resembling a rainbow, only brighter and clearer; after a further day's journey they entered this light and could then look down its axis and see the ends of it stretching from the heaven; to which they were tied; for this light is the tie-rod of heaven which holds its whole circumference together like the braces of a trireme. And to these ends is fastened the spindle of Necessity, which causes all the orbits to revolve; its shaft and its hook are of adamant, and its whorl a mixture of adamant and other substances. And the whorl is made in the following way. Its shape is like the ones we know; but from the description Er gave me we must suppose it to consist of a large whorl hollowed out, with a second fitting exactly into it, the second being hollowed out to hold a third, the third a fourth, and so on up to a total of eight, like a nest of bowls. For there were in all eight whorls, fitting one inside the other, with their rims showing as circles from above and forming the continuous surface of a single whorl round the shaft, which was driven straight through the middle of the eighth. The first and outermost whorl had the broadest rim; next broadest was the sixth, next the fourth, next the eighth, next the seventh, next the fifth, next the third and last of all the second. And the rim of the largest and outermost was many-coloured, that of the seventh was the brightest, the eighth was illuminated by the seventh, from which it takes its colour, the second and fifth were similar to each other and yellower than the others, the third was the whitest, the fourth reddish and the sixth second in whiteness. The whole spindle revolved with a single motion, but within the movement of the whole the seven inner circles revolved slowly in the opposite direction to that of the whole, and of them the eighth moved fastest, and next fastest the seventh, sixth and fifth, which moved at the same speed; third in speed was the fourth, moving as it appeared to them with a counter-revolution; fourth was the third, and fifth the second. And the whole spindle turns in the lap of Necessity. And on the top of each circle stands a siren, which is carried round with it and utters a note of constant pitch, and the eight notes together make up a single scale. And round about at equal distances sit three figures, each on a throne, the three Fates, daughters of Necessity, Lachesis, Clotho, and Atropos; their robes are white and their heads garlanded, and they sing to the siren's music, Lachesis of things past, Clotho of things present, Atropos of things to come. And Clotho from time to time takes hold of the outermost rim of the spindle and helps to turn it, and in the same way Atropos turns the inner rims with her left hand, while Lachesis takes inner and outer rims with left and right hand alternately.

'On their arrival the souls had to go straight before Lachesis. And an Interpreter first marshalled them in order and then took from the lap of Lachesis a number of lots and types of life and, mounting on a high rostrum, proclaimed: "This is the word of Lachesis, Daughter of Necessity. Souls of a day, here you must begin another round of mortal life. No Guardian Angel will be allotted to you; you shall choose your own. And he on whom the lot falls first shall be the first to choose the life which then shall of necessity be his. Goodness knows no master; a man shall have more or less of her according to the value he sets on her. The fault lies not with God, but with the soul that makes the choice." With these words he threw the lots among them, and each picked up that which fell beside him, all except Er himself, who was forbidden to do so. And when each had taken up his lot he knew what number he had drawn. Then the Interpreter set before them on the ground the different types of life, far more in number than the souls who were to choose them. They were of every conceivable kind, animal and human. For there were tyrannies among them, some life-long, some falling in mid-career and ending in poverty, exile and beggary; there were lives of men famed for their good looks or athletic prowess, or for their good birth and family connexions, there were lives of men with none of these claims to fame. And there was a similar choice of lives for women. There was no choice of types of character since of necessity each soul must assume a character appropriate to its choice; but wealth and poverty, health and disease were all mixed in varying degrees in the lives to be chosen.

'Then comes the moment, my dear Glaucon, when everything is at stake. And that is why it should be our first care to abandon all other forms of knowledge, and seek merely for that which will show us how to find the man who will teach us how to tell a good life from a bad one and always choose the better course so far as we can; we must reckon up all that we have said in this discussion of ours, weighing the arguments together and apart to find out how they affect the good life, and see what effects, good or ill, good looks have when accompanied by poverty or wealth or by different types of character, and what again are the effects of the various blends of birth and rank, strength and weakness, cleverness and stupidity, and all other qualities inborn or acquired. If we take all this into account and remember how the soul is constituted, we can choose between the worse life and the better, calling the one that leads us to become more unjust the worse, and the one that leads us to become more just the better. Everything else we can let go, for we have seen that this is the best choice both for living and dead. This belief we must retain unshaken when we
619 enter the other world, so that we may be unmoved there by the temptation of wealth or other evils, and avoid falling into the life of a tyrant or other evil-doer and perpetrating unbearable evil and suffering worse, but may rather know how to choose the middle course, and avoid so far as we can, in this life and the next, the extremes on either hand. For this is the surest way to human happiness.

'But to return. Er told us that the Interpreter then spoke as follows: "Even for the last comer, if he chooses wisely and lives strenuously, there is left a life with which he may be well content. Let him who chooses first look to his choice, and him who chooses last not despair." When he had spoken, the man with the first lot came forward and chose the greatest tyranny he could find. In his folly and greed he chose it without examining it fully, and so did not see that it was his fate to eat his children and suffer other horrors; when he examined it at leisure, he beat his breast and bewailed his choice, and forgot the Interpreter's warning that the fault for his misfortunes was his own, blaming fate and heaven and anything but himself. He was one of the souls who had come from heaven, having lived his previous life in a well-governed state, but having owed his goodness to habit and custom and not to knowledge; and indeed, broadly speaking, the greater part of those who came from heaven, being untried by suffering, were caught in this way, while those who came from earth had suffered themselves and seen others suffer and were not so hasty in their choice. For this reason and because of the luck of the draw there was a general change of good for evil and evil for good. Yet it is true also that anyone who, during his earthly life, faithfully seeks wisdom and whose lot does not fall among the last may hope, if we may believe Er's tale, not only for happiness in this life but for a journey from this world to the next and back again that will not lie over the stony ground of the underworld but along the smooth road of heaven.

620 'And to see the souls choosing their lives was indeed a sight,' Er said, a sight to move pity and laughter and wonder. For the most part they followed the habits of their former life. And so he saw the soul that had once been Orpheus choose the life of a swan; it was unwilling to be born of a woman because it hated all women after its death at their hands. The soul of Thamyris chose the life of a nightingale, and he saw a swan and other singing birds choose the life of a man. The twentieth soul to choose chose a lion's life; it was the soul of Ajax, son of Telamon, which did not want to become a man, because it remembered the judgement of the arms. It was followed by Agamemnon, who also because of his sufferings hated humanity and chose to be an eagle. And Atalanta's turn came somewhere about the middle, and when she saw the great honours of an athlete's life the attraction was too great and she chose it. After her he saw Epeius, son of Panopeus, turning into a skilled craftswoman, and right among the last the buffoon Thersites putting on the form of an ape. And it so happened that it fell to the soul of Odysseus to choose last of all. The memory of his former sufferings had cured him of all ambition and he looked round for a long time to find the uneventful life of an ordinary man; at last he found it lying neglected by the others, and when he saw it he chose it with joy and said that had his lot fallen first he would have made the same choice. And there were many other changes from beast to man and beast to beast, the unjust becoming wild animals and the just tame in every kind of interchange.

'And when all the souls had made their choice they went before Lachesis in the order of their lots, and she allotted to each its chosen Guardian Angel, to guide it through life and fulfil its choice. And the Guardian Angel first led it to Clotho, thus ratifying beneath her hand and whirling spindle the lot it had chosen; and after saluting her he led it next to where Atropos spins, so making the threads of its destiny irreversible; and then, without turning back, each soul came before the throne of

Necessity and passing before it waited till all the others had done the same, when they proceeded together to the plain of Lethe through a terrible and stifling heat; for the land was without trees or any vegetation.

'In the evening they encamped by the Forgetful River, whose water no pitcher can hold. And all were compelled to drink a certain measure of its water; and those who had no wisdom to save them drank more than the measure. And as each man drank he forgot everything. They then went to sleep and when midnight came there was an earthquake and thunder, and like shooting stars they were all swept suddenly up and away to be born. Er himself was forbidden to drink, and could not tell by what manner of means he returned to his body; but suddenly he opened his eyes and it was dawn and he was lying on the pyre.

'And so, my dear Glaucon, his tale was preserved from perishing, and, if we remember it, may well preserve us in turn, and we shall cross the river of Lethe safely and shall not defile our souls. This at any rate is my advice, that we should believe the soul to be immortal, capable of enduring all evil and all good, and always keep our feet on the upward way and pursue justice and wisdom. So we shall be at peace with God and with ourselves, both in our life here and when, like the victors in the games collecting their prizes, we receive our reward, and both in this life and in the thousand-year journey which I have described all will be well with us.'

Chapter 10

Phaedo

Translated by John Warrington

CHARACTERS OF THE DIALOGUE

PHAEDO,[1] on a visit to Phlius in Argolis, describes to ECHECRATES[2] the last hours of SOCRATES in conversation with himself, APOLLODORUS, CEBES, SIMMIAS and CRITO. An incidental speaker is the servant of the Eleven.

[St. I, p. 57.] ECHECRATES. Phaedo, were you yourself with Socrates on the day when he drank the poison[3] in prison, or did you hear about it from someone else?

PHAEDO. I was there myself, Echecrates.

ECH. Ah, then you can tell us what he said before he died and the manner of his ending. I should be glad to hear. Nobody from Phlius ever goes to Athens nowadays; a long while ago someone came from there, but he could give us no definite information, except that Socrates drank poison and died.

PHAE. [58] Didn't you even hear about the circumstances of his trial?

ECH. Yes, someone told us about it, and we were surprised that the execution took place so long afterwards. Why was that, Phaedo?

PHAE. It was quite accidental, Echecrates. The stern of the ship which the Athenians send to Delos happened to be garlanded on the day before the trial.

ECH. What ship?

PHAE. The one that commemorates a traditional voyage to Crete made long ago by Theseus with fourteen youths and maidens, whose lives he saved together with his own. According to tradition, the Athenians made a vow to Apollo that if Theseus and his companions got back safely the State would send an annual mission to Delos, and from that day to this they have sent one every year in honour of the god. Now Athenian law prescribes that once the mission has begun the city must

From "Phaedo" in *Plato: The Trial and Death of Socrates* translated with an introduction by John Warrington, 1963, J. M. Dent & Sons Ltd. Reprinted by permission of Everyman's Library, Northburgh House, 10 Northburgh Street, London EC1V 0AT.

remain pure, and no one must suffer capital punishment until the ship returns from Delos; but sometimes, when contrary winds detain it, this takes a long time. The mission begins with the garlanding of the ship's stern by the priest of Apollo; and this ceremony took place, as I say, on the day before the trial. That is why Socrates spent a long time in prison between his trial and his death.

ECH. What happened at his death, Phaedo? What was said and done? Which of his friends were with him? Or did the authorities forbid their presence and oblige him to die alone?

PHAE. Not at all. Some of his friends were there—quite a number of them, in fact.

ECH. Well, if you are not too busy, do please tell us all about it with as much detail as possible.

PHAE. I have plenty of time and I will try to give you an account of what happened. Nothing pleases me more than to be reminded of Socrates, whether by speaking of him myself or by listening to someone else.

ECH. Depend upon it, Phaedo, you will be talking to men who feel as you do; so try to tell us everything as accurately as you can.

PHAE. Speaking for myself, I experienced some strange emotions that day. I was not filled with pity as I might naturally have been when present at the death of a friend. The man's words and whole bearing, Echecrates, showed me he was happy, meeting death so fearlessly and nobly. This convinced me that in departing for the Underworld he was not setting forth without divine protection, and that on arrival all would be well with him, [59] if ever it was with any man. And so I was by no means filled with pity, as might have been expected of me at a scene of mourning; nor on the other hand did I feel pleasure, although our conversation was as usual of philosophy. No, the strangest feeling came over me, an unaccustomed mixture of pleasure and pain, when I remembered that Socrates would very soon be gone. All of us there felt much the same, sometimes laughing and sometimes weeping, especially one of us, Apollodorus; you know him, of course, and the kind of man he is.

ECH. Indeed I do.

'In fact then, Simmias,' he said, 'true philosophers train themselves for death, which is less formidable to them than to any other human beings. Look at it in this way. They are implacable foes of the body, and long to have the soul in isolation. It would surely, therefore, be worse than foolish if they were beset with fear when such isolation is on the verge of accomplishment, and experienced no joy at the prospect of going to a place where [68] they may hope to attain what they yearned for throughout their lives—I refer, of course, to wisdom—and to escape the companionship of that which they detested. Many men, after the death of their favourite wives or sons, have gladly made the journey to Hades in hope of seeing and being reunited there with those for whom they longed; and shall he who is really in love with wisdom and who is firmly convinced that he can find it nowhere else than in the land beyond the grave lament when he dies and not rejoice to go there? We cannot believe that, my friend, if he is really a philosopher; for he will be assured of finding wisdom pure and undefiled nowhere else than in the Beyond. This being so, would it not be the height of folly for such a man to fear death?'

'The very height of folly,' he replied.

'In that case,' said Socrates, 'when you see a man troubled at the prospect of death, is it not a clear sign that he was a lover not of wisdom but of the body. And the same man is also a lover of money or of honour—or of both.'

'You are perfectly right,' he said.

'Well, Simmias,' he went on to ask, 'isn't that which we call courage a peculiar characteristic of philosophers?'

'Definitely,' said he.

'And how about that which is commonly called self-control and which consists in not being dominated by the passions, in subduing them and in rigid propriety? Isn't self-control characteristic of those alone who despise the body and devote all their time to philosophy?'

'Without any possible doubt,' he answered.

'Yes,' said Socrates, 'if you care to ponder the "courage" and "self-control" of other men, you will find them to be mere mockeries.'

'How so, Socrates?'

'You know, don't you, that all other men reckon death among the great evils?'

'They certainly do.'

'And when brave men face death, isn't it through fear of greater evils?'

'That is so.'

[80] While the soul and the body are united, nature appoints one of them subject and servant, the other ruler and master. This being so, which do you think is like the divine, and which like the mortal? Don't you consider that the divine is naturally equipped to command and lead, the mortal to obey and serve?'

'Yes, I do.'

'Which then does the soul resemble?'

'Clearly, Socrates, the soul is like the divine and the body like the mortal.'

'Then surely, Cebes, it follows from all we have said that the soul is most like the divine and immortal, the intellectual and uniform, the indissoluble and always unchanging; whereas the body is most like the human and mortal, the multiform and unintellectual, the dissoluble and ever changing. Can we say anything, dear Cebes, to show that this is not so?'

'No, we cannot.'

'Well then, if that is the case, isn't it natural for the body to undergo speedy dissolution, and for the soul, on the contrary, to be virtually if not entirely indissoluble?'

'Of course.'

'You see then', he continued, 'that when a man dies the visible part of him, the body—which lies in the visible realm and is called a 'corpse', which is naturally liable to decay and dissolution—does not undergo these processes immediately, but remains for an appreciable time, and even for a very long time if death takes place when the body is in good condition and at an appropriate season. And when it does eventually decay, some parts of it, e.g. the bones, sinews, etc., are more or less indestructible. Isn't that true?'

'Yes.'

'The soul, on the other hand, the invisible part, goes to another place which is, like herself, noble and pure and invisible; she goes, in fact, to the realm of Hades, a good god and a wise, to whom my own soul (God willing) is soon to depart. Is this soul, I ask you, which has such a nature and such qualities, forthwith scattered and destroyed when she leaves the body, as most people say? Far from it, dear Simmias and Cebes. No indeed, here rather is the truth. Suppose she departs pure, trailing after her nothing of the body, with which she has never voluntarily associated during life, her constant study having been to shun the body and hold herself strictly aloof therefrom. In other words, suppose she has been a true devotee of philosophy and [81] has practised being in a state of death—unless, of course, you don't agree that real devotion to philosophy is the practice of death.'

'Oh yes, I agree to that.'

'Very well then, if the soul is thus disposed she departs into that which is like herself, into the invisible, the divine, immortal and wise. When she reaches her destination she is happy, freed from error and folly, fear and lust and all other human ills; as adherents of the Mysteries say, she "truly lives ever after with the gods". Is this our belief, Cebes; or not?'

'Indeed yes,' said Cebes.

'Suppose, on the other hand, that when she leaves the body she is defiled and impure, because she always treated the body as her friend and ally—pampering and loving it, fascinated by it and by its pleasures and desires, to such an extent that she thought that nothing was true except the corporeal, which one can touch and see, drink and eat, and use for venereal delights—and invariably hated and shunned what is dark and invisible to the eyes but intelligible and accessible to philosophy. Suppose all that, and then say whether you think a soul thus disposed will depart pure and uncontaminated.'

'She most certainly will not,' said he.

'No; she will be interpenetrated, I imagine, by the corporeal, which familiarity and communion with the body have rendered part and parcel of her nature because the body has been her constant companion and the object of her solicitude.'

'Exactly.'

'Yes, my friend, we must regard the corporeal as burdensome, heavy, earthbound and visible. Such a soul, through fear of the invisible and of the world beyond the grave, is weighted down by the corporeal and continually dragged back into the visible realm; and there she flits about the monuments and tombs, where shadowy shapes have been seen, figures of those souls which left the body not in a state of purity but retaining something of the visible.'

'Quite likely, Socrates.'

'Indeed yes, Cebes. It is also likely that those are not the souls of the good, but of inferior men, and that they are doomed to wander about in such localities as punishment for their former evil way of life. They wander thus until, through desire for the corporeal which clings to them, they are once again imprisoned in a body. It is probable, too, that they are imprisoned in natures which correspond to the practices of their former life.'

'What do you mean by that, Socrates?'

'I mean, for example, that those who have indulged in gluttony, violence and drunkenness, without taking any steps to avoid them, are likely to pass into the bodies of asses and other such beasts. Don't you think so?'

[82] 'That seems more than likely.'

'And those who have followed the way of injustice, tyranny and robbery pass into the bodies of wolves, hawks or kites. Where else can we suggest that they go?'

'Undoubtedly', said Cebes, 'it is into such creatures that they pass.'

'Then', said he, 'it is clear where all the others go, each in accordance with its own habits.'

'Yes,' said Cebes, 'perfectly clear.'

'Surely then', continued Socrates, 'the most fortunate of such impure souls, those which go to the best place, are those of men who, by nature and habit, and not as the fruits of rational philosophy, have practised the social and civic virtues known as practical wisdom and justice.'

'How are these the happiest?'

'Why, isn't it likely that they pass again into some such social and gentle species as that of bees, wasps or ants; or into the human race itself, where worthy men spring from them?'

'Yes.'

'No one who has not been a philsopher and who is not wholly pure when he departs this life is permitted to associate with the gods on his arrival in the other world. Only the lover of knowledge may do that. It is for this reason, dear Cebes and Simmias, that true lovers of wisdom firmly and successfully resist the impulses of all bodily desires, not because they fear poverty or loss of property, as most men in their love of money do; nor is it because they fear the dishonour or disgrace of wickedness, like those who esteem honour and power.'

ENDNOTES

1. A native of Elis in Peloponnesus; taken prisoner and sold as a slave at Athens in 401 B.C. He obtained his freedom and became a disciple of Socrates. After the latter's death he returned to Elis and founded a school of philosophy, which was subsequently transferred by Menedemus to Eretria.
2. Last of the Pythagoreans.
3. Hemlock.

Chapter 11

Tibetan Book of the Dead

David Chidester

The separation of the consciousness from the body at death was thought by Tibetan Buddhists to take as long as four days to complete. That process could be assisted, however, by a specialized Buddhist teacher known as the "extractor of consciousness." Sitting on a mat at the head of the body, the teacher guided the consciousness out of the body. Like a shaman, that Buddhist specialist was a psychopomp, a guide for the dead. He chanted, prayed, and went into a trance to be with the consciousness as it began its journey to another world. Surrounded by the fragrance of incense, the flickering of candles, and the deep resonance of chanting by the monks, the teacher whispered instructions that would aid the consciousness in its encounter with the world, of death.

Instructions given to the dying and whispered into the ear of the deceased were taken from a text that has been called *The Tibetan Book of the Dead*. The Tibetan Buddhists called that text the *Bardo Thödol,* which could be translated "Liberation by Hearing in the Other World" (Evans-Wentz, 1927; Rinpoche, 1992; Thurman, 1994). The text, which was prepared and used by schools of Tibetan Buddhists from around the eighth century, served as a map and guidebook to the world that followed death. The extraordinary territories of that other world had been explored in meditation, but they were expected to be encountered in their full splendor, as well as terror, by the consciousness during its passage through death.

Funeral rites and observances lasted about two lunar months. An astrologer was called in to cast a horoscope that showed the arrangement of the heavens at the time of death. The horoscope would influence the types of rites performed as well as the precise time and place for the funeral. While the corpse was placed in a fetal position within a death chamber, a carved image of the deceased was kept in the home or monastery for forty-nine days. During that interim time in the death ritual, survivors made offerings of food and drink to that effigy. Priests performed magical rites to assist the dead (Beyer, 1973). After the interim period, the body was disposed of by means of cremation, burial, or exposure in a final funeral ceremony.

As Robert Hertz observed in many death rituals, the Tibetan Buddhists treated the corpse in a way that reflected the progress of whatever remnant of the person was thought to survive death. The Ngaju Dyak, for example, had buried the bones at the exact time that they thought the soul entered the world of the dead. The bones were identified with the soul. For the Tibetan Buddhists, the surviving remnant of the person was not an immortal soul but a moving consciousness that passed out of the body on a trajectory toward rebirth. The funeral rites took forty-nine days; the entire process from death to rebirth was thought also to take forty-nine days to complete. In this way, ritual mirrored a mythic transcendence that imagined the transition of consciousness into another embodiment.

As there was an interim period in the ritual disposition of the body, so Tibetan Buddhists imagined an interim in the transition of consciousness from death to rebirth. During that period, the consciousness was expected to travel through an extraordinary realm of lights and sounds, dazzling visions, and terrifying horrors. Riding the karmic waves that had been set in motion during life, the consciousness was overwhelmed by attractive but also by repulsive and frightening visions in the other world. The consciousness was battered about by the winds of karma until it finally dissolved into unconsciousness in the womb of a new embodiment.

Primarily, the *Bardo Thödol* was a ritual text used in the ceremonies in which Tibetan Buddhist priests helped the deceased achieve liberation—nirvāṇa—during that passage through death (Brauen and Kvaerne, 1978). But this book may also have been used as a visionary text for meditation. It gave detailed descriptions of everything a consciousness could expect to encounter in the strange world after death. A person could prepare for those encounters by meditating on the visionary imagery of the *Bardo Thödol* during life. The temple, the monastery, and even the home could be decorated with pictures of the other world that would familiarize the consciousness with it. By being prepared, a person would be less likely to be overwhelmed by the powerful sights and sounds experienced in the passage through death.

During the first centuries of the common era, Buddhist missionaries had followed the trade routes from India into China. By the year 500, some had moved into the Himalayan country of Tibet. Different Tibetan Buddhist schools were formed, some gaining considerable power and political influence. They combined Buddhist meditation disciplines with shamanic practices that had developed in the indigenous Tibetan Bon religion (Powers, 1995; Samuel, 1993; Snellgrove, 1967). The Tibetan Buddhists also developed the unique institution of the *lāma,* or reincarnated Bodhisattva, who stood as the religious and political leader of the community. In established monasteries under the centralized authority of the lāma, Tibetan Buddhist monks practiced meditation techniques that would liberate them from the cycle of rebirth. The text of the *Bardo Thödol* contained much of the dramatic and intense imagery that was the focus of those meditations.

The *Bardo Thödol,* however, was also a visionary journey through death. As an imaginative text of mythic transcendence, it related everything that could be expected to occur to a consciousness after it was separated or extracted from the body. That journey was imagined to take place in three stages: the moment of dying, an interim stage of illusions, and the process of rebirth. Each of these stages after death was an alternative reality, a *bardo,* through which consciousness passed. The term *bardo* was used by the Tibetan Buddhists for any state of consciousness that was other than the reality experienced by ordinary waking consciousness. Three bardos were experienced in the course of an embodied life: in the womb, in dreams, and in meditation. Disembodied, the consciousness traveled through three alternative realities in the moment of dying, in the interim stage of illusions, and in the process leading to rebirth.

After death, the consciousness passed through each of those three stages. At every stage, however, it was exhorted to recognize everything it saw or heard as a projection of itself. When consciousness encountered the light and sound of the Buddha nature at the moment of dying, it was told, "Know that as you." When consciousness met the merciful and wrathful Buddhas in the interim stage of illusions, it was told, "Know them as you." Even when it was being judged, punished, and finally forced back into a body, the consciousness was instructed to recognize the whole process as a projection of itself. "Know it as you," the consciousness was told. Failing those tests of recognition, the consciousness remained locked in the cycle of rebirth. At every moment the person was bound, but at every moment there was an opportunity to get free. The *Bardo Thödol* was not only a road map to the other world, it was an instruction manual for liberation.

DYING

When breathing stopped, the energy that had served as a breathlike, vital force in the body was imagined to contract. That energy (*rlung* in Tibetan; *prāṇa* in Sanskrit) moved down the psychic nerves on the left and right sides of the body, draining vitality from the spinal column and the entire nervous system. The process of dying was described as a sensation of pressure, like the body sinking into the earth; it was a clammy coldness, like "earth sinking into water"; it was feverish heat, like "water sinking into fire"; and finally it felt as if the body were being smashed to atoms, "like fire sinking into air." Moving through the four elements, the body seemed to dissolve in the experience of dying. Although the body was beginning to be dispersed back to its elements, the consciousness passed out of the body into a strange new level of experience.

Chikhai Bardo

At the moment of dying, the consciousness entered the first bardo after death, the Chikhai Bardo. As consciousness left the body, it encountered a powerful, radiant, and reverberating void. That pure void was alive with light and sound. The text described this encounter as a vision of the "Clear Light of Reality." A lāma or a spiritual teacher stood by to remind the deceased that this was the light and sound of infinite Buddha nature. Since the transcendent Buddha essence was without any qualifying characteristics, it appeared as pure, undifferentiated light and sound.

Although that reverberating radiance was overwhelming, the consciousness was instructed to recognize the light and sound as its own nature. In the void entered at the moment of dying, the person could recognize that his or her own consciousness was the same as that Buddha essence. "Thine own consciousness," the deceased was reminded, "shining, void, and inseparable from the Great Body of Radiance, hath no birth, nor death, and is the Immutable Light." By recognizing that light and sound as its own, the consciousness could achieve liberation from rebirth in that first bardo at the moment of dying.

The pure light and sound of Buddha, nature dispelled all past karma. According to the principle of karma, consequences of past actions would have bound the consciousness to rebirth. But the object of the Buddhist path was to be liberated from the entire cycle of cause and effect. That liberation was possible in the moment of dying and did not depend on merit gained from past actions. Rather, liberation was a radical change of consciousness that allowed the person to abandon the body and merge into the pure light and sound of the Buddha nature. Like the sun driving away darkness, the pure light of reality broke the bonds of karma that would have led to rebirth.

Recognition was all that was required. In an instant of recognition, an enlightenment was achieved that guaranteed freedom from rebirth. By recognizing the pure light and sound as a manifestation of consciousness, the person remained in that state of Buddhahood. Summarizing the moment of dying, the *Bardo Thödol* stated,

> When thy body and mind were separating, thou must have experienced a glimpse of the Pure Truth, subtle, sparkling, bright, dazzling, glorious, and radiantly awesome. . . . Be not daunted thereby, nor terrified, nor awed. That is the radiance of thine own true nature. Recognize it. From the midst of that radiance, the natural sound of Reality, reverberating like a thousand thunders simultaneously sounding, will come. That is the natural sound of thine own real self (Evans-Wentz, 1927: 104)

When a person died, he or she was instructed not to cling to life but to recognize that luminous, thundering essence of Reality. Emerging from the body, the consciousness could merge into its own true nature as Buddha. That Buddha nature may have been recognized in life during meditation, but it was realized as the ultimate reality in the moment of dying. That moment, therefore, provided a supreme opportunity for liberation.

As the first stage in the journey after death, the Chikhai Bardo was thought to last as long as three and a half days. The consciousness was suspended in a swoon, lost in the void of the pure light and sound of Buddha nature. If the light and sound were recognized, liberation was achieved; however, most people were too bound by a sense of ego, by desire, and by illusion to recognize the Buddha nature as their own. They remained attached to a personal identity. Awed by the light and sound, they passed that first stage after the moment of dying in a hazy dream. Unable to recognize the void as themselves, they were carried along on the currents of their karma out of the first bardo and into the second, where they would be given further opportunities for liberation if they could recognize the Buddha forms.

The Hour of Death

The hour of death has been regarded in many different religious traditions as a moment of crucial importance for the fate of the dying person. In some cases, the disposition of the dying person's mind or heart in that last moment has been thought to determine the direction that person could be expected to take after death (Edgerton, 1926–27). Ritual arts of dying, therefore, have been important religious practices for preparing a person's consciousness or conscience. Besides allowing the dying to depart the world freely, they have been regarded as crucial techniques for directing the deceased on the right path to the next world.

The art of dying developed in the *Bardo Thödol* was almost exclusively concerned with the person's consciousness. Death was understood as the transition, release, or extraction of the consciousness from a body that was undergoing a reduction to its elements. As the body became earth, water, fire, and air, the consciousness emerged. Immediately, the consciousness was freed from the body to encounter its own nature.

Since Tibetan Buddhists were convinced that the consciousness continued after the cessation of all vital signs in the body, they remained by the body to direct instructions to the deceased as the consciousness passed into the first bardo. The art of dying developed in Tibetan Buddhism did not end with biological death but continued in the exhortations given to the consciousness by the priests and attendants. In this respect, dying was understood to occur not in a single moment but in an extended process of transition as the consciousness was given opportunities to establish itself in another reality and to liberate itself from rebirth.

The first opportunity for liberation was presented in the Chikhai Bardo. In the encounter with the pure, undifferentiated light and sound of the Buddha nature, the consciousness could merge into its own Buddhahood and achieve liberation. The Buddha nature encountered in that first bardo was understood by the Tibetan Buddhists to be the boundless, spiritual body of the Buddha. The spiritual body of the Buddha was one of three bodies of the Buddha as they came to be conceived in

Mahāyāna Buddhist thought (Reynolds, 1977). In fact, each stage in the consciousness' passage through the world of death was identified with one of those three bodies of the Buddha: the formless spiritual body, the formed spiritual body, and the formed physical body.

The formless spiritual body of the Buddha, the Dharmakāya, was the body of ultimate truth, or ultimate reality. That body was without form, without limit, without any of the conditions that applied to things in time and space. This eternal, formless, spiritual body of the Buddha was symbolized by the pure light and sound of the first bardo. The formless spiritual body of the Buddha—also called the Buddha nature or the Buddha essence—was to be recognized as one's own. Because the consciousness was also formless in the first stage of death, it had the opportunity to merge into the formless spiritual body of the Buddha.

Significantly, the Dharmakāya was symbolized as an extraordinary transsensory experience of light and sound. In normal perception, lights are seen and sounds heard; the visual and the auditory are separate. But in the encounter with the Buddha nature, the consciousness was imagined to experience an extraordinary light that resonated like a thousand thunders, a sound that was radiant. In perceptual psychology, the experience of seeing sounds or hearing lights has been called *synesthesia* (Chidester, 1992; Marks, 1978). Such experiences are unusual, but so may be the experience of dying. In symbolizing that experience, the text described it as an extraordinary synesthetic fusion of light and sound.

In recent research on near-death experiences (NDEs), some investigators have argued that the reports of people who have regained consciousness after being declared clinically dead bear a marked resemblance to the account of the *Bardo Thödol*. The experience of sound and light in particular has received much attention. Many survivors of NDEs have reported that the moment of clinical death they heard a loud ringing or buzzing sound. Often feeling like they were moving through a void or down a long, dark tunnel, many have also reported extraordinary experiences of light. A survivor reported to Raymond Moody, for example, that he had seen "a pure crystal clear light." Insisting that the light was not like any seen on earth, the person concluded that it was "a light of perfect understanding and perfect love" (Moody, 1975).

Using somewhat more controlled scientific procedures, cardiologist Michael Sabom found that more than 50 percent of NDEs involved some experience of light. A fifty-six-year-old executive from Florida described floating toward a source of light, "going through this shaft of light. . . . It was so bright, and the closer we got, the brighter it got, and it was blinding." A forty-five-year-old pharmaceutical salesman during a cardiac arrest experienced a light that he compared to sun shining on clouds as seen from an airplane. A fifty-four-year-old mechanic described the radiance not as light coming from a source but as the total absence of darkness. "This light was so total and complete," he reported, "that you didn't look at the light, you were *in* the light" (Sabom, 1981: 43–44).

Were these experiences of light the same as the experience described in the *Bardo Thödol?* Did the executive, the salesman, and the mechanic have the same encounter at the moment of dying that was anticipated by the Tibetan Buddhists? One difference certainly lies in the context within which the experience was reported to occur. Rather than a spontaneous, unexpected near-death event, the encounter with the light and sound of the Buddha nature was an experience that a Tibetan Buddhist prepared for through meditation and was guided through by priests and attendants. In other words, the experience was part of an entire ritual cycle that included a lifetime of meditation and the ritual procedures of the art of dying.

A second difference is found in the symbolism of the *Bardo Thödol,* which may have described the encounter with the formless spiritual body of the Buddha as light and sound because it was an experience that could not in fact be described. Calling that experience light and sound—particularly, a light that was heard and a sound that was seen—may have been a way of saying that it was so extraordinary that it was beyond description. Nevertheless, research on NDEs has suggested the intriguing possibility that scientific investigations could confirm the expectations of the Tibetan Buddhists that the moment of dying involved a powerful experience of light and sound (Epstein, 1990).

ILLUSIONS

After passing through the first bardo, the consciousness was thought to enter into a longer interim period of illusions, the Chönyid Bardo. This second stage was identified with the formed spiritual body of the Buddha, or Sambhogakaya, which was actually understood to be manifested in the many personalized forms of spiritual Buddhas that would be met in the interim stage after death. Assuming splendid, beautiful, but sometimes horrible forms, those Bodhisattvas were the formed spiritual body of the Buddha. In the second stage, the consciousness itself assumed a form, a thought body, which was its vehicle on its journey through the other world after death.

Experiences in that middle period assumed the quality of an extended dream, with vivid and dramatic images projected from the consciousness appearing as if they were real. Since the consciousness was traveling in a thought body, it did not need to fear those apparitions. They could not kill it because it was already dead. The consciousness had only to recognize them to get free.

Nevertheless, the consciousness still might not recognize the illusions of the second bardo as projections. It might be awed, overwhelmed, or even terrified by what it saw there. Therefore, the text of the *Bardo Thödol* advised the person to recognize everything encountered during that interim stage of illusions as a projection from consciousness. "Whatever may come—sounds, lights, or rays—are, all three, unable to harm thee: thou art incapable of dying," the text assured. "It is quite sufficient for thee to know that these apparitions are thine own thought-forms" (Evans-Wentz,

1927: 104). Recognizing all those appearances as projections from itself, the consciousness might achieve liberation from rebirth in the Chönyid Bardo. Failing that recognition, however, the consciousness continued on its trajectory toward rebirth, back into another body in another world.

Chönyid Bardo

On the fourth day after it had separated from the body, the consciousness, awakening from its swoon and wondering, "What has happened?," entered the second stage of its journey through the afterlife. The Chönyid Bardo was revolving, spinning around the thought body in which the consciousness was now clothed. Before the person could gain any sense of orientation, divine Buddha forms began to appear from all the directions of the compass. From east, south, west, north, and the center, the magnificent, merciful Buddhas appeared. In every appearance, the person was given a chance to achieve liberation. By merging into the forms that appeared, the person would be freed from rebirth.

But at the same time that the Buddha forms appeared, dull colored lights symbolizing the six worlds of desire where a person might be reborn also appeared, distracting and tempting the consciousness to turn back toward another birth. The white light of the heavens; the gray, smoky light of the hells; the red light of the ghosts; the green light of the demons; the blue light of the animal kingdom; and the yellow light of the human world—these six colored lights came from and led back to the lokas of rebirth.

If attracted to those lights, the consciousness would continue to whirl around on the cycle of human suffering. The text of the *Bardo Thödol,* therefore, exhorted the person to ignore those alluring, multicolored lights of the lokas. The consciousness was to resist any attraction to them by focusing on the rainbow splendor of the Buddha forms that appeared in the second bardo.

In this second stage after death, a new element was introduced: faith. The moment of dying had required a pure, conscious recognition of Buddha nature. The second stage offered opportunities for liberation through the quality of faith. In loving devotion to the divine Buddha forms that appeared, the consciousness could still attain Buddhahood by their grace. Merciful Buddhas came forward one after another to offer salvation in the second bardo. Beholding the "hook-rays of the light of grace," the consciousness could merge into those Buddhas through faith.

Although they awakened a liberating sense of devotion in the consciousness, those divine Buddha forms were nevertheless explained as spiritual forms projected from the person's own consciousness. The merciful Buddhas that appeared were all projections from the person's heart, manifestations of loving grace that could be recognized and embraced. But in all their splendor and magnificence, the Buddha forms were illusions, projections from consciousness. Repeatedly, the *Bardo Thödol* advised, "Recognize them as you." Like the Buddha nature beheld in the moment of dying, the spiritual Buddha forms were also identical to the genuine nature of the consciousness. Recognizing itself in the Buddha forms, the consciousness achieved liberation from rebirth.

The second bardo provided many opportunities to achieve liberation through faith, devotion, or love directed toward the Buddha forms. Unfortunately, most people failed to recognize the Buddha forms as themselves. At each appearance of a merciful Buddha, the consciousness recoiled from its splendor. Still attached to a personal ego identity, the consciousness failed to see that it was itself a gracious Buddha form, offering salvation for itself from the cycle of rebirth.

The symptoms of attachment to a personal ego identity were emotions—anger, pride, greed, jealousy, and so on—that separated the consciousness from the Buddha forms. They were like walls that protected the personal interests of the consciousness but at the same time blocked it from its ultimate liberation. At each appearance of a merciful Buddha, a selfish, egotistical, personal emotion blocked the consciousness, keeping it from merging into the rainbow lights of the Buddha forms.

As the entire bardo glowed a deep blue, the divine Buddha form of Vairochana suddenly appeared from its center, radiating a pure bluish-white light. In his splendor, that divine Buddha sat on a lion, holding the eight-spoked wheel of Buddhist wisdom. Each divine Buddha had a consort; the Buddha Vairochana was accompanied by his wife, the Mother of the Space of Heaven. "From the heart of Vairochana as Father-Mother," the text said, that wisdom "will shoot forth and strike against thee with a light so radiant that thou wilt scarcely be able to look at it" (Evans-Wentz, 1927: 106). Although that light of wisdom was overwhelming in its intensity, the person was exhorted to look at it in deep faith, praying earnestly for saving grace from Vairochana. In humble prayer, the consciousness could merge in a halo of rainbow light into the heart of Vairochana and attain Buddhahood.

Off to the side, however, pulsated the dull white light of the heavens, which distracted and tempted the consciousness. "Do not look over there," the text warned. That way led to rebirth. At this stage, the light of the heavenly loka was a distraction from the saving grace of the divine, merciful Buddha. Later, it would lead the consciousness back into another embodiment.

By focusing in love on the divine Buddha, the consciousness could achieve liberation. But it probably would not do that. The emotions of fear, terror, and anger could block the person from recognizing the Buddha form and merging into it. In order to protect a sense of personal ego identity, the consciousness might try to run away from the divine Buddha. In this case, anger arose from the person's past karma. Unable to get free from that karmic influence, the consciousness was propelled forward on its journey through the afterlife world.

Having been blocked from liberation by the personal emotion of anger, the consciousness was confronted on the next day by the divine Buddha Vajra-Sattva, riding from the east on an elephant throne. He held the lightning bolt of illumination in his hand, glowing with the pure white light of Mirror-like Wisdom. Surrounded by his wife and family like a constellation of divine Buddhas, Vajra-Sattva offered saving grace for those who recognized and took refuge in him. The text exhorted the consciousness not to flee but to place its faith in the light of the divine Buddha form. Recognizing that merciful Buddha as a projection from itself, the consciousness could achieve liberation by merging into its gracious form. However, it would probably be distracted by the dull, gray, smoky light pulsating off to the side, which came from the hell loka. Once again, the consciousness would probably also try to defend its separate, personal identity. Trying to run away, anger turned into pride as the consciousness was carried along on the currents of its karma.

The next day, the consciousness encountered the magnificent Buddha form of Ratna-Sambhava coming from the south, riding a horse and holding aloft the jewel of wisdom. Again, the merciful Buddha was accompanied by his wife and family, offering salvation for any consciousness that merged into him in loving devotion. But once again, a loka light—this time the dull blue-yellow light of the human world—appeared off to the side to distract the consciousness. That loka represented the personal emotion of egotistical pride that tempted the consciousness back into rebirth. Instead of merging into the divine Buddha by recognition and faith, the consciousness would probably hold on to its separate ego identity. As it tried to run away from the merciful Buddha, the consciousness was locked into egotistical emotions that blocked faith and prevented liberation.

With the dawning of the following day, the emotion of greed arose. On that day, the divine Buddha Amitābha appeared on a peacock throne, holding a lotus in his hand, and accompanied by his divine family to offer his liberating grace. Off to the side, the dull red light of the ghost world—the loka of the preta, or hungry ghosts—radiated its dim but alluring glow. In the preta-loka, ghosts were consumed by desires but had no means to achieve their satisfaction. It was a world of all-consuming greed. If that emotion blocked the consciousness, it was prevented from merging into the Buddha form of Amitābha and receiving that merciful Buddha's saving grace. In fear, terror, and egotistical greed, the consciousness tried to run away. But it remained trapped in the bardo by its own karma and egotism.

As greed became jealousy, the consciousness moved on to the fifth and final confrontation with a divine Buddha form. On that day, the Buddha Amogha-Siddhi appeared. Riding a mythological bird, holding the thunderbolt, and surrounded by his family, that divine Buddha also offered grace. But the dull green light of the demon loka—the world of the *asuras*—distracted and attracted the consciousness that was wrapped up in jealousy, envy, and egotistical desires. As on the previous days, the consciousness was not to look over there but to focus in recognition and faith on the luminous, divine Buddha. In love, the consciousness could merge into its radiant form and attain liberation.

Since it probably would fail to do that, the consciousness was propelled on by its own evil, egotistical inclinations. On the next day, the consciousness was given one final chance. Appearing all at once in their magnificent rainbow light, the five Buddha forms presented one more opportunity for the person to receive their grace.

At the same time, however, the lights of the lokas—now including the dull blue light of the animal world, along with the lights of the demon, ghost, human, hell, and heaven worlds—glowed off to the side. "Do not look over there," the text exhorted. In the purity of prayer, devotion, and love, the person was instructed to merge into the rainbow light of the merciful Buddhas and achieve liberating Buddhahood in the Chönyid Bardo.

The *Bardo Thödol* described the merciful Buddhas as projections from a person's heart. They were manifestations of divine love that promised salvation from rebirth. Failing to recognize them, the consciousness was forced to continue on its journey to rebirth. Suddenly, the experience of the consciousness shifted from mercy to a violent, shocking encounter with fifty-eight flame-enhaloed, ax-swinging, blood-drinking, wrathful deities. For twelve days, these terrifying Buddha forms attacked the consciousness. If the awesome majesty of the merciful Buddhas had been frightening, those wrathful Buddhas were terrifying beyond description. Consumed by terror, the consciousness was chased all over the bardo by them.

Those horrible Buddhas were only the merciful Buddhas appearing in different forms, however, shocking and terrifying the consciousness into a ruder awakening. Like the merciful Buddhas, these wrathful, vengeful Buddha forms were also projections from consciousness, but now they were projections from the intellect rather than the heart. Still, liberation was possible. If even these frightening Buddhas could be recognized as projections from consciousness, a person could achieve liberating enlightenment.

"When the fifty-eight Blood-Drinking Deities emanating from thine own brain come to shine upon thee," the text said, "if thou knowst them to be the radiances of thine own intellect, thou wilt . . . obtain Buddhahood" (Evans-Wentz, 1927: 146). Recognition may have been more difficult, as the Buddhas pursued, tortured, and terrified the fleeing consciousness. Nevertheless, it was still possible to recognize the mercy behind the vengeance and to achieve liberation through that recognition.

Since that liberating recognition had become so difficult by that point, most people were carried on to the next bardo that would prepare them for rebirth. After being chased all over the Chönyid Bardo by the terrifying Buddhas, the consciousness probably found the idea of rebirth attractive. Even if life in a body had been suffering, at least it was familiar.

Mental Life After Death

In the second stage after dying, everything was illusion. The Buddha forms appeared because they were projected from the consciousness. Merciful Buddhas emanated from the heart; wrathful Buddhas came from the mind. No matter how attractive or repulsive, they were to be recognized as projections. By recognizing the Buddhas as projections, the consciousness dissolved any separation between itself and its own Buddha nature. In recognition and faith, it merged into its own Buddhahood by merging into the rainbow lights of the Buddha forms. Although they were illusions, the Buddha forms nevertheless offered a saving grace to the person after death. They provided opportunities for giving up any sense of permanent personal identity, the egotistical attachment that bound consciousness to the cycle of rebirth.

Salvation was achieved, therefore, by a radical change of consciousness. In the bardo of illusions, the consciousness had to abandon any sense of separate personal identity in order to be liberated; it had to lose itself to be saved. If liberation from the cycle of rebirth was a type of salvation, it was a salvation from the ultimate illusion—the illusion of having a personal identity. The illusion of being a separate person was supported by the egotistical emotions of pride, anger, greed, and jealousy. Those were the sins from which consciousness had to be saved by a radical transformation into its enlightened Buddha nature. When a separate identity dissolved, all that remained was an enlightened freedom from the cycle of rebirth, a liberated Buddha.

If the illusions that appeared in the second bardo were all projections from consciousness, how did they get into the consciousness in order to be projected out after death? One answer to this question may be that after death a person projected what he or she had dwelled on during life. Consciousness may have been understood something like a movie projector running film that had been shot during life. In other words, the illusions that a person met after death were the images, sights, sounds, hopes, and fears that had preoccupied consciousness during life. The pattern of afterlife experience—from the moment of dying through the interim period of illusions to preparation for rebirth—might have been understood to be the same for everyone. But the precise content of the sights and sounds was determined by the consciousness that projected the illusions it encountered.

Tibetan Buddhists dwelled on the images of the five merciful Buddhas, meditating on their forms, their symbols, and everything associated with them, during a lifetime of spiritual discipline. Colorful statues of the five merciful Buddhas stood in an alcove in the monastery. Vivid designs depicting the Buddha forms were used to focus meditation. In this way, the consciousness was prepared to recognize what it encountered after death. More than that, however, the consciousness was prepared to recognize what it saw as projection. By recognizing projection as projection, the consciousness was freed from the web of illusion that tied it to the process of rebirth.

Taking this consideration of afterlife projections a step further, perhaps the content of the projected illusions was determined by the kind of training a consciousness had received during life. If the consciousness were trained in disciplined meditation, perhaps its afterlife illusions would appear in greater focus. But this also suggests the possibility that different trainings could produce different projections from consciousness after death. A Tibetan Buddhist might have been expected to see Buddhist imagery, but a Christian could be expected to encounter Christian imagery; a Hindu, Hindu imagery; a Muslim, Muslim imagery; and so on. In other words, each religious tradition would prepare a consciousness to project different content after death.

The *Bardo Thödol* seemed to imply that afterlife experiences would be specific to the religion and culture in which a consciousness had been trained. As a twentieth-century Tibetan Buddhist noted, "The illusory *Bardo* visions vary, in keeping with the religious or cultural tradition in which the percipient has grown up, but their underlying motive-power is the same in all human beings" (Evans-Wentz, 1927: lxii). The pattern might be the same, but the precise content would vary from religious tradition to tradition.

Obviously, some religious traditions would find it difficult to recognize that their God, or gods, or saviors, or saints were simply illusions projected by the human consciousness. Insisting on the ultimate reality of their divine beings, many religious traditions would find it hard to accept the Tibetan Buddhist claim that those divine beings were only projections. Nevertheless, that claim was central to the Tibetan Buddhist mythic transcendence outlined in the *Bardo Thödol.* By recognizing the divine forms as projections, the consciousness gained freedom from the imprisoning illusion that it was a separate, personal ego identity. In that change of consciousness, the person after death gained a deathless liberation, penetrating the illusions of self and gods to achieve the reality of a transcendent freedom from rebirth.

As an intriguing footnote to the afterlife illusions described in the *Bardo Thödol,* we might consider the theory of a purely mental afterlife proposed by the philosopher H. H. Price. In 1953, Price published an article, "Survival and the Idea of 'Another World,'" in which he suggested that dreams might provide a model for experience in the world after death.

Drawing his analogies from dream experience, Price suggested that a coherent picture of life after death could be imagined. If afterlife experience were similar to mental experience in dreams, it would consist of illusions projected by consciousness. Like a dream world, the afterlife would be a world of mental images. Experience would consist of a stream of consciousness. The person might still have the feeling of being alive if the consciousness continued to project mental images as in a dream after death. Experiencing those images as real, the person might not even realize that he or she was dead. Mental images would continue to provide the basis for an experiential sense of being alive even after death.

Price argued that such an image world would be just as "real" as the present world. Sights, sounds, and experiences would be familiar because they were projected from the person's own consciousness. But the projections would be based on the memories of the person before death. Since death was the end of life experience, no new images could be encountered. Memory provided the raw material of imagery with which a surviving consciousness could project its experience after death. In other words, the consciousness continued to experience the imagery that it had dwelled on during life.

Experience in that image world after death, however, would not have to consist merely of reruns of past experience. The imagery might be changed, arranged, and rearranged by a person's desires. In this way, afterlife experience might be an ongoing process of wish fulfillment, in which images were projected to satisfy desires. The raw material of the image world might come from memory, but the forms those images would take could be determined by the person's hopes, expectations, and wishes. Perhaps images might also be arranged according to a person's fears. Like the stuff of dreams, mental experience in such an afterlife image world would be derived from memory but shaped by desire. Survival in that image world would consist in the continuity of a self-contained consciousness that projected its own experience after death.

Survival in a projected mental world, of course, would make communication with other minds problematic. If all experiences were merely projections from consciousness only to be seen and heard by the same consciousness, how could two minds occupying such independent afterlife worlds communicate? Perhaps they could not. Or perhaps some type of extrasensory perception would bridge the gap between mental worlds, providing a means of telepathic communication. H. H. Price argued for the possibility of such a telepathy that would enable impressions to be shared among the different, independent image worlds occupied after death. Price even imagined that a variety of shared worlds might be constructed by like-minded individuals whose memories and desires might be similar enough to form image worlds that they could live in after death.

In some respects, the purely mental afterlife imagined by H. H. Price was similar to the afterlife experience anticipated by the *Bardo Thödol.* First, all experience was projected from the person's consciousness. Everything seen or heard could be (but probably would not be) recognized as projection. Second, the raw materials for those projections were derived from memory, particularly from the imagery that a person had dwelled on during life. A memory that had been trained within the Tibetan Buddhist religious and cultural tradition could be expected to project the vivid imagery of the merciful and wrathful Buddhas that had served as focuses for meditation. Other trainings might fill the memory with different content. Third, the raw material was shaped by desire. In the *Bardo Thödol,* however, the mental life of the other world was not an extended process of wish fulfillment. In fact, personal wishes, emotions, and desires blocked fulfillment. Only by giving up those personal desires could liberation be achieved. Unlike Price's image worlds, the *Bardo Thödol* saw the afterlife as a series of opportunities for achieving a Buddhist liberation from desire.

The Buddhist logic of desire, therefore, distinguished the afterlife of the bardos from the image worlds imagined by the philosopher H. H. Price. In the Chönyid Bardo, the interim stage of illusions, the emotions of anger, pride, greed, jealousy, and all other ego-centered desires, blocked the consciousness from merging into Buddhahood. Those desires, therefore, shaped an afterlife experience that was increasingly terrifying, as the consciousness tried to retreat from its real nature into a familiar sense of personal identity. By trying to hold on to what was familiar, the consciousness perceived the Buddha forms as unfamiliar, awesome, and finally as horrible monsters that threatened its sense of separate personal identity.

Ultimately, survival of death—in the sense of achieving a liberating deathlessness—was not shaped by desires but only made possible by eliminating personal desires. Failing to eliminate egotistical desires, the consciousness could not see through the illusions of the second bardo. In that failure, the consciousness was carried along on the currents of karma into the third and final stage of the afterlife in which it was made ready to be reborn in another body.

REBIRTH

If it failed to achieve liberation during the interim stage of illusions, the consciousness moved into the last bardo, the Sidpa Bardo, where it began preparations for rebirth. The six colored lights of the lokas appeared as possible destinations. Before rebirth, however, the consciousness was subjected to a process of judgment and punishment for its past actions. Battered by the winds of karma, the consciousness suffered its final purgation before it entered another body.

Like the punishments in the Chinese Buddhist hells, those punishments were remedial rather than permanent retribution for past deeds. They were part of the increasingly violent shock therapy after death designed to awaken the consciousness to its true nature. Even when judged and punished by the Lord of Death, the consciousness could still achieve liberation if it recognized the entire process as projection.

The pain and suffering were experienced as real, but the Lord of Death, the judgment, and the punishment were explained in the *Bardo Thödol* as projected hallucinations from a consciousness that did not know its true Buddha nature. If that ignorance persisted, the consciousness would end up in another body in one of the six worlds of desire to perpetuate the cycle of birth, suffering, and death.

Sidpa Bardo

After fourteen days in the bardo of illusions, the consciousness shifted into the grayish twilight of the last stage before rebirth. No longer surrounded by the dramatic rainbow splendor of the Buddha forms, the deceased proceeded into a dimmer state of consciousness. For the first time, the person became aware that he or she was in fact dead. Before that point the unenlightened consciousness had not had time to reflect on its condition. It had been too preoccupied with the overwhelming encounters with Buddha forms to realize that those experiences were not dreams but death. In the final bardo, however, the consciousness experienced the anguish of loss and separation. In misery, the person cried out, "I am dead! What shall I do?"

Lost and alone, the person looked back to the personal attachments he or she had formed during life. The consciousness saw dreamlike visions of friends and relatives left behind. To weeping friends and relatives, the person called out, "Here I am, weep not." But the survivors did not hear the anguished cries of the dead. In misery, the consciousness was blown about like a feather on the winds of karma.

Propelled by the powerful gusts of karmic wind, the consciousness was terrified by hallucinations. Demons struck terror with their war cries, fierce faces, and dangerous weapons. Terrible beasts of prey attacked. Under pursuit, the consciousness was swept through snow, rain, and darkness while all around it crashed the sounds of mountains crumbling down, seas overflowing, fires roaring, and fierce winds rushing. Trying to run away, the person was blocked by three cliffs, representing anger, lust, and ignorance. Like everything else in the bardo, these cliffs were illusory, but nevertheless these obstacles of anger, lust, and ignorance prevented the consciousness from getting free of the terrors it experienced as real.

In the midst of all this terrifying chaos, the *Bardo Thödol* promised, liberation was still possible. If the consciousness could remain undistracted by these hallucinations, it might still take refuge in the compassionate mercy of the Buddha. Dissolving the barriers of anger, lust, and ignorance, the consciousness might still achieve liberation from rebirth.

But liberation by that point had become very difficult. Instead of achieving a tranquil indifference that might set it free, the consciousness tended to be consumed by panic. Trying to escape the terrors of the bardo, the consciousness became obsessed with the desire to retreat into the safe familiarity of a body. "O what would I not give to possess a body!" the consciousness cried out. Unfortunately, its former body was no longer available. The old body had been frozen if death had occurred in winter, decomposed if in summer, and relatives may have already had it cremated, buried, thrown into water, or exposed on the ground for the birds. Although the text advised giving up any desire for a body, the consciousness heading toward rebirth started looking for a new body that would replace the old.

Before acquiring a new body, however, the consciousness had to go through a final judgment. The person's good deeds were counted out with white pebbles, bad deeds with black. In awe and fear, the consciousness appeared before the Lord of Death. Questioned about its previous life, the consciousness might lie and say, "I have not committed any evil deed." The Lord of Death, however, simply consulted the Mirror of Karma, in which the truth about all good and evil past deeds was reflected. The mirror revealed a judgment that could not be avoided. Disclosing the character of the person's past actions, the Mirror of Karma exposed the person to judgment.

Following that disclosure, the consciousness was punished in its thought body by the agents of the Lord of Death. The punishments were particularly horrible. Dragging the person along by the neck, an angel of death might "cut off thy head, extract thy heart, pull out thy intestines, lick up thy brain, drink thy blood, eat thy flesh, and gnaw thy bones" (Evans-Wentz, 1927: 166). Though under terrible torture, the person could not die because he or she was already dead. The thought body revived, only to be punished again.

Perhaps the punishment was intended as a violent form of shock therapy, a remedial punishment that might break attachments to having a body. Liberation might still be achieved at this point. The *Bardo Thödol* exhorted the consciousness to recognize that its thought body, its torturer, and even the Lord of Death were all hallucinations. Although the pain was experienced as real, the entire process of judgment and punishment was a projection from consciousness. Like everything else in the bardos, experience was determined by consciousness. If that experience was recognized as projection, liberation could be achieved. If not, the consciousness would continue to be carried along by the impetus of its past karma into another body.

The duration and intensity of punishment depended on a person's past deeds. After punishment was completed, the consciousness moved into the final stages of preparation for rebirth. As the colored lights of the worlds of desire appeared, the thought body began to glow with the light of the loka into which it would be reborn: white for the heaven world, smoky gray for the hell world, red for the ghost world, green for the demon world, blue for the animal world, or yellow for the human world. Even at this stage, liberation could still be achieved. Ignorance could be overcome by recognizing that even the process leading to rebirth was determined by consciousness.

For most, however, it was too late. By this point, the consciousness was probably consumed with desire for the safety, security, and familiarity associated with having a body. After all the intensity of the bardos, a body might seem like a safe haven. So the consciousness had one final vision of a mating couple in the world in which it would be reborn. If about to be reborn as a male, the consciousness would be attracted to the female; if about to be female, it would be attracted to the male. In that Tibetan Buddhist variation on the Freudian Oedipus-Electra complex, the consciousness began to reenter the worlds of desire.

In a moment of bliss in the union of sperm and ovum, the consciousness dissolved into unconsciousness in the womb. While that unconsciousness was probably a welcome rest from the splendors and terrors of the afterlife bardos, it signified a return to the cycle of suffering. Occupying another body in one of the six worlds of desire, the person would once again endure birth, life, and death, only to once again go through the entire process of afterlife experience outlined in the *Bardo Thödol.* That cycle would continue until the radical change in consciousness that led to liberation was finally achieved.

Reincarnation

In the Tibetan Buddhist visionary journey through the moment of dying, the interim stage of illusions, and the final return to embodiment, mythic transcendence of death was imagined within a theory of rebirth. Being born again in a different body provided a kind of transcendence; a genuine transcendence, however, was expected to be achieved only in liberation from the entire cycle of rebirth. Nevertheless, rebirth accounted for a certain degree of continuity from lifetime to lifetime. Although Buddhist thought in general emphasized the discontinuity that made every moment, let alone every lifetime, part of a process of constant change, the theory of rebirth involved the continuity of personal attributes over a series of lifetimes.

In Upaniṣadic Hindu thought, personal continuity over lifetimes was explained as a result of the existence of an eternal self, the ātman. In one sense, the ātman was incarnated in each lifetime, as the spiritual core of the person. Each embodied, living person was a *jīvātman*, a living eternal self. In another sense, however, the ātman was above and beyond the entire process of life, death, and rebirth, like a bird sitting on a branch, looking down on the person who was going through a series of lifetimes. Ultimately, as the eternal power diffused through the universe, the self in its supreme transcendence was unaffected by the whole process. The self merely waited for the person to awaken and to get free from the cycle of rebirth.

In Buddhist thought, however, the permanent, abiding, eternal self was denied. What continued after death was a set of influences in motion. A bundle of dispositions and inclinations persisted, but they did not add up to any eternal self. Instead, the very notion of a permanent, personal self was part of the ignorance that kept the bundle of dispositions and inclinations together and propelled it along in the process of rebirth. Seeing through that illusion, the consciousness radically changed and enabled the person to attain the liberating deathlessness of enlightenment. In that liberation, Buddhists imagined no eternal self. Although Buddhists were clear that nirvāna did not imply an immortal soul, they refused to specify precisely what that state would be like.

Regarding rebirth, Hindu thought emphasized continuity, whereas Buddhist thought stressed change. Both perspectives, however, evaluated the whole process of rebirth negatively. The reason for their negative assessment could be found in their understanding of karma. In karmic theory, actions were regarded as having good or bad consequences depending on their ethical merit. Good actions produced good effects, bad actions produced bad effects, but, as we have seen, the object was to gain liberation from the entire karmic process of cause and effect.

Failing to achieve liberation—whether it was called mokṣa, nirvāna, or satori—the person remained in the cycle of rebirth. In that case, the next best thing that could be expected would be a better rebirth. In order to be born again in better situations and circumstances, a person had to gain merit through good actions that would produce positive karmic results in the next life. Gaining merit and avoiding demerit became a secondary goal in the transcendence of death within forms of popular Hindu and Buddhist religion.

Not every religious tradition that has supported belief in reincarnation has evaluated that process negatively. In some Australian religions, after returning to the ancestral world at death a person might be transformed into a spirit child to come back again for another lifetime. That rebirth was imagined to occur within the same clan. Reincarnation, therefore, was regarded positively because it supported the ancestral and cultural transcendence of the clan. By being reborn in the same clan, a reincarnated person reinforced the continuity of that kinship group.

Similarly, the Trobriand Islanders of Melanesia studied by the anthropologist Bronislaw Malinowski imagined that after death a person's soul *(balōma)* descended to an underworld paradise called Tuma, where life went on much as it did on earth. When souls grew old, however, they were rejuvenated to become young again. They continued to live in Tuma until they became bored or were weakened by the evil effects of sorcery. Souls then reverted back to spirit infants in order to be reborn in the human world. Every birth, therefore, was regarded as a reincarnation of a spirit, a person born again in a different body but in the same clan and family lineage in which it lived before (Malinowski, 1927: 32). From the perspective of the Trobriand Islanders, the birth of every child was to be celebrated as the return of an ancestral spirit. Reincarnation was regarded not as resulting from an ancestor's failure to achieve liberation but as a welcome return to human life.

Among the Igbo of Nigeria, reincarnation was viewed positively because it gave people additional opportunities to achieve their goals and realize their destinies. Each person was assumed to have been given certain objectives in life by God. If a person did not achieve those goals, he or she would survive death in the world of the dead. The dead lived there much as they had during life: Spirits were organized by their clans, they continued in their occupations, and they thought and felt as if they were still alive. After spending time in the world of the dead, however, spirits were reborn on earth for another chance to achieve their personal goals in another lifetime. Reincarnation gave people numerous opportunities to improve their status, skills, and accomplishments. In that respect, reincarnation was regarded positively by the Igbo (Stevenson, 1985).

Tribal religions of India also seem to have held beliefs in reincarnation as a positive process (Fürer-Haimendorf, 1953). But in Hindu, Buddhist, Jain, and other Indian traditions, reincarnation came to be regarded as a cycle of bondage. The cycle of rebirth was understood as a trap to get out of, a wheel to get off of, or a prison to escape. The visionary journey through the world after death presented in the *Bardo Thödol* illustrated this negative evaluation of the entire process of rebirth.

This negative evaluation resulted from the development of the idea of karma. No concept similar to the Hindu or Buddhist notion of karma appeared in the reincarnation beliefs of the Trobriand Islanders or the Igbo of Nigeria. The principle of karma was central to the Hindu and Buddhist "ethicization" of life and death (Obeyesekere, 1980). All actions during life were given ethical significance that would carry consequences after death. A person was not reborn in the same family, clan, or kinship group but was reincarnated in a situation determined by the ethical quality of his or her past actions. Reincarnation, therefore, did not support the ancestral transcendence of a kinship group; rather, it reduced each person to an individual who was held accountable for the merits and demerits of past actions.

Over a series of lifetimes, cognitive continuity was broken by the loss of any memory of past lives. Only in rare cases, such as the Buddha's enlightenment, did a living person recover a detailed memory of past lives that would provide a sense of cognitive continuity. In the Buddha's case, of course, those memories were not worth remembering because they recalled a continuity that was ultimately seen as illusory. But many cases have been documented of claims to recollections and other circumstantial evidence for reincarnation (Stevenson, 1974, 1975, 1976). Memory of past lives is important for any theory of reincarnation because memory is the only basis for establishing a cognitive continuity that would guarantee that the person living now is the same as the person who lived before.

Although memory of past lives may be rare during life, a person might recall past lives during the interim period after death and before rebirth. After death, a person might recover a sense of cognitive continuity over lifetimes. As we have seen, memory was important in the *Bardo Thödol,* particularly in the recollection of personal attachments to relatives and friends that had been formed in the previous life or perhaps in a series of lifetimes. But the text instructed the consciousness to break free of all selfish, egotistical attachments that only contributed to its continuing suffering. In that respect, memory reinforced personal identity and personal relationships that needed to be broken in order for the person to achieve liberation from the cycle of karma.

A more binding forensic continuity, therefore, was determined by karma. A person remained the same person on account of ongoing karmic responsibility for actions. Even if unconscious of past deeds, a person nevertheless experienced their consequences. To a large extent, past actions determined present situations and circumstances; present actions determined the future. The cycle of rebirth was kept in motion by karma, resulting in a mechanical, automatic, and basically unconscious process of cause and effect over a series of lifetimes. A person's forensic identity was tied to that karmic cycle of consequences for action.

Transcendence of death could not be achieved within the cycle of rebirth. Even a good, moral life led to another life and another death in that mechanical cycle. Ultimately, in order to transcend death, a person had to get out of the mechanical cycle of cause and effect. Therefore, a genuine transcendence of death—a permanent deathlessness—required breaking out of the forensic identity that had been formed by karma. That breakthrough was a radical transformation of personal identity that dissolved karma and achieved the supreme freedom from the cycle of life and death.

Chapter 12

Orientation to the Existence Between

Translated by Robert A. F. Thurman

POWERS AND PROBLEMS OF A BETWEEN-BEING

If the power of negative evolution still makes recognition of the light difficult, you should again speak as follows:

Hey, noble one! Listen without your mind wandering! "Senses all complete, moving unobstructed" means that even if in life you were blind, deaf, crippled, and so on, now in the between, your eyes clearly discern forms, your ears hear sounds, and so forth. Your senses become flawlessly clear and complete; so, "senses all complete." Recognize this as a sign that you have died and are wandering in the between! Remember your personal instructions!

Hey, noble one! What is "unobstructed" is your mental body; your awareness is free from embodiment and you lack a solid body. So now you can move hither and thither everywhere, through walls, houses, land, rocks, and earth, even through Meru, the axial mountain; except through a mother's womb and the Vajra Throne at Bodhgaya. This is a sign that you are wandering in the existence between, so remember the instructions of your spiritual teacher! Pray to the Lord of Great Compassion!

> The between-being cannot pass through a mother's womb because that is the place where he or she will take rebirth—a being that can go through mountains cannot get through that delicate membrane. The Vajra throne at Bodhgaya is the place where Supreme Emanation Body Buddhas attain enlightenment in this world and the place is believed to have a special physical density as well as a special sanctity. So no between-being can pass through it.

Hey, noble one! "With evolutionary magic powers" means that you, who have no special abilities or magic powers whatsoever, now have magic powers arising as the result of your evolution. In a split second, you can circle this four-continent planet with its axial mountain. You now have the power just to think about any place you wish and you will arrive there in that very instant. You can reach anywhere and return just as a normal man stretches out and pulls back his arm. But these various magic powers are not so miraculous; if you don't specially need them, ignore them! You should not worry about whether or not you can manifest this or that, which you may think of. The fact is you have the ability to manifest anything without any obstruction. You should recognize this as a sign of the existence between! You should pray to your spiritual teacher!

> The person in the between-state naturally has all these supernormal abilities. However, they should not become a diversion, a distraction from the main issue of the between, the opportunity to attain liberation from the compulsive lifestyle by confronting the nature of reality; or at least, the opportunity to obtain a new life favorable to such an attainment, avoiding any horrid states or lives shorn of liberty and opportunity.

Hey, noble one! "One sees similar species with pure clairvoyance" means that beings of the same species in the between can see each other. Thus if some beings are of the same species, all going to be reborn as gods, they will see each other. Likewise, other beings of the same species, to be reborn in whichever of the six realms, will see each other. So you should not be attached to such encounters! Meditate on the Lord of Great Compassion!

"With pure clairvoyance" refers also to the vision of those whose pure clairvoyance has been developed by the practice of contemplation, as well as to the vision of those whose divine power of merit has developed it. But such yogis or deities cannot always see between-beings. They see them only when they will to see them, and not when they do not, or when their contemplation is distracted.

> If a clairvoyant were forced to perceive all between-beings around, she would have no time to see anything else. Infinite numbers of beings of all species are dying and traversing the between all the time, and their subtle embodiments can effortlessly penetrate solid objects, or coexist in the same coarse space with other things. Therefore, they are everywhere evident to one with clairvoyant abilities, whether natural or developed. What many cultures refer to as "ghosts" clearly fit the description of the between-state wanderer (which is why the pretan, who has become reborn in that horrid form, should not be translated "hungry ghost"). Indeed, the hero in the recent film *Ghost* is presented as having many of the characteristics of the between-being.

Hey, noble one! As you have such a ghostly body, you encounter relatives and familiar places as if in a dream. When you meet these relatives, though you communicate with them, they do not answer. When you see your relatives and dear ones crying, you will think, "Now I have died, what can I do?" You feel a searing pain, like a fish flopping in hot sand. But however greatly you suffer, tormenting yourself at this time does not help. If you have a spiritual teacher, pray to your spiritual teacher. Or else pray to the compassionate Archetype Deity. Don't be attached to your loved ones—it is useless. Pray to the Compassionate Ones, and do not suffer or be terrified!

Hey, noble one! Driven by the swift wind of evolution, your minds helpless and unstable, riding the horse of breath like a feather blown on the wind, spinning and fluttering. You tell the mourners, "Don't cry! Here I am!" They take no notice, and you realize you have died, and you feel great anguish. Now do not indulge in your pain! There is a constant twilight, gray as the predawn autumn sky, neither day nor night. That kind of between can last for one, two, three, four, five, six, or seven weeks—up to forty-nine days. Though it is said that for most people the suffering of the existence between lasts twenty-one days, this is not always certain due to people's different evolutionary histories.

This disclaimer of precision in timing comes as something of a relief. The time in the death-point between has been mentioned above as seeming to be four and a half days of unconsciousness to the ordinary person, though developed practitioners can prolong it indefinitely. Then there are twelve days mentioned in the reality between. If you add the twenty-one days of the existence between, you have a total of thirty-seven and a half days. Then there is the traditional number of forty-nine days, mentioned in various Buddhist sources. The bottom line is that waking-reality time-lines cannot convey with precision the experience of the between.

Now begins the experience of the existence between. The fierce deity apparitions in the reality between were interventions by the compassionate deities into a level of the person's consciousness where primal impulses were lodged. Powerful emotions were stirred up in those areas of being. Now, the person's conviction about the substantiality of reality and attachment to the ordinary, delusion-driven lifestyle have been so persistent that a further birth in the realm of ordinary existence appears imminent. It is only natural then, that this threshold is attended by psychic simulations of the most dramatic and terrifying sort of experiences.

Hey, noble one! At this time the great red wind of evolution will drive you from behind, fiercely, unbearably, terrifyingly. Don't be afraid of it! It is your own hallucination! A frightening thick darkness draws you from the front, irresistibly. You are terrified by harsh cries, such as "Strike!" "Kill!" Don't be afraid of them! Heavy sinners will see cannibal ogres brandishing many weapons, shouting war cries, "Kill!

Kill!" and "Strike! Strike!" You will see ferocious wild animals. You will be hunted by troops in blizzards, storms, and fogs. You will hear sounds of avalanches, flood waters, forest fires, and hurricanes. In panic you will escape by any means, only to stop short on the brink of falling down a yawning triple abyss, red, black, and white, bottomless and horrifying.

Hey, noble one! It is not really an abyss. It is lust, hate, and delusion. You should recognize this as the moment of the existence between! Call upon the Lord of Great Compassion, and pray intensely, "O Lord of Great Compassion! Spiritual teacher! Three Jewels! I am named So-and-so—please don't abandon me to the horrid states! Don't forget me!"

Those who have gathered merit, virtuous and sincere in Dharma practice, are entertained with various delights and enjoy various excellent pleasures. And those dominated by delusion, who have neither strong virtue nor strong vice, have neither happiness nor suffering, but feel only stupefaction and indifference.

O noble one, whatever happens along those lines, don't crave! Don't long for pleasures or joys! Offer them all to the jewel of the spiritual teacher! Abandon attachment to them! Even without any visions of pleasure or pain, with only feelings of indifference, set the mind on the experience of the Great Seal, free of both concentration and distraction! That is most important.

Hey, noble one! At that time, structures such as bridges, temples, cathedrals, huts, and stupas will seem to shelter you for a moment—but don't cling to them at length. Since your mind lacks a body, it cannot settle down. You feel cold, you become angry and distraught, and your awareness seems erratic, volatile, and unsteady. Then you will have the thought, "Now I have died—what can I do!" Your heart will feel cold and weak. You will feel fierce and boundless suffering. The fact is you must travel and cannot be attached to any one place. So don't worry about it, and let your mind come to rest.

From now on you have no food except for what is dedicated for you. There is no certainty about your friends. These are signs of your mentalbody wandering in the existence between. Your present joys and sorrows are determined by your evolution. When you see your lands, friends, loved ones, and your own corpse, and you think, "Now I have died, what can be done?" at that time, your mental body feels greatly stressed.

> The guide here implicitly accepts the magical efficacy of food ritually dedicated to a deceased person, that a portion of food set out for the recently deceased can provide the between-state embodiment a sense of nourishment. The guide reminds the deceased that her body is mental, made by pure imagery. Her sensation of feeling hungry, weak, and distressed is purely mental.

You think, "How nice it would be to have a new body!" Then you will have visions of looking everywhere for a body. Even if you try up to nine times to enter your old corpse, due to the length of the reality between, in the winter it will have frozen, in the summer it will have rotted. Otherwise, your loved ones will have burned it or buried it or given it to birds and beasts, so it affords no place to inhabit. You will feel sick at heart, and will have visions of being squeezed between boulders, stones, and dirt. This kind of suffering is in the nature of the existence between. Even if you find a body, there will be nothing other than such suffering. So give up longing for a body! Focus yourself undistractedly in the experience of creative nonaction!

Having been oriented in this way, she can attain liberation in this between.

AVOIDING THE DULL LIGHTS TO BLOCK REBIRTH

Even though you say this many times, it may still be hard for recognition to arise, due to the power of strong negative evolution. There is great benefit in further repetition. Calling the deceased by name, you should say as follows:

Hey, noble one! If you have not recognized the clear light by remembering what we have already said, from now your sense of your body from the preceding life will become vague, and your sense of your body of the emerging life will become more distinct. Then you will feel sad and think, "I am suffering so—now I will seek whatever body comes along!" Then you will move toward whatever appears, gradually and uncertainly, and the six lights of the six realms will dawn. The realm toward which evolution impels your rebirth will dawn most clearly.

Hey, noble one! Listen to me! What are the six lights? The dull white light of the gods will dawn; and also the red light of the titans, the blue light of the humans, the green light of the animals, the yellow light of the pretans, and the dull smoky light of the hells—all these will dawn. These are the six lights. So your body's color will become that of the light of the realm of rebirth.

Hey, noble one! At that time the essence of the instruction is very important. Contemplate the particular light that arises as the Lord of Great Compassion! When the light arises, hold the thought, "It is the Lord of Great Compassion." This is the extremely profound key of instruction. This is crucial to block rebirth.

> One of the six dull lights emerges in the deceased's awareness at this point, to indicate the realm of his rebirth. The trick here is not to accept that light as leading to that realm, but to align that light itself with the Bodhisattva Avalokiteshvara, the Lord of Great Compassion (Jesus for the Christian, Krishna for the Hindu, the Prophet for the Moslem, the most beloved figure for the secularist).

Again, meditate long and carefully that, whoever your Archetype Deity is, he or she appears like a magic illusion, lacking intrinsic reality. It is called the "pure Magic Body." Then, contemplate that Archetype Deity as dissolving from the edges inward, and enter the experience of not holding rigidly to the insubstantial, the clear light of voidness. Again contemplate that as the Archetype Deity! Again contemplate it as clear light! Thus meditating deity and clear light in alternation, then let your own awareness dissolve from the edges; where space pervades, let awareness pervade. Where awareness pervades, let the Truth Body pervade. Enter comfortably into the experience of the ceaseless nonproliferation of the Truth Body.

Having aligned the dull light of one of the realms with the Lord of Compassion, here the deceased is instructed in something more advanced, in contemplating the nonduality of the supreme integration of magic body and clear light. He contemplates the form of the archetype deity as magic illusion, as a dream apparition. He then dissolves the image into transparency and contemplates that as the deity. He then alternates contemplating the deity as magic body and as transparency, oscillating toward contemplating their non-duality. He then contemplates his subjective awareness of deity-transparency integration as itself dissolving, contemplating the non-duality of insentient space and awareness, voidness and clarity. He then rests in the inconceivable integration of the Truth Body as the integration of voidness and awareness, magic body and clear light. The Truth Body does not proliferate or fabricate anything because it already *is* everything—it is the actual reality of everything in every possible state. Again, Padma Sambhava guides even the most ordinary between-being in the highest possible meditation, showing that he takes most seriously the concept that a person's between-awareness is nine times more intelligent than his ordinary coarse awareness of the previous life.

From within that experience, rebirth is prevented and enlightenment is attained.

BLOCKING THE DOOR OF THE WOMB

Those whose practice was weak and inexpert will still not recognize the light. They will err and wander to the door of a womb. Since for them the instruction about blocking the door of the womb is very important, call the deceased by name and say as follows:

Hey, noble one! If you have not understood from the above, at this time, by power of evolution the vision will arise of your proceeding upward, on the level, or downward with head hanging. Now meditate on the Lord of Great Compassion! Remember him! Then, as already explained, you will have visions of hurricanes, blizzards, hailstorms, dense fogs, and being chased by many men, and you will seem to escape. Those without merit will seem to escape to a miserable place, but those with merit will seem to escape to a happy place. At that time, noble one, all the signs will arise showing the continent and place where you will be reborn. For this time there are many profound keys of instruction, so listen carefully! Even though you did not recognize freedom from the previous keys of orientation, here even those of the weakest practice can recognize freedom through the following keys, so listen!

Now, here, the method of blocking the womb door is very effective and important. There are two methods of blocking that door; blocking the entering person and blocking the womb door entered. First, the instruction for blocking the enterer.

> "Blocking the womb door" refers to using the *Natural Liberation* art—relaxed focusing on the presence of the archetype or patron deity as indivisible from the natural transparency of all things—as a way of intervening in the mechanical processes of assuming rebirth.

Hey, noble one! You named So-and-so! Clearly visualize your Archetype Deity appearing like magic without intrinsic reality like the moon in water. If you are unsure about your Archetype Deity, then vividly envision Avalokiteshvara, thinking, "He is the Lord of Great Compassion!" Then dissolve the Archetype from the edges and contemplate the void clear light transparency of ultimate nonperception. That is the profound key. Using it, the Buddhas said, the womb will not be entered; so meditate in that way!

But if this still does not block the way and you are just about to enter a womb, there is the profound instruction to block the door of the womb about to be entered. So listen! Repeat after me the following from *The Root Verses of the Six Betweens!*

> Hey! Now when the existence between dawns upon me,
> I will hold my will with mind one-pointed,
> And increase forcefully the impulse of positive evolution;
> Blocking the womb door, I will remember to be revulsed.
> Now courage and positive perception are essential;
> I will give up envy, and contemplate all couples
> As my Spiritual Mentor, Father and Mother.

Repeat this loud and clear and stir your memory. It is important to meditate on its meaning and put it into practice. As for its meaning, "Now when the existence between dawns upon me" means that you are now wandering within the existence between. A sign of that is that when you look in water you will not see your reflection. You have no shadow. You have no substantial flesh-and-blood body. These are signs that your mental body is wandering in the existence between. Now you must hold one-pointed in your mind the unwavering willpower. This one-pointed will is of chief importance. It is like reins to guide a horse. You can achieve whatever your will intends, so don't open your mind to negative evolution, but remember the teachings, instructions, initiations, authorizations, and inspirations you received in the human realm, such as this *Great Book of Natural Liberation Through Understanding in the Between,* and intensify the result of all good evolutionary actions. This is very important. Don't forget it! Don't be distracted! This is the exact time that determines whether you go up or you go down. Now is the time when indulgence in laziness definitely will bring on suffering. Now is the time when one-pointed positive willpower definitely brings on happiness. Hold one-pointed goodwill in your mind! Sustain forcefully the result of good action!

Now is the time to block the door of the womb! As the root verse says, blocking the womb door, remember to be revulsed! Now courage and positive perception are essential! That time is now. You should block the door of the womb. There are five methods to block the womb door; fix them well in your mind.

Hey, noble one! At this time you will have visions of couples making love. When you see them, don't enter between them, but stay mindful. Visualize the males and females as the Teacher, Father and Mother, prostrate to them, and make them visualized offerings! Feel intense reverence and devotion! Aim a strong will to request them to teach the Dharma, and the womb door will definitely be blocked.

If that does not block it, and you are about to enter the womb, then visualize them as Mentor Father-Mother, Archetype Deity Father and Mother, or Compassion Lord Father and Mother. Offer them visualized offerings! Form the powerful intention to receive spiritual attainments from them, and that will block the womb door.

If that does not block it, and you are again about to enter a womb, then third there is the instruction for reversing lust and hate. There are four modes of birth; egg birth, womb birth, magic birth, and warm-moisture birth. Egg birth and womb birth are alike. As before, you begin to see males and females engaged in love-making. If you enter the womb under the influence of lust and hate, whether you are reborn as horse, bird, dog, or human, if you are going to be male, you arise appearing to be male; you feel strong hate toward the father, and attraction and lust toward the mother. If you are going to be female, you appear as a female; you feel strong envy and jealousy toward the mother, you feel strong longing and lust for the father. Conditioned by that, you enter the path of the womb. You experience orgasmic bliss in the center of the union between white and red drops, and within the experience of that bliss you faint and lose consciousness. Your body develops through the embryonic stages of "custard," "gelatin," and so forth. Eventually you will be born outside the mother's womb. Once your eyes are open, you realize you have been born a puppy. Having been a human, now you are a dog. In the dog's kennel, you suffer. Or in the pig's sty, or in the anthill, or in the wormhole, or in the herds of cows or goats or sheep—born there you cannot return to the human state. Being extremely stupid, in the state of delusion you suffer various miseries. In this way you will cycle through the hells and the pretan realms, and will be tortured by limitless suffering. There is nothing more powerful, nothing more terrible than this. Alas! Alas! Those lacking the holy spiritual teacher's instruction fall down this deep abyss into the life cycle. They are tormented uninterruptedly by unbearable sufferings. So listen to what I say! Hold my personal instruction in your mind!

Now I will teach you an instruction to close the womb door by reversing lust and hate. Listen to it and remember it! As the verse says:

Blocking the door of the womb, I will remember to be revulsed.
Now courage and positive perception are essential;
I will give up envy and contemplate all couples
As my Spiritual Mentor, Father and Mother.

As before, you will have strong feelings of envy; if reborn as a male, you will lust for the mother and hate the father, if reborn as a female you will lust for the father and hate the mother. For that time, there is this profound instruction.

Hey, noble one! When such lust and hate arise, meditate like this. "Alas! Such a creature of negative evolution as myself will wander in the life cycle under the influence of lust and hate. If I still persist in lust and hate, I will know no end to my wanderings. I am in danger of being sunk forever in the ocean of miseries. Now I must give up lust and hate entirely. Alas! I must hold intensely the one-pointed will never to entertain lust and hate." The Tantras state that this meditation itself will close the door of the womb .

Hey, noble one! Don't waver! Hold your will one pointed in your mind! Even though you have done that, if the womb door did not close and you are about to enter the womb, you should block the womb door by the instruction of truthless magical illusion. Meditate as follows: "Male and female, father and mother, the thunderstorm, the hurricane, the thunder, terrifying visions, all phenomena are naturally like magical illusions. However they arise, they are truthless. All things are untrue and false. Like mirages. Impermanent. Noneternal. Why be attached to them? Why fear and hate them? It is to see nothing as something. All of these are but visions of my mind. The mind itself is as originally nonexistent as a magical illusion. So where—out there—do they come from? Since I never understood this in the past, I held the nonexistent to exist. I held the untrue to be true. I held illusion as truth. So for this long time I wandered in the life cycle. If I still now do not recognize the illusoriness of things, I will wander even longer in the life cycle, and I will be stuck in the quicksand of various miseries. So now I will recognize all these things as like a dream, a magical illusion, an echo, a fairy city, a mirage, a reflection, an optical illusion, the moon in water, lacking even a moment's truth-status, definitely untrue, and false."

"Truth-status" is the state of something's existing by virtue of its intrinsic reality. If things were not empty, if they existed by virtue of a fixed, absolute, real core, then that core would be discovered by truth-seeking scientific awareness and those things would be acknowledged as possessing "truth-status." The involuntary habit of all beings is to assume that things do have such status. When we see a thing, it seems to us to exist in its own right, as an independently established thing-in-itself. This habitual perception is called our "truth-habit." It is equivalent to our misknowledge, the root of all our delusionary existence. The Buddha's key liberative insight is that all things lack such truth-status, and that therefore our truth-habits are misguided. Our experience of

> this is called wisdom, and is the antidote for our delusionary grasping at life. Freedom from truth-habits does not mean that our consciousness is annihilated, only that it is less grasping, less dominating, allowing things to be the relative, fleeting, dreamlike, fluid things that they are, and not insisting that they conform rigidly to our set of preconceived categories. This is the most advanced teaching of all. Though it is not complicated, it is emotionally challenging, as releasing the habitual perception of truth-status in things can be frightening, can feel like succumbing to annihilation. Yet Padma Sambhava again uses these advanced teachings for between-beings, considering their extreme malleability, their ninefold intelligence, and their unique opportunity.

Thus, holding these thoughts one-pointedly in mind, the truth-habit erodes, and, as the resulting freedom is impressed in your continuum, the deeper self-habit is reversed. As you thus deeply understand cosmic unreality, the womb door will definitely be blocked.

Yet even doing that, if the truth-habit does not erode, the womb door is not blocked, and you are about to enter the womb, again there is a profound instruction.

Hey, noble one! Even doing that, if the womb door is not blocked, now, fifth, you should block the womb door by meditating on the clear light. This is how to contemplate. "Hey! All things are my own mind. That mind is voidness, free of creation and destruction." Thinking thus, do not artificially compose your mind. Like water being poured in water, let the mind flow into its own reality condition; release it into its own nature. Letting it relax easily and openly will decisively and definitely block the womb door for all four forms of rebirth. Thus meditate again and again until the womb door is blocked.

Up to here, you have given many authentic and profound instructions for blocking the womb door. Using them, it should be impossible for any person, whether bright, mediocre, or dull, not to become liberated. Why is that? The deceased's between-consciousness has a mundane form of clairvoyance, so whatever you say, it can understand, experience, and embody. Even if persons were deaf and blind in life, in the between their faculties are complete and they can understand whatever you say. They have hypermindfulness, being constantly overwhelmed by terror and panic, so they always listen to what you say. Their consciousness is without coarse embodiment, so wherever they aim their will, they reach immediately; they are easy to direct. Since their intelligence is nine times more clear, even if persons were stupid in life, in the between, by the power of evolution, their intellect is extremely clear, and they have the quality of knowing how to meditate on whatever they understand. These are the key reasons why it is useful to perform prayers and rites of teaching for the deceased. They can be very important for them. And it is very important to make the effort to read this *Book of Natural Liberation* during the nine days after death. If the deceased is not liberated by means of one orientation, he or she will be liberated by another. That is why there are many different orientations.

Chapter 13

The Undertaking

Thomas Lynch

Every year I bury a couple hundred of my townspeople. Another two or three dozen I take to the crematory to be burned. I sell caskets, burial vaults, and urns for the ashes. I have a sideline in headstones and monuments. I do flowers on commission.

Apart from the tangibles, I sell the use of my building: eleven thousand square feet, furnished and fixtured with an abundance of pastel and chair rail and crown moldings. The whole lash-up is mortgaged and remortgaged well into the next century. My rolling stock includes a hearse, two Fleetwoods, and a minivan with darkened windows our pricelist calls a service vehicle and everyone in town calls the Dead Wagon.

I used to use the *unit pricing method*—the old package deal. It meant that you had only one number to look at. It was a large number. Now everything is itemized. It's the law. So now there is a long list of items and numbers and italicized disclaimers, something like a menu or the Sears Roebuck Wish Book, and sometimes the federally-mandated options begin to look like cruise control or rear-window defrost. I wear black most of the time, to keep folks in mind of the fact we're not talking Buicks here. At the bottom of the list there is still a large number.

In a good year the gross is close to a million, five percent of which we hope to call profit. I am the only undertaker in this town. I have a corner on the market.

The market, such as it is, is figured on what is called *the crude death rate*—the number of deaths every year out of every thousand persons.

Here is how it works.

Imagine a large room into which you coax one thousand people. You slam the doors in January, leaving them plenty of food and drink, color TVs, magazines, and condoms. Your sample should have an age distribution heavy on baby boomers and their children—1.2 children per boomer. Every seventh adult is an old-timer, who, if he or she wasn't in this big room, would probably be in Florida or Arizona or a nursing home. You get the idea. The group will include fifteen lawyers, one faith healer, three dozen real-estate agents, a video technician, several licensed counselors, and a Tupperware distributor. The rest will be between jobs, middle managers, ne'er-do-wells, or retired.

Now for the magic part—come late December when you throw open the doors, only 991.6, give or take, will shuffle out upright. Two hundred and sixty will now be selling Tupperware. The other 8.4 have become the crude death rate.

Here's another stat.

Of the 8.4 corpses, two-thirds will have been old-timers, five percent will be children, and the rest (slightly less than 2.5 corpses) will be boomers—realtors and attorneys likely—one of whom was, no doubt, elected to public office during the year. What's more, three will have died of cerebral-vascular or coronary difficulties, two of cancer, one each of vehicular mayhem, diabetes, and domestic violence. The spare change will be by act of God or suicide—most likely the faith healer.

The figure most often and most conspicuously missing from the insurance charts and demographics is the one I call The Big One, which refers to the number of people out of every hundred born who will die. Over the long haul, The Big One hovers right around . . . well, dead nuts on one hundred percent. If this were on the charts, they'd call it *death expectancy* and no one would buy futures of any kind. But it is a useful number and has its lessons. Maybe you will want to figure out what to do with your life. Maybe it will make you feel a certain kinship with the rest of us. Maybe it will make you hysterical. Whatever the implications of a one hundred percent death expectancy, you can calculate how big a town this is and why it produces for me a steady if unpredictable labor.

They die around the clock here, without apparent preference for a day of the week, month of the year; there is no clear favorite in the way of season. Nor does the alignment of the stars, fullness of moon, or liturgical calendar have very much to do with it. The whereabouts are neither here nor there. They go off upright or horizontally in Chevrolets and nursing homes, in bathtubs, on the interstates, in ERs, ORs, BMWs. And while it may be that we assign more equipment or more importance to deaths that create themselves in places marked by initials—ICU being somehow better than Greenbriar Convalescent Home—it is also true that the dead don't care. In this way, the dead I bury and burn are like the dead before them, for whom time and space have become mortally unimportant. This loss of interest is, in fact, one of the first sure signs that something serious is about to happen. The next thing is they quit breathing. At this point, to be sure, a *gunshot wound to the chest* or *shock and trauma* will get more ink than a CVA or ASHD, but no cause of death is any less permanent than the other. Anyone will do. The dead don't care.

Nor does *who* much matter, either. To say, "I'm OK, you're OK, and by the way, he's dead!" is, for the living, a kind of comfort.

It is why we drag rivers and comb plane wrecks and bomb sites.

It is why MIA is more painful than DOA.

It is why we have open caskets and all read the obits.

Knowing is better than not knowing, and knowing it is you is terrifically better than knowing it is me. Because once I'm the dead guy, whether you're OK or he's OK won't much interest me. You can all go bag your asses, because the dead don't care.

Of course, the living, bound by their adverbs and their actuarials, still do. Now, there is the difference and why I'm in business. The living are careful and oftentimes caring. The dead are careless, or maybe it's care-less. Either way, they don't care. These are unremarkable and verifiable truths.

My former mother-in-law, herself an unremarkable and verifiable truth, was always fond of holding forth with Cagneyesque bravado—to wit: "When I'm dead, just throw me in a box and throw me in a hole." But whenever I would remind her that we did substantially that with everyone, the woman would grow sullen and a little cranky.

Later, over meatloaf and green beans, she would invariably give out with: "When I'm dead just cremate me and scatter the ashes."

My former mother-in-law was trying to make carelessness sound like fearlessness. The kids would stop eating and look at each other. The kids' mother would plead, "Oh Mom, don't talk like that." I'd take out my lighter and begin to play with it.

In the same way, the priest that married me to this woman's daughter—a man who loved golf and gold ciboria and vestments made of Irish linen; a man who drove a great black sedan with a wine-red interior and who always had his eye on the cardinal's job—this same fellow, leaving the cemetery one day, felt called upon to instruct me thus: "No bronze coffin for me. No sir! No orchids or roses or limousines. The plain pine box is the one I want, a quiet Low Mass and the pauper's grave. No pomp and circumstance."

He wanted, he explained, to be an example of simplicity, of prudence, of piety and austerity—all priestly and, apparently, Christian virtues. When I told him that he needn't wait, that he could begin his ministry of good example even today, that he could quit the country club and do his hacking at the public links and trade his brougham for a used Chevette; that free of his Florsheims and cashmeres and prime ribs, free of his bingo nights and building funds, he could become, for Christ's sake, the very incarnation of Francis himself, or Anthony of Padua; when I said, in fact, that I would be willing to assist him in this, that I would gladly distribute his savings and credit cards among the worthy poor of the parish, and that I would, when the sad duty called, bury him for free in the manner he would have, by then, become accustomed to; when I told your man these things, he said nothing at all, but turned his wild eye on me in the way that the cleric must have looked on Sweeney years ago, before he cursed him, irreversibly, into a bird.

What I was trying to tell the fellow was, of course, that being a dead saint is no more worthwhile than being a dead philodendron or a dead angelfish. Living is the rub, and always has been. Living saints still feel the flames and stigmata of this vale of tears, the ache of chastity and the pangs of conscience. Once dead, they let their relics do the legwork, because, as I was trying to tell this priest, the dead don't care.

Only the living care.

And I am sorry to be repeating myself, but this is the central fact of my business—that there is nothing, once you are dead, that can be done *to you* or *for you* or *with you* or *about you* that will do you any good or any harm; that any damage or decency we do accrues to the living, to whom your death happens, if it really happens to anyone. The living have to live with it. You don't. Theirs is the grief or gladness your death brings. Theirs is the loss or gain of it. Theirs is the pain and the pleasure of memory. Theirs is the invoice for services rendered and theirs is the check in the mail for its payment.

And there is the truth, abundantly self-evident, that seems, now that I think of it, the one most elusive to the old in-laws, the parish priest, and to perfect strangers who are forever accosting me in barber-shops and cocktail parties and parent-teacher conferences, hell-bent or duty-bound to let me in on what it is they want done with them when they are dead.

Give it a rest is the thing I say.

Once you are dead, put your feet up, call it a day, and let the husband or the missus or the kids or a sibling decide whether you are to be buried or burned or blown out of a cannon or left to dry out in a ditch somewhere. It's not your day to watch it, because the dead don't care.

Another reason people are always rehearsing their obsequies with me has to do with the fear of death that anyone in their right mind has. It is healthy. It keeps us from playing in traffic. I say it's a thing we should pass on to the kids.

There is a belief—widespread among the women I've dated, local Rotarians, and friends of my children—that I, being the undertaker here, have some irregular fascination with, special interest in, inside information about, even attachment to, *the dead*. They assume, these people, some perhaps for defensible reasons, that I want their bodies.

It is an interesting concept.

But here is the truth.

Being dead is one—the worst, the last—but only one in a series of calamities that afflicts our own and several other species. The list may include, but is not limited to, gingivitis, bowel obstruction, contested divorce, tax audit, spiritual vexation, cash flow problems, political upheaval, and on and on and on some more. There is no shortage of misery. And I am no more attracted to the dead than the dentist is to your bad gums, the doctor to your rotten innards, or the accountant to your sloppy expense records. I have no more stomach for misery that the banker or the lawyer; the pastor or the politico—because misery is careless and is everywhere. Misery is the bad check, the ex-spouse, the mob in the street, and the IRS—who, like the dead, feel nothing and, like the dead, *don't care.*

Which is not to say that the dead do not matter.

They do. They do. Of course they do.

Last Monday morning Milo Hornsby died. Mrs. Hornsby called at 2 A.M. to say that Milo had *expired* and would I take care of it, as if his condition were like any other that could be renewed or somehow improved upon. At 2 A.M., yanked from my REM sleep, I am thinking, put a quarter into Milo and call me in the morning. But Milo is dead. In a moment, in a twinkling, Milo has slipped irretrievably out of our reach, beyond Mrs. Hornsby and the children, beyond the women at the laundromat he owned, beyond his comrades at the Legion Hall, the Grand Master of the Masonic Lodge, his pastor at First Baptist, beyond the mailman, zoning board, town council, and Chamber of Commerce; beyond us all, and any treachery or any kindness we had in mind for him.

Milo is dead.

X's on his eyes, lights out, curtains.

Helpless, harmless.

Milo's dead.

Which is why I do not haul to my senses, coffee and quick shave, Homburg and great coat, warm up the Dead Wagon, and make for the freeway in the early o'clock for Milo's sake. Milo doesn't have any sake anymore. I go for her—for she who has become, in the same moment and the same twinkling, like water to ice, the Widow Hornsby. I go for her—because she still can cry and care and pray and pay my bill.

The hospital that Milo died in is state-of-the-art. There are signs on every door declaring a part or a process or bodily function. I like to think that, taken together, the words would add up to The Human Condition, but they never do. What's left of Milo, the remains, are in the basement, between SHIPPING & RECEIVING and LAUNDRY ROOM. Milo would like that if he were still liking things. Milo's room is called PATHOLOGY.

The medical-technical parlance of death emphasizes disorder. We are forever dying of failures, of anomalies, of insufficiencies, of dysfunctions, arrests, accidents. These are either chronic or acute. The language of death certificates—Milo's says "Cardiopulmonary Failure"—is like the language of weakness. Likewise, Mrs. Hornsby, in her grief, will be said to be breaking down or falling apart or going to pieces, as if there were something structurally awry with her. It is as if death and grief were not part of The Order of Things, as if Milo's failure and his widow's weeping were, or ought to be, sources of embarrassment. "Doing well" for Mrs. Hornsby would mean that she is bearing up, weathering the storm, or being strong for the children. We have willing pharmacists to help her with this. Of course, for Milo, doing well would mean he was back upstairs, holding his own, keeping the meters and monitors bleeping.

But Milo is downstairs, between SHIPPING & RECEIVING and LAUNDRY ROOM, in a stainless-steel drawer, wrapped in white plastic top to toe, and—because of his small head, wide shoulders, ponderous belly, and skinny legs, and the trailing white binding cord from his ankles and toe tag—he looks, for all the world, like a larger than life-size sperm.

I sign for him and get him out of there. At some level, I am still thinking Milo gives a shit, which by now, of course, we all know he doesn't—because the dead don't care.

Back at the funeral home, upstairs in the embalming room, behind a door marked PRIVATE, Milo Hornsby is floating on a porcelain table under florescent lights. Unwrapped, outstretched, Milo is beginning to look a little more like himself—eyes wide open, mouth agape, returning to our gravity. I shave him, close his eyes, his mouth. We call this *setting the features*. These are the features—eyes and mouth—that will never look the way they would have looked in life when they were always opening, closing, focusing, signaling, telling us something. In death, what they tell us is that they will not be doing anything anymore. The last detail to be managed is Milo's hands—one folded over the other, over the umbilicus, in an attitude of ease, of repose, of retirement.

They will not be doing anything anymore, either.

I wash his hands before positioning them.

When my wife moved out some years ago, the children stayed here, as did the dirty laundry. It was big news in a small town. There was the gossip and the goodwill that places like this are famous for. And while there was plenty of talk, no one knew exactly what to say to me. They felt helpless, I suppose. So they brought casseroles and beef stews, took the kids out to the movies or canoeing, brought their younger sisters around to visit me. What Milo did was send his laundry van around twice a week for two months, until I found a housekeeper. Milo would pick up five loads in the morning and return them by lunchtime, fresh and folded. I never asked him to do this. I hardly knew him. I had never been in his home or his laundromat. His wife had never known my wife. His children were too old to play with my children.

After my housekeeper was installed, I went to thank Milo and pay the bill. The invoices detailed the number of loads, the washers and the dryers, detergent, bleaches, fabric softeners. I think the total came to sixty dollars. When I asked Milo what the charges were for pick-up and delivery, for stacking and folding and sorting by size, for saving my life and the lives of my children, for keeping us in clean clothes and towels and bed linen, "Never mind that" is what Milo said. "One hand washes the other."

I place Milo's right hand over his left hand, then try the other way. Then back again. Then I decide that it doesn't matter. One hand washes the other either way.

The embalming takes me about two hours.

It is daylight by the time I am done.

Every Monday morning, Ernest Fuller comes to my office. He was damaged in some profound way in Korea. The details of his damage are unknown to the locals. Ernest Fuller has no limp or anything missing so everyone thinks it was something he saw in Korea that left him a little simple, occasionally perplexed, the type to draw rein abruptly in his day-long walks, to consider the meaning of litter, pausing over bottle caps and gum wrappers. Ernest Fuller has a nervous smile and a dead-fish handshake. He wears a baseball cap and thick eyeglasses. Every Sunday night Ernest goes to the supermarket and buys up the tabloids at the checkout stands with headlines that usually involve Siamese twins or movie stars or UFOs. Ernest is a speed reader and a math whiz but because of his damage, he has never held a job and never applied for one. Every Monday morning, Ernest brings me clippings of stories under headlines like: 601 LB MAN FALLS THRU COFFIN—A GRAVE SITUATION or EMBALMER FOR THE STARS SAYS ELVIS IS FOREVER. The Monday morning Milo Hornsby died, Ernest's clipping had to do with an urn full of ashes, somewhere in East Anglia, that made grunting and groaning noises, that whistled sometimes, and that was expected to begin talking. Certain scientists in England could make no sense of it. They had run several tests. The ashes' widow, however, left with nine children and no estate, is convinced that her dearly beloved and greatly reduced husband is trying to give her winning numbers for the lottery. "Jacky would never leave us without good prospects," she says. "He loved his family more than anything." There is a picture of the two of them, the widow and the urn, the living and the dead, flesh and bronze, the Victrola and the Victrola's dog. She has her ear cocked, waiting.

We are always waiting. Waiting for some good word or the winning numbers. Waiting for a sign or wonder, some signal from our dear dead that the dead still care. We are gladdened when they do outstanding things, when they arise from their graves or fall through their caskets or speak to us in our waking dreams. It pleases us no end, as if the dead still cared, had agendas, were yet alive.

But the sad and well-known fact of the matter is that most of us will stay in our caskets and be dead a long time, and that our urns and graves will never make a sound. Our reason and requiems, our headstones or High Masses, will neither get us in nor keep us out of heaven. The meaning of our lives, and the memories of them, belong to the living, just as our funerals do. Whatever being the dead have now, they have by the living's faith alone.

We heat graves here for winter burials, as a kind of foreplay before digging in, to loosen the frost's hold on the ground before the sexton and his backhoe do the opening. We buried Milo in the ground on Wednesday. The mercy is that what we buried there, in an oak casket, just under the frost line, had ceased to be Milo. Milo had become the idea of himself, a permanent fixture of the third person and past tense, his widow's loss of appetite and trouble sleeping, the absence in places where we look for him, our habits of him breaking, our phantom limb, our one hand washing the other.

Chapter 14

Megaliths, Temples, Ceremonial Centers

Mircea Eliade

STONE AND BANANA

The megalithic constructions of western and northern Europe have fascinated investigators for over a century. Indeed, it is impossible to look at a good photograph of the alignments at Carnac or the gigantic trilithons of Stonehenge without wondering what their purpose and meaning could have been. The technological ability of these farmers of the Age of Polished Stone arouses astonishment. How did they manage to set 300-ton blocks in an upright position and lift 100-ton slabs? Then, too, such monuments are not isolated. They form part of a whole megalithic complex, which extends from the Mediterranean coast of Spain, covers Portugal, half of France, the western seaboard of England, and continues into Ireland, Denmark, and the southern coast of Sweden. To be sure, there are significant morphological variations. But two generations of prehistorians have made every effort to demonstrate the continuity of all the European megalithic cultures—a continuity that could be explained only by dissemination of the megalithic complex from a center situated at Los Millares, in the province of Almeria.

The megalithic complex comprises three categories of structures: (1) the menhir (from Breton *men* = "stone" and *hir* = "long") is a large stone, sometimes of considerable height,[1] set vertically into the ground; (2) the cromlech (from *crom* = "circle, curve," and *lech* = "place"), which designates a group of menhirs, set in a circle or half-circle (the most monumental is the cromlech of Stonehenge, near Salisbury); sometimes the menhirs are aligned in several parallel rows, as at Carnac in Brittany;[2] (3) the dolmen (*dol* = "table" and *men* = "stone") is made up of an immense capstone supported by several upright stones arranged to form a sort of enclosure or chamber. Originally the dolmen was covered by a mound.

Strictly speaking, dolmens are burial places. Later and in certain regions—western Europe, Sweden—the dolmen was transformed into a covered passage by the addition of a sort of vestibule in the form of a long corridor covered with capstones. Some dolmens are gigantic; the one at Soto (near Seville), for example, is 21 meters long and has as pediment a granite block 3.40 meters high, 3.10 meters wide, and 0.72 meters thick and weighing 21 tons. At Los Millares a necropolis of about a hundred covered passages has been excavated. Most of the graves are under enormous mounds. Certain burials contain as many as a hundred dead, representing several generations of the same *gens*. Sometimes the burial chambers have a central pillar, and remains of painting can still be discerned on the walls. Dolmens are found along the Atlantic, especially in Brittany, and as far as the Netherlands. In Ireland the funerary chambers, which are comparatively high, have walls decorated with sculptures.

All this undoubtedly testifies to a very important cult of the dead. Whereas the houses of the Neolithic peasants who raised these monuments were modest and ephemeral (and in fact have left almost no traces), the dwellings for the dead were built of stone. It is obvious that there was an intention to construct imposing and solid works, capable of resisting time. The complexity of lithic symbolism and the religious valences of stones and rocks are well known.[3] The rock, the slab, the granite block reveal duration without end, permanence, incorruptibility—in the last analysis a modality of *existing* independently of temporal becoming.

When we contemplate the grandiose megalithic monuments of the earliest agriculturalists of western Europe, we cannot but call to mind a certain Indonesian myth. In the beginning, when the sky was very near to the earth, God hung his gifts on a cord in order to bestow them on the primordial couple. One day he sent them a stone, but the ancestors, surprised and indignant, refused it. Some days later God let the cord down again, this time with a banana, which was immediately accepted. Then the ancestors heard the creator's voice: "Since you have chosen the banana, your life shall be like the life of that fruit. If you had chosen the stone, your life would have been like the existence of stone" unchangeable and immortal."[4]

As we have seen (§ 12), the discovery of agriculture radically changed the conception of human existence: it proved to be as frail and ephemeral as the life of plants. Yet, on the other hand, man shared in the cyclical destiny of vegetation: birth, life, death, rebirth. The megalithic monuments could be interpreted as a response to our Indonesian myth: since man's life is like the life of cereals, strength and perenniality become accessible *through death*. The dead return to the bosom of Mother Earth, with the hope of sharing the destiny of sown seed; but they are also mystically associated with the stone blocks of the burial chambers and consequently become as strong and indestructible as rocks.

For the megalithic cult of the dead appears to include not only a certainty of the soul's survival but, above all, confidence in the power of the ancestors and the hope that they will protect and help the living. Such a confidence differs radically from the concepts documented among other peoples of antiquity (Mesopotamians, Hittites, Hebrews, Greeks, etc.), for whom the dead were pitiable shades, unhappy and powerless. What is more: whereas for the megalith-builders, from Ireland to Malta and the Aegean islands, *ritual communion with the ancestors* constituted the keystone of their religious activity, in the protohistorical cultures of central Europe, as in the ancient Near East, *separation between the dead and the living* was strictly prescribed.

In addition to various ceremonies (processions, dances, etc.), the megalithic cult of the dead involved offerings (food, beverages, etc.), sacrifices performed in the vicinity of the monuments, and ritual meals on the burial places. A certain number of menhirs were erected independently of burials. In all probability, these stones constituted a sort of "substitute body," in which the, souls of the dead were incorporated.[5] In the last analysis, *a stone "substitute" was a body built for eternity.* Menhirs are sometimes found decorated with human figures; in other words, they are the "dwelling," the "body" of the dead. Similarly, the stylized figures depicted on the walls of dolmens, together with the small idols excavated from the megalithic burial places of Spain, probably represented the ancestors. In certain cases a parallel belief can be discerned: the ancestor's soul is able to leave the tomb from time to time.[6] The perforated stones that close certain megalithic tombs, and which, furthermore, are called "soul holes," allowed communication with the living.

The sexual meaning of menhirs must also be taken into consideration, for it is universally documented, and on various levels of culture. Jeremiah (2:27) refers to those "who say to a piece of wood, 'You are my father,' to a stone, 'You have begotten me.'"[7] Belief in the fertilizing virtues of menhirs was still common among European peasants at the beginning of this century. In France, in order to have children, young women performed the *glissade* (letting themselves slide along a stone) and the *friction* (sitting on monoliths or rubbing their abdomens against certain rocks).[8]

This generative function must not be explained by the phallic symbolism of the menhir, though such a symbolism is documented in certain cultures. The original, and fundamental, idea was the "transmutation" of the ancestors into stone, either by the device of a menhir as "substitute body" or by incorporating an essential element of the dead person—skeleton, ashes, "soul"—into the actual structure of the monument. In either case the dead person "animated" the stone; he inhabited a new body that, being mineral, was imperishable. Hence the menhir or the megalithic tomb constituted an inexhaustible reservoir of vitality and power. By virtue of their projection into the structures of the funerary stones, the dead became masters of fertility and prosperity. In the language of the Indonesian myth, they had succeeded in taking possession of both the stone and the banana.

CEREMONIAL CENTERS AND MEGALITHIC CONSTRUCTIONS

Certain megalithic complexes, such as the one at Carnac or the one at Ashdown, in Berkshire (containing 800 megaliths in a parallelogram 250 by 500 meters), undoubtedly constituted important ceremonial centers. The festivals included sacrifices and, it may be presumed, dances and processions. Indeed, thousands of men could move in procession along the great avenue at Carnac. Probably most of the festivals were connected with the cult of the dead. Like other similar English monuments,[9] the Stonehenge cromlech was situated in the middle of a field of funeral barrows. This famous ceremonial center constituted, at least in its primitive form,[10] a sanctuary built to insure relations with the ancestors. In terms of structure, Stonehenge can be compared with certain megalithic complexes developed, in other cultures, from a sacred area: temples or cities. We have the same valorization of the sacred space as "center of the world," the privileged place that affords communication with heaven and the underworld, that is, with the gods, the chthonian goddesses, and the spirits of the dead.

In certain parts of France, in the Iberian Peninsula, and elsewhere, traces have been found of a cult of the Goddess, the guardian divinity of the dead. Yet nowhere else did megalithic architecture, the cult of the dead, and worship of a Great Goddess find such spectacular expression as on Malta. Excavations have brought to light very few houses; but up to now seventeen temples have been discovered, and their number is thought to be still greater, which justifies the opinion of certain scholars that during the Neolithic period Malta was an *isola sacra.*[11] The vast elliptical terraces that stretched before the sanctuaries or between them certainly served for processional and ritual choreography. The temple walls are decorated with admirable spirals in low relief, and a number of stone sculptures representing women lying on one side have been excavated. But the most sensational discovery is the enormous statue of a woman—certainly a goddess—in a seated position.

The excavations have revealed an elaborate cult, with animal sacrifices, food offerings and libations, and rites of incubation and divination, indicating the existence of an important and well-organized sacerdotal body. The cult of the dead probably played the central role. In the remarkable necropolis at Hal Saflieni, now called the Hypogeum and comprising several chambers cut into the rock, the bones of some 7,000 persons have been exhumed. It is the Hypogeum that has yielded the statues of recumbent women, suggesting an incubation rite. Just as in other megalithic monuments, the inner rooms have their walls sculptured and painted. These large chambers served for certain religious ceremonies reserved for priests and initiates, for they were isolated by carved screens.[12]

Whereas the Hypogeum was at once necropolis and chapel, no burials have been found in the temples. The curvilinear structure of the Maltese sanctuaries seems to be unique; the archeologists describe it as "kidney-shaped," but according to Zuntz their structure more nearly suggests that of the womb. Since the temples were covered by a roof and the rooms were without windows and rather dark, entering a sanctuary was equivalent to entering the "bowels of the earth," i.e., the womb of the chthonian Goddess. But the rock-cut tombs are also womb-shaped. One would say that the dead person is placed in the bosom of the earth for a new life. "The temples reproduce the same model on a large scale. The living who enter them enter the body of the goddess." Indeed, Zuntz concludes, these monuments constitute the stage for "a mystery-cult in the exact sense of the word."[13]

We will add that the surfaces of the dolmens and menhirs of Iberia and western Europe also display other magico-religious signs and symbols—for example, the image of a sun with rays, the sign of the ax (peculiar to storm gods), the snake, symbol of life, associated with figures of the ancestors, the stag, etc. To be sure, these figures have been discovered in different regions and belong to cultures of different ages, but they have in common the fact that they are bound up with the same megalithic complex. This may be explained either by the variety of religious ideas held by the different "megalithic" peoples or by the fact that the cult of ancestors, despite its importance, was associated with different religious complexes.

THE "ENIGMA OF THE MEGALITHS"

A decade ago archeologists explained the megalithic cultures by influences from colonizers arrived from the eastern Mediterranean, where, in fact, collective burials are already documented in the third millennium.[14] In the course of its dissemimition into the West, the construction of dolmens ("chamber tombs") was transformed into cyclopean architecture. According to Glyn Daniel, this transformation took place on Malta, in the Iberian Peninsula, and in southern France. The same writer compares the dissemination of megalithic architecture with the Greek and Phoenician colonization in the Mediterranean or the expansion of Islam into Spain. "It was a powerful, compelling, Aegean-inspired religion that made them build their tombs (or their tomb temples?) with such labor and preserve . . . the image of their tutelary and funerary goddess. The goddess figure, the axe, the horns, and other symbols take us back from the Paris Basin, from Gavrinnis, from Anghelu Raju to Crete, the Aegean, even Troy. It cannot be disputed that a powerful religion of east Mediterranean origin informed and inspired the builders of the megalithic tombs as they spread through western Europe."[15] But religion was not the primary cause of their migrations; religion was only "the solace of their exile in the far west and the north of Europe." The emigrants were seeking new countries to live in and ores for their trade.[16]

In his last book, Gordon Childe discussed a "megalithic religion," disseminated by Mediterranean prospectors and colonizers. Once accepted, the idea of building megalithic tombs was adapted by the various societies, without, however, affecting their specific structures. Each tomb probably belonged to a nobleman or to the head of a family; the labor was supplied by his companions. "A megalithic tomb should be compared to a church rather than a castle, and its occupants to Celtic saints rather than to Norman barons."[17] The "missionaries" of the megalithic faith, a religion above all of the Mother Goddess, attracted a large number of agriculturalists to their communities. And in fact the dolmens and cromlechs are located in the regions most suitable for Neolithic agriculture.[18]

Similar explanations of the megalithic complex have been proposed by other eminent prehistorians.[19] However, these explanations were invalidated by the discovery of dating by the radioactivity of carbon and by dendrochronology.[20] It has been possible to show that the megalithic sepulchers ("chamber tombs") of Brittany were built before 4000 B.C. and that in England and Denmark stone tombs were being built before 3000 B.C.[21] As for the gigantic complex of Stonehenge, it was thought to be contemporary with the Wessex culture, which was linked with the Mycenaean civilization. But analyses based on the recent methods prove that Stonehenge was finished before Mycenae; its last rebuilding (Stonehenge III) dates from 2100–1900 B.C.[22] So too on Malta, the period represented by the Tarxien temples and the necropolis of Hal Saflieni had ended before 2000 B.C.; hence certain of its characteristic features cannot be explained by an influence from the Minoan Bronze Age.[23] So the conclusion is inescapable that *the European megalithic complex precedes the Aegean contribution.* We are dealing with a series of original autochthonous creations.

However, the chronological "upset" and the demonstration of the originality of the western populations have not advanced the interpretation of the megalithic monuments. There has been much discussion concerning Stonehenge, but, despite some noteworthy contributions,[24] the religious function and the symbolism of the monument are still disputed. Furthermore, in reaction against certain risky hypotheses (for example, that of Sir Grafton Elliot Smith, who derived all the megalithic constructions from the one source of pharaonic Egypt), investigators no longer dare to attack the problem as a whole. But this timidity is regrettable, for "megalithism" is an exemplary, and probably unique, subject of study. Indeed, comparative research should be able to show to what extent the analysis of the numerous megalithic cultures that were still flourishing in the nineteenth century can contribute to an understanding of the religious concepts held by the originators of the prehistoric monuments.

ETHNOGRAPHY AND PREHISTORY

It is well known that, outside of the Mediterranean and western and northern Europe, megaliths of prehistoric and protohistoric origin are spread over a vast area: Algeria, Palestine, Abyssinia, the Deccan, Assam, Ceylon, Tibet, and Korea. As for the megalithic cultures that were still alive at the beginning of the twentieth century, the most notable are documented in Indonesia and Melanesia. Robert Heine-Geldern, who devoted part of his life to studying this problem, held that the two groups of megalithic cultures—those of prehistory and those of cultures at the ethnographic stage—are historically connected, for in his view the megalithic complex was disseminated from a single center, very probably the eastern Mediterranean.

We shall later return to Heine-Geldern's hypothesis. For the moment, we may appropriately summarize his conclusions regarding the beliefs typical of the living megalithic societies. Megaliths have a relation to certain ideas concerning existence after death. The majority of them are built in the course of ceremonies intended to defend the soul during its journey into the beyond; but they also insure an eternal postexistence, both to those who raise them during their own lifetime and to those for whom they are built after death. In addition, megaliths constitute the unrivaled connection between the living and the dead; they are believed to perpetuate the magical virtues of those who constructed them or for whom they were constructed, thus insuring the fertility of men, cattle, and harvests. In all the megalithic cultures that still flourish, the cult of ancestors plays an important part.[25]

The monuments serve as the seat of the souls of the dead when they come back to visit the village, but they are also used by the living. The place where the megaliths stand is at once the outstanding cult site (ceremonial choreography, sacrifices, etc.) and the center of social activity. In the megalithic-type cult of the dead, genealogies play an important part. According to Heine-Geldern, it is probable that the genealogies of the ancestors—that is, of the founders of villages and of certain families—were ritually recited. It is important to emphasize this fact: *man hopes that his name will be remembered through the agency of stone;* in other words, connection with the ancestors is insured by memory of their names and exploits, a memory "fixed" in the megaliths.

As we have just observed, Heine-Geldern claims for the megalithic civilizations a continuity extending from the fifth millennium down to the contemporary "primitive" societies. However, he rejects G. Elliot Smith's and J. W. Perry's pan-Egyptian hypothesis. In addition, he denies the existence of a "megalithic religion," for the simple reason that certain "megalithic" beliefs and concepts are documented in connection with many religious forms, both elementary and higher. The Austrian scholar compares the megalithic complex with certain "mystical" movements—for example, Tantrism, which can be indifferently either Hindu or Buddhist. He also denies the existence of a "megalithic cultural circle," made up, according to certain authors, of particular myths and characteristic social or economic institutions; and in fact megalithic ideas and practices are documented among populations that possess a great variety of social forms, economic structures, and cultural institutions.[26]

The analysis of the megalithic complex accomplished by Heine-Geldern still has value. But his hypotheses concerning the unity of ancient and contemporary megalithic cultures are today disputed, or simply ignored, by many investigators. The problem of the "continuity" of the megalithic complex is substantial and must remain open. For, as a certain author put it recently, it represents "the greatest enigma of prehistory." In any case—and whatever hypothesis is adopted, whether continuity or convergence—it is impossible to speak of *one* megalithic culture. For our purpose, it should be noted that, in the megalithic religions, the sacrality of stone is chiefly valorized in relation to postexistence. The attempt is made to "found" a particular mode of existence after death by means of the ontophany peculiar to stones. In the megalithic cultures of western Europe, the fascination exercised by stone in masses is obvious; but it is a fascination aroused by the desire to transform collective burials into spectacular and indestructible monuments. By virtue of the megalithic constructions the dead enjoy an exceptional power; however, since communication with the ancestors is ritually assured, this power can be shared by the living. To be sure, other forms of the cult of ancestors exist. What characterizes the megalithic religions is the fact that the ideas of *perenniality* and of *continuity between life and death* are apprehended through the *exaltation of the ancestors as identified, or associated, with the stones.* We will add, however, that these religious ideas were not fully realized and perfectly expressed except in a few privileged creations.

ENDNOTES

1. The menhir located near Locmariaquer measured more than 20 meters in height. In Brittany certain isolated menhirs are associated with burials.
2. The alignments at Carnac comprise 2,935 menhirs on a terrain 3,900 meters long.
3. See our *Patterns in Comparative Religion,* §§ 74 ff.
4. A. C. Kruijt, cited by J. G. Frazer, *The Belief in Immortality* (1913), vol. 1, pp. 74–75. We have commented on this myth in "Mythologies of Death" (chap. 3 of *Occultism, Witchcraft, and Cultural Fashions*).
5. Horst Kirchner, "Die Menhire in Mitteleuropa und der Menhirgedanke," pp. 698 ff. (pp. 90 ff. of the offprint).
6. Certain Breton menhirs, set up in front of the galleries of dolmens, have been explained by the Egyptian belief that the souls of the dead, transformed into birds, left their tombs to perch on a pillar in full sunlight. "This notion appears to have been entertained throughout the Mediterranean area and also in western Europe" (Maringer, *The Gods of Prehistoric Man,* p. 235). Carl Schuchhardt put forward the same interpretation for the obelisks painted on the sarcophagus of Hagia Triada (see § 41), on which birds are perched. But see the critique by Kirchner, "Die Menhire," p. 706 (offprint, p. 98). In the megalithic cultures of Southeast Asia, the menhir serves as "seat" for souls (cf. § 36).
7. Nevertheless, even such a vigorously Yahwistic treatise as Deuteronomy still uses the ontological metaphor of stone when it proclaims the absolute reality of God as sole source of creativity: "You forget the Rock who begot you, unmindful now of the God who fathered you" (Deut. 32:18).
8. See some examples and the bibliography in *Patterns in Comparative Religion,* § 77, to which Kirchner, "Die Menhire," pp. 650 ff. (offprint, p, 42) should be added.
9. For example, Woodhenge, Avebury, Arminghall, and Arbor Low; see Maringer, *The Gods of Prehistoric Man,* p. 247.
10. Stonehenge was not all built at once. It is now known that the original work underwent several rehandlings. See Colin Renfrew, *Before Civilization,* pp. 214 ff.
11. Gunther Zuntz, *Persephone,* p. 4, n. 1.
12. J. D. Evans, *Malta,* p. 139; Glyn Daniel and J. D. Evans, *The Western Mediterranean,* p. 20.
13. Zuntz, *Persephone,* pp. 8, 25.
14. The Minoan collective tombs were either natural caves or circular enclosures, usually called *tholoi;* see Glyn Daniel, *The Megalithic Builders of Western Europe,* 2d ed. (1962), p. 129.
15. Ibid., p. 136.
16. Ibid., pp. 136–37.
17. Gordon Childe, *The Prehistory of European Society,* pp. 126 ff. The author (p. 128) compares the megalithic tombs with the little chapels founded by the Welsh and Irish saints in the same parts of the British Isles.
18. Ibid., p. 129.

19. Stuart Piggott derives the megalithic monuments from the eastern Mediterranean and compares them with Christian churches or mosques; see his *Ancient Europe,* p. 60. For Grahame Clark, the Aegean rite of collective burials, associated with the cult of the Mother Goddess, was disseminated in the West by prospectors and explorers for mines; see his *World Prehistory,* pp. 138–39.
20. For this "tree-ring calibration of radiocarbon," see a clear exposition in Colin Renfrew, *Before Civilization,* pp. 48–83. As is well known, the two "revolutions"—dating by carbon 14 and by dendrochronology—radically altered the chronology of European prehistory.
21. It should be born in mind that in Egypt the earliest stone pyramids were erected about 2700 B.C. It is true that these pyramids had predecessors of brick, but the fact remains that, before 3000 B.C., we know of no Egyptian stone monument comparable to the megaliths of western Europe; see Renfrew, *Before Civilization,* p: 123.
22. See the documentation ibid., pp. 214 ff.
23. Ibid., p. 152. See also Daniel and Evans, *The Western Mediterranean,* p. 21. Zuntz, however, thinks of an Egyptian or Sumerian influence (*Persephone,* pp. 10 ff.).
24. Since the tectonic structure of Stonehenge seems also to imply the function of an astronomical observatory, it is probable that the chief festivals were related to the changes of the seasons, as among the Hopis and the Cherokees; see Renfrew, *Before Civilization,* pp. 239 ff.
25. R. Heine-Geldern, "Prehistoric Research in the Netherlands Indies," p. 149, and "Das Megalithproblem," pp. 167 ff.
26. See "Das Megalithproblem," pp. 164 ff.

Chapter 15

Magic and Ritual for the Dead

John H. Taylor

The transition from life to afterlife was a complex process involving uncertainties and dangers. Major concerns were that the offerings should be supplied in perpetuity, and that the deceased should not fall victim to the many dangers which threatened the unwary or ill-prepared. Mortuary rituals and texts assisted the deceased on his passage to the next life and equipped him with the special knowledge he would need to protect and sustain himself in the hereafter. This special knowledge could only be made to function by magic.

The term 'magic' as used here simply denotes the use of supernatural means to produce desired effects. The power by which this was done was termed *heka* by the Egyptians. *Heka* was a creative power, possessed by all the gods, and to which the dead also had access.

Magic pervaded life in ancient Egypt. Far from having the negative connotations of irregularity and subversiveness which are associated with the term in many cultures, it played a regular part in orthodox religion at all levels of society. Recourse was had to magic when confronted by situations which required more than ordinary human powers to deal with. In these circumstances practical approaches would be used as well as magic. Magic was preventative as well as responsive: it was used to avert an undesirable situation, as well as to solve one. It was also used to serve both positive and negative ends.

Egyptian magic was founded on a belief in the power of the spoken and written word, and the use of amulets and ritual objects. It was used in the the temple cult, in everyday life (in healing and protecting against illness) and for the dead. Magic was performed *on behalf* of the dead by priests and relatives during mummification, in the funeral rites, and in the offering cult; it was also made available for the *personal use* of the dead in the tomb via texts, images and amulets.

RITUALS FOR THE DEAD

The most conspicuous use of magic for the dead was in the context of rituals. The uttering of prescribed words, together with the performance of appropriate acts, was regarded as the most effective way of achieving results. According to Egyptian belief in the 'performative' power of speech, to pronounce something made it so; hence attributing qualities or status to someone in a ritual context endowed them with those qualities. Like the cult of the gods in the temples, funerary ritual was usually enacted at a sacred location, a place perceived as a boundary between the world of the living and that of the gods and the dead. This was usually the tomb, but might also be a mortuary temple, a cult temple or a memorial chapel. As the foregoing description of the tomb has shown there was a parallelism between the status of the transfigured deceased in funerary ritual and that of the god in temple cult, emphasising the new divine quality of the dead person.

We have already encountered the offering ritual which was intended to sustain the dead. This was incorporated into a long sequence of funerary rituals, which began shortly after the death and culminated in the rites at the tomb on the day of burial. This long sequence included ritual acts accompanying the embalming, and the various episodes which constituted the 'funeral'.

Rituals of Embalming

There can be no doubt that the process of mummification was heavily ritualised at all periods, but actual information on this is rare. The main source of details is the *Ritual of Embalming*, which survives in manuscripts dating to the Roman Period (first to second centuries AD), but probably represents a much older tradition, perhaps dating back as far as the New Kingdom. The text contains eleven episodes, with spells to be recited and instructions for the correct application of particular wrappings and amulets.

Rites on the Day of Burial

At the end of the period of mummification, the relatives of the deceased collected the body from the embalmers. The day of burial was the occasion for a series of acts and rituals which correspond approximately to the modern notion of the 'funeral'. This is described and illustrated in many tombs and funerary papyri, particularly those of the New Kingdom, although interpretation of such depictions is complicated by their sometimes incorporating episodes which would in reality have happened at other times, such as the transportation of the body to the embalmer's workshop, and symbolic journeys to places of pilgrimage such as Abydos.

At its most elaborate the funeral was a heavily ritualised procedure. The mummy in its coffin was taken from the deceased's house and either carried by servants or placed inside a shrine-shaped catafalque. This was mounted on a boat-shaped base, the whole edifice resting on a sledge. This would be drawn by oxen or by male friends of the deceased, although at the funeral of the king the catafalque was pulled by a group of high officials, an episode depicted in the tomb of Tutankhamun (*c.* 1336–1327 BC). Sometimes the coffin was transported on a wheeled cart.

The catafalque, adorned with floral bouquets, was the focus of a procession, which also included the relatives and friends of the deceased. Those taking part observed the formalities of mourning. The period of mourning began immediately after death. Herodotus describes how the female relatives of the deceased 'smear their heads with dust, and sometimes also the face, and then they leave the corpse in the house and themselves wander through the town and beat their breasts with garments girt up and revealing their breasts . . . And the males beat their breasts separately, these too with their garments girt up.' These actions were repeated during the funeral. In New Kingdom depictions the dead man's widow is often shown kneeling beside his mummy, and at the burial of a person of wealth there would also be professional mourners. Old Kingdom scenes show men and women segregated in mourning, women indoors, men outside. In New Kingdom scenes, the most conspicuous mourners are the women, recognisable in the depictions by their dishevelled hair, exposed breasts, mouths open in lamentation, and contorted postures, which conveyed a highly specific 'semaphore' of grief. Herodotus' account notwithstanding, men generally adopted a less dramatic pose, squatting on the ground with their faces downcast, a gesture described in the story of Sinuhe, where the courtiers who lament the death of the king sit 'head-on-knee'. In addition to these groups, there were sometimes two women who personified Isis and Nephthys, the mourners for Osiris.

The procession also included the embalmer and various priests, headed by the lector priest carrying a scroll, from which the appropriate incantations were read out. Servants brought the burial goods, particular attention being given to the canopic container, which was dragged on a sledge. Since most tombs were on the west bank, it was usually necessary to cross the Nile. At the river the coffin was placed on a boat, towed by rowing boats. The coffin was laid beneath a canopy in the middle, with the two principal lamenting women at the prow and stern. The boat crossed the river and arrived at the west bank, where it was received into the *wabet*. This structure (perhaps the same in which the embalming had been carried out) was the place in which the mummy was subjected to purifying rituals, before resuming the journey to the tomb.

At the tomb a further series of rituals took place. Here the *muu* dancers performed a ritual dance wearing tall headdresses made of vegetal material. Brief processions were made representing journeys to different cult centres in Egypt, which were represented by chapels. These included a visit to Sais, with rituals believed to derive from the ceremonies enacted at the burials of the Predynastic rulers of Buto in Lower Egypt. Finally, both the *tekenu* and the canopic container were brought to the tomb entrance.

The Opening of the Mouth

Once the deceased had arrived at his tomb, the threshold of the next world, the *sakhu* rituals were performed, to bring about his transfiguration. This was the moment for the most important of the funerary rites, the Opening of the Mouth, the basic purpose of which was to re-animate the mummy. This originated as a ritual to endow statues with the capacity to support the living *ka*, and so to receive offerings. By the Old Kingdom it had been adapted from a statue-rite to one performed on the mummy, its purpose being to restore to the dead person the use of his mouth, eyes, ears and nose enabling him to see, hear, breathe, and receive nourishment to sustain the *ka*. Texts offer no clear indications as to what became of the *ka, ba* and other non-physical aspects of a person during the seventy-day interval between death and burial; possibly their activity was imagined to be suspended until the mummification process was complete. The Opening of the Mouth, however, renewed the relationship of these aspects with the corpse.

Depictions of the ritual from the New Kingdom show the mummy placed upright on a patch of clean sand at the entrance to the tomb. The liturgy was recited while the appropriate acts were carried out; in its fullest form, the ritual incorporated elements from a number of different sources. Purifications and offerings similar to those performed in temple rites were enacted. The most important episodes were those adapted from the original statue-ritual, involving the priest touching the mouth of the mummy-mask with a chisel, an adze and other implements, including a bifurcate object called the *pesesh-kef*, by which the faculties were symbolically renewed. The ritual was directed by an official called the *sem*-priest. This individual, originally the eldest son of the king, acted as the intermediary between the deceased and the netherworld; through his filial relationship to the deceased, like that of Horus to Osiris, the identification of the dead man with the resurrected god was strengthened. From the New Kingdom onwards this role was often conceived as being carried out by Anubis; at least, he is often depicted taking part, either holding the mummy upright while the ritual is performed or bending over the mummy on its bier, holding the adze and actually carrying out the ritual himself.

The words of the Opening of the Mouth ritual occur in the *Pyramid Texts*. In the New Kingdom, a revised version of the ritual was produced, illustrated with seventy-five individual scenes, copies of which are found in several tombs, notably that of Sety I (*c.* 1294–1279 BC) in the Valley of the Kings. The main elements of this revised version were purification, the sacrifice of a bull, the mouth-opening itself, and the presentation of offerings. The ritual ended with an invocation to the gods at the placing of the mummy or statue in the tomb.

Because of the importance of the Opening of the Mouth, tombs were sometimes supplied with sets of implements which enabled the deceased to perform the ritual for himself if the need should arise. In the Old Kingdom, these implements are usually models, set into stone slabs with receptacles specially cut to receive them. More elaborate models of some of the implements and vessels are known from the New

Kingdom, and some tombs of the Late Period have also been found to contain groups of objects relating to the ritual. The tomb of Tjanehebu at Saqqara (26th Dynasty) contained a group of these, including a *sekhem* sceptre, the ram-headed serpent rods called *wer-hekau* instruments, and models of vessels in faience, calcite and wood.

The Offering Ritual

As noted previously, the Offering Ritual supplied the deceased with nourishment for eternity. It was performed for the first time immediately after the Opening of the Mouth, and, like the latter, was composed of several individual rituals: purifications, libations, the burning of incense, and the presentation of food and drink. Actual food and drink were placed on the offering table of the chapel, and the *hetep di nesu* formula was pronounced. This was the most important ritual in the long term, since it was the one which would ensure the continued survival of the deceased. It was accordingly repeated at intervals after the burial.

The last element in the 'funeral' was the actual burial. The body and its funerary goods were placed in the tomb and the entrance to the burial chamber was sealed. Cattle were slaughtered, and the choicest parts of the animal were offered to the dead. The remainder was consumed by the relatives and mourners at a feast. The remnants of this banquet were sometimes ritually buried, and from such a deposit found in the Valley of the Kings we know that the guests at Tutankhamun's funeral feast consumed beef, sheep or goat, duck and goose. The participants then withdrew, returning to their homes, while final rituals to protect the tomb were performed.

FUNERARY TEXTS

The collective term for all ancient Egyptian funerary texts was *sakhu* (literally, 'that which makes *akh*'). This emphasises the principal purpose of all the texts, which was to enable the deceased to make the successful transition to the transfigured state, *akh*. The placing of funerary texts in the tomb—on the walls of the chapel, on papyri, on coffins, stelae and amulets, or on the mummy wrappings—sought to make possible the replication by magic of the ritual acts which the texts described. The deceased was thereby equipped with the special knowledge needed to attain the afterlife.

Funerary texts in ancient Egypt had a long history, stretching from the late third millennium BC to the early centuries AD. Originally reserved for the sole use of the dead king, they ultimately became available to a broader range of the population.

The Pyramid Texts

The earliest collection is the texts inscribed on the internal walls of pyramids of kings and queens buried in the Memphite necropolis, from Unis, last ruler of the 5th Dynasty, to Ibi, an obscure king of the 8th Dynasty (early First Intermediate Period), i.e. *c*. 2350–2150 BC. They are carved in vertical columns on the walls chiefly of the burial chamber and antechamber. The hieroglyphic signs were filled with green pigment, symbolising regeneration, but there were no images. Although principally for royal use, some sections of the *Pyramid Texts* were used in non-royal burials even before the end of the Old Kingdom, and sporadically at later periods. It is possible that the entire corpus derived from a 'master' source in which the main protagonist was not consistently the king.

These texts are in fact a compilation of earlier sources, and represent various traditions which apparently arose at different times, though they probably do not (as was once believed) go back to the Predynastic period. Some allude to the dead king's ascent to the stars, others to his association with Osiris, while others place emphasis on his connections with the sun god. Hence already at this formative stage in the tradition of Egyptian funerary literature we observe the 'multiplicity of approaches' which characterises so much of Egyptian religious belief and practice. Apparently contradictory doctrines are accommodated simultaneously. Far from being a random compilation of old spells, the *Pyramid Texts* are structured, and organised into three different categories. Their function is expressed not only through the wording of the spells but also through their positioning on the walls of the pyramid's internal chambers.

One category consists of 'incantations' of a protective nature, designed to ward off the attacks of dangerous creatures such as snakes, or other hostile entities. A second category comprises the words to be spoken at the enactment of important funerary rituals carried out for the benefit of the dead. In these texts the deceased is equated with Osiris, the ruler of the Underworld, and the words are put into the mouth of the king's son, who takes the role of Horus. Within this group of texts—which are inscribed in the burial chamber—are 'offering' rituals and 'resurrection' rituals. The former, written on the north wall, gives the words to accompany the Opening of the Mouth to revitalise the deceased, and the offering of food and drink to sustain the spirit. The 'resurrection' ritual, inscribed on the facing wall, consists of spells relating to the dead king's passage from earth to the afterlife.

The third category comprises the 'personal' spells designed for the deceased's own use. They cover a variety of themes, particularly the transition to the next world expressed in metaphorical terms (such as crossing water, or ascending a ladder to the sky). These are inscribed on the walls of the antechamber and the passage leading to the exterior of the pyramid; it is important to recognise that the spatial arrangement of the texts is for the convenience of the dead king in leaving his sarcophagus and making his way *out* of the pyramid to the next world. Spells from the *Pyramid Texts* were also inscribed in the tombs and on the sarcophagi of some officials in the Middle Kingdom and the New Kingdom, and more extensively in the Late Period.

The Coffin Texts

After the end of the Old Kingdom, the corpus of Egyptian funerary literature underwent further development. This period saw the emergence of another compilation of funerary texts, known to modern scholars as the *Coffin Texts*. The name derives from the circumstance that the majority of examples are found inscribed in cursive hieroglyphic script on the surfaces of wooden coffins, but they also occur on tomb walls, on mummy masks and occasionally on papyri. Many of these texts were identical to, or adapted versions of spells from the *Pyramid Texts* corpus, with additions from other sources. During the First Intermediate Period and Middle Kingdom, these texts were not restricted to royalty and occurred in the burials of officials and their families in various parts of Egypt. These texts articulate, for the first time, the possibility that all Egyptians, and not the king alone, could attain divine status in the afterlife.

This adoption by private individuals of funerary texts previously reserved for royalty is commonly termed 'democratisation of the afterlife'. It is a somewhat misleading term, as it implies a removal of the distinction between king and subject which the evidence does not warrant. The king continued to be distinguished from his subjects both in life and in the provision made for him after death, as exemplified by the restriction of the pyramid-tomb for the use of royalty alone. What funerary texts were used for Middle Kingdom rulers is not known, but they were not necessarily the same as those provided for non-royal persons. It is noteworthy that several centuries later, in the New Kingdom, new royal funerary texts were created, but that these were, as a rule, distinct from those of private individuals.

The organisation of the *Coffin Texts* is related to that of the *Pyramid Texts*, the internal surfaces of the wooden coffin equating to the stone interior walls of the king's pyramid. The 'resurrection' ritual continues to be used, while in place of the 'offering' ritual an offering-list is often included; the offerings are further illustrated in the 'frieze of objects', a narrow band of pictures of various commodities which is one of the most characteristic features of coffin decoration in the Middle Kingdom.

The *Coffin Texts* develop the notion of the two main contrasting concepts of the afterlife: the heavenly travels of the *ba*, and existence in the earthly netherworld, through the preservation of the corpse and the nourishing of the *ka*. The content of the *Coffin Texts* is heavily indebted to that of the *Pyramid Texts*, and includes many of the 'personal' spells. There were, however, innovations, the most important of which was a new genre of spells, collectively termed 'guides to the hereafter'. These texts were usually accompanied by a map showing the topography of the netherworld, and the means of access to it. The texts provided information and special knowledge to assist the deceased in making a safe journey into the next life. The most important of these guides was the *Book of Two Ways*. This composition was probably formulated at the Residence and first employed in the cemeteries of Dahshur and Lisht. From here it seems to have spread to other regions, most notably to the province of Hermopolis. The rectangular wooden coffins of governors and officials from Deir el-Bersha, the necropolis of that city, are the major source for the *Book of Two Ways*. On the coffins, the floor is usually occupied by the map, generally presenting two paths consisting of earth and water. The coffins of the physician Gua in the British Museum are among the finest examples. Different versions of the book were in use simultaneously. In the version painted on the outer and inner coffins of Gua, the main goal of the deceased is to join the sun god Ra.

The Book of the Dead

The Second Intermediate Period brought an interruption in the funerary text tradition, but by the beginning of the New Kingdom, a series of new corpora of texts had been assembled. The main composition developed at this time was the collection of texts called the *Spells for Going Forth by Day*, better known by the modern term, the *Book of the Dead*. This comprised approximately 200 spells, the bulk of which can be traced back in earlier guises to the *Pyramid Texts* and *Coffin Texts*, although new spells were also added. The *Book of the Dead* was probably created at Thebes in the 17th Dynasty. It perhaps owed its existence to the need for a new compilation of funerary texts when the transfer of the court from Itj-tawy to Thebes severed direct contact with the sources of older text-traditions based at Memphis and Heliopolis. Early examples of *Book of the Dead* texts were written on coffins and on linen mummy-shrouds. These texts on shrouds were succeeded in the middle years of the 18th Dynasty by the *Book of the Dead* written in ink on a roll of papyrus. The spells were also inscribed on tomb walls, coffins and mummy-bandages.

The *Book of the Dead* provided instructions and access to magical power to assist the deceased in his passage to the afterlife and in his existence there. Most of the texts are 'personal' spells. Unlike its precursors, the *Book of the Dead* was extensively illustrated with vignettes. The most important addition to the text corpus was spell 125, relating to the judgement of the deceased to determine his worthiness to receive new life. Many of the spells begin with rubrics giving instructions for their proper use. Certain spells were inscribed separately on objects such as on *shabtis* and on heart scarabs.

Although the whole corpus of *Book of the Dead* spells comprised about 200 separate texts, it was usual for only a selection of these to be made and inscribed on a roll of papyrus. Certain spells were meant to function as charms to protect or assist the deceased, and according to the rubrics, were to be written out on a separate sheet. The rubric to spell 100 states that the words were to be pronounced over the appropriate design which was to be drawn on a clean, unused sheet of papyrus with powder of green glaze mixed with myrrh-water, the sheet to be placed on the breast of the deceased without coming into direct contact with the body. If this is done, the text states, the deceased will be able to enter the barque of Ra. A rare example of the carrying out of these instructions in a New Kingdom burial is the papyrus from the mummy of Henutmehyt, which bears the text and vignette of spell 100 written unusually in red and white inks.

The *Book of the Dead* remained the most important collection of funerary texts until the Ptolemaic Period. In the version used in the New Kingdom (the 'Theban recension') the spells do not occur in a standard sequence. A major revision of the corpus in the 25th to 26th Dynasties (the 'Saite recension') resulted in a fixed sequence of chapters dealing in turn with the burial of the dead, their equipping with divine power and knowledge, their judgement and, finally, transfiguration. It is this later version that is the basis of the numbering sequence used today.

Books of the Underworld

Whereas the *Pyramid Texts, Coffin Texts* and *Book of the Dead* were concerned primarily with the destiny of the deceased in the afterlife, the other major set of compositions of the New Kingdom deal chiefly with the sun god's nightly journey and rejuvenation. These are the *Books of the Underworld,* the most important texts used in kings' tombs of the New Kingdom. They were descended from the 'guides to the hereafter' of the Middle Kingdom. The major ones, in chronological order of their appearance are: the *Amduat,* the *Book of Gates* and the *Book of Caverns.* All these 'books' are concerned with the journey of the sun through the subterranean underworld during the twelve hours of the night. The god is envisaged as travelling from the western to the eastern horizon by barque along an underworld river (the counterpart of the Nile). In the course of this journey the god is united with Osiris (the two of them regarded as halves of a single divine being) and there takes place the all-important rejuvenation of the sun god, which makes possible the new day. The god's progress is opposed by the forces of chaos, chief among whom is the serpent Apep who has to be defeated and restrained. The books also provide details of the experience of the dead; the righteous are rewarded with new life, while the unrighteous are punished. As in earlier periods, there is a distinction between the texts supplied for the king's use and those available to his subjects. The *Books of the Underworld* were primarily a royal prerogarive throughout the New Kingdom (although in rare cases they were used by private individuals). The king's rebirth is assured through his close identification with the sun god throughout his journey. These compositions are primarily pictorial guides with commentaries. The *Amduat* and *Book of Gates* are distinguished by their layout in three registers, the central one representing the sun god's path. Each has twelve divisions corresponding to the hours of the night; this aspect is emphasised in the *Book of Gates* by the depiction of large fortified doorways guarded by serpents, at the entrance to each division—from which the composition takes its modern name.

Mortuary Liturgies

The three great corpora of funerary writings, the *Pyramid Texts,* the *Coffin Texts* and the *Book of the Dead,* represent the most conspicuous stages in the development of the textual tradition. Another important category of funerary texts, however, is that of the 'mortuary liturgies', the words of the rituals carried out at the time of burial. Although designed for the welfare of the dead, they were not primarily meant to be read by them for their own benefit, but were intended for use by the mortuary priests who carried out the rites. Although, as noted above, a substantial number of them are found incorporated within the *Pyramid Texts* and *Coffin Texts,* they are far more widely distributed in time, from the Old Kingdom to the Roman Period. They also occur in various contexts, being inscribed in tombs, on coffins, on stelae, on papyri and on statues. With the passage of time, the main funerary text corpora and the mortuary liturgies followed independent courses of development, and the two became more clearly differentiated.

Late Funerary Texts

Funerary texts of earlier periods were revived in the Late Period, including the *Pyramid Texts* and *Books of the Netherworld,* inscribed in sarcophagi and on tomb walls. The production of long *Book of the Dead* papyri declined in the late Ptolemaic Period, though short selections continued to be used until the Roman era. From the 4th century BC, the *Book of the Dead* was increasingly replaced by other texts. These included liturgies used in temple rituals, which were usually written on papyri. Some of these texts were originally mortuary liturgies. There were also new compositions such as the two *Books of Breathing* and the *Book of Traversing Eternity.* The opening phrases of the *Books of Breathing* demonstrate that the texts have the character of divine decrees to grant new life to the deceased, notably giving him the ability to breathe. They also acted as letters of recommendation to the inhabitants of the hereafter. These 'passports' to the afterlife were sometimes folded up like letters and placed at the head and legs of the mummy, so that the deceased might present them to the gods on reaching the next world. Such late texts were also sometimes inscribed on wooden boards placed under the mummy.

The provision of funerary texts had been abandoned by the 4th century AD, together with most of the other features of traditional pharaonic burial practices.

MAGICAL OBJECTS FOR THE DECEASED

Objects were believed to convey magical power no less efficiently than texts. Magical objects and images placed in the tomb could function independently through the associations of their form, colour or material, as well as in conjunction with texts which would activate them. The strong belief in the power of the image is strikingly emphasised in some funerary inscriptions of the Middle Kingdom and Second Intermediate Period. In these texts, hieroglyphic signs representing potentially harmful creatures were deliberately 'mutilated'—snakes were drawn without tails or with the head severed from the body, birds appear without legs—as a precaution lest the images should inadvertently be activated within the tomb and cause harm to the deceased.

Funerary Jewellery

Egyptian burials have yielded an enormous quantity of jewellery, and this was one of the main temptations to ancient tomb-robbers. From the point of view of the deceased, however, its importance was manifold. Jewellery not only beautified the body and marked the social status of the wearer for eternity; much of it also conveyed magical power and protection, through its form, its iconography, and the materials of which it was made. Some people were buried with treasured jewellery which they had worn when alive, but there was also jewellery made specifically for the tomb. This superficially resembled real jewellery but was flimsy in construction. Like the tomb models and model vessels, they were substitutes which would function as well as the real thing by magic.

The most important items of funerary jewellery were collars. The *wesekh*, or 'broad', collar usually had terminals in the shape of falcon heads. This collar conveyed magical protection over the deceased as did the vulture collar. The magical functions of these collars, and the manner prescribed for their placing on the body are described in spells in the *Book of the Dead*.

Funerary Amulets

Another important means of protecting and empowering the deceased was through amulets. In ancient Egypt, amulets were widely used by the living as well as by the dead. Their purpose was to give the wearer supernatural power or protection. They depended for their potency on their shape and colour, the material from which they were made, and the particular ritual acts and incantations associated with them which rendered them effective. Certain spells in the *Book of the Dead* prescribe the correct materials, form and colour of important amulets and how they were to be positioned on the body. Similar details are also included in the *Ritual of Embalming*.

Some amulets were placed within the wrappings during the mummification process, while others were laid on the outer surface. Small numbers of simple amulets were being included with the dead even in the Predynastic period. They began to increase in number from the First Intermediate Period onwards. The growth in popularity of amulets in the Middle Kingdom was perhaps as a substitute for funerary literature, which was absent in many burials. By the New Kingdom, the wrappings of royal mummies were filled with a wide range of amulets, as the body of Tutankhamun (*c.* 1336–1327 BC) testifies; in the burials of private individuals, however, amulets were generally few in number and restricted to a few types, such as the *tit*, the *djed* pillar, papyrus column and heart amulet. After the New Kingdom there was a substantial increase in the range and quantity of amulets provided for the dead; many mummies of the Late Period possessed a profusion of amulets, and a single body might even contain several groups positioned between different layers of the wrappings.

One of the commonest amulets, closely associated with Osiris, was the *djed*, a pillar or column, which perhaps originally represented a tree with lopped branches. Originally associated with Sokar and Ptah, it featured in an ancient ritual called the 'Raising of the *Djed*,' in which the pillar was hauled into an upright position using ropes. Later it became a symbol of Osiris and was reinterpreted as a representation of his backbone. As an amulet, it conferred stability on the deceased, and the ability to stand upright. The *djed* was often paralleled by the *tit*, a depiction of a girdle-tie, which was associated with Isis. Spell 156 of the *Book of the Dead* directed that it be made of red jasper, and explained that if placed on the mummy's throat it would convey the power of Isis to protect the body.

In the myths about Horus, originally a god of the skies, his eyes were equated with the sun and moon. Seth stole the eye of the moon, and the two gods came into conflict. Seth disposed of the eye, which was later found in pieces by Thoth and restored. This story perhaps enshrines the explanation of the name *wedjat*, 'that which is whole', which was assigned to the eye of Horus; eye amulets in the form of the *wedjat* became very common as protective devices, guaranteeing that the wearer, like the healed eye of the god, was whole and sound.

Symbols such as the *wadj*, or papyrus column, were usually made of green stone or blue-green faience. This amulet connoted rebirth and resurrection, as manifested in the new growth of plants, of which the papyrus was a familiar example to the ancient Egyptians. The predominantly green colouring of this amulet played a significant part in establishing its effectiveness.

A large number of amulets are miniature representations of a particular god or goddess. When used in funerary contexts these placed the wearer under the protection of that god, or identified him with the deity, so as to endow him with the god's powers or attributes. The most common deities represented in this form are those associated with the myth of Osiris: figures of Isis and Nephthys are common, either individually or as members of a miniature triad incorporating Horus. Amulets representing Osiris himself are rare, probably because the deceased was himself identified with Osiris in the context of the tomb.

The scarab (a representation of the beetle *scarabeus sacer*) was another of the most popular amulets. Small representations of scarabs were commonly used by the living as seals, but they also served as funerary amulets to be placed on mummies. The scarab was associated both with the sun god and with the notion of rebirth. The adult beetle was observed to propel before it a ball of dung in which its eggs were embedded. The sight of the ball from which newly hatched beetles emerged apparently prompted in the minds of the Egyptians a comparison with the sun-disc at dawn as the source of renewed life. Hence the scarab was regarded as the form adopted by the sun god in the morning, and is depicted propelling the solar disc across the sky. This powerful image of rebirth occurred repeatedly on coffins, mummy-trappings and pectorals, sometimes showing the beetle alone, but often with outspread falcon-wings.

One of the most important of all funerary amulets was a special type of scarab which protected the heart of the deceased. The heart was regarded as one of the modes of human existence, and was considered to be the location of the human intelligence. Moreover, it contained a record of its owner's deeds and behaviour in life, and it would be examined by the gods of the judgement hall to determine whether or not its owner merited eternal life. It was therefore important that the heart should be retained in the hereafter. It was deliberately left inside the mummified body by the embalmers, and spells in the *Book of the Dead* were designed to guard against its loss. Since it could reveal potentially damning information about the deceased, texts such as spell 30B of the *Book of the Dead* also prevented the heart from testifying against its owner in the presence of the gods. This text was often inscribed on the 'heart scarab'. The rubric of the spell prescribed that this amulet should be carved from green stone and mounted in gold. It was to be anointed and vitalised by the

Opening of the Mouth, then placed on the breast of the mummy. Many heart scarabs are indeed of green stone (jasper seems to have been the preferred material), though others were of faience or Egyptian blue. One of the earliest known examples of a heart scarab is that inscribed for King Sebekemsaf of the 17th Dynasty (*c.* 1600 BC). It is mounted in gold, as prescribed in the spell-rubric, and bears a representation of a human face in place of the head of the beetle, emphasising that the heart encompasses the being of the deceased. A number of heart scarabs of the 18th Dynasty were also bound by gold bands, and were suspended on a gold wire or chain around the neck of the mummy.

While spell 30B is the most common, some heart scarabs carry other spells from the *Book of the Dead,* though the texts are always concerned with the heart. These include spell 26, to ensure that the deceased retains his heart in the netherworld; spell 27, to prevent the taking away of the deceased's heart in the netherworld; and spell 29B, relating to the *bennu,* or heron, which is identified as the *ba* of Ra. The *bennu* bird is frequently represented both on heart scarabs and on heart-shaped amulets. These latter also protected the heart. They were commonly placed inside the mummy wrappings, and the amulet was sometimes depicted being worn as a pendant by the deceased in scenes such as the weighing of the heart.

A characteristic feature of mummies of the middle and late 1st millennium BC was a large net of blue-green faience tubular beads, threaded in a lozenge pattern, with small spherical beads of different colours at the junctions and amuletic figures attached. These were placed on the front of the body, over the outer wrappings. The bead-nets were evidently related to the bead-garment worn by Osiris, and hence the placing of such a net on the mummy probably enhanced the assimilation of the deceased with Osiris. The nets also carried celestial symbolism, illustrated in the blue colouring and the incorporarion of the face of Nut into some examples. This also recalls the astral associations of Osiris; in at least one late depiction of Osiris wearing the net (in a tomb at Kom el-Shugafa) the lozenge spaces are occupied by moon, star and solar disc.

A few sporadic instances have been reported from the the Third Intermediate Period, but it was only in the 25th Dynasty that the nets were introduced on a regular basis, continuing in use until the Ptolemaic Period. The earliest version of the net usually extended only from the shoulders to the ankles, and amuletic figures were limited to a faience winged scarab and the four Sons of Horus on the breast. Later examples (26th Dynasty and later) were more elaborate, covering the head as well as the body. The finest ones incorporate a face mask of gold (occasionally silver), often with a *wesekh* collar, and a wider range of amuletic figures. To the Sons of Horus were added a winged Nut, mourning Isis and Nephthys, and a band of inscription giving the name and titles of the deceased; these could be of gold leaf, gilded wood or cartonnage. Some Memphite examples incorporated a flat face of the goddess Nut, frontally depicted, recalling frontal images of the goddess on coffins. Particularly rich burials had more elaborate nets. That of the chief of royal ships Hekaemsaf, buried at Saqqara in the reign of Ahmose II (570–526 BC), consisted of beads of gold, lapis lazuli and amazonite, with an integral gold mask, bead-collar with gold falcon-head terminals, and figures of Nut and the Sons of Horus and an inscription all in gold. Another type of net incorporated a face of tiny coloured beads, directly over the face of the mummy. Some examples have a collar and divine figures in the same 'mosaic bead' technique threaded into the open lozenge-pattern net. These have been found at sites such as Saqqara, Abusir, Lahun and el-Hiba.

Magic Bricks

Depictions of the mummy in the burial chamber occur in the *Book of the Dead,* and these illustrate the protection of the deceased by a range of deities and tutelary symbols. One important means of providing magical protection was the placing of four bricks of unbaked mud in niches in the burial chamber. These are attested for high status burials of the New Kingdom and 21st Dynasty, and were apparently reintroduced in the Late Period, the latest example dating to year 15 of Nectanebo I (*c.* 365 BC). They occur in both royal and private burials, so apparently no royal privilege was attached to them, though examples for kings usually have inscriptions in hieroglyphic, and those for non-royal persons in hieratic. The bricks have rarely survived in good condition, the best preserved set being those of Henutmehyt (reign of Ramesses II, *c.* 1279–1213 BC).

Each brick supported an amulet—a *djed* pillar, jackal, torch, and mummiform figurine—and each had a text, which reveals that their purpose was to ward off hostile forces from the four cardinal points. This text, part of spell 151 of the *Book of the Dead,* contains specifications for the bricks and what the figures were to be made of. The *djed* brick was to be placed on the west, and the torch at the south—this was to be of reed, containing a wick. An Anubis of unbaked clay mixed with incense was to be placed on the brick for the east wall while the brick with the human figure guarded the north. The inscriptions and placing of the bricks seem to have confused the personnel who deposited them, for the texts often contain mistakes, and the positioning of the bricks in the tomb did not always follow the prescribed pattern. In some tombs the bricks were placed in two pairs of niches in opposite walls, and even in royal tombs, the pattern was not always followed, suggesting that the positioning may reflect notions of a localised geography within the burial chamber.

Other Magical Figures

At different periods, a range of other magical objects was placed in the tomb. Some of these, once introduced, became a fixed part of the standard burial outfit for centuries; others were in vogue only briefly. A complex methodology underlay the selection of objects; texts on coffin, mummy-shroud and papyrus were sometimes complementary, each component forming part of a ritual unit indispensable to the deceased's welfare. In the same way, at periods when funerary texts were rarely placed in the tomb, other types of object appeared, perhaps to compensate for the absence of the texts. Hence, from the middle of the 12th Dynasty the custom of providing models of servants declined, while model food offerings were introduced and *shabtis* grew in importance. The same period witnessed a reduction in the use of *Coffin Texts,* corresponding with the addition to the burial outfit of a range of magical items.

Some of these were objects used in everyday life: serpent-shaped staffs, 'magical rods' bearing figures of turtles and other creatures, and curved ivory wands of apotropaic significance. The latter carry carved figures of animal deities holding knives, with which they were to ward off harmful influences. Some examples are worn, or have been damaged and repaired in ancient times, so it is clear that they were used to protect the living—particularly mothers and young children. The placing of these wands in tombs in the Middle Kingdom and Second Intermediate Period indicates that they also protected the dead and promoted their rebirth. Some of these objects carried symbolic allusions to the victory of the sun god over his enemies. Because of this association they too might have functioned as replacements for the texts, now often absent from the tomb, which alluded to the same concepts.

It was also in the Middle Kingdom that fertility figurines began to be placed in tombs with frequency, a custom which continued into the New Kingdom. These include figures representing naked females, often with the sexual organs emphasised, and others in the form of a woman lying on a bed, sometimes accompanied by a child. Such objects, which are also found in domestic contexts and at cult places, were probably intended to promote fecundity. Placed in tombs, they might have been intended to give the dead sexual powers as well—but more probably acted as symbols of rebirth and regeneration.

The kings' tombs of the New Kingdom contained a range of magical items and images all of which served to protect the dead king and assure his rebirth. Most of these objects are peculiar to royal burials. Notable among these are the pairs of life-size or larger statues of the king. The best preserved examples were found in the tomb of Tutankhamun (*c.* 1336–1327 BC). The statues were of wood, covered with black varnish and the headdresses, kilts and other trappings were originally gilded. In the tomb of Tutankhamun, the statues flanked the sealed doorway to the burial chamber. Similar statues, stripped of their gilding in antiquity, have been found in other tombs of the 18th to 20th Dynasties. The statues were differentiated by the types of royal headdress depicted: one wears the striped *nemes,* the other the bag-like *khat.* Those from Tutankhamun's tomb also bore different inscriptions. These indicate that the figures represented the two main aspects of the sun-god with whom the dead king was identified. The statue wearing the *nemes,* positioned on the eastern side, represented the king as the manifestation of Ra-Horakhty, the daytime form of the sun god, while that on the west (wearing the *khat*) was an image of the king as Osiris, equated with the nocturnal *ka* of the sun god.

Equally imposing are the couches in animal form. Three of these were found in Tutankhamun's tomb. Made of gilded wood, they have cow, lion and hippopotamus heads, and were intended to facilitate the king's passage to the afterlife. Heads from similar couches in black-varnished wood have been found in other tombs. Among the smaller figures were statuettes of the king as Horus, harpooning Seth, or riding on the back of a black panther, and standing and seated figures of deities. After the Amarna Period, the range of figures in the royal tomb was enlarged by the inclusion of a series of protective deities—often inaccurately termed 'demons of the underworld', but better described as apotropaic deities. Most are in human form, but with a variety of heads, including those of a ram, gazelle or turtle. They grasp knives, snakes and lizards to symbolise their power over hostile forces. Some of these gods are deities well known from other contexts—such as the Sons of Horus, chiefly associated with the protection of the viscera—while others are cognate with deities listed in the *Book of the Dead*, who guarded the gateways that led to the netherworld, and turned back the unrighteous. Examples of this type were found in the tombs of Horemheb (*c.* 1323–1295 BC), Ramesses I (*c.* 1295–1294 BC) and other kings. Comparable figures were depicted on the walls of royal tombs of the 19th and 20th Dynasties, as well as on papyri, sarcophagi and coffins of the Third Intermediate Period. These sources throw light on the purpose of the images, which appear to have been arranged around the mummy as if forming a protective cordon. The later depictions show that access to this form of protection was no longer restricted to royalty after the New Kingdom, but sculptural representations occurred only once more; the Theban governor Montemhat (early 26th Dynasty, *c.* 650 BC) arranged for a set of statuettes of these guardians to be carved from stone and placed in his tomb in the Asasif.

Corn-Mummies and Osirian Statues

The god Osiris was closely associated with vegetation, and particularly with germinating grain. The emergence of young growth shoots from the fertile mud of Egypt was regarded as a powerful metaphor for human resurrection, and this notion was given physical form in Osirian images and figurines in which earth and corn were basic constituents. Some royal tombs of the New Kingdom contained an 'Osiris bed', a seed bed in a wooden frame or on a piece of textile, made in the shape of an image of Osiris. This bed was planted with barley, which germinated in the tomb, symbolising the renewal of life for the dead king via the agency of Osiris. A similar concept underlay the creation of 'corn mummies', figurines composed of earth or mud mixed with grains of barley and fashioned into a miniature mummiform image of Osiris. These figures were manufactured in an elaborate temple ritual during the month of Khoiak, and then buried in areas with sacred associations. The majority of examples date to the Late and Ptolemaic periods, but comparable figures have occassionally been found in private tombs of earlier periods, and a few instances have been reported of small roughly shaped mummiform figurines found buried with mummies of the 22nd Dynasty.

Towards the end of the Third Intermediate Period, a new type of funerary statuette was introduced. These mummiform figures of wood often had a cavity either within the figure or in the base to contain a rolled funerary papyrus. Their antecedents probably stretch back to the royal burials of the New Kingdom. As early as the reign of Amenhotep II (*c.* 1427–1400 BC), the king's burial included a mummiform statuette hollowed out to contain a papyrus. Similar figures, representing Osiris, were used in non-royal burials from the 19th Dynasty, but hollow figures fell out of use in the 22nd Dynasty, when the provision of funerary papyri temporarily ceased. The mummiform figures were re-introduced in the 25th Dynasty, now representing not Osiris alone but Ptah-Sokar-Osiris, a syncretistic deity who embodied the concept of resurrection.

These statuettes possessed a standard range of attributes: a shrouded mummiform body, from which the hands occasionally protrude; a tripartite wig; a red, green or gilded face; and a headdress composed of twin plumes, ram's horns and a solar disc. The figure was supported on a long base. Many of these images contain a cavity, either within the figure itself or in the plinth. Instead of a papyrus roll, they contained a small corn-mummy. This symbol of the deceased's resurrection, when placed in the base of the statue, was often covered by a miniature sarcophagus or an image of a mummified falcon. This last represented Sokar, the god who protected the necropolis. The tendency to merge Osiris and Sokar with Ptah had begun as early as the Middle Kingdom, but Osiris and Sokar predominated, Ptah always playing a minor role. The importance of this god as a symbol of resurrection is emphasised in the texts on the Late Period statuettes, according to which the deceased shared the renewal of life experienced by Osiris. In consequence, a Ptah-Sokar-Osiris statue became an indispensable feature of the standard burial assemblage in the Late-Ptolemaic periods.

Chapter 16

The Hindu Rite of Entry into Heaven

David M. Knipe

With few exceptions, the Hindu rites at the time of death and the procedures for cremation *(antyeṣṭi)* are fairly uniform throughout the regions of India. Similarly, the series of rites for the departed (*śrāddhas*), where it has been retained, is performed according to traditional archaic standards. The basic structures of the antyeṣṭi and the śrāddha rites proceed from vedic models, models prefigured in the saṃhitās and brāhmaṇas, detailed in the gṛhyasūtras, and then conveyed with continuing elaboration in two thousand years of dharmśāstra literature. This conformity in ritual across vedic, epic, purāṇic, and āgamic periods, and on into modern practice, is remarkable considering that the answer to the question, "Where does a Hindu go when he dies?," had varied considerably within each one of these periods.[1]

Perhaps the question should be rephrased, "*Who* is a Hindu after death?," because the reply then would necessarily articulate the complex of stages that the deceased traverses between earthly expiration and eventual acceptance among his ancestors.

I shall examine the rite of *sapiṇḍīkaraṇa,* the moment of entry of the deceased into the world of the ancestors (*pitaraḥ*—literally, the Fathers, *pitṛ* in the singular), and the series of bodily constructions and dissolutions the deceased undergoes before becoming established in the world beyond. Contemporary practice of the post-cremation srāddhas, as performed by some traditions in Varanasi (Banaras), Uttar Pradesh, will be an ancillary focus of discussion,[2] and attention will be accorded the history and structure of the rites in the literature of the ritual tradition of Hinduism.

Of all the complex stages in the Hindu rites of death and dying, the most arresting moment comes at the sapiṇḍīkaraṇa, the time-filled action of blending the deceased with his forefathers, of transforming the vulnerable, disembodied spirit (*preta*) of this world into the secure pitṛ of that other world. The sapiṇḍīkaraṇa, or *sapiṇḍana* as it is sometimes called, is a "creating of the *sapiṇḍa*" relationship, that

"Sapindīkarana: The Hindu Rite of Entry into Heaven" as it appeared in *Religious Encounters with Death* edited by Frank E. Reynolds and Earle H. Waugh, based on a paper originally prepared for the Annual Convention of the American Academy of Religion held in Chicago, November 1973. Reprinted by permission of David M. Knipe, Professor Emeritus, University of Wisconsin-Madison.

is, an establishing of the ritual bond between the generations of those (living) who *offer* and those (deceased) who *receive* the *piṇḍa,* a symbolic meal of food pressed into a ball. The rites before death have their own mixture of tough and tender realism. The preparations after death are hurried and shocked, followed swiftly by the stark vigil of cremation, an occasion, perhaps, for reverie and insight. Then the successive days of piṇḍa offerings are a recovery and recuperation for the mourning family, even as the temporary body of the deceased is symbolically constructed in the rites. But the moment of transition—however elaborate and sumptuous a rite it may be for the wealthy, or however brief and poorly performed it may be for the masses—is one of profound religious awareness. It is one of the great spiritual dramas of man. And yet it is one of the least studied aspects of Hinduism.

NEW BODIES FOR THE EMIGRANT DEAD

The non-Hindu who examines the system of postcremation śrāddha, that is, the prescribed offerings for the nourishment and promotion of deceased ancestors, might conclude that priorities somehow have been muddled. If the basic Hindu doctrine of transmigration (*saṃsāra*) is operative (and the dharmaśāstra literature never suggests its suspension), then rebirth in another terrestrial existence is an eventual concomitant of death. The self (*ātman*) is known to discard the body of each lifetime and then collect itself toward a new one (*Bṛhadāraṇyaka-upaniṣad* 4.4.3–4), commuting as readily as a caterpillar from leaf to leaf or an artifact of gold formed in the hands of a smith. It takes on new bodies as effortlessly as a man puts on new clothes (*Bhagavadgītā* 2.22). Moreover, a new body after death is as natural a transformation for the self as the changes a child's body undergoes in becoming an adult (*Yājñavalkya-smṛti* 20.49).

But if transmigration of the imperishable self is thus assured, why is a great company of deceased ancestors still existent in some extraterrestrial world? Further, if the inescapable laws of *karman* stand effective, how can it be that these ancestors subsist in continued dependence on the ritual activities of their descendants? Is it the case that the simpler, unsophisticated vedic desire to prevent the dissolution of an afterlife for the deceased has prevailed? Did the pre-upaniṣadic fear of repeated death institute procedures for the ritual maintenance of ancestors in the "other" world, procedures that later demonstrated the peculiar capacity of death rites generally to resist change? The doctrines of transmigration and liberation transformed the whole of ancient Indian speculation and practice, but the rites accorded the ancestors bear a stamp of rigorous antiquity. They appear to endure beside the newer sentiments of saṃsāra and mokṣa.

The poets of the Ṛgvedic hymns did not frequently chant on death and the afterlife. Most of their funerary verses are collected in an early section of the tenth maṇḍala; these hymns to Yama, Agni as the cremation fire, and the ancestors are just as obscure as those on other subjects addressed to other beings. But among the prominent features is a concern that the deceased obtain a new body for his life in a new home among the Fathers in heaven (Agni *kravyād,* "eater of flesh," having consumed the old one).[3] *Ṛgveda* 10.14.8, for example, directs the deceased to join Yama and the ancestors in the highest heaven, where he will unite in radiance with a body. Another hymn has the deceased proceed to the third celestial "light," there to unite with a body (10.56.1). Sometimes it is Agni who is requested to supervise this unison of the departed with his new life and new body (10.16.5; 10.15.14).

Nothing of the deceased's former body, mind, or spirit remains below, according to the *Atharvaveda* funeral liturgy,[4] which shows specific concern that all traces of the dead body be consumed in the pyre. Whether Agni acts to translate to heaven the life-principle alone (variously called *manas, asu, ātman, prāṇa*), or whether the dead body is itself somehow transmuted into the celestial one, is unclear. Two intriguing references in this same *Atharvaveda* liturgy seem to indicate that a single limb surviving the pyre can become the entire celestial body.[5] One may gauge the religious values inherent in burial and expectation of rebirth in rites associated with the soil: the bone fragments are collected from the pyre in a jar, buried in preseeded ground, and carefully nourished with milk and water.[6] The liturgy for that classical rite of the gṛhyasūtras, which in medieval and modern times has largely been replaced by Ganges or other river burial of the bone fragments or ashes, involves part of the *Ṛgveda* 10.18 burial hymn.

Yet another fate of the corpse lies in the vedic-upaniṣadic notion of the redistribution of cosmic elements. The well-known ritual circulation of elements that undergirds the saṃsāra expressions of the upaniṣads (e.g., the journey of the self [*puruṣa*] after death in the five-fire doctrine in *Chāndogya-upaniṣad* 5.4–9) has prefigurations in the final maṇḍala of the *Ṛgveda.* In 10.16.3 the deceased on the pyre is ritually dismissed to the cosmos, his eye to the sun, his life-breath (ātman) to the wind, his body to the plants. He is thus projected back into the three-leveled world according to the cosmic law (*dharman*).[7] This is an obvious reversal of the cosmogonic process outlined in the *puruṣasūkta* (*Ṛgveda* 10.90.13), where the sun is born from the eye of the sacrificial god, Puruṣa, the wind from his breath (prāṇa), the moon from his mind.

In the powerful prayer that concludes the *Vājasaneyi-saṃhitā,* the one about to die declares: "Now my breath (*vāyu*) is the immortal wind, this body is ashes" (40.15ab). *Śatapatha-brāhmaṇa* 14.6.2.13 raises the eschatological question precisely: What becomes of the self (puruṣa) of the dead man after all of his components have gone back to their respective elements?[8] The answer could only be sought in the brāhmaṇical doctrine of sacrifice itself, wherein the victim (e.g., the horse in the great two-year drama of the horse-sacrifice, the *aśvamedha*) is collective space-and-time, reintegrated, consecrated, immolated, and offered as the manifest cosmos that Puruṣa, the sacrifice-person, first became.[9] This sense of ritual reunification, of a return to the beginning when space-and-time is clean and all unused, is perpetuated at the personal, microcosmic level in the "final offering," the antyeṣṭi, the cremation-sacrifice that recapitulates cosmogonic totality and potentiality, and dramatizes death as the matrix for a new being.

It appears that, in matters of death and continuation, "all ways are the Queen's ways." In this respect, modern India has conserved the vedic heritage. If questioned about the fate of a recently deceased person, Hindu villagers today could summon more or less vague and successive replies, all with scriptural, folk-literary, or proverbial supports, to indicate that the departure was in the direction of some immediate terrestrial rebirth or cosmic dispersal reminiscent of the classical return to the five elements,[10] or transmission to heaven, or an unhealthy lingering in the locales of life, death, and the cremation site. This simultaneity of presence of the deceased in varied, even contradictory situations appears to be more the norm than the exception in the history of religions.

Having reviewed these vedic conceptions of human mortality and afterlife, we must now examine the mature system of postcremation śrāddhas. In the ritual tradition of Hinduism ceremonies during the first ten or eleven days after death are known as *nava-śrāddhas,* their principal function being the ritual construction of a temporary body for the deceased.[11] It is no longer the case, as it was in Ṛgvedic eschatology, that a complete new body awaits the deceased in heaven. He requires exact assistance of the living in order to emigrate from this world to that higher one, to pass from the dangerous condition of a disembodied spirit[12] to the secure role of pitṛ among his own pitaraḥ. In order to negotiate that passage he must have a proper body (or series of bodies) and regular nourishment. According to some authorities,[13] this requires a full year of daily ritual activity from the day of death until the day of the sapiṇḍīkaraṇa and release from "pretahood." It is understandable that efforts were made to condense such a demanding calendar, and sapiṇḍīkarana in its modern form generally occurs on the twelfth day after death, that is, at the end of a symbolic year. Another cause for abbreviation is that perpetual concerns regarding ritual purity and pollution are better served by a shorter period of ritual impurity (*sūtaka*) borne by the family of the deceased during the mourning period. So inauspicious are the cremation and pre-sapiṇḍīkaraṇa rites that many ritual texts covering the rites of passage (*saṃskāras*) omit the funeral ceremonies altogether. Others, like the *Prayogaratna,* append a separate manual on the subject. Some texts point out, not imprudently, yet another reason for moving the sapiṇḍīkaraṇa to within a few days of the cremation: were the eldest son, or other relative serving as the sacrificer (*yajamāna*) for the deceased, to die during the course of the year, the preta would be stranded by the truncated ritual.

One must appreciate here the fact that *jñānakāṇḍa* (the texts dealing with liberating knowledge) and *karmakāṇḍa* (the texts dealing with rites) have disparate concerns and priorities. The *Vedānta-sūtras,* which are concerned with knowledge, proceed from the ambiguities of upaniṣadic statements on perishable and imperishable constituents of being and describe the soul as wrapped in the intangible, subtle aspects of the elements during its journey from material body to body. This distinction of the intangible body (*sūkṣma-* or *liṅga-śarīra*), which survives cremation, from the tangible body (*sthūla-śarīra*), which is eliminated by cremation, is always set in a soteriological discussion. The spirit with its subtle body that is the continuing "mark" of individuality, transcending death upon death, will finally lose even that *liṅga* when it merges with *bráhman.*[14] Thus the soul in its subtle vehicle, escaping from the heart upward through the cranium,[15] has an ultimate residence in view. There is no concern in the vedānta texts for the ritual necessity of constructing an intermediate body.

The ritual texts and other smṛtis, on the other hand, do not focus on the long-range mokṣa ideal. Their preoccupation is with the immediate task of transmitting the spirit of the deceased to his place among the ancestors. Their method, consistent with the brāhmaṇical sacrificial schema, has recourse to the ancient *mantras* and ancient offering procedures. The smṛtis do not all agree on the nature and longevity of the intermediate body or, in fact, the number of bodies that the preta requires,[16] but they are uniform in their understanding of the creation as a *ritual* task. As far as this temporary body for the preta is concerned, it is no less than a replication of cosmogony and the primordial sacrifice-person. Modern dharmaśāstra literature appears to have lost sight of this central drama. There are, classically, sixteen Śrāddhas to be performed prior to the sapiṇḍīkaraṇa. Man (puruṣa), like Puruṣa-Prajāpati and like the whole of space-and-time, is sixteenfold, according to a *Śatapatha-brāhmaṇa* account of creation (11.1.6.1–36), and remarkably, the pre-sapiṇḍīkaraṇa *śrāddha* system of re-creation seems to follow suit. Although temporary and intermediate, this new body is nonetheless the fruit of sacrifice and, as such, a microcosm spun anew.

On the first day after death the sacrificer bathes and dresses, then creates a single tennis-ball-sized mass of cooked white rice[17] (called piṇḍa) and, at a quiet place near a river or temple tank, and perhaps with the assistance of his family priest and a special priest acting as the watchful presence of the deceased, places it on a tiny altar of loose earth no more than half an inch high. This rice-ball represents the preta (i.e., the spirit of the sacrificer's father), endowed only with its briefest, subtlest body, and is therefore accorded all the honors of worship: incense, flowers, a tiny ghee lamp, and white threads as symbolic clothing. Most important, a small clay cup of water containing sesame seeds is poured out onto the ball. Each day this procedure will be repeated with a single ball of rice as the preta on the altar. The cups of water offered, however, increase by one each day until there are ten on the final day. And each day of the rites results in a new portion of the preta's intermediate body, the head being created on the first day, then in succession the neck and shoulders, the heart and torso, the back, the stomach, the thighs and bowels, the lower legs and skin, the knees and hair, the genitals, and, on the tenth day of the offerings, the preta receives digestive powers so that the sufferings of hunger and thirst now experienced by the "body of nourishment" duly created may be allayed by continued offerings of piṇḍas and water from the living.[18]

In contemporary practice it appears usually to be the wealthy and the devout who fulfill this entire sequence of offerings. All such rites are performed "according to one's capacity." The results are the same, Banaras paṇḍitas will admit, if offerings are made only on the first, third, and seventh days, or on the tenth day only.[19]

A less expensive form of attention to the deceased in these ten days, however, is not abbreviated. That is the custom of hanging two clay pots by strings from a peg in a *pīpal* tree near a river or a temple tank, one pot containing water for the deceased, who lingers in or near the tree until the rite of sapiṇḍīkaraṇa, and in the other pot a ghee lamp to light the way for the preta. Early each morning the sacrificer bathes, then refills the hanging water pot with river or tank water from his bath. On the tenth day, when the subtle body disappears in favor of the newly ritualized intermediate body, the pots are taken down and smashed.

This ends the ten-day period of ritual impurity suffered by the mourning household. The sacrificer and all the male members of the family will bathe and be shaved by barbers, and they will return home purified of death's defilement. Technically, according to later ritual authorities, the nava-śrāddhas during this defilemcnt period were not true śrāddhas at all. Only now with purity regained on the eleventh day can the first *ekoddiṣṭa* (rites for a single deceased person),[20] with the requisite feeding of invited brāhmaṇas who represent the company of the ancestors, take place. No deceased ancestor (and certainly no brāhmaṇa surrogate nowadays!) would consent to be entertained as guest in a house of defilement.

There is not space here to detail the "mixed" śrāddhas of the eleventh day, a day that may, in the more elaborate postcremation śrāddha schedule, involve as much as a ten-hour sequence of a half-dozen major events, including the establishment of the deceased in sixteenfold time and sixteenfold space, the worship and ritual payment of a priest who has served during the nava-śrāddhas as a ritual surrogate for the deceased, the feeding of eleven brāhmaṇas, and such occasionally performed rites as the *nārāyaṇabali*. In some parts of India the giving away of a cow, a substitute for the ancient bull-sacrifice, may also be performed on the eleventh day.[21]

Since the sapiṇḍīkaraṇa was originally a year subsequent to cremation there was time to observe twelve (lunar) monthly piṇḍa offerings in the ekoddiṣṭa pattern. These plus a three-fortnight offering (after one-and-a-half months), and offerings on days immediately prior to the first, sixth, and twelfth months made a total ritual year of sixteen. Variant texts allow for an intercalary month, still observing the sacred totality of sixteen. Thus in collapsing the anniversary śrāddha to the twelfth day, only the eleventh day remains to celebrate these sixteen offerings. The modern rite dispenses in this fashion with a whole "year" of sacrifices in about two hours, using sixteen cooked-rice piṇḍas plus 360 barley piṇḍas for the requisite daily rites. Somewhat more artificial is the other carryover from the sixteenfold *soma* pattern, the placement of the preta in a line of sixteen deities, all of whom receive elaborate worship from the sacrificer. These include Viṣṇu, Śiva, Yama, Soma, Agni, and Mṛtyu.

The nārāyaṇabali, in its full form a rite of tremendous power, is designed to promote the deceased, after the sapiṇḍīkaraṇa, to the Vaikuṇṭha heaven of Viṣṇu. It involves a *Viṣṇu-tarpaṇa* with milk and water, and a sixteenfold worship of the preta in the company of Brahmā, Viṣṇu, Maheśa (Rudra), and Yama, utilizing the sixteen verses of the *puruṣasūkta.* Simultaneously, *havanas* of ghee and grains are made in the offering fire.[22]

But the dramatic focus of the eleventh day comes with the worship and ritual payment of the priest who has served as ritual surrogate for the dead. This is one of the most extraordinary roles in all of Hindu ritualism. The priest is a *mahāpātra,* a brāhmaṇa who performs the necessary role of silent, watchful stand-in for the preta. It is an unenviable priestly function. Connections with the defilement of death have brought mahāpātras as a class, at least in many parts of north and central India, to a low and ill-regarded status, cut off from the Sanskritic traditions of the priestly caste. Because they perform all too well the ritual presence of the deceased, making claims on the finances and emotions of the living, who must ritually maintain them, they are dismissed as a greedy, cantankerous, illiterate lot. For the common man they perform whatever passes for the nava-śrāddhas. For the elaborate rites of the wealthy, however, the mahāpātras is the continued presence of the preta, observing every detail of the rites promoting the preta to the ancestors. He is permitted to say or do nothing whatever. But when he receives all the lavish *dakṣiṇās* in the form of gold, utensils, bed, linens, clothes, food, and paraphernalia intended to maintain the deceased and satisfy his every need for the coming year, the mahāpātra always begs, cajoles, and argues for more. And more he receives, lest the deceased take offense.

The eleven brāhmaṇa guests on the eleventh day are all mahāpātras. This feeding of brāhmaṇas who represent the ancestors is a focal point of the ancient śrāddha system. However, the increased fear in later times of the defilement of death, even *after* the ten-day period of recognized impurity, created a scarcity of willing brāhmaṇa guests, and the low-status mahāpātras, today invariably poor despite an occasional windfall in the demise of a wealthy patron, make themselves available, and therefore despised, for the ritual task. The number eleven is not idle, for they represent the eleven Rudras, and therefore the deceased's ancestors. (On the following day, twelve days after death, the deceased is ritually joined to his ancestors.)

THE TRIPLE WORLD OF THE IMMIGRANT DEAD

Thus far the rites have focused on the deceased in his vulnerable preta condition. First, he has been the vague ghost in the tree. Then, in his more demonstrable presence as mahāpātras, he has made claims on the living for his continued support. And he has brought a company of ancestors, in the form of invited brāhmaṇas, to come and sit for a ritual feast. From where have these ancestors arrived? As early as the *Ṛgveda* (e.g., 10.15.1) there is understood to be a tripartite hierarchy of the Fathers (pitaraḥ). From the cremation fire the deceased ascends to the triadic *lokas,* earth, midspace (atmosphere) and sky (heaven), according to the *Atharvaveda* funeral hymn.[23] This ascension through the trileveled cosmos is precisely dependent on the ritual activities of the living: the ancestors are in fact *brought into being* in the three worlds by offerings.[24]

Further, the upward mobility of the ancestors is complemented by the fact that they are mortal. Unlike the gods, the Fathers are themselves subject to repeated death (*punarmṛtyu*),[25] a conception that the epics and purāṇas perpetuated in higher drama with a world view in which these very lokas themselves died periodically.[26]

More to the point of homogeneity of the Fathers, however, is the identification of three generations of deceased paternal ancestors with three classes of deities residing in the three levels of the cosmos. An individual's deceased father (pitṛ) is to be found among the eight Vasus in the earth (pṛthivī), the Vasus being presided over by Indra or Agni or both. A deceased grandfather (*pitāmaha*) is a temporary resident of the midspace (*antarikṣa*) where the eleven Rudras, under the leadership of Rudra himself, are located. And a deceased great-grandfather (*prapitāmaha*) is in the company of the twelve Ādityas in heaven (*svarga*), where either the god Varuṇa or Aditi, their mother, rules.

These three closest generations of the ancestors thus inhabit the three-layered cosmos in close association with the gods. They are, in fact, "on call" precisely like the deities who are invoked for sacrifices, and when, for example, eleven brāhmaṇas are required to attend the sixteen ekoddiṣṭa rites (now condensed to the eleventh-day rite), the "grandfathers" leave their midspace home in the form of "the Rudras" to accept the piṇḍa offerings. Similarly, the "fathers" appear as the eight Vasus, with that number of living surrogate brāhmaṇas taking part.[27] These three paternal generations are the recently deceased, the powerful immigrants to the three worlds who exist in symbiotic ritual connections with their living descendants. They require sustenance for their continuing journey to the unmanifest, the ocean of dissolution that lies beyond these three worlds. And the living have need of these celestial intermediaries for health and long life, for wealth and progeny.

Significantly, these three ranked but cohesive generations contrast with those gone before as well as those coming after. If the preta undergoing a symbolic year of nava-śrāddhas may be said to exist in the dawn of death, the full power of day belongs to the unit of his Fathers with the Vasus, Rudras, and Ādityas, while death's twilight is the phase of the three preceding generations, the remote dead. The remote dead (a sacrificer's great-great-grandfather and *his* father and grandfather), although still venerable and nominally included in the sevenfold sapiṇḍa lineage with the sacrificer and the intermediate triad, are distant and relatively inaccessible. They are, in fact, on the frontiers of dissolution to other life forms, where the doctrine of saṃsāra, however contrastive with purāṇic chronologies for an individual's sojourn in heavens and hells, seems not so disjunctive after all. These remote dead require scant ritual attention from the living since their physiological presence is necessarily diminishing. Graphically, Manu and the purāṇas call them *lepabhāgins,* because they receive not the full piṇḍa or the full water cup, but only the remnants, the "wipings" (*lepa-*) of the hand *after* he has served the basic (nearer) triad in *pārvaṇa-śrāddha*.[28] The purāṇas extend to them an emotional benefit of the doubt by referring to them collectively as the *nāndīmukh, a-pitaraḥ*. "Fathers having faces of joy," as distinguished from the *aśrumukha-pitaraḥ,* the father, grandfather, and great-grandfather, "having faces of tears."[29] Whether the happiness of the further triad, vis-à-vis the nearer triad's grief, has to do with its distance *from* the fact of death or its proximity *to* prolonged heavenly rewards, rebirth, *or* liberation is a matter of some significance, but one that the purāṇas douse more with shadow than light. Such collectivities allow little margin for individual merit or demerit, and would appear to presume a common destiny for the generations.

To return to the Fathers in the three worlds, it is necessary to look again to the sacrificial schema of the *Śatapatha-brāhmaṇa* to understand the underlying cosmography of death and rebirth. The funeral hymn, *Ṛgveda* 10.15.1, declares that the Fathers (pitaraḥ) enjoy soma (a sacred inebriating drink). As in the general sixteenfold symbolism or in the connections of the śrāddhas to lunar phenomena, there is the strong presence of the soma sacrifice. Soma, pressed three times daily—morning, noon, and evening—is offered to the Vasus, the Rudras, and the Ādityas, respectively.[30] In the section of the *Śatapatha-brāhmaṇa* that concerns the ritual construction of the fire-basin (6.5), the cosmos is ritually assembled by the sacrificer following the model of the gods: first, on the bottom, is the earth, originally made by the Vasus, and now recreated by the sacrificer. Second is midspace and third is heaven, originally created by the Rudras and the Ādityas, respectively. "He [the sacrificer] then completes the fire-altar [= the cosmos] by a fourth, the Viśvedevāḥ," representing the four quarters of space. Thus the ātman (6.5.3.5) of Agni, at once Puruṣa/Prajāpati/the sacrificer, is composed of the three worlds plus a transcendent fourth.[31] (See Figure 1.)

4	**Transcendent**	**Viśvedevāḥ**	**Remote ancestors**
3	heaven	Ādityas	great grandfather
2	midspace	Rudras	grandfather
1	earth	Vasus	father
			son

Figure 1. The correspondence of cosmic, divine, and human triads, completed by a transcendent fourth. At the point of the sapiṇḍīkaraṇa, the deceased, or preta, moves from the level af "son" to the level of "father" and is thereafter dependent upon his son as sacrificer of offerings.

This pattern is ancient, and highly significant. *Ṛgveda* 10.125 knits together the essential components in a hymn that precisely connects the sacred utterance (*Vāc*, cf. bráhman) to the sacrifice for ancestors. It is ritual speech that carries the Vasus, Rudras, Ādityas, and even the transcendent fourth, the Viśvedevāḥ, to the (śrāddha) sacrifice, and ritual speech that carries soma to them. Most important, it is ritual speech that "brings forth the pitṛ,"' even to the highest level (vs. 7), by which the transcendent level of the Viśvedevāḥ, the realm of the remote, long-gone ancestors may be understood.[32] This early vedic conception is perpetuated in the gṛhyasūtras and in such texts as the *Viṣṇudharmaśāstra*, thus assuring liturgical longevity in the ritual manuals of classical and medieval India. *Kāṭhakagṛhyasūtra* 50.10 addresses the ancestors in earth, midspace, heaven, and the (transcendent) ocean with the ritual utterance "*svadhā*!"[33] in a series of prayers equating Vāc and immortality (*amṛta*) with the sacrifice of life-strength (*ūrj*), which is the essential, saplike "vigor" of the piṇḍa and water. Here again is the continuity with the ancient soma rites: cooked-rice balls are not soma, but their powers in the context of the soma-mantras are life-sustaining to the point of re-creativity.

From these and other vedic contexts it can be seen, turning to the sapiṇḍīkaraṇa, that the prior worship of the Viśvedevāḥ is *not* simple recognition of "the All-Gods," as is the contemporary paṇḍitas' explanation. Rather it is the *ritual presence* of the remote ancestors who are dispersed to the four quarters of the transcendent region beyond these worlds. They are worshiped first, their representation being to the immediate right of the sacrificer's right knee as he sits facing south. (See Figure 2.) Directly in front of him is a row of four leaf-plates, which now receive four large cooked-rice piṇḍas. Two low earth-altars are prepared directly before the sacrificer's right knee, a small one to receive the *preta-piṇḍa*, an elongated mass of cooked rice, and a larger one to receive a row of the three round piṇḍas of the Fathers.

After making numerous offerings to the east-west row of all four generations, the sacrificer takes up the preta-piṇḍa and places it on the western altar. Then he takes up the piṇḍa representing the preta's father (his own grandfather) and places that on the closest place before him, the other two piṇḍa following away from him in a north-south line. He now recites mantras from the *Ṛgveda* (including the last three verses of the *Ṛgveda*, 10.191.2–4) and the *Vājasaneyi-saṃhitā* (twice repeating 19.45–46), these mantras stressing the unity and equality of the ancestors. As he recites he blends the water cups of the Fathers into that of the preta, reciting the names of the ancestors along with his deceased father's and declaring that he unites them. Then cutting the preta-piṇḍa into three slices he blends each slice into one of the three piṇḍas of the ancestors, reciting the name of each, and the act of uniting each with the deceased, "Go to your father (grandfather, great-grandfather)" are the words he addresses to each slice of the preta-piṇḍa as it mixes with its ancestral counterpart. Finally, the three are blended into one, and in *that moment* the deceased has passed from the preta to the pitṛ stage and has joined the revered company of the ancestors at home in the three worlds, his father and grandfather having advanced to new lev-

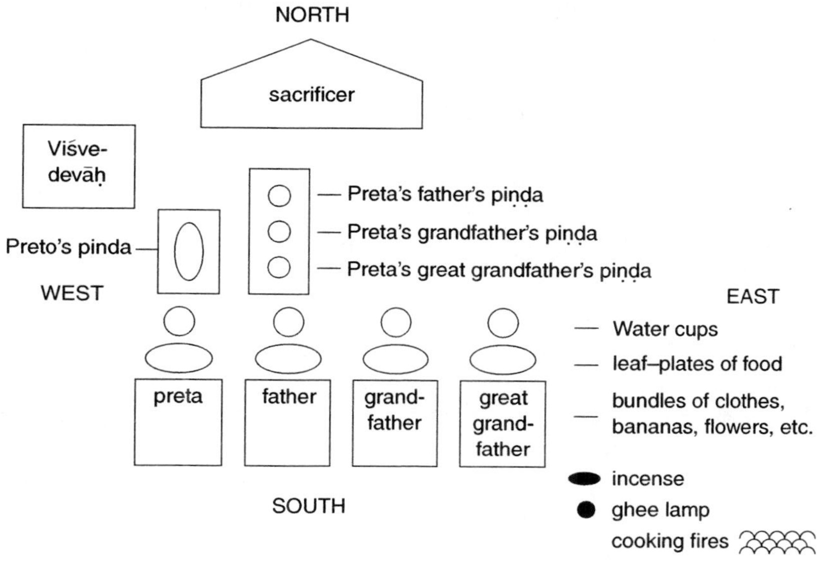

Figure 2. Sapiṇḍīkaraṇa, just before the ritual blending of the deceased (preta) into his three paternal ancestors by his son (sacrificer).

els and divine groupings in the cosmic and ritual hierarchy, and his great-grandfather having been regenerated into the realm of the remote dead as one of the Viśvedevāḥ.[34]

Another conflation of vedic-Hindu liturgical practice and probable indigenous folk religion occurs in a ceremony that sometimes concludes the sapiṇḍīkaraṇa. The *Prayogaratna* and some other manuals direct the sacrificer to the border of his village where he should throw the piṇḍas into "the Gaṅgā" (meaning the local river), then return home to bathe and present offerings to the Viśvedevāḥ.[35] This closing sacrifice to the Viśvedevāḥ seems to have been replaced in many regions by offerings to crows, the crow having widespread folkloric associations with the souls of the dead. Not only the collective remote ancestors but perhaps also the preta may be personified by the crow. At the Rāmakuṇḍa in Nāsik, a special śrāddha site for western India, the crow may clearly be seen as yet another commanding presence of the deceased. When the sacrificer, upon concluding the sapiṇḍīkaraṇa, goes outside of the ritual pavilion he carefully lays out on a leaf plate the special piṇḍa intended for a crow, then waits to observe reactions from the first crow to approach. If the piṇḍa is acccpted and eaten immediately, all is well, but if, as is sometimes the curious case, the crow struts about the piṇḍa with disinterest, if not hesitation or naked aversion, the sacrificer and mourners understand that the deceased is declaring to them his dissatisfaction and they then must remember how and where they have failed him.

In conclusion, the period of the brāhmaṇa texts (*Aitareya, Kauṣītaki, Śatapatha,* and so on) was the crucial one for myths, rites, and symbols of death and rebirth. It was then that the application of the Puruṣa-Prajāpati cosmogonic model to an *individual's* postcremation passage was first conceptualized and concretized liturgically, and there that the cosmically renewing potency of the soma rites and mantras was first brought to bear on human regeneration and perpetuation. The ritual world view of early vedic religion could abide through several strenuous periods via the directives of the sūtras and śāstras for individual funeral and ancestral rites, with remarkably little tampering from the innovative doctrines, theologies, and cosmographies that gradually eroded the official, institutional structures of vedic religion. Although the concern shifted from the early vedic desire for a state of perpetual nondeath or immortality to the dilemma of saṃsāra and the ideal of mokṣa, the intention of the śrāddhas survived, and the understanding of the passage of the deceased as a cosmogonic progression, with an individual's salvation dependent on the correct ritual activity of his descendants, permitted these archaic ceremonies for the dead to continue to the present day.

The continuity of life forms and the mutual responsibility of the living and the dead for one another are borne out by the often repeated liturgies. The sacrificer, as he offers food and water to his Fathers, addresses them directly, contractually, hopefully:

> This life-strength is for *you,* this "*svadhā*" is for *you*! Eat and drink! Do not allow *us* to perish![36]

ENDNOTES

1. By "vedic" is meant the period of composition and compilation of *śruti* from the *Ṛgveda* (ca. fourteenth century B.C.) to the early upaniṣads (ca. sixth century B.C.). The śrauta-, gṛhya-, and dharma-sūtras succeeded in the next half millennium. The gṛhya- and dharma-sūtras were the anchors of dharmaśāstra to the vedic substratum. The first centuries of the present era witnessed completion of the two epics as well as beginning production of the legal-ritual smṛtis (*Manu, Yājñavalkya,* and so on). The period of composition of the purāṇas and āgamas begins before the middle and extends to the close of the first millennium. Although production of the legal-ritual smṛtis dwindled by the seventh and eighth centuries, the writing of commentaries (ṭīkās) and annotated digests (nibandhas) based on the whole of dharmaśāstra and the vedic mantra traditions had just begun. Numerous ṭīkās and nibandhas were produced up until the eighteenth century. One such digest among those of current authority in Banaras, where it was composed by Nārāyana Bhaṭṭa in the sixteenth century, has an extensive section on *antyeṣṭi* and *śrāddha*. This is the *Prayogaratna,* cited occasionally below.
2. Narratives of observed rites that are included here with historical and interpretive materials do not presume, of course, to represent typical or exemplary ceremonies. Rites of the same name taking place in Poona, Calcutta, Madras, or, for that matter, in Banaras as well, although structurally and functionally the same, could display a wide variety of details due to vedic and śāstric traditions, sectarian persuasions, class, caste, and economic status, or to employ that phrase of convenience in all ritual manuals, due to "local customs."

3. Excepting, of course, possible references to direct inhumation such as *Ṛgveda* 10.18. Cremation evidently became, and remained, normative for all but exceptional funerals during the vedic period. On the exceptions, see Willem Caland, *Die altindischen Todten- und Bestattungsgebräuche* (Amsterdam, 1896; reprint, Wiesbaden, 1967), pp. 85–98.
4. 18.2.24; cf. the *Kauśika-sūtra* utilization of these *Atharvaveda* stanzas, 82.29 and 85.26.
5. 18.2.26; 18.4.64. This brings to mind the later purāṇic belief that a bone or fragment of the deceased's body will bring him mokṣa or astronomical periods of time in heaven if it is thrown in the Ganges. Cf. *Viṣṇudharmasūtra* 19.10-12. The cremation rite at Banaras always concludes with the sacrificer flipping the last unburned fragment of the body into the Ganges.
6. The *asthisañcayana*, or bone-gathering rite, described as part of the burning-ground (*śmaśāna*) procedures in *Śatapatha-brāhmaṇa* 13.8.3.1ff.
7. Not, as later authorities presumed, according to his "merit." In pada c, *āpo*, the "waters," can be construed as the poet's reference to the atmosphere or midspace, located beyond *dyu*, the sky, and *pṛthivī*, the earth. On diffusion to the elements, cf. also *Ṛgveda* 10.58.7.
8. Speech (*vāc*) to Agni, *prāṇa* to the wind (*vāta*), the eye (*cakṣus*) to the sun (*āditya*), the mind (*manas*) to the moon (*candra*), the ear (*śrotra*) to the quarters (*diśaḥ*) of heaven, the body (*śarīra*) to the earth (*pṛthivī*), *ātman* to midspace (*ākāśa*), body hair (*loman*) to plants (*oṣadhī-*), head hair (*keśa*) to trees (*vanaspati-*), blood and semen (*lohita* and *retas*) to the waters (*āpah*).
9. Cf. *Aitareya-brāhmaṇa* 2.6.13; *Śatapatha-brāhmaṇa* 13.5.2.13–16; *Sāṅkhāyana-śrautasūtra* 16.6.3–4; *Bṛhadāraṇyaka-upaniṣad* 1.1.1–2.
10. Sanskrit *mahābhūtāni*. According to *Aitareya-brāhmana* 3.3 the ātman *is* the five great elements. Cf. *Taittirīya-upaniṣad* 2.1; *Praśna-upaniṣad* 4.8. In popular belief, there is, and was anciently, a vague homology between *bhūta*, "element," and *bhūta*, "ghost, malevolent spirit"; both words derive from the past passive participle of *bhū-*, "be"; thus bhūta, "become, gone; being, existing, present."
11. Technically, the śrāddhas of the "new" (*nava*) or recently deceased are those of the first ten days, while the "mixed" (*miśra*) śrāddhas include remaining rites up to the sapiṇḍīkaraṇa. Thus, in the modern ritual calendar, *miśtra-śrāddhas* are crowded into the eleventh day. Some authorities, however, count the eleventh day, too, among the nava-śrāddhas.
12. The same word *preta* also indicates "dead body" in the ritual texts. Literally, "gone, out, departed," preta in the sense of the dead occurs in the *Śatapatha-brāhmaṇa* (e.g., 10.5.2.13), but not in the saṃhitās. Cf. in the śrāddha sections of *Sāṇkhāyana-gṛhyasūtra* (4.2.7; 4.3.5–6) and *Pāraskara-gṛhyasūtra* (3.10.49–55) the distinction of the preta prior to the sapiṇḍīkaraṇa.
13. The rites for a single deceased person are collected under the rubric *ekoddiṣṭa*, pertaining to "one" (*eka*) only, to distinguish these śrāddhas from those for *groups* of ancestors previously deceased. The paradigmatic form of śrāddha, which the ekoddiṣṭa adopts mutatis mutandis, is the *pārvaṇa-śrāddha*, which is celebrated for the father, grandfather, and great-grandfather on the paternal side of the sacrificer's ancestry.
14. Saṅkara, in his commentary on 3.1.1, describes the *sūkṣma* aspects of the elements as "seeds" of the *next sthūla-śarīra*. Cf. *Vedānta-sūtra* 1.4.2–3; 4.2.1 ff. Śaṅkara cites *Bṛhadāraṇyaka-upaniṣad* 4.4.1–4. On the *liṅga*, see *Maitrāyanīya-upaniṣad* 6.10 and the vaguer references in *Kaṭha-upaniṣad* 2.3.8 and *Svetāśvatara-upaniṣad* 6.9. In vedānta literature *ātivāhika* is an epithet of the liṅga (śarīra). This word becomes in the purāṇas a reference to the subtle and immediate body that requires no ritual construction.
15. Thus the still current practice of breaking the skull of the corpse after it has burned on the pyre for an hour or two. The ātman in its *sūkṣma-śarīra* might otherwise be unable to exit through the *brahmarandhra* suture at the crown of the skull. On this upaniṣadic eschatological physiology, see *Chāndogya-upaniṣad* 8.6.6 and *Kaṭha-upaniṣad* 2.3.16; cf. also *Aitareya-upaniṣad* 1.3.12, the *sīman* or *vidṛti* being the door by which the ātman *enters* the body.

16. In addition to the ātivāhika (the "carry-over" body) that appears to compare with the vedāntic sūkṣma-śarīra, the purāṇas employ terms for intermediate śarīras (*bhogadeha, pretadeha, yātāniya*) that express particular functions. In purāṇic belief the automatic subtle body enveloping the spirit escapes from the corpse but then must itself be replaced by a ritual body, more physical in nature, so that offerings of food and water can be enjoyed and utilized by the preta. Then after sapiṇḍīkaraṇa, yet a third body becomes the spirit's vehicle to heaven and hell to "endure" the rewards and punishments due to previous karman. (Again the symbolic year appears when the purāṇas speak of the twelve-day journey of the soul to reach the kingdom of Yama.) Thus in the ten days of piṇḍa offerings folling death, the ātivāhika body, composed of fire, wind, and space (*tejas, vāyu, ākāśa*) but *not* of the other two elements, earth and water (*pṛthivī, āpah*), daily shrinks away to nothingness in size and strength. For references to the purāṇas and nibandhas, see P. V. Kane, *History of Dharmaśātra,* vol. 4 (Poona, 1953), pp. 265–66, and Dakshina Ranjan Shastri, *Origin and Development of the Rituals of Ancestor Worship in India* (Calcutta, 1963), pp. 58ff.
17. Sesame seeds (*tila*) are an essential ingredient, and the boiled rice may also contain milk, ghee, honey, sugar, and so on.
18. Authorities vary in recounting this ten-day physiological assembly. Nārāyaṇa Bhaṭṭa's *Prayogaratna,* ed. By Vasudeva Sharma, 2nd ed. (Bombay, 1937), *Antyeṣṭipaddhati,* pp. 12–13, gives details. Cf. also p. 27. Incidentally, among the *saṃskāras* (vedic-Hindu rites of passage), it is remarkable to note the parallel structures of these post-cremation śrāddhas and the rites at birth (*jātakarman*). In each case, following the day of birth/death there are ten days of offerings of rice, sesame, and so on, ten being a homology to the human gestation period of ten (lunar) months. It may well be the case, then, that the completion of the temporary body on the tenth day is an intentional *re*birth expression. In the case of both sets of rituals the twelfth day marks the resumption of offering fires, the completion of purification and the transition out of the great time (twelve days representing the twelve-month year) into routine ritual time.
19. From the gṛhyasūtras on through the whole of dharmaśāstra the number of *nava-śrāddhas* prescribed varies considerably, but a predilection for certain odd-numbered days, among days one to eleven after cremation, persists. Cf. Nārāyaṇa Bhaṭṭa, *Prayogaratna* p. 11, on these nava-śrāddhas that cumulatively remove *pretatva,* the condition of "pretahood."
20. See no. 13.
21. Often detailed in purāṇic descritions of the afterlife is a twelve-day journey of the preta to the kingdom of Yama, prior to the punishments and rewards that await the deceased in the various *narakas* and *lokas.* To cross the dread netherworld river Vaitaraṇī the deceased must hold on to the tail of this cow that has been sacrificed (given). Without elaboration Nārāyana Bhaṭṭa's calls the *vṛsotsarga* the most important part of the śrāddhas.
22. Cf. *Prayogaratna, Antyeṣṭipaddhati,* p. 14.
23. 18.4.5, 78–80; cf. *Kauśika-sūtra* 87.8.
24. *Śatapatha-brāhmaṇa* 2.6.1.1–3; subsequent vss. (4–7) make it clear that a threefold system of the Fathers, homologized to the three-fire schema, ranks them hierarchically according to the substances that they themselves had offered while they existed in life (*soma,* cooked food, or nothing at all being their offerings.) This is an intriguing prefiguration of upaniṣadic eschatology: ritual activity (karman) in life bears results—advantages and disadvantages—in the mobile ranks of the ancestors.
25. *Śatapatha-brāhmaṇa* 2.1.3.4: *amṛtā devā . . . martyāḥ pitaraḥ.* Cf. 2.1.4.9.
26. In the world view of periodic dissolution (*pralaya*) the number of "heavens" had proliferated far beyond the original triad.
27. See e.g., *Prayogaratna,* pp. 17–18, the Vasus Dhruva, Adhvara, Soma, Āpa, Anila, Anala, Pratyūṣa and Prabhāsa being the pole-star, sky, moon, water, wind, fire, dawn and light, respectively. Cf. *Manu* 3.189 on the relationship of the pitaraḥ to the brāhmaṇas in śrāddhas.
28. *Manu* 3.216; *Matsyapurāṇa* 18.29; and so on.

29. Cf. Kane, *History of Dharmaśāstra,* 4: 528–529.
30. *Śatapatha-brāhmaṇa* 4.3.5.1. "Vasus, Rudras and Ādityas are the three classes of gods." Cf. also 1.3.4.12.
31. For a discussion of the transcendent fourth beyond the triads, see my article, "One Fire, Three Fires, Five Fires: Vedic Symbols in Transition," *History of Religions* 12 (1972): 28–41. *Chāndogya-upaniṣad* 3.1–10 provides an example of the example of this triad to the pentad, with the addition of a transcendent pair, the Maruts (with Soma as deity) and the Sādhyas (with Brahmā as deity), at the fourth and fifth levels respectively. Horizontally, with orientation in plan, the five classes are in the east, south, west, north, with the Sādhyas at the center or zenith. Further, the five are associated, again in the correct ascending order, with the sequence of the four vedas, and bráhman, the sacred utterance itself, completing the pentad at the zenith.

    Similarly, the septadic cosmography of the purāṇas reveals, like the vedic-Hindu pentad, an interior structural triad (e.g., earth, midspace, heaven), although now with *two* interstices opening up each segment of the triad instead of one only. The macro-microcosmic correspondences that evolve in purāṇic Hinduism (mythology, cosmogony, eschatology) and in tantric *yoga* (the seven *cakras* as seven lokas, and so on) are relevant to our understanding of the septadic *sapiṇḍa* structure.
32. This hymn is rearranged, probably for liturgical benefits in the rites, in *Atharvaveda* 4.30, where the juxtaposition of speech-born soma and the rebirth of the pitṛ is more clearly indicated.
33. *svadhā* is both the ritual utterance and the offering to the pitaraḥ; traditionally, it is said that the *devas* enjoy hearing "*svā hā,*" the benediction accompanying offerings to them, as the Fathers delight in hearing "*svadhā.*" Cf. *Ṛgveda* 10.14.3.
34. It is difficult to convey the power of this and related rites for the dead without visual materials. A color videocassette of the antyeṣṭi and śrāddha rites is available from the South Asian Language and Area Center, Univ. of Wisconsin, Madison. This is Program 15, "Death and Rebirth in Hinduism," of my series, *Exploring the Religions of South Asia* (Madison, 1975).
35. *Antyeṣṭipaddhati,* p. 20. An apparent mystical connection between the Viśvedevāḥ, sacrificial remnants, and the beings of animals and birds may be seen in *Aitareya-brāhmaṇa* 3.31.
36. *Kāṭhakagṛhyasūtra* 50.11; emphasis added.

Chapter 17

Gods, Ghosts, and Ancestors

Arthur P. Wolf

In the rural areas along the southwestern edge of the Taipei Basin, conservative families burn three sticks of incense every morning and every evening.[1] One of these is placed in a niche outside the back door for the benefit of wandering ghosts; one is dedicated to the Stove God, whose image resides above the large brick structure on which all meals are prepared; and the third is placed in a burner before the tablets of the family's immediate ancestors. The purpose of this essay is to examine the significance of these three acts of worship. I will argue that this significance is largely determined by the worshippers' conception of their social world. The reader should therefore note at the outset the limited scope of this exploration. My informants have been farmers, coal miners, and laborers, as well as a few shopkeepers and petty businessmen. Thirty years ago the homes of many of these people were constructed of mud bricks and roofed with straw thatch. Thus my social perspective is that of a poor and politically impotent segment of the society. It is also that of the layman rather than of the religious specialist. Were we to look at the same acts of worship from the perspective of government officials, wealthy landlords, or the Taoist priest, we would find they had very different meanings. The most important point to be made about Chinese religion is that it mirrors the social landscape of its adherents. There are as many meanings as there are vantage points.

The geographic scope of my study is most appropriately defined with reference to the Ch'ing Shui Tsu Shih Kung temple in San-hsia. In 1895, when Taiwan was ceded to Japan, this god was regarded as the super natural governor of much of the Taipei Basin. The area of his jurisdiction extended from the outskirts of Shu-lin in the north to just beyond Ying-ke and Chung-chuang in the south, embracing the entire valley that is bounded on one side by the Kuei-lun Hills and on the other by the lower reaches of the central mountain range. In cultural terms the boundaries of Tsu Shih Kung's domain were coterminous with the limits of an area dominated by the descendants of eighteenth-century immigrants from An-ch'i. To the west T'ao-yuan and

Ta-ch'i were controlled by Chang-chou people, while to the east Tsu Shih Kung's subjects faced Ting-chiao and T'ung-an people at Shu-lin and Chang-chou people in the direction of Pan-ch'iao and Tu-ch'eng. Until the Japanese administration brought an end to years of internecine strife, An-ch'i people worshipped An-ch'i gods and married An-ch'i women. Although Hsia-ch'i-chou, the site of my first fieldwork, is only fifteen minutes' walk from villages controlled by Chang-chou people, it was not until 1918 that the first Chang-chou woman married into the community.

This is not to say that Tsu Shih Kung's domain existed as an isolated, self-sufficient kingdom. At the turn of the century at least half a dozen families in Hsia-ch'i-chou made their living as boatmen, and San-hsia's position as the area's leading commercial center depended on its role as a riverport. The area sent camphor, tea, coal, and wood down the river to Wan-hua and Tamsui, and received in return cotton, paper, and tobacco from Amoy, sugar and sweetmeats from Hong Kong, and occasionally flour and kerosene from the United States. Recognition of the area's position as part of the Chinese empire is clearly reflected in the natives' conception of their supernatural governor. The most enthusiastic of Tsu Shih Kung's subjects would never have claimed that he was an autonomous ruler. It was universally understood that his authority was delegated by a higher power, responsible for a much larger community. Tsu Shih Kung is but the local representative of a vast supernatural bureaucracy, headed by a deity whose every characteristic marks him as the spiritual equivalent of the human emperor.

I have probably given the reader the impression that my subject is a community that disappeared shortly after the turn of the century. There is a sense in which this is true. The bandits who used to parade through the streets of San-hsia shouting, "You trust the mandarins; we'll trust the mountains," have long since been dispersed (MacKay 1895: 159–60). The river that once carried the burden of all commerce was supplanted by the railroad seventy years ago. By the time I began my research in the area in 1957 many residents were commuting to jobs in Taipei City, and by 1970 the area's leading employers included Sony and Motorola. Everything has changed, and yet nothing has changed. Even new houses have ancestral altars and a Stove God as well as a television set, and I have seen a fire-walking performed on a baseball diamond. The reader will have to exercise some historical imagination to understand the conditions that gave rise to the beliefs I discuss, but he must not forget that these beliefs endure and will influence the future.

The Stove God, Tsao Chün, is not a god of the culinary arts, nor is his location above the stove a matter of convenience or coincidence. In northern Taiwan the large brick cooking stove on which most meals are prepared stands as a substantial symbol of the family as a corporate body. Possession of a stove identifies a family as an independent entity. The new independent segments of a recently divided household often share many of the facilities of a single house, including, occasionally, the kitchen, but independent families never share a stove, not even when the heads are brothers. When brothers divide their father's household the eldest inherits the old stove, while his younger brothers transfer hot coals from the old stove to their new ones, thereby inviting the Stove God to join them. For this reason, family division is commonly spoken of as *pun-cau,* "dividing the stove." In the view of most of my informants, the soul of a family, its corporate fate, is somehow localized in their stove. When a shaman informed one family that there were "ants and other things" in their stove, they demolished the structure and threw the bricks into the river. A neighbor explained, "There was nothing else they could do. A family will never have peace if they don't have a good stove."

The association of Stove God and stove is thus an association of god and family. The character of the relationship is essentially bureaucratic. The family is the smallest corporate unit in the society, and the Stove God is the lowest-ranking member of a supernatural bureaucracy. In the Yangtze delta village of Kaihsienkung, Stove Gods were viewed as the spiritual remains of foreign soldiers forcibly billeted in the houses of the region to act as spies and informers (Fei 1939: 99–102). In San-hsia the god is usually described as "a kind of policeman." The metaphors chosen to describe the god vary from one area of China to another, possibly as a result of political experience, but the god is everywhere looked upon as representing a supernatural bureaucracy. The glutinous rice cakes offered him at the New Year are explained as a means of forestalling an unfavorable report on the family. According to one of my informants in Hsia-ch'i-chou, "You have to give the god something so that he won't say things about your family and cause you a lot of trouble."

The prototype of the many gods in the Chinese pantheon is, in my view, Fu Te Cheng Shen, commonly known as T'u Ti Kung. This "earth god" is often introduced as the Chinese god of agriculture, but this is only partially accurate. "T'u-ti" is better translated as "site" or "locality" than as "earth" or "soil." T'u Ti Kung is a tutelary deity, the governor of a place, concerned with agriculture, to be sure, but no more so than any official responsible for the welfare of a rural community. T'u Ti Kung are just as common in the towns and cities of Taiwan as in the villages. Older residents of Tainan City claim that in former times every neighborhood had its own T'u Ti Kung, and evidence gathered by Kristofer Schipper appears to bear them out. A Taoist manuscript dated 1876 lists all of the city's divine agents from whom one must request forgiveness in time of disaster. Among the 138 cults mentioned in the list, 45 are devoted to T'u Ti Kung (Schipper 1975).

T'u Ti Kung is seen as having two functions, one of which is to police the *kui (kuei),* the "ghosts," the supernatural equivalent of bandits, beggars, and other dangerous strangers.[2] The association between T'u Ti Kung and the earth is in part a consequence of this role. The kui are creatures of the soil, spiritual residues of the most material part of man, often represented in experience by bones uncovered in digging a foundation or plowing a field. It is T'u Ti Kung's task to protect the living from the depredations of these unhappy, wandering spirits. Although the god thus serves the best interests of the human community, he is not that community's agent. His other role is to spy on the affairs of his human charges, keep records of their activities, and report regularly to his superiors. Commenting on H. A. Giles's view that T'u Ti Kung are worshipped "for anything that can be got out of them," Clarence Day (Day 1940: 65) notes, "Not only that, but all local events and proceedings must be duly reported to them: births, marriages, misfortunes, deaths." Most people in the San-hsia area report vital events to their neighborhood T'u Ti Kung as well as to the local police station, and in many villages people customarily ask the god's permission to build a new house or demolish an old one.

In imperial China every local official was responsible for a discrete administrative district, and this was as true of the supernatural bureaucracy as it was of their human counterparts. Until only recently the jurisdiction of many T'u Ti Kung in the San-hsia area was defined by means of a circulating plaque, a piece of wood about twenty inches long and eight inches wide, inscribed on one side with the name of the god and on the other with the name of the community.[3] This token of the god's authority was passed from family to family, day by day, moving through the community along an irregular but exhaustive route. The family holding the plaque on any given day was responsible for making an offering of incense, fruit, and tea at the T'u Ti Kung temple. This it did in the morning after receiving the plaque and again in the evening before passing it on to a neighbor. In this way every family participated in honoring the local T'u Ti Kung and in so doing identified itself as part of the community.

This practice implies a conditional relationship between the god and his subjects. The family that moves from one community to another should see themselves as leaving the authority of one T'u Ti Kung and entering that of another. And so it is. R. F. Johnston's description of Weihaiwei at the turn of the century is entirely applicable to the San-hsia area in the 1960's. After describing a procession of mourners "wending their way along the village street in the direction of the shrine of T'u Ti to report the death of a relative or fellow villager," Johnston continues: "It is noteworthy . . . that no village in Weihaiwei, or elsewhere as far as I am aware, possesses more than one T'u Ti, though there may be two or more 'surnames' or clans represented in the village; moreover, when a man migrates from one village to another he changes his T'u Ti, although his connection with his old village in respect of ancestral worship remains unimpaired" (Johnston 1910: 372–73).

Johnston's point is that T'u Ti Kung serve localities, not kinship groups. This is right and explains why farmers in San-hsia who own land in more than one locality worship more than one T'u Ti Kung. However, Johnston makes an avoidable error when he observes that no village ever has more than one T'u Ti Kung. The library of the School of Oriental and African Studies contains Johnston's copy of Arthur Smith's *Village Life in China*. The book is inscribed "R. F. Johnston, Government House, July 6th, 1901," a year or two after Johnston's arrival in Weihaiwei and nine years before he published his *Lion and Dragon in Northern China*. Had Johnston consulted Smith on the T'u Ti Kung, as he did on many other subjects, he would have found this passage: "If the village is a large one, divided into several sections transacting their public business independently of one another, there may be several temples to the same divinity. It is a common saying, illustrative of Chinese notions on this topic, that the local god at one end of the village has nothing to do with the affairs of the other end of the village." (Smith 1899: 138.)

Smith, too, errs in implying that T'u Ti Kung temples are always thought of as independent of one another. In fact, many T'u Ti Kung are the delegated representatives of other T'u Ti Kung. This is sometimes made explicit in the ritual process by which a new temple is established or an old one refurbished. During my most recent trip to Taiwan, in 1970, the people of Chung-p'u on the west side of San-hsia decided to rebuild the residence of their local deity. On the day the old temple was to be demolished, the head of the village bent six long strips of bamboo into circles and tied them together with red string to form a large hoop. Before the god was invited out of the temple for the duration of the repairs, this bamboo hoop was lowered over the roof and thus made to encircle the entire building. I was told that the hoop represented the boundaries of the district governed by the god. The purpose of encircling the temple was to keep the god from deserting the community while his home was under repair. "This is the god of this place. We do not want him to leave and take up residence somewhere else."

This step of the ritual identified the god with the district for which he is responsible. The next made it clear that he is not conceived of as a sovereign ruler, but as the local representative of a higher authority. Once it had been ascertained by divination that the god agreed to leave the temple, the village head took a spoonful of ashes from the incense burner and wrapped it up in red paper. This packet was then conveyed to the town of San-hsia, where it was deposited in the incense burner of what is known as the Big T'u Ti Kung temple. The village head explained that this was done because "our temple in Chung-p'u is only a substation of the big temple in town." He also told me that upon completion of the new temple, he would get ashes from the temple in town and deposit these in the new burner in Chung-p'u. "This is like asking the god in the big temple to send someone to live in our temple and protect us."

The view that the T'u Ti Kung temples in villages and neighborhoods are substations of larger temples is not an unusual one. There are fourteen other temples in San-hsia and its immediate environs that are commonly regarded as branches of the Big T'u Ti Kung temple on the main street. Until the changing character of the town led to a reorganization in 1947, these relationships were given explicit recognition on T'u Ti Kung's birthday. The puppet shows provided for the entertainment of each of the fourteen neighborhood gods were always organized and paid for by the individual neighborhoods. The responsibility for the far more expensive opera performed to entertain the Big T'u Ti Kung was rotated among the fourteen neighborhoods on an annual basis. Even today the special status of the Big T'u Ti Kung receives occasional acknowledgment. When families invite gods to their home for some special occasion, they usually include the Big T'u Ti Kung as well as their neighborhood T'u Ti Kung. "It's the same as inviting both the mayor and the head of your village."

In considering the implications of this equation of god and bureaucrat, it is important to remember that one side of the equation is objective, the other subjective. A T'u Ti Kung and the administration he serves do not partake of the same reality as the human bureaucracy. People with different perspectives can interpret the supernatural hierarchy in different ways. An interesting case in point is provided by the T'u Ti Kung temples in Ch'i-nan, across the river from San-hsia. The community comprises four hamlets, each of which is dominated by a single lineage and its ancestral hall. At one time all four hamlets were united under the jurisdiction of one T'u Ti Kung. One T'u Ti Kung plaque circulated from family to family and then from hamlet to hamlet, and the four hamlets rotated the responsibility for the show presented to the god on his birthday. Then, sometime in the late 1950's, the hamlet dominated by the Ong lineage decided to build its own T'u Ti Kung temple. Residents of the Ong hamlet continued to take their turn in sponsoring the show for "old T'u Ti Kung's" birthday, but stopped accepting the plaque from the old temple and began instead to make daily offerings at the "Ong temple."

According to a member of the Ong lineage who now lives in the town of San-hsia, this decision was prompted by the Ongs' fear that the old T'u Ti Kung was neglecting them. "All our pigs and chickens suddenly died, and so someone called a geomancer who told us that it was because the old temple faced away from the Ong settlement. The god couldn't see us." Emily Ahern has since discovered that there were other reasons for the Ongs' dissatisfaction, but I will leave that story to her.[4] The important point for my purpose is that the present situation in Ch'i-nan is reflected in differing accounts of the Ong temple's origins. My Ong informant claims that the incense used to found the temple came from the Big T'u Ti Kung temple on the main street of San-hsia. A senior member of the Lou lineage in Ch'i-nan insists that the incense came from the old T'u Ti Kung temple in Ch'i-nan. The disagreement reflects the social perspectives of the two informants. The Ong lineage would like to put their settlement on an equal footing with the rest of Ch'i-nan. The other three lineages put the Ongs down by insisting that their temple is only a branch of the Ch'i-nan temple.

I emphasize the influence different social perspectives have on what is said about T'u Ti Kung temples in order to underline my primary thesis. People would not argue about the age of temples or the source of their incense if they did not see this as a question of the relative rank of the gods in question and hence the relative status of the communities they govern. Conflicts are expressed in these terms because everyone thinks of the gods in terms of a bureaucratic hierarchy. John Shryock reports that the followers of a certain Tung Yo in Anking advanced his claims for godhood by claiming for him the governorship of the entire province. Skeptics countered by arguing that the god's activities were confined to the East Gate suburb. Even Buddhists and Taoists expressed their perennial opposition in the same idiom. A Taoist monk told Shryock that the Ch'eng Huang responsible for Anking prefecture was a Taoist deity, while the god responsible for the hsien, who differed from the prefecture god in no way except for the smaller size of the district he governed, was Buddhist (Shryock 1931: 87–88).

The view of the gods as bureaucrats is so pervasive that evidence to the contrary is itself explained away in bureaucratic terms. The picture of the pantheon with which many families decorate their ancestral altar has the Stove God in the lower left-hand corner and T'u Ti Kung in the lower right-hand corner. The reason for this has to do with the ritual specialist's view that the left side is the *iong (yang)* side and the right side the *im (yin)* side.[5] One of T'u Ti Kung's tasks is to escort the souls of the dead to the underworld, the im world, so he appropriately appears on the im side of the picture, the right side. But since etiquette makes the left superior to the right in seating guests, this positioning of the gods conflicts with the laymen's view of their relative status. T'u Ti Kung should be at the left and the Stove God at the right because Tu'Ti Kung governs a community while the Stove God is responsible only for a single family. I first noticed the contradiction while attending a feast in San-hsia, and immediately raised the problem with my fellow guests. One of the older men present explained that the T'u Ti Kung and the Stove God are not comparable. "T'u Ti Kung is like a policeman who wears a uniform. He can only report to lower gods like the Ch'eng Huang. The Stove God is more like a plainclothesman. He reports directly to T'ien Kung [the supernatural emperor]." I asked: "But how is it that a little god like the Stove God can report directly to T'ien Kung?" Another old man answered: "The Stove God is not a small person like T'u Ti Kung. He is T'ien Kung's younger brother." The apparent departure from bureaucratic principles is thus explained away as nepotism.

Popular mythology in northern Taiwan as in other areas of China has it that T'u Ti Kung's immediate superior in the supernatural bureaucracy is Ch'eng Huang, the so-called City God, a deity posted to govern the spirits residing in each of the major administrative districts of the empire. When a small T'u Ti Kung temple in a mountain village near San-hsia was enlarged in 1967, the village head obtained incense from the Ch'eng Huang temple in Taipei City as well as the Big T'u Ti Kung temple in San-hsia. He felt this was necessary "because the Taipei Ch'eng Huang is overseer of all the T'u Ti Kung in Taipei hsien. There is no point in building a new temple if you do not ask the Ch'eng Huang to send someone to live in it." The residents of Hsia-ch'i-chou also obtained incense from the Taipei Ch'eng Huang when they built a new temple to replace the one destroyed by a typhoon in 1962. They were afraid that if they did not inform the Ch'eng Huang, he might post a new T'u Ti Kung without recalling the old one. Two gods in one temple might quarrel and thereby bring the village further misfortune.

As his relationship with T'u Ti Kung implies, Ch'eng Huang is also conceived of as a scholar-official. The god's image is always dressed in official robes and usually appears on a curtained dais flanked on either side by secretaries and fearsome lictors; his temples are laid out on precisely the same lines as a government yamen, even to the details of red walls in the courtyards and flagstaffs at the entrance. In most cities the god appeared in public three times a year to *ke-kieng (kuo-ching),* "tour the boundaries," or, as other informants put it, "to inspect the frontiers." Preceded by heralds carrying his gold boards of authority and his banners, the god passed through the streets in a covered sedan chair, accompanied by hundreds of young men dressed as servants, soldiers, secretaries, and lictors. By all accounts, the procession was awe-inspiring. Shryock says the tour in Anking commenced about nine in the morning and did not return to the temple until after midnight, the god visiting every street whose inhabitants had made known their desire to welcome him in the proper manner:

> The parade took more than an hour to pass my point of observation. There were hundreds of ghosts like the wildest nightmare visions, their faces painted and lined with every colour under heaven, their robes bright with embroidered silks, beads, and tinsel glittering in their high head gear and banners streaming from their shoulders like wings. Soldiers with gags in their mouths, lictors bearing staffs of office, secretaries, giants and dwarfs passed two by two down the narrow, crowded street, until finally, to a continuous roar of firecrackers exploding under the feet of the marching men, and a deafening clash of cymbals and drums, came the god in the sedan chair of an official, curtains drawn for fear pictures might be taken. I caught a glimpse of his dark, impassive face, and he was gone. (Shryock 1931: 105.)

A somewhat subtler indication of the god's assimilation to the imperial bureaucracy is his loss of individual identity. Although some tales of the god's origins give him a specific identity, most people now treat Ch'eng Huang as a position rather than a person. For example, deceased notables are commonly assigned the status of Ch'eng Huang. Ch'ü T'ungtsu identifies the Ch'eng Huang of Lou hsien in Kiangsu as a former magistrate, Li Fu-hsing, who died there in 1669 (Ch'ü 1962: 311), and, according to Florence Ayscough, the god governing Shanghai is a former member of the Hanlin Academy, Ch'in Yü-poi, who was assigned to his present position by the founder of the Ming dynasty (Ayscough 1924: 140–41). This is a particularly interesting case because it led commentators on the Shanghai gazetteer to recognize that the term Ch'eng Huang is nothing more than a bureaucratic label. Ayscough quotes one commentator as asking, "How is it that we know nothing of a former P'usa [bodhisattva]? Did the seat of Spiritual Magistrate wait for Ch'in Yü-poi?" Another commentator she cites comes to the conclusion that officials in the im world are moved around just like those in the iong world (1924: 141).

Ritual specialists and people who take more than a casual interest in temple affairs commonly distinguish two types of deities. On the one hand, there are the *su (shih),* the "officials," the most notable of whom are the T'u Ti Kung and the Ch'eng Huang; on the other, there are the *hu (fu),* the "sages" or "wise men," a category represented in the San-hsia area by such gods as Tsu Shih Kung, Pao Sheng Ta Ti, Shang

Ti Kung, and Ma Tsu. The former are explicitly compared with the imperial bureaucracy and are often treated as administrative positions that can be occupied by different people. The latter are usually thought of as particular deified persons with saintly qualities, the emphasis being on the deity's moral character and good works rather than on his bureaucratic functions.

Most laymen, though aware of this distinction, do not trouble much about it. From the point of view of farmers, coal miners, coolies, and the keepers of small shops, all gods are bureaucrats. Whereas the managers of San-hsia's Ch'ang-fu Yen, the residence of Tsu Shih Kung, insist that the god is hu, "a wise man like your Lincoln," the great majority of the population think of the god as their supernatural governor. Local legend says that many years ago a god named Ang Kong saved San-hsia by warning its inhabitants of an impending raid by head-hunting aborigines. To thank the god for this timely warning, San-hsia now sends a delegation every year to invite Ang Kong to attend a festival in his honor. The god is brought from his home temple in Hsin-tien on a sedan chair, and is met at the San-hsia border by Tsu Shih Kung, riding in another chair. Asked why Tsu Shih Kung goes to meet Ang Kong at the San-hsia border, people explain that it is because "Tsu Shih Kung is the god in charge of this place and so must meet Ang Kong and show him the road." The custom is precisely parallel to that by which a hsien magistrate greeted a visiting colleague and escorted him to the yamen.

Elsewhere in this volume Wang Shih-ch'ing's account of the history of the Ch'i-an Kung temple in Shu-lin provides another example. Although the god enshrined in the temple, Pao Sheng Ta Ti, is classified as hu by ritual specialists, the populace treat him as the town's chief bureaucrat, comparable in many ways to the Ch'eng Huang found in administrative centers. He makes an annual inspection tour and is looked upon as the official responsible for the many T'u Ti Kung temples in the area. When a village or neighborhood decides to build a new temple or enlarge an old one, they usually invite Pao Sheng Ta Ti to choose the temple's site and orientation. There is even a legend to the effect that Pao Sheng Ta Ti was once an official in Ch'üan-chou *fu* and that he was deified in recognition of meritorious service.

The same habit of thought molds the views of people whose gods are not responsible for communities as large as San-hsia and Shu-lin. The small village in which I initiated my research in Taiwan is one of five hamlets that together constitute a rural community known as Ch'i-chou. The local gods are two T'u Ti Kung, one for each half of the community, and Shang Ti Kung, who is considered the supernatural governor of Ch'i-chou. The five hamlets rotate the responsibility for Shang Ti Kung's annual inspection tour on the occasion of his birthday. Preceded by the village band and the clatter-bang of firecrackers, the god visits the four landmarks that define the boundaries of Ch'i-chou, stopping along the way to exchange incense with the head of every family that resides in the community. The whole affair is a country version of the grand tours undertaken by the Ch'eng Huang of important towns. The only difference is in the number: of people involved and the magnificence of the god's equipage, a matter of magnitude rather than meaning.

Shang Ti Kung's bureaucratic character is most evident in his relationship to the local T'u Ti Kung. Although the T'u Ti Kung are always invited to witness a play or puppet show performed for Shang Ti Kung, people are careful to place Shang Ti Kung in the center of the viewing platform with the two T'u Ti Kung at his right. Shang Ti Kung is thought of as a proud, somewhat arrogant official, who would take offense were he denied the seat of honor. A person can use the same foodstuffs to make offerings to the two gods, but he must present the offering to Shang Ti Kung before he presents it to T'u Ti Kung. A series of misfortunes that befell one family was widely blamed on a careless daughter-in-law, who thanked T'u Ti Kung before she thanked Shang Ti Kung. I was told that on one occasion Shang Ti Kung refused to leave his temple for his annual inspection tour because only two men were assigned to carry his chair. A god of his status would not deign to sally forth in a sedan chair carried by fewer than four men.

The relative status of the two gods is also apparent at the fire-walking that is held every year "to cleanse the gods and make them efficacious." Riding in sedan chairs carried by young men chosen by lot, the various images of the two gods are carried two or three times across a bed of hot coals. Every year some of the men carrying the chairs occupied by Shang Ti Kung are possessed by the god and carry on as though he were in complete command of their senses. The chairs charge the crowd and one another, sometimes meeting in violent collisions, causing bloody if not very serious injuries. This display of energy is looked upon by the villagers as evidence of Shang Ti Kung's great vitality. It therefore says something about their conception of T'u Ti Kung that the men carrying his chairs are never possessed, despite their exposure to the excitement of the occasion and the example of Shang Ti Kung's bearers. I think it is simply that people consider T'u Ti Kung "a little god," who lacks the strength and authority to take command of a person's body.

The greatest power the peasant can imagine does not escape the impress of the imperial bureaucracy on his thought. Yü Huang Ta Ti, Pearly Emperor and Supreme Ruler, the mightiest god in the peasant's pantheon, is but a reflection of the human emperor. Although there are temples for Yü Huang Ta Ti in some parts of Taiwan, there are none in San-hsia or Shu-lin. People say this is because "Yü Huang Ta Ti is a long way away and cannot be spoken to directly." All communication with the god must be by way of another god, who must himself be one of the higher-ranking deities. Lowly deities like the T'u Ti Kung cannot approach Yü Huang Ta Ti any more than a district magistrate could approach the emperor. As the Rev. Justus Doolittle puts it on the basis of his observations in Foochow, "In strict theory, the great gods, the divinities of high rank, may worship him, while the gods of lower rank may not properly worship him, in accordance with the established practice that only mandarins of high rank may wait upon the emperor in person and pay their respects, while officers of lower grade may not approach into the emperor's presence" (Doolittle 1865: II, 257).

In traditional China not all officials were assigned to territorial posts. Some served as general inspectors, traveling from one area to another and reporting their observations to the central government. The same practice is followed by the supernatural government. In her brief account of religion in a fishing village in southern Taiwan, Norma Diamond describes "two wandering inspector gods" who visit the village periodically. Their visits are announced through a shaman, who cries the news through the village streets. During their stay in the village the gods are housed in the village temple, where each household worships them in the morning and again in the evening. Diamond notes that there is some disagreement about what the gods do while they are present, but the opinions expressed by her informants suggest that most people think of them as carrying out bureaucratic functions:

> One informant was of the opinion that the god came only to bring protection, to prevent illness, and to help people earn more money, and that he did this of his own volition during a pleasure trip. Another felt that he was specifically sent by the Jade Emperor to investigate men's activities, parallel to the secret police being sent by the government. A third informant explained that while the god himself was benevolent in his intentions, the troops that followed him were a mixed breed, some of whom would bring misfortune and harm. And some felt that illness or misfortune would strike evildoers shortly after the god reported back to his superiors. (Diamond 1969: 94.)

It is not only bureaucratic organization that is replicated in the world of the supernatural; the gods also display many of the most human characteristics of their worldly counterparts, including their fallibility. A temple history translated by Shryock (1931: 113–14) tells the story of a Ch'eng Huang who allowed an innocent boy to be identified as a thief. The boy, knowing he was innocent, wrote a report condemning the god and burnt it. The report was picked up by one of the wandering inspector gods mentioned by Diamond and brought to the attention of the Jade Emperor, who "immediately issued a decree banishing the City-God 1,115 *li* from his city for three years." Thus castigated, the penitent Ch'eng Huang testified on the boy's behalf and thereby managed to get his sentence reduced to 15 *li*. "So the City-God has a temple in San K'ou Cheng, because that place was just 15 *li* from the city. Anyone who does not believe this may go to San K'ou Cheng and see the temple."

In this case a culpable deity is punished by his superior in the supernatural bureaucracy. In other instances irresponsible gods are punished by human officials. The bureaucracy of the other world is not thought of as superior to the human bureaucracy with authority over it. Rather the two are parallel systems, in which the higher-ranking members of one bureaucracy have authority over the lower-ranking members of the other. When drought strikes part of a province, the governor does not appeal to the local gods to bring rain. Instead, he orders them to see to their duty, treating them with as little ceremony as he would treat one of his county magistrates.

Gods who failed in their duties could be tried and condemned to a public beating. Shryock writes: "A year or so ago, at Nanling Hsien during a drought, a god was publicly tried by the magistrate for neglect of duty, condemned, left in the hot sun to see how he liked it himself, and finally, after enduring every kind of insult, was broken in pieces" (1931: 97).

Like their human counterparts in the imperial bureaucracy, the gods are far more powerful than ordinary men. They can quell rebellions, check epidemics, apprehend criminals, dispatch ghosts, cure illnesses, control the weather, and otherwise intervene in natural and social processes for the benefit of their subjects. One of the T'u Ti Kung in Ch'i-chou is credited with the important capacity to control the market price of pork. Yet the gods are far from omnipotent Like the capacities of powerful human bureaucrats, those of their supernatural counterparts have limits. One day while I was attending a shamanistic session an elderly woman appeared and asked the god to save her seriously ailing husband. The shaman, speaking with the authority of the god, told her that although her husband's fate was due, his death could be postponed one year. My assistant happened to be present when the woman returned a little over a year later. Again her husband was seriously ill, and again she appealed to the god. This time the shaman refused to hear her appeal, bluntly informing her that nothing could be done. "Your husband's time is up. He will die no matter what I do. If I were to tell you that he will live, he would still die, and then what kind of a god would people think I am?" Although this answer may have been the shaman's way of saving himself from an almost certain loss of credibility, the idea that the god was powerless was accepted without surprise by everyone present.

The resemblance between the gods and their human counterparts extends even into the realm of their personal lives. The temples of the gods often include living quarters for their families as well as the hall in which they conduct their public business. Behind the main hall of the Ch'eng Huang temple in Shanghai is a room for the god's father and mother and an apartment occupied by his wife and four daughters (Ayscough 1924: 147). Even the lowly T'u Ti Kung is usually provided with a wife, and some take it upon themselves to add a concubine. On inquiring why a T'u Ti Kung in Weihaiwei was accompanied by two female images, R. F. Johnston was informed that "the lady on his left (the place of honour) was his wife and the lady on his right his concubine. . . . Two explanations were offered as to why this particular T'u Ti Kung had been allowed to increase his household in this manner: one was that he had won the lady by gambling for her, the other was that the T'u Ti Kung had appeared to one of the villagers in a dream and begged him to provide him with a concubine as he had grown tired of his wife." (1910: 374.)

In sum, what we see in looking at the Chinese supernatural through the eyes of the peasant is a detailed image of Chinese officialdom. This image allows us to assess the significance of the imperial bureaucracy from a new perspective. Historians and political scientists often emphasize the failure of most Chinese governments to effectively extend their authority to the local level. Certainly many governments had difficulty collecting taxes, and some allowed this function and others to fill into the hands of opportunistic local leaders. Judged in terms of its administrative arrangements, the Chinese imperial government looks impotent. Assessed in terms of its long-range impact on the people, it appears to have been one of the most potent governments ever known, for it created a religion in its own image. Its firm grip on the popular imagination may be one reason the imperial government survived so long despite its many failings. Perhaps this is also the reason China's revolutionaries have so often organized their movements in terms of the concepts and symbols of such foreign faiths as Buddhism and Christianity. The native gods were so much a part of the establishment that they could not be turned against it.

Although the gods and the ancestors differ in many important respects, they also have a great deal in common. The extreme contrast, from the Chinese point of view, is between the gods and the ancestors on the one hand, and ghosts on the other. The gods and the ancestors are granted the respect due social superiors; ghosts are despised, "like beggars." Where the gods and the ancestors can be appealed to for protection and help, ghosts offer men nothing but misfortune of every kind. The terms used to refer to the two forms of the supernatural denote the sharpest spiritual and moral opposition. The gods and the ancestors are sin, "gods" or "deities"; the generic name for ghosts is kui, "demons" or "devils. In Chinese metaphysics the positive, immaterial, and celestial aspect of the human soul is termed sin; the negative, material, and terrestrial side of the soul is called kui. Philosophers associate sin with growth, production, and life, and hence with light and warmth; kui is identified with decline, destruction, and death, and, by extension, with darkness and cold.[6]

The catalogue of human misery attributed to ghosts is a lengthy one. Accidents, barrenness, death, and all varieties of illness are laid to their agency, as are crop failures, business losses, bad luck in gambling, and the wasteful and disruptive habits of individual men and women. One woman in Ch'i-chou blames ghosts for her husband's frequent visits to wine houses and prostitutes, and another sees their malevolent influence at work in her son's lack of enterprise and her daughter-in-laws stubborn independence. Any contact with ghosts, however brief, is likely to result in misfortune. One night Tan Chun-mui was returning home late from the market town and saw "something black" ahead of her on the path. Frightened by the apparition, she stopped, thinking it might be wise to return to town and spend the night with friends. While she hesitated, "the black thing flipped over into the field and was gone." Tan Chun-mui was so shaken she had to crawl all the way home to the village, and she and her friends now say the encounter resulted in an illness "lasting for months and months."

Some ghosts are purposely harmful, "like a man who is mad at you," whereas others are only passively dangerous, "like a hot stove." In the view of most of my informants the character of a ghost depends upon his social and economic circumstances. Most dead people have descendants obligated to make offerings for their benefit, and their souls are therefore supplied with all the means of a comfortable existence in the next world. The spiritual remains of these people are content and bear no malice toward the living. The malicious ghosts are those discontented souls who are forced by their circumstances to prey on the living. They include the neglected dead—those who have no descendants because they died childless or as children, and those who died away from home and were forgotten—and also those hateful souls who receive no sacrifices because they remain at the scene of death seeking revenge—murder victims, suicides, and the unjustly executed. Some are angry because they are hungry and homeless, and some are hungry and homeless because they are angry. The weaker of these unhappy beings gather outside temples to beg for a living like the derelicts of this world, while the more powerful among them roam the countryside like so many bandits.

Although people in San-hsia differ on how one should deal with these malevolent creatures, they agree that dealing with a ghost is like dealing with *lo-mua:*, the gangs of young toughs who use threats of violence as a means of extortion. According to Ong Thian-co, "You have to make offerings to ghosts. They are just like the lo-mua:. If you don't give them something so that they will go away, you will never have any peace." Ong Zi-ko also views an offering to a ghost as comparable to paying off a lo-mua:, but he takes a more defiant attitude toward the use of such offerings. In his view it is a mistake to make an offering to a ghost "because the more you offer them the more often they come. They are like the lo-mua:. If you give a lo-mua: something when he comes to your house, he'll come back every day." As poor men with little means of defending themselves, Ong Thian-co and Ong Zi-ko fear both the ghosts and the lo-mua:. Their affluent and politically powerful neighbor, Li Bun-tua, fears neither. One day at a funeral Li told me that his relatives would not have to burn spirit money to keep the ghosts from harassing his soul on its journey to the underworld. "The next world is just like this one. If you are a strong man like me, big and fat, no one will bother you, but if you are old and weak, the ghosts will bully you just as the lo-mua: bully the old and weak in this world."

When pressed to explain their conception of ghosts, most of my informants compared them to bullies or beggars. Why do you have to make offerings to ghosts? "So that they will go away and leave you alone. They are like beggars and won't leave you alone if you don't give them something." Why is it that people usually call ghosts "the good brothers"? "Because they would be angry if you called them ghosts. Calling a ghost kui is like calling a beggar 'beggar.'" Ghosts ordinarily appear to the living as evil, formless objects, seen lying next to an irrigation channel or lurking in a dense bamboo grove. The one exception in Hsia-ch'i-chou was a creature who was said to walk through the village every night "beating two bamboo sticks just like a beggar." The dozen or so villagers who claimed to have seen this particular spirit agreed that it was the spiritual remains of a former beggar. "He used to come here all the time before he died. That was a long time ago now, but he still comes every night. He didn't have any children, so there is no one to make offerings."

The association of the destitute of this world with those of the next is also clear in the Reverend Doolittle's description of funeral customs in Foochow in the 1860's: "When burials connected with wealthy families take place on the hills, or the regular sacrifices to the dead are about to be performed in the spring at their graves, beggars often interfere for the purpose of getting food or money. . . . Oftentimes a considerable sum of money is distributed on such occasions among the beggars before they will allow burial or the sacrifice to proceed without interruptions, and with the desirable solemnity and silence." (1865: II, 262.) Just as the mourner must bribe the beggars to keep them from interfering, he must also pay their supernatural counterparts to save the deceased from similar annoyances. After the coffin has been lowered into the grave, "an offering is also made to the distressed and destitute spirits in the infernal regions, such as the spirits of lepers and beggars. . . . According to the general supposition, they, on receiving what the friends of the dead are disposed to bestow upon them, allow the sacrifice to the dead to go on without interruption." (Doolittle 1865: I, 206.) Each year when people return to the grave to make offerings to the deceased, they must also offer something to the ghosts. This, Doolittle says, is "in order to prevent departed friends from being molested by the importunity of beggars and lepers in the unseen world" (1865: II, 49).

In the Chinese view a beggar's request for alms is not really begging. It is a threat. Beggars are believed capable of laying terrible curses on anyone who ignores their entreaties. The man who sends a beggar away empty-handed risks the possibility of illness or damage to property. Beggars are thus like bandits and ghosts in that they are feared, and bandits and ghosts are like beggars in that they are socially despised. The social identities of the three are so similar that bandits and beggars are sometimes treated like ghosts. It was once the practice in northern Taiwan for every village and town to make a massive offering to the ghosts during the seventh lunar month. A high bamboo structure was erected in some central place, a market or a village square, and then hung with firecrackers and a wealth of food: chickens and ducks, both dead and alive, slices of pork and pigs' heads, fish of every kind, rice cakes, bananas, pineapples, melons, etc. This great feast was first offered up to all the wandering spirits who had answered the summons of the gongs, and then, after the ghosts had had time to satisfy themselves, the entire collection was turned over to the destitute humans who had gathered for the occasion. The Rev. George MacKay witnessed one of these festivals in Taipei City in the 1880's:

> It was a gruesome sight. When night came on and the time for summoning the spirits approached, the cones were illuminated by dozens of lighted candles. Then the priests took up their position on a raised platform, and by clapping their hands and sounding a large brass gong they called the spirits of all the departed to come and feast on the food provided. "Out of the night and the other world" the dead were given time to come and gorge themselves on the "spiritual" part of the feast, the essence, that was suited to their ethereal

> requirements. Meanwhile, a very unspiritual mob—thousands and thousands of hungry beggars, tramps, blacklegs, desperados of all sorts, from the country towns, the city slums, or venturing under cover of the night from their hiding-places among the hills—surged and swelled in every part of the open space, impatiently waiting their turn at the feast. When the spirits had consumed the "spiritual" part, the "carnal" was the property of the mob, and the mob quite approved of this division. . . . At length the spirits were satisfied, and the gong was sounded once more. That was the signal for the mob. . . . In one wild scramble, groaning and yelling all the while, trampling on those who had lost their footing or were smothered by the falling cones, fighting and tearing one another like mad dogs, they all made for the coveted food. (MacKay 1895: 130–31.)

All ghosts are like bandits and beggars, but not all ghosts are the spiritual remains of bandits or beggars. The reader will remember the case of the young man who saw "a white thing" moving across the paddy. His argument for labeling this apparition a "ghost" was his belief that it was the soul of another man's mother. This woman had not been a beggar during her lifetime, and she was not destitute in the next world. She was on her way to her son's house to receive deathday offerings made in her honor. I suggest that the category "ghosts" includes the souls of all people who die as members of some other group. They are not all malicious because the great majority are cared for by their living descendants, but they are all potentially dangerous because they are all strangers or outsiders. The malicious among them are malicious for the same reason some strangers are malicious. They are souls who have been insulted or injured in this life or the next, or souls who can support themselves only by begging or banditry. The crucial point is that the category "ghosts" is always a relative one. Your ancestors are my ghosts, and my ancestors are your ghosts, just as your relatives are strangers to me, and my relatives strangers to you.

This is not a point one can prove by asking people if the ghosts they see are their neighbors' ancestors, or, worse yet, by asking them if their own ancestors are ghosts to their neighbors. The two categories are polar opposites, like day and night, good and bad, and iong and im. Hence it is impossible for people to seriously consider the idea that what is an ancestor from one point of view is a ghost from another. The few informants on whom I tried such questions replied, "How could your ancestors be ghosts? Your ancestors are your own people and help you. Ghosts make you sick and cause trouble." Only the rare informant can look at his own society from a vantage point other than his own. Tan Cin-chiong was such a man because of his education and his academic interest in Chinese folklore. In his view kui is the generic term for all spirits or souls of the dead. "Sin is just a polite name for kui. Your ancestors are sin to you, but they are kui to other people. It just sounds better to call them sin."

Most people realize that their ancestors are other people's ghosts only when unusual circumstances make them look at their own dead from another point of view.

One of my best examples was recorded by Ch'en Cheng-hsiung, who worked as my field assistant for a few months in 1967. A woman named Peq A-mui was telling Ch'en that her mother had once quarreled over water with one of her husband's cousins. "That man went to see a famous *hu-a-sian* and got something and put it in my mother's tea. Ten days later a red stripe appeared on my mother's neck and she died. Exactly one year later his neighbors heard that man scream, saying that someone was squeezing his testicles. When the neighbors ran to see what was happening, they saw my mother coming out of the house." Ch'en then alertly asked his informant if her mother was a ghost to that man. She seemed surprised by the question, but agreed that her own mother was a ghost from the other man's point of view. "If he wanted to make an offering to my mother, he would have to do it outside the house rather than in the house."

Maurice Freedman has kindly allowed me to report another striking case in point, which he collected in Hong Kong. Talking to a man who had grown up in Kwangtung province, Freedman asked him about the difference between *shan* and *kwai* (the Cantonese equivalents of sin and kui). "He was horrified at the suggestion that the ancestors were other than shan; kwai are evil, ancestors never are, they help. But when I got him on to the festival of the hungry ghosts in the seventh lunar month, it occurred to him that other people's ancestors could be kwai and therefore harmful." A few weeks later Freedman asked the same informant to explain the use of the term kwai in the context of female mediums who are hired to call up customers' ancestors. One term of these mediums in Cantonese is *man kwai p'o*, "old women who talk to ghosts." "My informant patiently explained that everybody else's dead are kwai to you: the word kwai in such expressions as *man kwai p'o* . . . refers to the fact that the customer's ancestors are not the medium's ancestors. Your own ancestors cannot possibly be kwai to you; kwai means (implies) stranger."

The essential point that ghosts are the supernatural equivalent of feared strangers need not rest on contemporary evidence alone. Thanks to the careful work of Shen Chien-shih, we have a detailed account of the evolution of the character *kuei* (the Mandarin equivalent of kui and kwai). Drawing on both paleographic and documentary evidence, Shen (1936–37: 19) reconstructs the character's history as follows:

1. *Kuei,* like *yü,* was originally the name given to some strange anthropoid or simian creature.
2. From the name of an animal, *kuei* was extended to denote a people or race of alien origin.
3. From the abstract idea of an animal, *kuei* was extended to express the abstract ideas of "fear," "strangeness," "large size," "cunning," etc.
4. *Kuei,* the name of a corporeal creature, was "transferred" to represent the imagined appearance of a spiritual being, i.e., the ghost of the dead.

One could argue that the meaning of the character kuei has not changed at all. The term still refers to strange creatures who are regarded as aliens and are feared. The only difference is that whereas kuei once referred to real beings, it now refers to their supernatural counterparts. As the horizons of the Chinese world expanded, aliens became fellow citizens, making it impolite and impolitic to refer to them as kuei. But from the point of view of the average villager, people who are nothing more than fellow citizens are still strangers, and still to be feared. Consequently, their souls become kuei.

Until the Japanese occupied Taiwan and established an effective police system, the average village was a small community surrounded by a largely hostile social environment. The mutual animosity of the various racial and ethnic groups occupying the Taipei Basin made it a cauldron of internecine strife. The Chinese settlers fought the aborigines; Hokkien-speaking Chinese fought their Hakka neighbors; while among the Hokkien, people from Chang-chou and Ch'üan-chou competed bitterly for land and control of ports. In the hills surrounding the Basin, law and order gave way entirely to the rule of bandit chiefs and fugitives from the mainland. Under these conditions much of a peasant's contact with strangers was with bandits, beggars, bullies, and equally rapacious yamen hirelings. When a man left his village it was usually to visit relatives in a neighboring community, and the only outsiders welcomed in the village were those recommended by ties of kinship. The world beyond the bamboo walls that encircled each community was dangerous because it was inhabited by strangers, and strangers were feared because they were represented in experience by bandits and beggars. The ghosts are the product of this experience. They are dangerous because they are strangers, and strangers are dangerous because experience has proved them dangerous.

The conception of the supernatural found in San-hsia is thus a detailed reflection of the social landscape of traditional China as viewed from a small village. Prominent in this landscape were first the mandarins, representing the emperor and the empire; second, the family and the lineage; and third, the more heterogeneous category of the stranger and the outsider, the bandit and the beggar. The mandarins became the gods; the senior members of the line and the lineage, the ancestors; while the stranger was preserved in the form of the dangerous and despised ghosts. At a more general level the ancestors and the gods, taken together as sin, stand for productive social relationships, while their spiritual opposites, the kui, represent those social forces that are dangerous and potentially destructive.

As an example of the Chinese peasant's singular and unscriptural sentiments" concerning the soul, the Reverend Doolittle observes (1865: II, 401–2) that people in Foochow believe "each person has *three distinct* souls while living. These souls separate at the death of the adult to whom they belong. One resides in the ancestral tablet erected to his memory, if the head of a family; another lurks in the coffin or the grave, and the third departs to the infernal regions to undergo its merited punishment." The soul enshrined in the ancestral tablet clearly represents the dead in his role as kinsman, while the soul subjected to judgment in the underworld is just as obviously the dead in his role as citizen of the empire. Although the Chinese peasant's conception of the underworld was inspired by the Buddhist imagination, it has long since become a multi-layered yamen staffed with supernatural bureaucrats. The great amounts of spirit money transmitted to the Bank in Hell at the end of a funeral are only partly intended for subsistence expenses. Everyone knows that most of it will be expended to bribe officials who might otherwise subject the deceased to his merited punishment and perhaps some unmerited punishment as well.

This leaves for identification the soul that goes into the coffin and the grave. In Freedman's view the rites performed at the grave are the reverse of those performed before the ancestral tablets in homes and lineage halls. Where the soul represented by an ancestral tablet is involved in a moral relationship with its descendants, the soul associated with the bones in the grave is the source of an amoral power that can be manipulated by impersonal means. The former is iong; the latter, im (1966: 140–42; 1967: 86–88). I am inclined to extend this interpretation, and to argue that the soul in the grave represents the social role of the stranger. Division of the social world into strangers, bureaucrats, and kinsmen means that every man plays the role of stranger as well as the role of kinsman and citizen. At death the kinsman takes his place on the ancestral altar, where he continues to perform many of his rights and duties as an ascendant; the citizen is conducted to the underworld by a representative of the supernatural bureaucracy and is there judged and punished; while the stranger goes into the grave and becomes the source of an amoral and impersonal power.

ENDNOTES

1. The first draft of this paper was written in 1965, for a seminar conducted at Cornell University by Maurice Freedman. The paper has since been revised several times to take account of new information and the comments of friends and colleagues. I am particularly indebted to Maurice Freedman, Margery Wolf, Robert J. Smith, Emily M. Ahern, and C. Stevan Harrell, all of whom have commented on earlier drafts. I am also indebted to Freedman, Ahem, and Harrell for permission to report data drawn from personal correspondence and unpublished field notes.
2. Place names and the names of familiar gods are romanized with their Mandarin pronunciation. Otherwise, all terms are given in Hokkien. Where Hokkien terms have a familiar Mandarin equivalent, I sometimes give the Mandarin in parentheses following the Hokkien.
3. Sung Lung-sheng, recently returned from field research, tells me that one of the T'u Ti Kung plaques in the San-hsia area also lists the names of the heads of all households that receive the plaque. Thus the plaque makes explicit the relationship between the god, the community, and the residents who worship the god.
4. A detailed account of the four Ch'i-nan lineages and the problems that led to the construction of the Ong temple is now available in Ahern's *The Cult of the Dead in a Chinese Village* (1973: 64–66). Readers who want another perspective on the topics discussed in this paper are urged to read Ahern's book and Wang Shih-ch'ing's paper in this volume. All three studies are based on fieldwork in San-hsia *chen* and its neighbor, Shu-lin chen.

5. I am following the Chinese convention of taking the ancestors' perspective in designating right and left. If one asks a native how he seats guests at a home banquet, he will almost always turm his back to his ancestral altar and say, "The guest of honor sits this way (with his back to the altar, facing the door), while the second guest sits at the left and the third at the right." Thus, right is stage right; left, stage left.
6. In his paper in this volume C. Stevan Harrell discusses cases in which ghosts acquire a reputation for great power and come to be regarded as gods. The important point with respect to my thesis is that powerful spirits become gods and are then clothed in bureaucratic trappings. It is as though the peasant cannot imagine great power that is not essentially bureaucratic.

Chapter 18

Hopi Stories of Witchcraft, Shamanism, and Magic

Ekkehart Malotki and Ken Gary

In general, the underworld is conceived by many shamanic traditions as a region where everything "takes place as it does here, but in reverse. When it is day on earth, it is night in the beyond . . . the summer of the living corresponds to winter in the land of the dead" (Eliade 1964: 205). This is certainly true for the Hopi, as reflected in their concept of the year's duality and the characteristics of the dead. One of these is the concept of "a dual division of time and space between the upper world of the living and the lower world of the dead" (Titiev 1944: 173–78) so that when it is day in the surface world, it is night down below. Similarly, when it is winter in the upper world, it is summer in the lower. This inversion or duality has a profound effect on the structure of the ritual cycle due to the fact that "life in the other world is supposed to reflect life on earth so exactly that corresponding ceremonies are performed simultaneously (with the seasons reversed) in the two spheres" (Titiev 1944: 173–78). Also, among many other inversions that could be mentioned, the dead eat only the essence or odor of food, not its material form (Voth 1905: 116), and when they see a live person in the underworld, the children there remark upon them as "skeletons" (Voth 1905: 118).

Finally, one of the operative concepts of the Hopi underworld is that "a person who dies on earth 'becomes like a baby' in the other world, and that spirits of the dead become embodied in children born on earth" (Titiev 1944: 176, quoting Parsons 1925: 75–76, n. 121). An example of this is contained in a story in the present collection, "How Coyote Came to Visit Maski, Home of the Dead." Here the storyteller observes, after Coyote comes across nothing but frolicking children there, "Apparently, when a Hopi dies, he becomes like a child again and for that reason, there were nothing but children there. No matter how much anyone suffers in life, upon their arrival in Maski, they are in perfect health again."

In the view of Eliade (1964: 182), "It is always the shaman who conducts the dead person's soul to the underworld, for he is the psychopomp par excellence . . . because his soul can safely abandon his body and roam at vast distances, can penetrate the underworld and rise to the sky." In Hopi oral literature, this role is often filled by Kwaakwant (One Horn) and Aa'alt (Two Horn) priests, who guide travelers on their perilous journey to Maski, separate the good from the evil, and carry out judgment on the wicked. Geertz (1987: 122) summarizes the role of the One Horn priests thus: "The most important part of their guardian nature is the role they play during an individual's journey to the land of the dead. . . . It is the spirit of Kwan members who not only keep watch over the paths of the dead, thus serving as psychopomps, but also act in judgment over the souls of the dead." This role forms a central theme in two stories in the present collection, "An Oraibi Boy's Visit to Maski, Home of the Dead" and "How Coyote Came to Visit Maski, Home of the Dead," and elsewhere, in the story "A Journey to the Skeleton House" (Voth 1905: 109). These themes are echoed in a delirium vision that Don Talayesva had when sick in the autobiography *Sun Chief* (Simmons 1942: 121–27).

In Hopi ritual practice, other than the kachinas, who are the prototypical journeyers between cosmic zones, Hopi clowns can also be seen as guides or conductors between worlds. In the underworld, "every attribute is reversed, which may account for the clowns saying the opposite of what they mean, for their association with the dead, and for their coming over the clouds to the villages. As inhabitants of both worlds, the clowns also become the caretakers, or 'fathers,' of the kachinas, able to announce their arrival, albeit in an obverse manner, care for their appearance as they dance, and serve as interpreters between the two worlds" (Wright 1994: 4). And "in the manner of a shaman, the clown becomes one with his patron and uses that being's powers to accomplish his ends. In the manner of a priest, the clown makes manifest the needs of both the Underworld and the villagers of the Upper World" (Wright 1994: 7).

AN ORAIBI BOY'S VISIT TO MASKI, HOME OF THE DEAD

Aliksa'i. People were living in Oraibi and various other settlements across the land. In Oraibi, there lived a boy named Honanyestiwa, along with his parents and a younger sister. They all resided at the far northeastern edge of Oraibi. Thus, when the sun came up in the morning, the inside of their home was the first to be lit by its rays.

Also along the northeastern side of Oraibi was a graveyard. Day in and day out, as the boy went to greet the sun in a morning prayer, he passed by this graveyard. In the beginning, he did not give much thought to it. As time went on, however, his curiosity about the place increased, and he thought, "I wonder if it's really true that upon one's death one goes somewhere. Does one really travel to some paradise? How could I go about reaching such a place and find out about it with my own eyes?" Each time while going by this location these thoughts were on his mind. However, he never confided his thoughts to his parents. Most likely they would harshly berate him for this, for no one in his right mind would willingly choose death. For this reason he never brought up the subject in front of his parents.

But as time passed, he became more and more determined to seek out this place. So he decided, "The next time I go and pray to the sun, I'll ask for guidance on how I may reach this place. People say that the sun goes along picking up everyone's wishes, even the bad intentions of those who are evil."

With this in mind, the following morning when he went to pray, he begged the sun to somehow arrange for him to visit the place where the dead go. Each morning now he made this desire known to the sun.

On the fourth morning, just as he turned back toward the village, someone spoke to him. "Wait a minute," the voice said.

Much to his surprise, when he looked back he saw a stranger standing behind him. It was a man, very handsome in appearance. He was dressed most beautifully and covered with colorful body paint. Each time he moved, bright light reflected from him. In addition, his breath exuded warmth. The boy, staring at the stranger in wonderment, did not respond immediately. At last he asked, "Are you the one who spoke to me?"

"Yes, I came just to see you," he replied.

From all appearances, it was the sun, so the boy asked, "Very well, what do you want?"

"I'm sure you recognize me," Sun continued.

"Yes, it's clear who you are by your costume and your breath," the boy answered.

"I suppose that is so. But you have come to pray several times in the morning now and begged for something that is not pleasant. In your village all the young people your age lead happy lives. They have no desire to die just yet. Why on earth you want this is beyond me," Sun said to the boy.

"Indeed, for a long time I've had this curiosity about where people go after they pass on. Not that I wish to go there permanently. If only I could somehow find the way there, I could go there and see for myself. I'd very much like to learn what life is like there," the boy confessed.

"Is that right? Very well, then," Sun replied. "If you truly want this, you must follow my instructions. You must do exactly as I say," he warned the boy.

"All right, that's fine. I promise to do that, for I really do want to see this place," the boy said.

With that, Sun instructed the boy as follows. "For four full days I want you to make prayer sticks and prayer feathers. Make four of the double male and female prayer sticks that are painted black and green. The rest must be prayer feathers without the breath strand. Make plenty of these, to present to the dead as you go along. They will lack breath strands because the dead no longer have any breath. The morning after you have completed this task, return here and I will give you additional instructions." The boy took his eyes off Sun for just a second, and when he looked again, he was gone.

So the boy returned home. Upon his arrival, he decided not to inform his mother and father about this, for he was sure that they would be very upset with him. They would not want this for their son, so he said nothing to them, quickly ate his breakfast, and then left. He took along all the various materials that he would need to make the prayer items, and grabbed his tobacco pouch and pipe. It was his intention to seek out a place where he would be undetected, so he first went to a point southwest of the village and then descended to the foot of the mesa. As he reached a place directly below Pöqangwwawarpi, he stopped and carefully scanned the cliff there. There was a rock overhang there that was quite deep. He chose this place, for apparently no one ever came through that area. So he began to work on his pahos, and continued until evening. Then he stopped, and heaped all the ones he had made onto a tray and smoked upon them. After completing this ritual smoke, he bundled up the finished prayer items, carefully hid them in a crevice, and sealed the opening with a large rock. Then he headed home.

His family was already having their supper when he arrived. They asked him where he had been because he had been gone so long. "We were waiting for you to come, but when you did not show up, we went ahead and started eating. Your father was hungry when he came home, so we started supper without you," his mother explained.

"You did the right thing. It was my own fault that I didn't come home at an earlier hour. I was out hunting and didn't realize how far I had wandered out, so that's why I was late." This was all the boy had to say for himself as he joined the others at their supper.

He did not eat much as he had plans to go on a journey. He had no fear, but rather looked forward to it. So he ate just a little and after leaving the area where the food was laid out, he went out and climbed up to the second story. There he sat on his bedroll and pondered the matter. "I wonder what I'll see. Perhaps I'll see people I know." These and other thoughts occupied his mind, so he failed to notice that the hour had gotten late.

So he spread out his bedroll and lay down. As he was lying there, he continued to think about these things and did not fall asleep for a long while. But finally he became so tired that he fell asleep without realizing it. The following morning, when it was time to go out and pray to the sun, he realized what had happened and with a start jumped up from his bed. He quickly grabbed his pouch of sacred cornmeal, dashed down from the upper story of their home, and headed out to the northeast side of Oraibi. He took his usual route when he went out to pray, and prayed again that he might be shown how to get to Maski. When he was done, he headed back home.

This time, no one approached him, and nobody spoke with him before his ascent to the mesa top. As soon as he had eaten breakfast, he departed again without informing his parents of his plans. He headed back to the same overhang where he had been the day before making the pahos. Without delay he retrieved his bundle from the place where he had hidden it and again started working. He followed the same routine as the day before. He worked all day without even stopping at noon to eat. When the sun was low on the western horizon, he smoked over the products of his labor and carefully wrapped everything up into a bundle. Once again, he hid it in the crevice and returned home.

His family was already at supper when he entered. This time they didn't pry into what he had been up to, but only invited him to join them. Just as before, he did not fill himself too full before getting up. Again he climbed to the upper level of the house and sat there, mulling things over. When night fell, he bedded down and this time fell asleep a little earlier. This was the routine he followed for four days.

On the evening of the fourth day the boy took all the pahos he had made home with him. This time he arrived back at the village during the night and hid the prayer items in the house. When he entered the living quarters, he saw that his family had already eaten their evening meal and were putting the leftovers away, so he ate alone. Neither his mother nor his father said anything to him for being late.

The moment he had finished eating he was gone again. He climbed to the upper story of the house, took out his bundle, and unwrapped the pahos. Then he smoked over them. After finishing this ritual, he spread out his bed and lay down. He never fell into a deep sleep that night, and when the dawn came he noticed it right away. Quickly he rose and went out for his morning prayers. This time Sun was there waiting for him. "You have come, then?" he inquired.

"Yes," the boy replied.

"Very well. And are you willing to make this journey?"

"Yes, I am. That's why I followed your instructions."

"All right then. You will depart tonight. But you must tell one person what you intend to do. This person will be your younger sister. There will be an opportunity for the two of you to be alone, and then you can tell her. When you start out, you will first head in the direction of Apoonivi. From there you will go on to Awat'ovi. As you reach Apoonivi you will pass through a house. Exiting it on the northwest side, you will descend some stairs and then travel across the plain below to Awat'ovi. From there you will go to Hootatsomi, where I'll be waiting for you. Mark my words now. If you follow my instructions, no harm will befall you prior to reaching me. Some of the dead have not yet reached that place and still have a long way to go. Some died long ago but because of their wrongdoings are traveling at a slow pace. You're bound to come upon more than a few of these wretched ones. As you encounter them, they will speak to you and ask you for something. You must not heed their pleas, though. That's all I want to tell you now. And tonight when you are about to go to sleep, I want you to eat this." With that, Sun handed him something resembling a sweet corn cake wrapped in cornhusk. "As soon as you taste this, your soul will depart from your body. At that moment you will embark on your journey. Also, you must tell your sister that no one is to bother you the next day. No one must take away your death shroud nor touch your body. You will probably be back by the time it gets noon." That's all Sun said before disappearing.

The boy now headed straight home and ate with his family. He then ascended to the upper story to ready the things he would take along. It was not yet noon when he finished with his preparations. After lunch he returned to the upper story and waited for the proper time. He was so anxious that the passage of time seemed painfully slow. When evening finally came and it was time for them to eat, his mother came and invited him down to supper. This time he did not feel like returning to the upper story, so he remained there with them. To while away the time he taught his younger sister how to play cat's cradle. They played for several hours until it was dark outside. At one point the girl said to him, "My brother, please go with me to relieve myself. I'm afraid to go out by myself."

"Sure, I'll go with you," he readily agreed.

The two walked out of the door and headed northeast to the mesa edge. At the spot where the girl was relieving herself, the boy told his sister of his intentions. He revealed all of his plans to her and told her that he would be departing that night. Upon hearing this, the poor girl burst into tears. Her brother tried to calm her down. "That's enough. Don't worry too much. I will return." With that, his sister's crying abated somewhat. He then added, "There's one thing I need to tell you though. Tomorrow someone is bound to find my lifeless body. I am telling you this because I want you to rise early, so that when someone comes to move my body you can prevent them from doing that. Tell them exactly what I told you. And especially remember this one thing: When the sun is high in the sky, I am supposed to come back to life." His sister agreed to carry out his instructions, and with that, the two returned to the house.

As soon as the boy had escorted his sister back home, he told her that he was going to bed. He climbed up to the second story, opened the bundle of pahos, and smoked over them once more. Then he carefully wrapped it shut again and tied it to his waist. Next, he spread out his bedroll and lay down and covered himself. He then ate the entire piece of the qömi-like paste the Sun had given him and immediately fell into a deep sleep. From all appearances he was dead. He became aware of how his soul was departing from his body. Before long, his soul had completely separated. He glanced back now and saw his body lying there.

He looked at it for a long while, but then went on his way, for surely there was someone out there waiting for him. Quickly he descended from his house and headed in a northwesterly direction. Weightless, he was able to move along rapidly. On his way he came across an old woman he had known who had passed away long ago. And yet here she was, so close to the village still. As he came up to here, she greeted him. "You are also going along here?"

"Yes," he replied.

"Please, have pity on me. Load me on your back and carry me at least four steps along your path. Then you can put me down again," she pleaded.

The boy's reply was brief. "I don't think I can do that. I'm in a great hurry."

That's all he said and then continued on his way. As he was leaving, though, the poor old woman began to weep. It was then that he remembered his bundle of pahos, so he turned around and returned to her, opened his bundle, and gave her one of the prayer feathers. She was elated about the gift and thanked him profusely. Then he went on his way again.

Eventually, the boy came to the crest of Awat'ovi. He had just passed this landmark when, much to his surprise, he found another woman sitting there, crying. As he strode by her, she beseeched him like the old woman before. The plea she uttered was similar, but his reaction was the same. He rejected her plea and gave her one of his pahos instead. Then he pressed on. He did not encounter anyone else as he descended the northwestern slope of Awat'ovi and reached Hootatsomi. Upon his arrival there Sun was already waiting for him. "You have come?" he inquired.

"Yes," the boy replied.

"Very well. Let's not be tardy then, for daylight comes quickly this time of the year. Come here," he ordered the boy. Obediently, the boy stood next to him. Sun now spread something out before them. Evidently it was a plain white ceremonial kilt. He told the boy, "All right, climb aboard this with me. The least I can do is to get you closer to your destination. It's quite a distance to where you're going." The boy did as bidden and squatted down on the garment. Just as Sun climbed aboard, the kilt rose gently up into the air and flew off with the two.

As the magic kilt made its flight, it finally neared a large pool. The edges of this pool were flanked with a great many burden baskets filled to the brim with small pebbles. At this point Sun said to the boy, "Some of the people who are on their way to Maski carry these baskets on their backs. Here is the place where the baskets are selected and put on their backs. For that purpose they are set out there, ready to be picked up."

A short distance later Sun spoke again. "Young man, look down below. The people moving that way have been traveling for a long, long time, yet they have only come this far. A person who dies without any sin reaches his destination without delay, but those who have done wrong in their lifetime are burdened down with heavy loads. Witches especially are forced to go at a very slow pace. Anyone who acquires the knowledge of sorcery and then dies is permitted only one step a year. So, although some of these people died long ago, they have not advanced farther than this. In addition, those witches are surrounded by a stone wall as they move along. Whenever one who is pure of heart passes them by, they beg them for a drink of water. When their plea is denied, they say, 'At least spit into my mouth.' But their request is never granted. It is their own fault that they suffer so severely as they journey along."

The boy stared at all this in great amazement. For truly, countless people were moving along there. Some of the women and men were traveling with burden baskets on their backs. The baskets were filled with large amounts of pebbles so that they, poor things, were burdened down with them. The women had to carry their loads with the straps that were designed for men. They deeply gouged their foreheads and caused excruciating pain. The men, on the other hand, carried their baskets by means of cords that women use to tie their hair. These people are known as Wiiwintses. Whenever an unmarried man weds a married woman, he supposedly must have one of these baskets. The same applies to unwed women who marry married men. He also saw women walking along with large strands of penises about their necks. Then also there were men who had dangling from their necks large strands made up of vulvas. These were women and men who had married more than once.

As the two continued their journey on the flying kilt, they arrived at a place where a man was removing the clothing of some women. The boy didn't know what to make of this, so he asked the Sun, "Why is he taking away the clothing of those women?"

"Well, some of those women were married several times. When a woman marries only once, all the items her husband makes for her belong to her. Occasionally, for one reason or another, a woman will have more than one husband. When she marries a man who had a wife prior to her marriage, and he makes a piece of clothing for her, it really belongs to the first wife. It does not properly belong to the woman he is living with at that time. Therefore, when she arrives here wearing that apparel, that man down there takes it away from her," he explained.

All these things the boy observed as he traveled along accompanied by Sun. He was familiar with some of the men and knew that they had been married more than once. The same was true for some of the women.

Much to his surprise he also noticed that there were mules among the people. Struck by this oddity, he pondered it but didn't know what to make of it. Eventually, he couldn't help himself any longer and blurted out to Sun, "Why are there mules going alongside the people? I thought it was only humans that entered Maski."

Sun snickered and replied, "That's right, those mules are part of the crowd. In truth, they are Hopis. They are the ones who took a Zuni spouse. Whenever a Hopi marries someone from that tribe, he is transformed into a mule. Therefore the elders warn against marriages with Zunis." He did not mention marrying members of other tribes.

After flying over all these beings, the two finally landed. Sun said to the boy, "Now, this is as far as I will go with you. From here on you will have to travel alone for a while. You will soon meet someone else who will assist you. Remember, though, not to help anyone along your way. There will be people pleading with you for a favor. But do not give in to any of them, he instructed the boy. With that, he let him off the flying kilt.

Thoughtful as he was, the boy now handed Sun one of the multihued pahos that he had made. What joy this brought to Sun! "Thank you so much. This is what I desire most from all people, but they so seldom make them for me. I'm grateful you made enough pahos so there is one to spare for me. Don't tarry now, but hurry on, for morning comes quickly." With this advice Sun left him there.

The boy now journeyed on alone. The trail was clearly marked, and people could be seen traveling along this route. At one place he came upon an elderly woman enclosed by a stone wall. She begged him, "Young man, please give me a drink. I'm very thirsty." However, the boy refused, telling her that he was in a rush. At this, the old woman reworded her plea. "Then at least spit into my mouth," she asked. He remained steadfast. He only gave her one of his pahos and continued on. And sure enough, each time he overtook a person, some sort of favor was sought of him. But he acted according to Sun's instructions and did not grant anyone any favors.

Once again, he covered quite a distance before he arrived at a pile of ashes and trash. Much to his amazement, there were some children playing there. He was still a good ways off when they noticed him, and said to one another, "Someone else is coming." That's all they said, staring at him as he went by. Not a single word did they say to him, apparently enjoying themselves. A woman with a burden basket on her back followed right behind the boy. As the children spotted her they exclaimed, "Look, someone else is coming!" As before, they closely eyed the oncoming woman. As she drew closer, they noticed the basket on her back. "How awful, there's a Wiiwintse coming," the children yelled and scattered to hide. Anyone with such a load on their back was known as a Wiiwintse.

Pressing on past this place, the boy continued at a rapid pace, overtaking lots of people. Each time he passed a person, he bestowed one of his prayer feathers on them.

After a while he reached a place where he heard a strange noise. Halting in his tracks, he listened. It was a clacking noise he heard. As he went on, he aimed his steps toward the origin of the noise. As he drew nearer, he saw that it was a man who was walking around there, all garbed in white.

When he stepped up to the man, he realized that he was an Aala'ytaqa, a member of the Two Horn society. At least he was dressed much like the initiates of the Oraibi Two Horn society. He wore two horns that were painted white and had a large piece of buckskin draped about his shoulders. Around his waist he had a ceremonial kilt. And just like the Oraibi Two Horns, he was barefoot.

The man's body was not painted; instead, white kaolin dots ran down from the top of his shoulders to his waist on both sides. To these dots adhered bits of eagle fluff. From his knees down to his feet he was decorated in exactly the same manner. In his left hand he held a mongko, a stick denoting his affiliation with the Two Horn society. His right hand was free. In addition, he wore turtle shell rattles on both legs. They were what was producing the clacking noise the boy had heard as the Aala'ytaqa strode back and forth.

The spot where he was walking to and fro was right along the edge of a cliff. As the boy glanced down, he found that it was a sheer drop-off. "You are just going along here?" the Two Horn man asked the boy.

"Yes," he answered. "Are you waiting for me?"

"Indeed I am. But let's not waste time, for it will soon be daylight. I am to take you down this cliff, for that's the task assigned to me. I must take down whoever arrives at this place."

With that, he too spread out something before them and instructed the boy. "All right, climb on this thing with me. We'll use it to descend the cliff. There is no trail down this place, so no one can go down without my aid," he explained. The boy did as bidden and stepped on the thing after the Two Horn man.

No sooner had the two climbed aboard than the thing rose off the ground. It first took them a little ways beyond the rim of the cliff, and then began its descent with both of them aboard. It was such a long cliff that it took them a while to reach the ground below.

After getting off the magic flier, the boy looked around. The area was covered with blooming flowers as far as the eye could see. The Two Horn man said to the boy, "All right, from here on you must continue on your own. Soon, however, you will meet someone else who will help you." With that, he ascended the cliff using the magic flier.

So the boy started out again. It was easy to see where the trail was leading. After a good length of time he came to an area studded with many rock spires. The spires stood quite tall, and as he walked among them, he suddenly heard a voice. He was not sure where the voice was coming from, nor could he make out what it said, so he paused and strained his ears. Apparently, the voice came from one of the rock spires. There, at the top, sat a man, who had spoken to him. Once more he repeated his words, "Young man, how fortunate to see you this far along! Have pity on me and help me down from here."

But the boy turned a deaf ear. He was probably up there for a reason, so the boy merely said, "I don't think I can help you. I'm in a great hurry." That was all he said, and then he went on.

As he continued his trek he realized that numerous people were perched on top of these rock towers. They all pleaded with the boy to help them down, but he refused, and he finally left the area behind. The people sitting atop these pillars apparently were evil. They too had approached the Aala'ytaqa, but since he recognized their evil nature, he merely pretended to help them down into the abyss. Instead of flying them down, he would take them directly to one of the pillars, where he abandoned them. In this way, they were paying for their wrongdoings.

Once more the boy pressed on, and it was not long before he clearly heard the ringing of a bell. Without stopping, he headed straight toward the sound. This time he encountered a Kwaani'ytaqa, a member of the Kwan or One Horn society. The Kwan man greeted him and said, "You've arrived?"

"Yes, I have. Are you waiting for me?" the boy inquired.

"Yes, indeed. But let's be on our way, for the morning light comes quickly. I will personally lead you for a ways," he said, and took the boy by the hand.

Together they went on and had not traveled very far when they came upon a fork in the road. There the Kwan man said, "All right, this is as far as I can accompany you. But I will show you which road to choose. One of them leads directly to your destination, the other does not. Onto that road I usher all the evil ones. You must take the other road. Also, you will meet someone else who will lead you to your next station. Make sure you don't stray off this trail, though." The Kwan man showed him the right trail to take and left him standing there.

Once more the boy set out alone. As he went on his way, he kept an eye on the other trail. Sure enough, there were people on it, and like some of the others, they were burdened by such things as baskets, vulvas, or penises. No doubt, those were evil people. Their road was rough and strewn with rocks. Plants with burrs or thorns grew in its midst, and tall cacti grew on both sides of it. While not so thick that they prevented seeing the other road, the cacti still prevented anyone from switching from one trail to the other. So those poor souls had to keep to that road.

At some point along his way, the boy heard the ringing of a bell again. This meant that he must be nearing his next station. So, without stopping, he briskly moved along. Sure enough, he found himself confronted by another member of the Kwan society, who had obviously been waiting for him there. "You've arrived?" the man inquired.

"Yes," the boy replied.

"All right, I'm glad you've made it. I've been waiting for you for quite some time, so come with me. It's been some time since you left your body. This time of the year, morning comes quickly. Let's not tarry, but press on." With that he grasped the boy's wrist and led the way. Soon the two came to a kiva. "We need to stop here first," he told the boy. At the kiva top he took the boy on his back and in this manner entered the kiva with him. Inside, he let the boy down to the right of the entrance ladder. At first the boy had difficulty making out the interior of the kiva. All he could see was the glow from the fire pit. As his eyes became accustomed to the dark and he scanned his surroundings, he realized they had entered a real kiva. Right underneath the entrance ladder was a fire pit around which some elderly men were squatting. No one had yet spoken a word to them. They were still engaged in their ritual smoking. Eventually, one of the men asked, "Have you brought him?"

"Yes," the Kwan man replied, "he's standing here alongside me." He spoke in such a low tone that the boy was barely able to discern his words.

The old men were all clad in old, worn kilts. The downy feathers adorning their hair were equally ragged. As the boy looked at their faces, he seemed to recognize some of them. One of the old men he knew for sure. He was the former village chief of Oraibi, who had been dead for seven years. According to the Oraibi people he had truly been a good leader. Under his leadership the Oraibis had not quarreled with one another, nor had they lacked anything. Apparently, only old Kwan society leaders occupied this place around the fire pit.

Their voices were low as they spoke to one another. No one used a strident tone. That's the way it was in the main kivas of the Hopi villages. Finally, one of the old-timers said to the boy, "All right, come down and have a seat here in front of us."

With that, the man at the extreme southwestern end took his pipe and filled it with tobacco. Then they all started smoking, handing the pipe from one person to the next. By the time it reached the last man, the tobacco in the pipe was almost gone. When he was finished, he passed the pipe back to the one who had lit it. He, in turn, smoked up the rest and then said, "All right, I hope they caught the fragrance." The others now picked up their rattles and, shaking them, commenced to chant.

The person at the extreme southwestern end now took the boy by the hand and led him to a spot northwest of the fire pit. There he ordered him to stoop over. He was still bent forward when a cumulus cloud floated into the kiva and hovered directly above the boy. Next, there was a loud thunderclap and then rain began to pour from the cloud. Apparently the old men meant to wash the boy's hair and they did this with the help of the rain. Next, they had the boy stand in front of them so that they could smoke over him. When they had finished, the old man said to him, "All right, there is still another place you need to visit. So don't waste any time, hurry on. At your home far away, dawn is nearing. This man here will lead you. So go with strength." With that, the boy and his guide left the kiva.

This time, the boy was not carried piggyback. As the two made their exit, they headed in a new direction. Before long they neared a place from where a glow of light came. Upon reaching the place, it turned out to be a pit oven in the middle of nowhere. Beside it squatted a person who was stoking the fire inside. Huge flames were leaping up from the oven, and the heat from it was tremendous. The two stopped, and soon eight people appeared from out of nowhere, headed for the fire pit. They positioned themselves, two each at the four directions, one behind the other, facing the pit.

The boy didn't know what to make of this. He had no idea what they were up to, nor did he bother to ask his guide. On the northwest side a man stood in the front position. On the southwest side, a woman was in this position. On the southeast, a man was at the front again, and on the northeast a woman was at the front. Those standing in the front were stark naked. After a while the person in charge of tending the fire said, "All right, when I give the word, you on the northwest begin. Next, it will be the turn of the one on the southwest, then that of the one on the southeast, and finally yours on the northeast." Suddenly, he commanded, "Now, throw them in!" At this, the designated people took their turns pushing their victims into the burning pit, beginning with the one on the northwest side and continuing around the pit. All this the boy witnessed there. Whenever one was cast in, a large puff of smoke rose from the oven.

After they had performed this, the Kwan man said to the boy, "All right, come over here and take a look into this pit." The boy did as bidden and stepped up to the edge of the pit. There, at its very bottom, he saw a black stinkbug, scurrying about.

But he found no trace of a human being inside the pit, nor did he spot any bones or other remains. Now the Kwan man explained, "Those people who were thrown into the pit were evil. They practiced sorcery while alive. Those who flung them in were the ones who died an early death because of them. It was not yet their time to die, but they were killed by those witches. The witches prolonged their lives by killing those people. If anyone with such great powers wants to get out of the burning pit, he transforms himself into a creature such as a fly or a stinkbug. Of course, a stinkbug is of no use for anything," he said. "Now, there is yet another place you need to see." Billowing smoke was still coming out of the pit oven and the entire area was filled with smoke. They had no choice but to go through it. So again the Kwan man took the boy by the hand and guided him along.

After their departure, new groups of people were herded to the pit. But the boy did not bother to look over his shoulder. He knew that they would meet the same fate as the others. As they passed through the smoke, the Kwan man explained that it stemmed from the burned bodies of the evil ones, which gave off an unusual amount of smoke. So much smoke filled the air that no light shone for quite a distance.

Soon thereafter they emerged from the darkness into the light again. Once more the air was clear, and as the boy looked about, he saw flowering fields in every direction. As they walked through them, all sorts of winged creatures flew about. There were the various songbirds, chirping their particular melodies, and there were butterflies and hummingbirds fluttering about amid the flowers. The hummingbirds were hovering, happily humming and sucking the nectar of the flowers. Cicadas could be heard chirping all over. The weather was so nice and warm that life there was pleasant. It was like the middle of summer except that it was not so humid.

Then, as the two traveled on, they came upon a field in which were growing large amounts of many different plants. The boy had never seen any field quite like this before. Everything imaginable was growing there. He saw watermelons and muskmelons and their vines were spread out all around. There were also squashes growing there, their round shapes jutting up through the vines. The stalks of corn stood tall, with tassels at their tops and long ears protruding from their leaves. Different kinds of beans, too, were there in large amounts. How he wanted to have such a marvelous field of his own! Surprisingly, there were no weeds visible among these plants. The field was so huge that it took them quite a while to traverse it. When they had, they came to a village.

It turned out to be a very large settlement, and as they approached it, the Kwan man said to the boy, "You can stay here for four days. During this time you'll be able to realize all your dreams of what life is like here. Back at your home white dawn has not yet appeared over the horizon. You will have four days here, before the sun rises there. So don't be bashful, go about and talk to the villagers as much as you'd like. They are not evil and will not ask you to do anything improper. I have to go now. So enter the village and enjoy yourself. Don't let anything trouble you. You won't come out of your death before you return. So don't worry about things back at home while you are here." That's all he told him, and then he departed.

On his own initiative, the boy now entered the village and walked about among the homes. The place was teeming with people. Every time someone came toward him, they would gaze at him, but no one had recognized him yet. Since they did not know him, they simply greeted him by saying, "You have just arrived? Fine, settle down like the rest of us and be happy here." That's all they ever said. He soon discovered that the people there were most cordial. Outside of the houses the children were playing. Some of them were snacking on such delicious things as freshly roasted corn, corn baked in pit ovens, boiled corn, muskmelons, watermelons, and the other crops harvested by people there. As he continued through the village, he encountered an old woman. "How nice to see you here," she exclaimed.

"Yes," the boy replied.

"Haven't you met anyone yet that you know?"

"No," he answered, but then he recognized her. It had not been a year since she had died. The old woman further questioned him, "That's odd. How is it that you're walking about here without a prayer feather adorning your hair?"

The boy was perplexed. "What could she mean by asking about this?" he wondered. "Am I supposed to be wearing something in my hair?" he inquired.

"Well, when a person dies, his relatives usually make a prayer feather for the deceased before they bury him," she explained.

The boy was familiar with this custom, but had never given it any thought. It was only now, when she asked him, that he thought about it. So he replied, "I'm going to return back home soon." And then he related to her how he used to go out and greet the sun with his fervent wish and how the sun had helped him to make this journey possible.

"Is that how it is?" the old woman asked. "Very well, then. And you haven't yet met an acquaintance?"

"No, you're the only one I've recognized so far."

The woman next inquired which village he was from, so he explained that he was from Oraibi. She then began questioning him as to who his parents and relatives were, and this he also let her know.

"I see. In that case, I'll escort you to your grandmother's home. She lives with your grandfather only a short way from here. I'm sure you don't know them. I don't believe you were born yet when they died, one right after the other. Your grandfather passed away first, and your grandmother, who missed him, followed soon thereafter. Come on, I'll take you to them," she said and led him off.

Soon they came to a house. Leading the boy, the old woman entered without announcing their coming. They were warmly welcomed by another old woman. "All right, have a seat. I'm surprised to see that you have someone with you."

"That's right, I came upon him northeast of here. He is your daughter's son. I pointed out to him that he was lacking the feather in his hair. But he tells me that he will be returning to the land of the living."

No sooner had the other old woman heard this than she embraced the boy, expressing her happiness. Right away she entered a back room, and came out with an old man. When she told him who the boy was, he too greeted him happily.

The boy still had not given away all his prayer feathers, so he gave one to the old woman who had brought him to his grandparents. Delighted with the precious gift, she took her leave.

The boy's grandparents now began to set out food for their grandchild. They brought out many things and placed them before him. They were an old couple, but they did not appear to live in want. So the boy sat down and started eating. He was anxious to sample all the foods, so he took a little bit of everything. To him it seemed a little wasteful, but in this manner he ate his fill. When he was finished, his grandparents asked him about life in Oraibi. They also wanted to know if he had any siblings, so he mentioned his younger sister. They kept plying him with all sorts of questions. In this way the boy came to know his grandmother and grandfather.

While he stayed with his grandparents, he would go out every so often and tour the village. What he discovered was awesome. He found that the people there were living a good life and that they were always happy. They also treated one another with respect and kindness, and whenever two people met, they had something polite to say to each other.

Every time he went about and met someone, he was asked which village he was from. When people found out that he was from Oraibi, they would inquire about those they had known and how they were faring. Others who had known him as a baby greeted him with great joy.

The fields there, full of lushly growing crops, made him envious as he explored them. They provided an ample food supply, so everybody had plenty to eat. From the crops he moved on to a huge field of sunflowers. He noticed that children were playing in it and having a good time. They kept climbing up and down on the stalks. As he stood there observing them, one of the children approached the boy and asked him to join them in their play. He declined the offer, but the child was so persistent that he finally gave in. He went up to them and at first only watched. Then another child prompted him, "Now, you have a turn."

Deciding to take a chance, no matter what happened, he tried to climb the sunflower, but it would not support him. Once more he tried, but again it could not bear his weight and collapsed. The children kept laughing at his futile attempts, but eventually they said, "You'll never be able to climb on that. We were merely teasing you when we urged you on. Only we who live here can climb these sunflowers because we are only souls and weigh nothing. That's also the reason why the ladders at our village are made from sunflower stalks."

Early in the morning on the fourth day of his stay there, the boy's grandparents said to him, "All right, you must get up and start back. At your home they are getting restless because they cannot revive you. You'll have to go without breakfast." So the boy had no choice but to get out of bed and get dressed.

His heart was not set on returning at all. He had gotten used to the good life there. But since they only allotted him four days, he obeyed and started out without eating. He had barely gone beyond the village boundary when he encountered the Kwan man again. He said to the boy, "I've been waiting for you for quite some time. You are late. The sun is probably just rising at your home, and people there are anxiously awaiting your return." Unfortunately, this time I can't escort you back myself. You'll have to go alone for a while. But you'll meet the person who will get you to the top of the cliff. Make sure you don't get tempted by anything as you leave. I know you haven't eaten yet and must be hungry, but if you eat anything on your way home, you won't live long after your return. That's why your grandparents did not feed you before they sent you off this morning." The Kwan man then urged, "All right, then, go without delay," whereupon the boy dashed off as fast as he could run.

By the time he reached the village fields, his hunger got the best of him. At first he tried not to pay any attention to the crops, but he saw so many delicious and appealing things that he craved food. He had the best intentions, but when he came to the melon patch he couldn't hold back any longer. He broke one off the vine, opened it, and feasted on it.

Then he continued his journey home. Now that he had some food in his stomach, he felt stronger. He had not forgotten the route he had traveled, so when he reached the place that was filled with smoke, he managed to get to the other side without any difficulty, even though he could barely see. As he ran past the fiery pit oven, there were still evil people being hurled into the flames. However, he pressed on without stopping.

Before long he came to the kiva. This time he did not enter, but continued right along. Eventually, he came to a group of children who asked him where he was going. He told them that he was returning home, but they replied that that would be impossible. The boy paid no heed to their warnings and ran on. Finally, he reached the place of the rock pillars. Just as before, there were Hopis perched on top of them. Once more they shouted their pleas to him, but without listening to them, he passed on by. At long last he stood in front of the precipitous cliff.

The person who had helped him down was expecting him. "You've returned?" he greeted the boy. "I've been waiting for you for quite a while. At your home they have found your corpse. Your sister told them exactly what you instructed her to say, but they don't believe her. So let's not waste any more time, because there's another person waiting for you up above. Come on, hurry. Your sister is anxious for you to return."

Once again the man spread out his flying thing, which flew them up the cliff. As they arrived at the top, Sun was already waiting for the boy. "You've brought him back then?" he asked the One Horn man.

"Yes, so you two hurry on, for the boy's relatives are getting nervous," he replied to Sun.

"That's true, it's already late in the morning. I thought he'd get here sooner. That's why I came much earlier. So let's be on our way," he said, whereupon the boy climbed aboard Sun's flier.

They rose into the air and flew off toward Apoonivi. Looking down, the boy could still see the people traveling this route. Some were hauling burden baskets and appeared not to be making much headway. At Apoonivi they passed again through the house on top and then headed in the direction of Oraibi. Sun let the boy off at the northwestern edge of the village. Then he said, "All right, you have had your wish fulfilled. You wanted this, so we have helped you realize your dream. From here on you must go by yourself. It's late in the morning and you've not yet returned. Your sister is unable to control your relatives any longer. They are eager to pull away your shroud." With that, Sun departed, and the boy hurried on toward the village. His greatest desire had now been achieved, and he had experienced many wondrous things.

As soon as he arrived at his home, he rushed up to the upper story. As he entered he found his relatives assembled there, crying. His sister was still trying to impress upon them what he had told her. "He definitely told me to wait and not to uncover him. He said he would come back to life on his own. He was very firm when he gave me these instructions last night." She repeated this over and over, but by now they were almost beyond restraint. He had been lying there without moving for much too long.

The boy now quickly slipped under his cover and began to stir. One of his family noticed this and cried out, "Look, I think he moved a little bit!"

Sure enough, all eyes were upon him as he began to stir. "Maybe he's not quite dead yet," someone said.

With that, they removed his death shroud. No sooner had they lifted it than the boy started getting up. "Thank goodness, we have you back," his father cried. "We were just about to go and bury you. I guess you had left instructions with your sister, but her story sounded so incredible that we didn't believe it. I'm so glad you did not journey there for good." He embraced his son, and now everybody else came toward him, weeping tears of joy.

After they all recovered, they fixed the boy a meal that he devoured with great appetite. Even though he had eaten the melon, he woke up with a craving for food.

The boy now told his parents and relatives, in great detail, about his adventure. They listened attentively to the wondrous tale he had brought back. Then the other villagers learned of this, and they too came flocking to the boy's home. They were curious, of course, whether he had by chance met any of their loved ones. If that was the case and he had indeed conversed with any of them, he let the inquirer know, without having to lie, that the person was doing well. He also mentioned that people were all very happy in the land of the dead. There was no need, he said, to worry about a deceased person who had been good. On the other hand, if he found that the person in question was an evildoer, he made an excuse and pretended not to have seen him. Eventually, people stopped coming to the boy's home and life went on as before.

Then one day the poor boy really died. Of course, the Kwan man had warned him specifically not to eat any fruit from the field or he would not have long to live. This turned out to be true. Now his family really had to bury him. Four days later, when he regained consciousness, he found himself inside a small chamber. He was all curled up with his knees flexed to his chest in a fetal position. As he looked about, he saw a ladder sticking out of the top of the chamber. Climbing up it, he emerged from his grave and scanned the surrounding area. Nearby, there were other ladders in the same position. He departed and headed directly northwest. He knew where Oraibi was, but he passed it by and soon came to Apoonivi. As before, he entered the house on top and then made his exit on the northwest end. From there he continued on toward Awat'ovi. At some point along his journey he thought, "Perhaps I'm going back to my grandmother and grandfather, for this is the same route I traveled before. Also, I remember that a good person, who dies without sin, gets to that place without delay." He had not encountered anyone prior to reaching the Two Horn man, who then helped him make his descent down the steep cliff. It now appeared to him as if he was not moving very rapidly, but he did not let it worry him. After all, this time he was on his own, so his progress was naturally much slower. Not once did he stop to rest, because he wanted to arrive quickly at his destination.

After a while, it struck him that he was indeed not moving very fast. He tried to increase his pace, but to no avail, so he had no choice but to go at the speed permitted to him. Once in a while he was overtaken by someone advancing much more swiftly. He attempted to stop one of these people by shouting at him, but in vain. No one even paused for him. Perhaps they thought of him as being evil; after all, he was moving along at a slow pace. In turn, when he overtook another person and was asked for a favor, he simply ignored the plea and pressed on.

Meanwhile, the boy became tired. He thought of stopping and resting for a while, but then reconsidered. "Why waste my time resting here? Who knows, if I stop here, that stop may become permanent." These and other thoughts crossed his mind.

Eventually, he reached the large pond with the many burden baskets filled to the brim with pebbles. He was aware, of course, that as an unmarried man, he did not have to fear this place.

It had been quite some time since his arrival there. At least seven days had gone by since his death, perhaps more. On his journey with Sun this place had not seemed to be far from Oraibi. Knowing that he had still a long way to go, he hurried on. Soon he began overtaking people with burden baskets on their backs. Then there were the men with vulvas and the women with penises hanging around their necks. Now and then he also passed a mule. By the time he reached the huge cliff, twenty days had passed. As he was drawing nearer, he could clearly hear the turtle shell rattle of the

Two Horn man and the clacking noise he was making. Apparently, he already knew of the boy's return and had been expecting him for some time. "You've come?" he asked.

"Yes, I had a hard time getting here. I didn't think it would take this long. I have no idea what has been slowing me down," the boy replied.

"Well, your own relatives can do that to you," the Two Horn man explained.

The boy didn't know what he meant, so he asked, "Really? Why is that?"

"Because you were still young when you died, they won't forget you so soon. It was their crying that slowed you down. Not until they stop lamenting your death will you reach your destination. But that's the way people are. When they lose a loved one and cry over his loss all the time, they hold him back after death," he explained.

"Is that right? What a shame. Couldn't I go back perhaps and make them aware of this?" he asked.

"Yes, we may let you do this, since you died pure of heart. Wait here for me while I go to find out what the others think of this idea." With that, the Two Horn man descended the cliff.

Before long he reappeared and said to the boy, "All right, this man here will be your guide and accompany you back. I must still help others down this cliff. That's why I can't go with you. Now, call your transportation," he ordered the guide.

This guide was about the same age as the boy. He had a small pouch hanging from his waist from which he took a whistle. He blew it and before long a large bird was winging toward them. When it got closer, he could see that it was an enormous eagle. "Come on," the guide said to the boy. "We'll use this bird. He'll take us back in a short time. With that they both climbed on the eagle and sat down, one behind the other. Next, the guide commanded the eagle, "Go!" and the bird took off, carrying both of them aloft.

The eagle was so strong that he easily carried the two passengers. While they were flying along, the guide instructed the boy what to do when they arrived at Oraibi. The boy listened carefully to his instructions. Soon they were nearing Apoonivi. The boy had focused all his attention on what the guide was telling him and didn't notice where they were traveling. According to the guide, they were back at Apoonivi already, but they were not moving as fast as on Sun's magic vehicle.

Flying directly over Apoonivi, they headed straight southeast and then landed at a field near Oraibi. The guide said to the boy, "This is as far as I'm taking you. Now you must go on your own. If you follow my instructions, you'll be back right away." With that, he flew off in a northwesterly direction. As the boy looked after him, the guide on his eagle quickly disappeared over the northwest side of Apoonivi.

As instructed, the boy did not enter the village, but instead went first to check on his father's field. His father would probably be there, trying to put the death of his son out of his mind by hoeing weeds.

At one point along the way, he looked at himself and saw that he had grown feathers and wings. He had actually been transformed into a snipe. His guide had informed him that he could not appear in front of his father in human form. So now he flew to his father's field. Sure enough, once he alighted at the edge of the field, he spotted his father working there. He appeared to be troubled, for he went about his work in complete silence. The boy knew that it was his nature to always sing as he did his chores.

When the boy realized this he felt sorry for him, so he approached his father and scurried back and forth right next to him. His father, however, whose mind was filled with other thoughts, paid no attention to the bird. When he saw this, the boy began to chirp and kept chirping until his father noticed. At first he only stared at the bird, but then he said "You are hopping around here with a happy heart? All right, go ahead. I won't bother you. You don't need to be afraid of me."

Now the boy ceased fluttering around and replied, "My father, it is I, your son." The man immediately ceased his work, but didn't say anything. "Father, it is I, Honanyestiwa. I came back to tell you something, so don't interrupt. Listen carefully to me."

With that, he explained how he had been slowed down on his way to the Maski because they were crying over his death. "So when you get home, inform the others not to weep anymore. The sooner I get to my destination, the happier I'll be. I know you all miss me, but somehow I'll come back and check in on you from time to time. We're all going there eventually. So never let thoughts about me trouble you, and live harmonious lives. If you do that, then one day we'll all meet again." That's all the boy said, and then he flew off.

That day, after the father told the others what he had learned, they did not weep as much as before. The boy then began to advance much faster. Thus, it was only a short time before he arrived at his destination. He sought out his grandmother and grandfather, who were overjoyed to have him back. They sympathized with the boy's parents and relatives but were glad because they were no longer alone. From that time on, the boy stayed there permanently.

At Oraibi, the boy's relatives put him out of their minds and carried on with their lives. Perhaps they still live there. This was how the boy learned about the road to the Maski and how he returned to it after his death.

And here the story ends.

Chapter 19

The Third Place

Jacques Le Goff

In the bitter disputes that pitted Protestants against Catholics in the sixteenth century, the former severely reproached the latter for their belief in Purgatory, to which Luther referred as "the third place." This "invented" world—the "other world"—is not mentioned in the Bible.

The aim of this book is to trace the formation of the idea of this third place through time, from its roots in Judeo-Christian antiquity to its final emergence with the flowering of medieval civilization in the second half of the twelfth century, when the idea of Purgatory finally took hold in the West, and beyond, into the next century. I shall try to explain why the idea of Purgatory is intimately bound up with this important moment in the history of Christendom and to show, further, the crucial role that Purgatory played in persuading people to accept (or, in the case of the heretics, to reject) the new society that was the result of two and one-half centuries of prodigious growth following the year 1000.

WHAT WAS AT STAKE?

It is rare that we can follow the historical development of a belief, even if—as is the case with Purgatory—it is made up of many very ancient elements, whose origins often seem to be lost in the depths of time. But belief in Purgatory is no mere adjunct, no minor addition to the great edifice whose foundations were first laid by primitive Christianity and which eventually developed into the medieval Church. Ideas about the other world are among the more prominent features of any religion or society. The life of the believer undergoes a change when he becomes convinced that life does not end with death.

The gradual emergence—or perhaps one should say, the lengthy construction—of the doctrine of Purgatory at once required and entailed a substantial modification in the spatial and temporal framework of the Christian imagination. Such mental structures are the framework within which society lives and thinks. In a society as thoroughly permeated with religion as was the Christian West from the end of antiquity down to the industrial revolution—an epoch to which I refer, with some license, as the "Middle Ages" in the broad sense—to change the geography of the other world and hence of the universe, to alter time in the afterlife and hence the link between earthly, historical time and eschatological time, between the time of existence and the time of anticipation—to do these things was to bring about a gradual but nonetheless crucial intellectual revolution. It was, literally, to change life itself.

Clearly, the emergence of such a belief is associated with far-reaching social change. The new way of thinking about the other world was related to specific changes in this one. What were these changes? What ideological role did Purgatory play? The fact that the Church exerted tight control over the new doctrine, going so far as to divide power over the other world between itself and God, shows that the stakes were high. Why not leave the dead to wander as they will, or to rest in peace?

BEFORE PURGATORY

Purgatory did indeed come to prominence as a "third place." Christianity inherited from earlier religions and civilizations a geography of the other world. Two models were set before it: Christianity might well have followed Judaism in choosing a monistic other world—*sheol*—rather than a dualistic one like the Roman Hades and Elysian Fields, the former a place of terror, the latter of happiness. But it adopted the dualistic model and even accentuated some of its features. Rather than send all the dead, good and bad alike, to repose underground for some portion of the interval between Creation and the Day of Judgment, Christianity decided that the just would reside in Heaven from the moment of their death. That is, at least some of them would—namely, the best: the martyrs and later the saints. Christianity even identified a place on the surface of the earth as the location of the Earthly Paradise. Thus Christianity took the ancient myth of a Golden Age and assigned it a place and not, as the ancients had been content to do, just a time, a nostalgic memory of the good old days. The Earthly Paradise figures on medieval maps in the Far East, beyond the great wall and the fearsome inhabitants of Gog and Magog. Through it flowed a four-branched river created by Yahweh "to water the garden" (Gen. 2:10). What is more, Christianity pushed the contrast between Heaven and Hell to the limit, drawing an analogy between Heaven and Hell on the one hand and earth and sky on the other. Though underground, Hell was still identified with earth, and in the Christian mind the infernal world contrasted with the celestial world, just as in the Greek mind the chthonic world contrasted with the uranian. Despite occasional impulses to look heavenward, the Ancients—Babylonians and Egyptians, Jews and Greeks, Romans and pagan barbarians—had been more afraid of the depths of the earth than drawn to the vastness of the sky, which in any case was often inhabited by angry gods. Christianity, in the first few centuries at any rate and subsequently during the medieval barbarization, did not try to focus attention exclusively on Hell. Rather, it lifted up man's eyes toward Heaven. Jesus himself had shown the way: after descending into Hell, he went up to Heaven. Whereas the Greeks and Romans had emphasized the contrast between right and left in their spatial symbolism, Christianity, while not abandoning a distinction mentioned in both the Old and New Testaments, nevertheless quickly accorded pride of place to the opposition between high and low. Throughout the Middle Ages it was the latter that oriented the inner dialectic of Christian values whenever thought was translated into spatial terms.

To ascend, to raise oneself, to move higher—the direction in which the compass of moral and spiritual life pointed was up, whereas in social life the norm was to stay in one's proper place, where God had placed one on this earth, guarding against ambition to escape one's condition while at the same time taking pains not to lower oneself, not to fail.

When, between the second and fourth centuries, Christianity set itself to thinking about the situation in which souls find themselves between the death of the individual and the Last Judgment, and when, in the fourth century, the greatest Fathers of the Church conceived of the idea (shared, with minor differences as we shall see, by Ambrose, Jerome, and Augustine) that certain sinners might be saved, most probably by being subjected to a trial of some sort, a new belief was born, a belief that gradually matured until in the twelfth century it became the belief in Purgatory; but the place where these souls were to reside and where this trial was to take place was not yet specified. Until the end of the twelfth century the noun *purgatorium* did not exist: *the* Purgatory had not yet been born.

It is a remarkable fact that the first appearance of the word *purgatorium*, expressing a newly acquired awareness of Purgatory as a place and thus the birth of Purgatory per se, has been neglected by historians, and in the first place by historians of theology and spirituality. Historians doubtless do not yet attach sufficient importance to words. The clerics of the Middle Ages knew better: whether realists or nominalists, they knew that words and things are as closely connected as soul and body. For historians of ideas and of *mentalités*, historians of the *longue durée*, historians of the deeply rooted and the slowly changing, words—certain words—offer the advantage of making their appearance at specific points in time. Their introduction can be dated with reasonable accuracy, thus providing the historian with valuable chronological evidence, without which no true history is possible. Of course a belief cannot be dated in the same way as an event, but the idea that the history of the *longue durée* is a history without dates is to be firmly rejected. A slowly developing phenomenon such as the belief in Purgatory may lie stagnant for centuries, or slowly ebb and flow, only to burst forth suddenly—or so it seems—in a kind of tidal wave that does not engulf the original belief but rather testifies to its presence and power. Anyone, however erudite, who uses the word purgatory in speaking of the period between the fall of the Roman Empire and the thirteenth century is missing an important point, perhaps the crucial point in the history of the idea: its spatialization, which first found expression in the appearance of the substantive sometime between 1150 and 1200. Worse still, he is missing an opportunity to shed some light on certain far-reaching social changes associated with a critical era in the history of medieval Christendom. And he is missing an opportunity to touch on one of the most important episodes in the whole history of ideas and *mentalités:* what I shall call the "spatialization" of thought.

SPACE: "GOOD TO THINK"

The idea that space plays an important part in scientific thought is a familiar one. Recent work on the history of this idea has done much to revitalize such disciplines as "geographical history," geography, and urban history. The potency of the idea of space manifests itself above all in symbolism. Following the zoologists, anthropologists have demonstrated the fundamental importance of territoriality. In *The Hidden Dimension,* Edward T. Hall has shown that for humans and animals territory is an extension of the organism itself and, further, that the perception of space depends in large part on culture (indeed, on this point he may be too much of a "culturalist") and that the idea of "territory" is an internalization of space, organized by thought. The way in which different societies organize "space"—geographic space, economic space, political space, and ideological space—has an important bearing on their history. Organizing the space of the other world had lasting consequences for Christianity. If one is looking forward to the resurrection of the dead, the geography of the other world is of no small moment. Indeed, it seems reasonable to suppose that there is a connection between the way Christian society lays out the other world and the way it organizes this one, since the two are related by the ties that bind the society of the living to the society of the dead. Between 1150 and 1300, Christendom gave itself over to a wholesale revision of the maps of both this world and the other. To Christians it seemed that things lived and moved here below as in the hereafter, more or less at the same pace.

THE LOGIC AND THE GENESIS OF PURGATORY

What exactly was Purgatory when, between 1150 and 1200 or so, it installed itself firmly in the mind of Western Christendom? Briefly, it was an intermediary other world in which some of the dead were subjected to a trial that could be shortened by the prayers, by the spiritual aid, of the living. But before the concept achieved this degree of specificity, a long prior history was necessary, a history of ideas and images, of beliefs and deeds, of theological debates and, as seems probable, of profound, hard-to-grasp social change.

The first part of this book will be devoted to the formation of the various elements that would finally be assembled in the twelfth century into what we know as Purgatory. It may be regarded as a reflection on the originality of the religious thought of Latin Christendom, a reflection on the traditions, discontinuities, and conflicts both internal and external out of which the theology of the Christian West was constructed.

Belief in Purgatory implies, in the first instance, belief in immortality and resurrection, since something new may happen to a human being between his death and resurrection. It offers a second chance to attain eternal life. Finally, belief in Purgatory entails the belief that immortality can be achieved in the life of a single individual. Thus religions such as Hinduism and Catharism, which believe in perpetual reincarnation and metempsychosis, cannot accommodate the idea of a Purgatory.

The existence of a Purgatory also depends on the idea that the dead are judged, an idea shared by any number of religions, though, to be sure, "the forms of judgment have varied widely from one civilization to another." The particular form of judgment that allows for the existence of a Purgatory is quite a novel one. In fact, two judgments are involved: one at the time of death and a second at the end of time. In between—in the eschatological interlude, as it were—every human soul becomes involved in complex judicial proceedings concerning the possible mitigation of penalties, the possible commutation of sentences, subject to the influence of a variety of factors. Belief in Purgatory therefore requires the projection into the afterlife of a highly sophisticated legal and penal system.

Furthermore, belief in Purgatory is associated with the idea of individual responsibility and free will. Though guilty by nature because of original sin, man is judged for the sins he himself is responsible for committing. There is a close connection between Purgatory, the "intermediary hereafter," and a type of sin that falls between the purity of the saints and the saved on the one hand and the unpardonable culpability of criminal sinners on the other. For a long time there had been a rather vague notion of "slight," "routine," or "habitual" sins, as Augustine and Gregory the Great were well aware, but it was not until shortly before the emergence of Purgatory that this idea finally gave rise to the category of sin known as "venial"—indeed, this was a prerequisite for the emergence of the doctrine of Purgatory. Broadly speaking, Purgatory developed as the place where venial sins might be expurgated—though in reality things were a bit more complicated, as we shall see.

In order to believe in Purgatory—a place of punishment—one must have a clear understanding of the relation between the soul and the body. From very early times Church doctrine on this point was as follows: the immortal soul separates from the body at death and is rejoined with it only at the end of time, when the body is resurrected. As I see it, however, the question whether the soul is corporeal or incorporeal seems not to have posed a problem for the development of Purgatory or its forerunners. Once separated from the body, the soul was endowed with a materiality *sui generis*, and punishment could then be inflicted upon it in Purgatory as though it were corporeal.

THE IDEA OF THE INTERMEDIATE

Purgatory is situated in a position that is intermediate in more than one sense. In respect of time it falls between the death of the individual and the Last Judgment. But before settling in this location, as it were, Purgatory had first to pass through a period of uncertainty. Though Augustine played a crucial role in locating the time of purgation, he himself never moored Purgatory firmly to any berth in the beyond. Whether the time of Purgatory was earthly time or eschatological time long remained a matter of controversy: Purgatory might begin here below in the form of penitence, only to be completed in the hereafter with a definitive purification at the time of the Last Judgment. But, later, Purgatory began to encroach on eschatological time, and Judgment Day, once a mere moment, swelled to fill a large expanse of time.

Spatially, Purgatory is also in an in-between position, between Hell and Paradise. Yet for a long time it tended to be confused with one or the other pole. Before it could begin to exist in its own right, Purgatory had to supersede both the *refrigerium*, that antechamber to Paradise invented by the early Christians, and the "bosom of Abraham" mentioned in the story of Lazarus and the wicked rich man in the New Testament (Luke 16:19–26). Above all it had to detach itself from Hell, of which it long remained a relatively undistinguished department, a sort of upper Gehenna. This wrangling between Hell and Paradise suggests that to Christians Purgatory was no minor issue. Before Dante could map the other world's three realms in his incomparable poem, the soil had to be prepared by long and arduous effort. Purgatory was not ultimately a true intermediary. Reserved for the purification of the future elect, it stood closer to Heaven than to Hell. No longer in the center, Purgatory was situated above rather than below the true middle. In other words, Purgatory was a part of one of those not quite balanced systems that are so characteristic of the feudal mentality. The feudal mind had a predilection for symbols of inequality within equality: consider, for example, the symbolism of vassalage and marriage. Everyone is equal, and yet the vassal is subordinate to the lord, the wife to the husband. It is therefore illusory to think of Purgatory as lying midway between the Hell escaped and the Heaven desired by the soul, all the more so because the soul's stay in Purgatory is merely temporary, ephemeral, not everlasting like its term in Heaven or Hell. And yet space and time in Purgatory were different from space and time here below, governed by different rules—rules that make Purgatory a part of the imagination to which the men of the Middle Ages referred as "marvelous."

At the heart of the matter, perhaps, was a question of logic. In order for Purgatory to be born, the notion of "intermediacy" had to take on some substance, had to become "good to think"* for the men of the Middle Ages. Purgatory was one component of a system—the system of the hereafter—and is meaningless unless viewed in conjunction with the other elements of that system. I ask the reader to keep this in mind. But since, of the three principal zones of the other world, Purgatory took longest

*As Lévi-Strauss would say.—Trans.

to define, and since its role proved the most problematic, I have thought it possible and desirable to treat Purgatory without going into detail about Heaven and Hell.

A logical, mathematical concept, "intermediacy" is an idea whose significance is closely bound up with profound changes in the social and intellectual reality of the Middle Ages. We see other signs of the increased importance attached to intermediate categories in the attempts made to introduce "middle classes" or third orders between the powerful and the poor, the clergy and the laity. To move from binary to tertiary schemes was to cross a dividing line in the organization of social thought, a step the importance of which Claude Lévi-Strauss has pointed out.

PENAL IMAGERY: FIRE

Unlike the Jewish *sheol*—a sad, disturbing place but one devoid of punishments—Purgatory is a place where the dead are subjected to one or more trials. As we shall see, these may resemble the tortures to which the damned are subjected in Hell. Of these, fire and ice are the most common, and trial by fire played a role of fundamental importance in the history of Purgatory.

Anthropologists, folklorists, and historians of religion are all familiar with fire as a sacred symbol. In medieval Purgatory and its precursors we find almost all the forms of fire symbolism that have been identified by anthropologists or religion: circles of fire, lakes and seas of fire, rings of fire, walls and moats of fire, fire-breathing monsters, burning coals, souls in the form of sparks, rivers of fire, and burning mountains and valleys.

What is sacred fire? "In initiation rites," G. Van der Leeuw tells us, "fire wipes out the past period of existence and makes a new period possible." Fire, then, is part of a rite of passage, quite appropriate to this place of transition. Purgatory is one of what Van Gennep calls "liminal rites," whose importance has sometimes been overlooked by anthropologists intent on the phases of "separation" and "incorporation" that open and close rites of passage.

But there is still more to the significance of fire. Using fairy tales, legends, and popular plays of both medieval and modern times, Carl-Martin Edsmann has clearly demonstrated the presence of regenerative fires analogous to those found in Greek and Roman mythology, and even earlier, in Iranian and Indian mythology, where the concept of a divine fire—*Ignis divinus*—seems to have originated. Accordingly, it may be that the rise of Purgatory is related to the resurgence of Indo-European folklore that seems to have taken place in Christendom between the eleventh and the thirteenth century. Roughly contemporary with that rise is the emergence (or reemergence?) of the trifunctional schema recently brought to light by Georges Duby and others. Fire was associated with oven, forge, and stake, and it is alongside these elements of popular culture that we must set the fire of Purgatory, upon which folklore also seized.

Fire rejuvenates and renders immortal: the legend of the phoenix is the most famous embodiment of this idea, a commonplace of medieval thought from the time of Tertullian on. The phoenix became the symbol of mankind waiting to be reborn. One text, erroneously attributed to Ambrose, applies to this legend the remark of Saint Paul, that "the fire shall try every man's work of what sort it is" (1 Cor. 3:13), which was destined to serve, throughout the Middle Ages, as the biblical basis for Purgatory.

This tradition helps to clarify, I think, three important characteristics of the idea of purgatory fire as it figures in the doctrine that interests us here. The first of these is that the fire that rejuvenates and renders immortal is a fire "through which one passes." Again it was Paul, in the same celebrated passage (1 Cor. 3:15), who said "he himself shall be saved; yet so as by fire." Purgatory is a transitory location (or state), and imaginary voyages in Purgatory, it is worth pointing out explicitly, may have been symbolic in intent. The more the passage through Purgatory came to be modeled after a judicial proceeding, the more trial by fire was emphasized. Trial by fire was an ordeal: an ordeal for the souls in Purgatory themselves, and also for the living souls allowed to pass through Purgatory not as mere tourists but at their own risk and peril. It is easy to see how this rite might have appealed to men who combined ancient Indo-European traditions of divine fire, handed down through Greece and Rome, with barbarian beliefs and practices. It is not hard to understand why one bit of natural geography attracted particular attention when it came to locating the site of Purgatory, or at least the mouths of Purgatory, on earth: volcanoes. As mountains that spit fire from a crater or pit at the center, these had the advantage of combining three key physical and symbolic ingredients of Purgatory's structure. We shall see presently how men roamed Sicily between Stromboli and Etna hoping to compile a map of Purgatory. But in Sicily there was no group capable of taking advantage of the opportunity offered by the local geography; by contrast, the Irish, their English neighbors, and the Cistercians who organized carefully controlled pilgrimages to the site of Saint Patrick's Purgatory were able to do this. The problem with Frederick II's Sicily was that it had a sovereign suspected of heresy, Greek monks, and Moslem inhabitants and so was thought to be insufficiently "catholic" to be the site of one of Purgatory's main portals. Mount Etna, moreover, had a long association with Hell, which proved difficult to overcome.

If fire came to occupy a place of paramount importance in the symbolic system of Purgatory and ultimately became the symbol of the doctrine par excellence, it generally figured in a symbolic pair, coupled with water. In texts properly belonging to the prehistory of the Middle Ages, we commonly find a pair of sites, one fiery, the other damp, one hot, the other cold, one in flames, the other frozen. The fundamental trial to which the dead are subjected in Purgatory is not merely to pass through fire but to pass in succession first through fire and then through water—through a probative sauna, as it were.

Carl-Martin Edsmann has discerningly pointed to certain texts dating from classical Rome in which one finds Caucasian ascetics described as living nude, now in flames, now in ice. Cicero speaks of "sages who live nude and withstand the snows of the Caucasus and the rigors of winter without pain and then hurl themselves into the fire and burn without a moan." Valerius Maximus also refers to "men who spend their whole lives in the nude, now hardening their bodies by throwing themselves into the harsh ice of the Caucasus, now exposing themselves to flame without uttering a cry."

The symbolic coupling of fire and water (or cold) recurs in a rite of early Christian times which must have played a part in the prehistory of Purgatory: baptism by fire. Christians were made familiar with this rite by the Gospels of Matthew and Luke, where they discuss John the Baptist. Matthew (3:11) puts the following words into the mouth of Christ's forerunner: "I indeed baptize you with water unto repentance: but he that cometh after me is mightier than I, whose shoes I am not worthy to bear: he shall baptize you with the Holy Ghost, and with fire." A similar speech is attributed to John the Baptist in Luke 3:16.

The idea of baptism by fire, which stems from ancient Indo-European myths about fire, took concrete shape in Judeo-Christian apocalyptic writings. The earliest Christian theologians, especially the Greeks, were aware of it. Commenting on Luke 3:16, Origen tells us that "baptism by fire and the spirit is necessary so that, when he who has been baptized comes to the river of fire, he can show that he has preserved the vessels of water and spirit and is therefore worthy of receiving baptism by fire in Jesus Christ as well" (*In Lucam,* Homily 24). Edsmann sees the pearls mentioned in Matthew 13:45–46 ("Again, the kingdom of heaven is like unto a merchant man, seeking goodly pearls, who, when he had found one pearl of great price, went and sold all that he had, and bought it") as a symbol of Christ, who had joined fire and water. In "orthodox" Christianity baptism by fire remained metaphorical. This was not true of certain sects (Baptists, Messalians, and some Egyptian ascetics, for example) or, for that matter, of the Cathari, who in the twelfth century were accused by Ecbert, an "orthodox" apologist, of not really practicing baptism "in fire" but rather "alongside" the fire.

In ancient mythology and religion the nature of fire is manifold and varied. We find great variety, for example, in Judeo-Christian fire symbolism and in particular in the many different functions and meanings attributed to the fire of Purgatory. In these various aspects of fire, "at once deifying and vivifying, punitive and destructive," Edsmann sees "the different sides of divinity's very being," and he consequently reduces fire's many faces to unity in the godhead. This explanation helps us to understand the variety of interpretations of purgatorial fire put forward by Christians from the earliest days of the religion until the thirteenth century. Although it may seem that a different kind of fire is being talked about, the apparent diversity can be traced to the polysemy of "divine fire" as it was understood in the ancient world. At times it was seen as purifying, at other times as punitive or probative. Sometimes it seems to exist in the present, sometimes in the future. Usually it is real but occasionally spiritual. Sometimes it affects only certain people, sometimes everyone. But the fire is always one and the same, the fire of Purgatory, whose complexity can be traced back to its origins in the Indo-European notion of a divine or sacred fire.

Augustine apparently understood this continuity, which, despite certain fundamental changes of meaning, links ancient and Christian concepts of fire: "The Stoics," he wrote in the *City of God* (book 8, chap. 5), "believed that fire, one of the four elements that constitute the visible universe, is endowed with life and wisdom, and is the creator of the universe and of all its contents; that fire, in fact, is actually God." To be sure, in Christianity, fire, as Francis of Assisi magnificently put it, is merely a creature. But as Edsmann rightly says, "all the complexity of the fire of the hereafter in either its general or special forms—for example the river of fire—can be understood as so many functions of one and the same divine fire." This assertion holds good for the fire of Purgatory. However, neither the men of the Middle Ages nor the bulk of medieval clerics had any idea of the rich past history of purgatorial fire, apart from a few passages in the Bible, which for medieval man constituted a necessary and sufficient guarantee of the authenticity of this sacred tradition. Nevertheless, I have felt the need to make mention of this lengthy heritage. It casts a revealing light on some disconcerting aspects of the history of Purgatory in the Middle Ages. It enables us to understand the reasons behind certain hesitations in regard to Purgatory, certain debates, and certain choices: a tradition proposes as much as it imposes. And above all it explains in part, I think, why the doctrine of Purgatory proved so successful: because it incorporated certain very ancient symbolic traditions. What is rooted in tradition is more likely to succeed than what is not. Though new to Christianity, Purgatory borrowed much of its baggage from earlier religions. When incorporated into the Christian tradition, divine fire underwent a change in meaning to which the historian must of course be sensitive. Yet, however dramatic the changes that history may bring, we must nevertheless remain attentive to a certain persistence of certain fundamental elements over the long term. Revolutions rarely create anything that is new. Rather, they change the meaning of what already exists. Christianity was, if not a revolution, then at least a key element in a revolution. From the past it took over the idea of a divine fire that rejuvenates man and renders him immortal; it made this idea, not into a belief coupled with a ritual, but rather into an attribute of God, the use of which is determined by human behavior in two ways: by the behavior of the dead while they were still on earth, which determines whether or not they will be subjected to purgatorial fire, and by the behavior of the living, which can modify the length of time a dead soul must remain in Purgatory. The fire of Purgatory, while remaining a symbol imbued with meaning and signifying salvation through purification, became an instrument to be wielded by a complex system of justice associated with a society quite different from those that believed in the regenerative power of fire.

THE SOLIDARITY OF THE DEAD AND THE LIVING

The last important characteristic of Purgatory to be mentioned is this: Purgatory is an intermediary other world in which the trial to be endured by the dead may be abridged by the intercessory prayers, the "suffrages," of the living. That the early Christians were persuaded of the efficacy of their prayers for the dead we know from funerary inscriptions, liturgical formulas, and the *Passion of Perpetua,* which dates from the early third century and is the first in a long line of spatial representations of what would one day be Purgatory. This belief in the efficacy of prayer began a movement of piety that culminated in the creation of Purgatory. It is significant that Augustine, in the *Confessions,* broaches for the first time the line of thought that would lead him toward the idea of Purgatory when he describes his feelings after the death of his mother Monica.

Christian confidence in the efficacy of prayer was not immediately linked to a belief in the possibility of postmortem purification. As Joseph Ntedika has clearly shown in the case of Augustine, the two beliefs were elaborated separately and had virtually nothing to do with one another. Before the idea of the suffrage or prayer in behalf of the dead could be evolved, solidarity had to be established between the living and the dead: institutions were required to finance intercessory prayer, namely, wills, and to execute it, namely, the confraternities, which took prayer for the dead as one of their daily obligations. Beyond that, it took time for the necessary links to be established.

What an enhancement of the power of the living there was in this hold over the dead! Meanwhile, here below, the extension of communal ties into the other world enhanced the solidarity of families, religious organizations, and confraternities. And for the Church, what a marvelous instrument of power! The souls in Purgatory were considered to be members of the Church militant. Hence, the Church argued, it ought to have (partial) jurisdiction over them, even though God was nominally the sovereign judge in the other world. Purgatory brought to the Church not only new spiritual power but also, to put it bluntly, considerable profit, as we shall see. Much of this profit went to the mendicant orders, ardent propagandists of the new doctrine. And finally, the "infernal" system of indulgences found powerful support in the idea of Purgatory.

PURGATORY: THE EVIDENCE

I invite the reader to examine along with me the evidence I have gathered concerning the history of Purgatory. I can think of no more cogent support for my interpretation than to put the reader in contact with the texts: the writings of great theologians as well as of obscure, sometimes anonymous compilers. Some of these texts are of great literary merit, others are mere instruments of communication, but many are translated here for the first time and most are imbued, in one degree or another, with the charm of imagination, the warmth of evangelical zeal, and the excitement of discovering a world within as well as a world without. There is no better way to get at the nature of the place called Purgatory, and the belief in that place, than to watch it being built up, piece by piece, slowly but not always surely and without leaving out any of history's complex texture.

These texts often repeat one another, for it is by repetition that a corpus is constituted and a history perpetuated. The echoes that reverberate through this book reflect reality. To have eliminated repetitions that actually occurred would have been to distort and falsify the past.

We shall see what happened to the geography of the other world as the first chapter of the Middle Ages unfolds, as the foundations of our Western world are being laid. This period of slow change, which extends from the third through the seventh century, used to be referred to as the Late Empire and the early Middle Ages. Now that it is much better known than it used to be, it is more properly called "late antiquity." This was a period when ancient traditions were being decanted, Christianity was shaping new habits, and mankind was struggling to survive physically and spiritually. Caught between Hell and Paradise, anticipating an imminent end to the world, men had no time for Purgatory, a superfluous luxury that remained hidden in the depths of their consciousness. Later, between the eighth and eleventh century, various precursors of Purgatory were proposed only to be left in suspense as progress in theology and religious practice came to a virtual standstill with the birth of feudalism, though the monastic imagination did depict the hidden recesses of the next world in chiaroscuro canvases slashed across by shafts of light. The great century of creation, the twelfth, was also the century in which Purgatory was born, and this birth can only be understood when set against the context of the feudal system then being given its definitive shape. The time that followed was one of restoration of order. The domestication of the next world that paved the way for Purgatory also made it possible to include the dead among the ranks of the social order. Purgatory gave this society a new lease on eternal life, as it were, a second chance at salvation, and this change entailed other modifications in the social system.

Chapter 20

The Otherworld Journey as Pilgrimage: St. Patrick's Purgatory

Carol Zaleski

The "spatialization" of purgatory is nowhere more evident than in the cycle of tales about a sacred site in Lough Derg, County Donegal, which achieved fame in the Middle Ages as a goal for pilgrims and a doorway to the other world. Here, according to legend, St. Patrick converted the pagan Irish by means of a graphic demonstration of the pains of the damned and the joys of the blessed.

Located in a cave or cavelike cell on a barren archipelago in the mysterious red waters of Lough Derg, far in the northwest of Ireland, this holy site was hospitable to pagan and Christian Celtic traditions that placed the realm of the dead in the west, beneath the waves, beyond the mist, or on a remote island. There are traces of an early Celtic monastic settlement and hints of a more ancient pre-Christian past. By the twelfth century, however, the sacred places of Lough Derg had come under the control of a community of Augustinian canons regular, who administered the rites of entry and departure. Thousands of pilgrims traveled to Lough Derg to be locked inside the Purgatory, where they might see extraordinary visions extending their pilgrimage into the other world. Those who survived this ordeal were said to be exempt from the pains of purgatory after death, and they returned to their parishes and monasteries with vivid stories of the terrors and wonders to be found on the other side of life's threshold.

Despite several attempts to dismantle the site, the Purgatory has a nearly continuous history up to the present day; since the final destruction of the cave in the eighteenth century, however, it has become a setting for penitential exercises rather than otherworldly excursions. Today, St. Patrick's Purgatory draws close to fifteen thousand pilgrims and tourists each year, having become, according to Victor and Edith Turner, "a kind of national totemic center."

During the period we are considering, the journey to St. Patrick's Purgatory received its greatest publicity in England and on the Continent, where hearsay accounts of the pilgrimage were amplified and transformed into works of didactic literature in the tradition of Gregory's *Dialogues* and the Vision of Drythelm. In this form, the Purgatory legend played a major role in the development of medieval conceptions of the otherworld journey; I will therefore conclude this chapter by examining it in detail.

The most famous account of this pilgrimage is the *Treatise on the Purgatory of St. Patrick*, relating the vision of the Knight Owen. Composed near the end of the twelfth century by an English Cistercian monk who calls himself H. of Sawtry, it was translated into nearly every European vernacular language, set to verse, and retold in chronicles, saints' lives, and sermons. The *Treatise* prospered because of its unique combination of didactic and popular appeal: it was at once a romantic tale of knightly adventure and a cautionary tale destined to be read from the pulpit; in addition, it rode in on the wave of enthusiasm for St. Patrick that followed the "discovery" of his relics and their solemn translation to Downpatrick in 1186. Although it was written with a monastic audience in mind, the story of Owen's visit to Lough Derg became, during the thirteenth century, a vehicle for lay religious instruction, gleefully employed by the preaching friars, who specialized in evoking dread of purgatory.

The apparently inexhaustible subject of travel to the other world by way of St. Patrick's Purgatory was also treated in countless letters, diaries, and poems by various other pilgrims to Lough Derg, both fictional and historical. Not surprisingly, the legend extended its influence far beyond the Middle Ages—Ariosto mentioned the Purgatory in *Orlando Furioso*, and Shakespeare alluded to it by having Hamlet say, "Yes, by Saint Patrick . . . Touching this vision here, / It is an honest ghost, that let me tell you." Rabelais treated it in a satiric vein, and Erasmus described it as a distant echo of the cave of Trophonius. In seventeenth-century Spain, Montalvan retold the H. of Sawtry account in his *Vida y Purgatorio de S. Patricio*, and Calderón turned it into a play *(El Purgatorio de San Patricio)*, which so affected Shelley that he saw a strange vision after reading it. Robert Southey made the legend the subject of his ballad, "Sir Owen"; as late as 1844, Thomas Wright felt entitled to ask, "who has not heard of St. Patrick's Purgatory?"

The widespread influence of the *Treatise* makes it worth our while to review its content. Its most striking feature is the way it links terrestrial to extraterrestrial topography: the protagonist steps through a physical doorway into the other world; he insists that his was not the visionary experience of an ecstatic. This peculiar detail seems to set the Purgatory legend apart from other Christian tales of rapture and return-from-death visions. H. of Sawtry says in a preface, however, that his account of Owen's journey simply follows the precedent of Gregory's *Dialogues*, and later commentators rarely discriminate between the testimony of the Knight Owen and that of the visionaries. Despite its idiosyncrasies, the *Treatise* can be read as a typical medieval vision story.

Like the visions of Drythelm, Tundal, and others, the *Treatise* is essentially a conversion narrative, in which the hero is a sinner who changes his way of life after a visit to the other world. The Knight Owen, a crusader under King Stephen (1134–54), returns to his native Ireland after a successful campaign and is suddenly seized with chagrin for having devoted his life "to violence and plundering, and, what he regretted more, the desecration of churches and theft of ecclesiastical property . . ."

To repair his rupture with God and society, Owen has only to submit to the machinery of the twelfth-century penitential system, with its prescribed tariffs and austerities. For crimes like Owen's that threatened the social order, pilgrimage would be considered an appropriate punishment. A form of banishment, the obligatory pilgrimage temporarily rid society of a menace who, ideally, came back reformed.

Not content to follow the routine, however, Owen tells his bishop, "Since, as you assert, I have offended my maker so greatly, I will assume a penance more severe than all other punishments. . . . I wish to go down into the Purgatory of St. Patrick."

Although the prior and canons in charge of the Purgatory attempt to dissuade him, Owen keeps his resolve, and after a fifteen-day retreat he has himself locked into the cave for the night. As is common in visionary topographies, this chamber, which appears small from outside, turns out to be cavernous within. Tentatively, Owen makes his way through a long, dark passageway, following a distant glimmer of light which finally brings him to a vast open cloister. Here he meets twelve men clothed in white and recently shaven, who look like monks. Like the canons on the earthly side of the threshold, these mysterious figures play an initiatory role: they warn Owen of the perils to come and instruct him to use the name of Jesus as a protective prayer; then they abandon him to his fate. The instant they leave, a cataclysmic uproar shakes the ground; it sounds as though the entire human and animal kingdoms were screaming in unison. Only by invoking the divine name does Owen preserve his sanity. He is then carried off on a tour of infernal sightseeing.

Owen visits four fields of punishment where, as in earlier visionry and apocalyptic accounts, sinners are devoured by dragons, set upon by serpents and toads, fixed to the ground with red-hot nails, baked in furnaces, immersed in boiling cauldrons, and hooked to a flaming version of Ixion's wheel. Moving south, Owen and his demonic guides come upon a well from which naked bodies shoot upward like sparks and then fall back into the sulphurous flames. "This is the mouth of hell," the demons say, and they cast Owen in. He falls endlessly, for this well is none other than the realm of utterly lost souls, the bottomless pit described in Rev. 20:1–3 and featured in the visions of St. Paul, Drythelm, and Alberic. No longer a mere spectator, Owen descends into a state of deadly oblivion, forgetting to call on the name of Jesus. At the last minute, however, a divine intervention causes Owen to remember the invocation, and he is lifted to safety on a tongue of flame.

From the well, the party travels to a river of fire and sulphur, spanned by a bridge which Owen must cross. If he should fall off, he will land in the clutches of demons and be dragged down to hell. The bridge has three great shortcomings: it is too slippery to stand on, it is too narrow to gain a foothold on it, and it rises to a vertiginous height. As Owen ventures to cross, however, he finds the bridge widening at every step, until there is enough room for two carriages to pass. Readers familiar with Western otherworld journey traditions will recognize that this bridge is at once test and testimony; Owen can make it across only because his harrowing tour through the realms of punishment has already cleansed him of his sins. He easily attains the other shore, leaving the demons shrieking in impotent rage.

His ordeals behind him, Owen walks up to a jeweled gate, which opens in welcome, leading him to a land of light more dazzling than the sun, where he meets a procession of clergy carrying crosses, banners, candles, and golden palm branches, singing an unearthly harmony. Two archbishops take Owen on a tour of the delightful meadows adorned with flowers, fruit, grass, and trees, "on whose fragrance he felt he could subsist forever." There is no night, no darkness, no heat, no cold—negatives are employed where superlatives are inadequate to describe fully the delights of this region. Yet this is only the earthly paradise, an intermediate realm where those who have been purified by purgatorial suffering await God's call to ascend to heaven. Owen's guides remind him that although everyone must undergo purgatorial torments after death, the duration and severity of the punishment can be lessened by the masses, prayers, and alms of the living. Only those confined in the well are beyond help. Thus the *Treatise,* like the otherworld visions related by Gregory and his successors, serves to promote not only private acts of penance and spiritual reform, but also liturgical practices that link the living with the souls of their departed kin.

The archbishops conduct Owen to the top of a mountain and bid him look up at the sky, which is the color of gold burning in a furnace. Here, at the entrance to the heavenly paradise, Owen receives his first taste of heavenly food. A flame comes down from heaven and irradiates each person.

> It descended on the head of the knight and entered him just as it entered the others. Then he felt such a sweet sense of delight in his body and his heart that he could scarcely tell, for the delight of the sweetness, whether he was living or dead; but the time passed in an instant.

Just when Owen is thinking that he wants to stay there forever, his guides tell him it is time to go back. If he lives well, they promise, he will return to this place when he dies. If not, he knows what is in store for him. Owen is afraid that if he returns to earth he will relapse into his old ways. Against his will, they lead him through the gate and close it after him: having begun his journey by being locked into the Purgatory, Owen ends it by being locked out of heaven.

Nothing remains for Owen but to go back the way he came. Fortunately, his ordeal has purified him; as he retraces his steps, the demons flee in dismay. Back at the starting point, Owen meets the twelve men who initiated his journey. They joyfully give him absolution and urge him to hurry to the doorway, which he reaches at dawn, just in time to be set free by the canons. After another fifteen-day retreat in the church, he takes a cross on his shoulder and sets out for Jerusalem, now a pilgrim rather than a crusader. Upon his return, he asks the king for permission to take up the religious life and is assigned to serve as interpreter for the Cistercian monk Gilbert of Louth on his mission to found a new abbey in Ireland. An eager recruit, Owen replies, "It is a joy to serve monks of the Cistercian order, and you should welcome them to your land since I own that in the other world I saw no others in such great glory as I saw them."

During their stay in Ireland together, Owen confides his experiences in the Purgatory to Gilbert. Once Gilbert returns to England to become abbot of Basingwerk, he cannot keep so edifying a story to himself. He spreads the word before large audiences, including the monk of Sawtry, who finally commits it to writing. Owen stays in Ireland, not suspecting his imminent rise to fame. This conforms to the principle set forth by Gregory in the first book of his *Dialogues:* for his own merit the visionary should wish to conceal his experience, but for the sake of others the story should be told. This twofold convention—the reticence of the visionary and the didactic purpose of the narrative—is a standard feature of medieval visions and one which we will have reason to compare to modern accounts.

C. M. van der Zanden has shown that the *Treatise* is in part a Cistercian manifesto, depicting the white monks as the best qualified to inherit St. Patrick's task of taming Ireland. As van der Zanden points out, the twelve men in white, whom other scholars have compared to the twelve apostles or the *doucepers* of the Charlemagne legend, look very much like Cistercians. When Owen returns from the Purgatory, he is convinced of the Cistercians' superior rank in heaven; he displays his rehabilitation by becoming a humble servant for the Cistercian mission to Ireland. H. of Sawtry also makes a point of showing the king's support for the Cistercian order.

This is not the first case in which Cistercian bias has shaped the content of an otherworld journey narrative; in fact, the Cistercians were especially sensitive to the propaganda value of an otherworld journey and contributed more to this genre than did any other religious order. Like Gregory and Bede, they turned the otherworld journey story into a conversion narrative, putting great emphasis on the transformation of the visionary after his return from death. During the twelfth and early thirteenth centuries; a period of intense controversy over competing vows and observances, they portrayed this transformation in an especially partisan light. The visions of Gunthelm and the Monk of Melrose and the Cistercian stories collected during the early thirteenth century by Peter of Cornwall offer visionary evidence for the favored position of Cistercians in heaven and for their especially intimate relation to the Virgin Mary.

Another remarkable feature of the story of Owen, as of all accounts of St. Patrick's Purgatory, Cistercian or otherwise, is the way in which it dramatizes one of the central religious conceptions of the Middle Ages: the idea that life is a pilgrimage.

It is well known that the high Middle Ages witnessed a virtual craze for pilgrimage discourse. After the lull in the barbarian invasions of the ninth and tenth centuries, travel became somewhat less dangerous, and interest in the symbolic value of pilgrimage kept pace with the increasing number of pilgrims on the road. This is not to say that pilgrimage as a metaphor was a medieval invention. The early Fathers often spoke of the church as a pilgrim or exile in the world, embarked on a collective journey through the *saeculum* to the day of judgment. In the high Middle Ages, however, pilgrimage became a symbol for the individual's journey through life and death. Romance and legend celebrated the solitary seeker: the desert hermit, the Irish seafaring saint, the knight on a quest, the courtly lover, the traveling penitent.

The Knight Owen is just such a solitary hero. The *Treatise* underlines his loneliness. First, the canons lead him to the door, lock him inside, and desert him. Then he is met by a reception committee of sorts, but they can only point the way and warn of its dangers; they cannot accompany him. A brief episode of desertion by the guide is a common feature of medieval visions, but Owen is one of the few who must travel the whole distance unescorted.

The purgatorial teaching of the *Treatise* also tends toward individualism. Each person's progress through the regions of the other world is governed by a separate timetable:

> No one who is in torment knows how long he will stay there. . . . And when they come to this land, they do not know how long they are to remain. . . . Here, as you can see, we dwell in great peace and joy, but after a certain period determined by God, each one of us will go beyond. Daily the number of our society increases and daily it decreases. For just as some come to us daily from the torments, having been purged, so some of us ascend from the earthly paradise to the heavenly paradise.

Inevitably, Christian pilgrimage came to be identified with the ultimate passage of death. Comparison of death with pilgrimage is found in pilgrim narratives with no explicit otherworld content as well as in vision narratives that do not concern actual travel. The St. Patrick's Purgatory accounts, which combine pilgrimage with otherworld vision, merely enlarge upon an already natural association. The usual pilgrim's goal is the tomb of a martyr or saint or the shrine that houses holy relics: in short, a visit to the venerated dead. In preparation for this journey, the pilgrim is instructed to fast, keep vigils, and put on special clothing (tunic, pouch, and staff) that separates him or her from ordinary life. He or she is now, in effect, "dead to the world."

During the period we are considering, moreover, a common purpose of pilgrimage was to work off one's debt of purgatorial suffering. In the drama of pilgrimage, with its real and mimetic ordeals, the penitent played the part of a soul in purgatory; and if he or she died before fulfilling the vow, understudies could step in: friends or relatives could perform the pilgrimage as proxies. In a number of medieval ghost stories, the dead return to berate their families for shirking the obligation to help one's kin in purgatory. Thus, as Victor Turner notes, "if pilgrims are companions to the dead, it is to the dead of the church suffering; and if pilgrims are equivalent to the dead, it is to the dead in Purgatory."

Those who entered St. Patrick's Purgatory followed an initiatory routine that amounted to a ritual imitation of death. Antonio Mannini, who visited the Purgatory in 1411, describes it thus in a letter he wrote to a friend soon after his experience:

> Having placed me flat on my back as though I were dead, he closed my eyes and commanded me not to open them until the office was over; he crossed my hands upon my breast, and having said over me the vigil and all the Office of the Dead, he signed me three times with holy water, with the same prayers and solemnity as is used for the dead, neither more nor less. Then he opened my eyes with his own hands, put the cross in my right hand, and made me stand up.

Given the hazards of travel in the Middle Ages, there were practical as well as symbolic reasons to equate preparation for pilgrimage with preparation for death. The author of a sermon for one of the feasts of St. James advises pilgrims to Compostela to settle their affairs before they set out:

> If one is legitimately intent on reaching the threshold of St. James, then before the journey begins he forgives those who have injured him, confesses and makes amends for every encroachment of which his neighbors or his own conscience accuse him, obtains permission from his parish priest, his lord, his spouse, or anyone else to whom he is obligated; if he can, he gives back whatever is not rightfully his, finds a peaceful solution for the conflicts that are within his control, accepts appropriate penance, puts his house in good order, and on the advice of his parish priests, distributes his property, setting aside a certain amount for alms in the event of death . . .

The pilgrim is singularly well prepared to travel the road to heaven because the perils of his or her earthly journey—treacherous bridges, flooded rivers, robbers, tariffs—have trained him or her to withstand the trials that must be faced after death. In the twelfth-century Vision of Tundal, the only soul who crosses the test-bridge with ease is a priest who holds a palm branch, signifying that in life he had gone on pilgrimage to Jerusalem; this reprises the episode quoted above from Gregory's account of the vision of a soldier in Rome. The pilgrim's letters of permission and safe conduct also have their otherworld counterparts: the Knight Owen relies on the name of Jesus as a kind of password to protect him from demonic assaults and to help him cross the test-bridge; and among the souvenirs of later visitors to St. Patrick's Purgatory, one finds official passports for travel to Lough Derg along with protective formulas, usually

"Lord Jesus Christ, son of the Living God, have mercy upon me a sinner," to secure safe passage once they have entered the Purgatory cave.

It was common for spiritual writers to compress pilgrimage and other-world journey into a single, densely packed image, which would symbolize the ordeals encountered on the soul's itinerary through life. As we have seen, Gregory reads the perilous crossing in moral terms, interpreting Stephen's struggle on the test-bridge as a conflict of virtues and vices; and the author of the pilgrimage sermon quoted above compares the arduous journey to Compostela to the narrow road that leads to life:

> The pilgrim's path is rich in goodness, but it is also a difficult strait. For strait is the way that leads man to life, and wide and broad is the way that leads to death. The pilgrim's path goes directly forward, for it is the departure from vices, the mortification of the flesh, the disclosure of virtues, the absolution of sinners, the fulfillment of penitence, the way of the just, the delight of the saints; it is faith in the resurrection and reward of the blessed; it is distancing from hell and drawing near to heaven.

Monastic authors of the Middle Ages were adept at allegorizing both pilgrimage and otherworld journey in order to express their conviction that the monk who stays in his monastery is in fact the celestial pilgrim par excellence. St. Bernard, who preached the Second Crusade, nonetheless told his monks, "Jerusalem is your cell," and Catherine of Siena urged a Carthusian monk who had been denied permission to visit St. Patrick's Purgatory to seek its finer analogue in spiritual exercises.

A vivid example of the allegorical treatment of travel can be found in the Vision of Gunthelm, a twelfth-century Cistercian tale designed to show that monastic vows are more sacred and binding than the vocations of crusader or pilgrim. Gunthelm, a worldly crusader-knight like Owen, repents of his sins and vows to make a penitential pilgrimage to Jerusalem. He consults a Cistercian abbot who persuades him to join the white monks instead. Although he is a dedicated novice at first, Gunthelm has second thoughts about breaking his pilgrimage vow and makes secret plans to depart for Jerusalem. That night a demon, in the guise of a monkey, appears at his bed and shakes him senseless. For three days, while his body lies near death, Gunthelm visits heaven and hell under the guidance of the archangel Raphael and St. Benedict (who better to teach him the value of monastic stability?). Benedict brings the frightened novice before the Virgin, who asks him to make up his mind whether he will keep his promise to stay in her house and serve her. Gunthelm renews his vow before the altar, and when he returns to life his wanderlust is entirely quenched.

In another account, also of Cistercian authorship but apparently oriented toward lay piety, the otherworld journey is offered as consolation to a peasant who cannot afford the expense of an earthly pilgrimage. Thurkill, an impoverished Essex farmer, is so hospitable to pilgrims and so devoted to St. James that his patron favors him with an aerial version of the pilgrimage to Compostela. Thurkill meets St. James in a basilica without walls which is both a heavenly replica of the shrine at Compostela and a gathering place for the dead; he also sees the test-bridge, the weighing of souls, the theater of hell, the Mount of Joy, and other spectacles, which he describes very much in the style of a pilgrim diary.

The Vision of Thurkill strongly suggests that otherworld journey narratives resemble pilgrimage narratives in content because they resemble pilgrimage in social form and function. The pilgrim who visits Canterbury or Calvary recreates and participates in events of cultural significance—as do all pilgrims in every period and society. So, too, the visit of a solitary knight to St. Patrick's Purgatory is a far from isolated affair; he explores a landscape whose contours are culturally formed. Imaginative rehearsal enables pilgrim and visionary alike to learn the roles they must play in order to live and die meaningfully.

The dual theme of pilgrimage–otherworld journey retained its orienting function when it passed from the literature of monastic propaganda and popular homily into the literature of spiritual allegory; this long-lived tradition reaches from *The Divine Comedy* to *Pilgrim's Progress* and still has its occasional representatives among modern works of symbolic fiction (René Daumal's *Mount Analogue* comes to mind). St. Patrick's Purgatory stands apart, perhaps, for the peculiar way in which it links inner and outer pilgrimage. Nonetheless, it seems to share a common purpose with these other and better-known accounts of spiritualized outer journeying or visualized inner travel: the overcoming of moral and spiritual dislocation. The protagonist who has lost his way in the "wilderness" or "dark wood" of an aimless life recovers his path by an imaginative pilgrimage through the culturally shaped regions of the other world. As a symbolic guidebook, the legend of St. Patrick's Purgatory belongs to an immense family of visionary and spiritual writings that seek to locate humanity in a divinely and socially sanctioned cosmic hierarchy and to map the perilous journey through life and death.

The four narratives considered in this chapter correspond roughly to four phases in the development of the Christian otherworld journey. The Vision of St. Paul brings apocalyptic narrative within the compass of the deathbed vision; the miracle tales of Gregory the Great celebrate experiences of ordinary folk sent back to life; the Vision Drythelm expands the return-from-death story into a full-blown visionary journey, resuming some apocalyptic themes; and the Vision of the Knight Owen, which represents the most fully realized form of the otherworld journey, gives us a sense of the narrative complexities attained by this genre during its peak years in the high Middle Ages.

Chapter 21

Stories of the Departed

Translated by Henry Snyder Gehman

THE STORY OF THE LIKENESS TO FIELDS

While the Blessed One was dwelling at Kalandaka-nivāpa[1] in Veluvana near Rājagaha, he told this story.

At Rājagaha there was an immensely wealthy banker known only by the name of Mahādhanaseṭṭhi.[2] He had an only son, who was amiable and charming. When he reached the years of discretion, his parents reflected thus: "If our son spends a thousand per day, even in a hundred years this accumulation of wealth will not come to an end." They did not teach him a craft, thinking: "Since the learning of a craft would be a fatiguing exertion, let him with sound body and mind comfortably enjoy his wealth." Instead, when he was come of age,[3] they procured him a charming bride, but totally lacking in a conception of Dhamma. With her he passed the time, given to enjoyment, delighting in and hankering after pleasure. At the death of his parents, he gave lavishly to dancers, singers, and others, and having wasted his wealth and become poor, he managed to live by borrowing money. But when he could no longer secure a loan and was pressed by his creditors, he gave them field and farm, house, and his other possessions, and became a beggar, and lived in the poor-house in that same city.

Now one day some robbers met him and thus addressed him: "Look here, man, what do you get out of this hard life? You are young and active. Come with us and make a comfortable living by stealing. We will train you." . . He agreed and went with them. The thieves gave him a large club; as they entered a house in which they had made a breach, they stationed him at the opening saying: "If anyone else comes here, strike and kill him." He, mentally dull and not knowing friend from foe, stood there, and awaited only the approach of others.

From *Stories of the Departed (Peta-Vatthu)* trans. by Henry Snyder Gehman, London: Routledge & Kegan Paul, 1974, pp. 1–3, 7–13, and 27–35.

Now the people of the house got up, and running very quickly and looking this way and that, saw the man standing at the breach. With the words, "Here they are, the rogues, the thieves," they seized him, and brought him before the king, saying: "Lord, this thief was caught house-breaking." The king commanded the town-watch: "Cut off his head." These took him into custody and led him to the place of execution, flogging him with whips as he went along after the execution-drum. At the same time the populace shouted "This plundering robber has been captured in this city."

Now at that moment in the same city, the town belle, Sulasā by name, was standing at a window. She saw him led along, and since she had been acquainted with him in the past, she felt sympathy for him, who had attained great prosperity in this very town, and sent out sweetmeats and water and had this message delivered to the town-watch: "May your honour wait until this man shall have eaten these sweetmeats and drunk the water."

Now while in this same city the venerable Mahāmoggallāna was contemplating clairvoyantly and noticed this man's predicament, his mind was moved with compassion, and he thought: "Since this man has not accomplished any merit, but done wickedness, he will be reborn in hell; now, if I go and he gives me the sweetmeats and the drink, he will be reborn among the terrestrial devas. Let me help this man." He accordingly appeared before the culprit as the drink and sweetmeats were being brought. When he saw the elder, his mind was at ease, and he thought: "What benefit shall *I* derive from eating these sweetmeats if I am put to death? Now these will become provisions for my journey to the other world." So he had the sweetmeats and the water given to the elder. When Moggallāna saw that his misery had grown into joy, he sat down, ate and drank and arose and went his way.

The man, however, was led by the headsmen to the place of execution and beheaded. On account of the pious act done to the elder Moggallāna, unsurpassed field of merit, he was worthy of rebirth in the sublime deva-world. But his affection went forth to Sulasā as he thought: "I attained this gift thanks to her," and so at the moment of death his heart became impure, and he was reborn in a lower state and became a dryad in a large banyan tree of dense shade in the jungle.

Now it came to pass that he seeing Sulasā in her garden bore her to his abode. Her mother lamenting, she bade him after a week take her back. And she told the people, who asked her, what had happened, and they were full of wonder and said: "The Arhans verily are the world's incomparable field of merit: even a small act of mercy done unto them gives men rebirth among devas." Monks narrated the affair to the Blessed One, who then spoke these stanzas in explanation of this:

1. "Like unto fields are the Arhans; the givers are like unto farmers; resembling seed is the gift; from this is produced fruit."
2. "This seed and cultivated field are for the petas and the giver. This the petas enjoy; the giver increases through the pious act."

3. "For doing a meritorious act here on earth and honouring the petas, to heaven[4] indeed he goes as his station, since he has done a good deed."

At the end of the discourse eighty-four thousand persons were converted to Dhamma.

THE STORY OF THE PETAS OUTSIDE THE WALL

While the Teacher was living at Rājagaha, he told this story.

Ninety-two cycles ago there was a city called Kāsipuri. In that place, king Jayasena was reigning; his queen was called Sirimā. Their son Phussa attained supreme enlightenment.[5] Now King Jayasena displayed pride, thinking: "Since my son, who is born as a Buddha, has made the great renunciation, I alone have the Buddha, I alone have Dhamma, I alone have the Church." All the time he alone was in attendance upon him and gave no opportunity to others.

The three younger brothers of the Blessed One, born of a different mother, thought: "The Buddhas indeed are born for the benefit of the whole world, not for the sake of just one person. Now our father gives no opportunity to others. How now can we serve the Blessed One and the Church? Come along, let us perform some stratagem." So they caused a disturbance, as it were, on the borderland. Then the king, when he heard about this disturbance, sent forth these three sons to pacify the border. They did so and, upon their return, the king in his pleasure granted them a boon, saying: "Take whatever you wish." They said: "We wish to wait upon the Blessed One." The king, denying this, said: "Take something else." They replied: "We do not care for anything else." The king said: "Well, you can take your choice."

They approached the Blessed One and said: "Reverend Sir, we wish to serve the Blessed One three months. Let the Blessed One consent to spend with us for three months the retreat of the rainy season." The Blessed One assented. The three sons personally sent a written message to the man appointed over the province, saying: "During these three months we must serve the Blessed One; beginning with a monastery; provide all his needs." Then they served with due honour the Blessed One and the Order of the monks. When they, as rulers of the province, had dedicated the monastery, they observed the retreat of the rainy season. One of them, a royal treasurer, the son of a householder, a believer, together with his wife, found faith. He duly gave a donation to the Order of monks at whose head was the Buddha. The man who was set over the province followed his example and with eleven thousand people dispatched gifts with all due honour. On that occasion some people were offended in heart; having hindered contributions, they themselves ate the gifts and burned with fire the refectory. After the king's sons with their retinue had honoured the Blessed One and bidden him farewell, they went directly to their father.

Upon his return, the Blessed One attained Nirvāṇa; the king's sons, and the man set over the province, and the royal treasurer, in the course of time, died and with the multitude were reborn in heaven, but the people who were offended in heart were reborn in hell. Thus ninety-two cycles passed by, as these two states of persons were reborn respectively from heaven to heaven and from hell to hell. Then in that auspicious cycle, at the time of the blessed Kassapa, the people who were offended in heart were reborn among the petas.

At that time, men themselves would give a gift for the benefit of their peta kinsmen and indicate: "Let this be for our relatives." Thereupon the petas received happiness. Then these petas too noticed this, and having approached Kassapa asked him: "How now, reverend sir; can we too attain such bliss?" The Blessed One said: "At this time, you cannot attain it, but in time to come, there will be a universal Buddha named Gotama; in the time of that Blessed One, there will be a king named Bimbisāra, who ninety-two cycles from now will be a kinsman unto you. He will give a gift to the Buddha and ascribe the credit to you; then you will attain (blessedness)." Now when this was spoken, it was as though one had said to those petas: "To-morrow you shall receive."

Then[6] after this Buddha-interval had passed, the Blessed One was born unto us in the world; the three princes too with a thousand men passed from the world of the devas and were reborn in the kingdom of Magadha in brāhman families. In course of time, having given up the worldly life, the three became ascetics with matted hair, sojourning at Mount Gayā; the man set over the province became King Bimbisāra; the royal treasurer, the son of a householder, became guild-leader by the name of Visākha; his wife became the daughter of a guild-leader and was known as Dhammadinnā; but the rest of the multitude were reborn as attendants of the king. Now our Blessed One, reborn in the world, at the end of seven weeks came to Benares, where he set rolling the wheel of Dhamma. He instructed the three ascetics, after he had begun with a group of five, and obtained as many as a thousand followers. Then he proceeded to Rājagaha and established King Bimbisāra in the fruits of the first way together with eleven myriads of brāhmans and laymen dwelling in Aṅga and Magadha.[7]

The petas, however, surrounded the house thinking: "Now the king will ascribe a gift to our credit." As the king gave a donation, he thought only, "Where now, I wonder, may the Blessed One be dwelling?" Accordingly he did not ascribe the credit of the gift to anyone. Thus, since the petas, who had not received a donation, were without hope, they uttered during the night dreadful outcry at the king's residence. The agitated king told the Blessed One at daybreak of what had occured and asked: "Did you hear a noise like that? Reverend sir, I wonder now what may happen to me." The Blessed One replied: "Do not fear, great king; no evil will befall you, but prosperity will come your way. Now verily, these are your kinsmen who have been reborn among the petas. For one Buddha-interval they have been wandering about, yearning just for this: 'He will bestow upon the Buddha a gift and ascribe to us its merit.' Yesterday when you presented a gift, you made no transfer of credit. Consequently they have lost hope and uttered outcry." The king said: "How now, reverend sir, could they obtain what is given as a gift?" The Buddha said: "Indeed they can, great king." The king said: "Then, reverend sir, let the Blessed One accept my invitation for to-morrow; I shall transfer to them the virtue of the gift." The Blessed One agreed.

Then the king had a generous bounty prepared and had the time announced to the Blessed One, who came to the royal palace. The petas came, thinking: "To-day we shall get something," and stood outside the walls and fences. The Blessed One then brought it about that everyone of them became visible to the king. As the ruler gave water to wash in, he ascribed to them the merit with the words: "Let this be for my kinsmen." Instantly there came into existence for the petas lotus-ponds full of lotuses and water-lilies. They bathed and drank there, and alleviated of their sufferings from distress, fatigue, and thirst, they became gold-coloured. The king handed out rice gruel and solid and soft food and made over, the merit of the gift. In a moment there came into being for them other, even deva-foods, of which they joyfully partook. The king made a donation of clothes and dwellings and made over the merit of the gift. There came into existence for them deva-clothes, deva-mansions, and couches, covers, and ornaments. The Blessed One so resolved that all this bliss of theirs should be manifest to the king, who, seeing this, was very much pleased. Then the Blessed One, having eaten and being invited, in order to thank King Bimbisāra, told the story of the petas outside the wall.

1. "They stand outside the walls and at the open spaces and at the cross-roads; they are standing at the doorposts, having gone to their own house.
2. "Although abundant food and drink, hard and soft, are served, no one needs these beings because of (their) acts.
3. "They who are compassionate give their kinsmen at the proper time pure, excellent, suitable food and drink (with the words): 'Let this be for our kinsmen; let the relatives be blessed!'
4. "And these coming together there, the departed spirits of the kinsmen who have assembled greatly rejoice at the abundant food and drink, saying:
5. "'Long live our kinsmen through whom we receive. Piety has been shown us, and the givers are not without reward.'
6. "'For there is no ploughing there, nor is cowherding found there; nor is there trading there as here, nor commerce with gold.'
7. "'With gifts from here, the petas, the dead in the other world, maintain themselves. As water rained on a height flows down to the low ground, even so the gift hence given supports the petas.'
8. "'Just as full streams of water fill the ocean, even so the gift hence given supports the petas.'
9. "'My kinsfolk and companions, each one gave to me, worked for me. May each one give gifts to the petas, remembering what was done in their past.'

10. "'For[8] mere weeping or grief or any other lamentation is of no avail; all this is of no help to the departed person. Such a practice have the kinsmen.'
11. "'But indeed this gift which is given and well established in the Church with immediate effect serves a long time for the benefit of the departed.'
12. "Now this is the duty defined for kinsmen; to the petas, moreover, high piety has been paid, and strength has been bestowed upon the monks. No little good has been pursued by you."

At the end of the discourse, insight into Dhamma was received by eighty-four thousand people whose understanding began, as it were, from the incident of rebirth in the realm of the petas. Their hearts were stirred with praise, and they made earnest efforts. On the following day, the Blessed One taught to devas and men this same discourse of "Outside the wall." Thus for as long as seven days there was such a conversion as this to Dhamma.

THE STORY OF THE DEVOURER OF FIVE CHILDREN

While the Teacher was living at Sāvatthī, he told this story. In a village not far from Sāvatthī a certain land-owner's wife was barren. His relatives said: "Let us procure you another girl." He was unwilling out of affection for his wife. Then, when his wife heard of this, she urged her husband to marry again and not cut off his lineage. But when the new wife was with child, the barren wife, who was overcome by envy, satisfied with food and drink a certain Wanderer,[9] and employed him to bring about abortion. The second wife told her mother, who summoned her kinsfolk and they spoke thus to the barren wife: "You have caused the death of her unborn child." She replied: "I am not guilty." The kinsmen said: "If you are not, take an oath." She took the oath, inviting, were she guilty, the date told below.

Not long afterwards she died, and was reborn, not far from that same town, as an ill-favoured petī. At that time, eight elders who were spending the rainy season in the province and were going to Sāvatthī to see the Teacher, came to a place in the forest supplied with shade and water, not far from this same village. Then the petī appeared unto the elders, of whom one asked her:

1. "You are naked and ugly in form; an ill-smelling and putrid odour you breathe forth; you are all covered with flies. Now who are you that are standing here?"

The petī:

2. "I, venerable Sir, am a petī, a wretched denizen of Yama's world. Since I had done a wicked deed, I went hence to peta-world.

3. "At daybreak I give birth to five sons, in the evening again to five others, all of whom I devour; even these are not enough for me.
4. "My heart is scorched and smokes with hunger; I get no water to drink. Behold the misfortune come to me."

When the elder had heard this, he asked her:

5. "Now what wicked deed was done by body, speech, and mind?[10] In retribution of what offence do you devour the flesh of your sons?"

Then the petī told the elder what she had done:

6. "The other wife of my husband was with child, and I devised evil against her; I myself with a corrupt spirit caused the fall of her unborn child.
7. "When it was two months old just blood flowed forth. Then her mother in anger brought her kinsfolk to me. And she both administered an oath to me and had me reviled.
8. "I, even I, took the terrible oath falsely: 'May I eat the flesh of children if it was done by me.'
9. "In consequence of both the deed and the perjury, I devour the flesh of children, stained with the blood of the past."

The elders, moved with compassion for her, went to the house of that landlord, and had him transfer to the petī the virtue of the alms-gift he made them. All at once the petī, freed from her misery, obtained great blessedness and showed herself (in a vision) during the night to her husband. Then the elders in due time came to Sāvatthi and told the matter to the Blessed One.

ENDNOTES

1. Usually translated as Squirrels' Feeding-ground.—Ed.
2. *Setthi,* lit.: best; often translated as treasurer: a 'guild-leader.' *Dhana* = wealth.—Ed.
3. Sixteen years old.
4. *Sagga, Svarga,* lit.: the bright (World).
5. The 18th Buddha after Dīpaṅkara. See Bv. XIX, etc.
6. From here the Commentary is more or less a duplicate of that on the 'Wall' verses in the Khuddakapātha (VII). Cf. *Minor Anthologies* I, S.B.B.—Ed.
7. There follows, briefly, the Sakka tribute from the Nidānakathā of the Jātaka.—Ed.
8. See I, 4, 3.
9. *Paribbājaka,* a roaming student.
10. Note that in the two Suttas (*A.* i, 138; *M.* iii, 179) of the post mortem tribunal great stress is laid on ill deeds as having been done "by you, yea, by you . . ." Here, in the following verses, the same notion becomes apparent.—Ed.

THE STORY OF THE FINDING RELEASE IN TRANSMIGRATION

While the Teacher was sojourning at Veluvana, he told this story.

In a village called Iṭṭhākavatī in Magadha and in Dīgharājī village dwelt many who, finding release in transmigration, held wrong opinions. And long ago a certain woman was reborn in one such family. Killing many beetles and grasshoppers she on dying was reborn a petī, enduring for five hundred years the pangs of hunger and thirst. Now our Blessed One was then at Rājagaha, when she was once more born into the same family at Iṭṭhākavatī. And one day when she was playing with other girls in the high road near the village gate, the venerable Sāriputta with twelve monks passed by and the girls hastened to salute him. But she stood there disrespectful. Then the elder, discerning her past and future, and moved with sympathy commented on her attitude to the girls. They took her hands and dragged her to pay homage. Dying subsequently in childbirth she was again born among the Petas. And she appeared by night to Sāriputta, who seeing her said:

1. "Naked and of hideous appearance are you, emaciated and with prominent veins. You thin one, with your ribs standing out, now who are you, you who are here?"

The petī:

2. "I, venerable sir, am a petī, a wretched denizen of Yama's world; since I had done a wicked deed, I went from here to the world of petas.

Sāriputta:

3. "Now what evil deed was done with your body, speech, or mind?[1] Because of what act have you gone hence to the world of petas?"

The petī:

4. "Reverend sir, I did not have compassionate relatives, father and mother, or even other kinsmen who would urge me, saying, 'Give, with devotion in your heart, a gift to recluses and brahmans.'
5. "From that time for five hundred years in this form I have been wandering, nude, consumed by hunger and thirst; this is the fruit of my wicked deeds.
6. "With a believing heart, I worship you, sir. O wise, powerful one, pity me! Go, give some gift in my name; free me from my misery, O venerable one."

The redactors continue the narrative:

7. Consenting with the words, "Very well," the compassionate Sāriputta gave to the monks a morsel of food, a handful of cloth, and a bowl of water and ascribed to her the donation.
8. Immediately thereupon, when this was transferred to her, the result came to pass. This was the fruit of the gift: food, clothing, and drink.
9. Then pure, having clean garments, wearing the best Benares cloth, dressed in various clothes and ornaments, she approached Sāriputta.

Sāriputta:

10. "O devi,[2] you are of excellent appearance, you who are illuminating all the regions like the morning star.[3]
11. "As a result of what is such an appearance? As a result of what is this your portion here, and why fall to your lot whatever pleasures are dear to the mind?
12. "This I ask of you, devī,[4] a very powerful one, you who have become human, what good deed have you done? Whence have you such radiant majesty, and why does your splendour illuminate all the regions?"

The petī:

13. "Me, with all my bones exposed,[5] emaciated, famished, naked, and with wrinkled skin, you, merciful seer, have seen here in my misery.
14. "When you gave to the monks a morsel of food, a handful of cloth and a bowl of water, you transferred to me the virtue of the gift.
15. "Behold the fruit of the morsel: desiring pleasure, I enjoy for ten hundred years food with many flavours.
16. "Behold what sort of result there is from the handful of cloth: as many clothes as there are in the kingdom of Nandarāja.
17. "Venerable sir, I have more than that number of garments and coverings, silken and woollen, linen and cotton.
18. "Many and precious are they; moreover they are hanging in the sky; and I wear whichever one, I assure you, strikes my fancy.
19. "Behold what sort of result there is from the bowl of water: four deep, well-laid-out lotus-ponds.
20. "They have clear waters and beautiful banks; they are cool and have pleasing fragrance; they are covered with the pink lotus and the blue lotus and full of the filaments of the water-lily.
21. "I for my part enjoy myself, play and rejoice, having no fear from any quarter. Reverend sir, I have come hither to the world to worship the compassionate seer."

THE STORY OF THE MOTHER OF THE ELDER SĀRIPUTTA

While the Teacher was dwelling at Veluvana, he told this story.

One day the venerables Sāriputta, Mahāmoggallāna, Anuruddha, and Kappina were sojourning in a certain spot in the forest not far from Rājagaha. Now at that time in Benares a certain brahman of great wealth and resources was a well unto recluses and brahmans, indigents, tramps, wayfarers and beggars, gave away food, drink, clothes, lodging and other benefits. He ordered his life and gave, according to opportunity and as was fitting, to those coming and going, everything necessary for the road.[6] He said to his wife: "Madam, do not neglect this business of giving, but carefully look after it, as has been appointed." She assented but when he was gone away, she cut short the rule of charity for the monks. Furthermore, to wayfarers who had come for shelter she pointed out an abandoned tumble-down shed behind the house, saying: "Stay there." When the wanderers came there for food, drink, and other things, she would utter a curse, enumerating to each one whatever was impure and loathsome, saying: "Eat dung! drink urine! drink blood! eat the brain of your mother!" Taken up at her death by the power of *karma,* she was reborn as a petī who endured misery in conformity with her misbehaviour. Remembering their kinship in her former existence and desiring to approach Sāriputta, she came to his abode. There the devas of his home refused her admittance. Wherefore she spoke as follows: "In the fifth previous life I was mother of the honourable elder Sāriputta; permit me to enter the door to see him." Upon hearing this, they granted her admittance. When she was inside, she stood at the far end of the cloister and saw him. As he noticed her, he was moved in his mind by compassion, and so he asked her:

1. "Naked and of hideous appearance are you, emaciated and with prominent veins. You thin one, with your ribs standing out, who are you now, you who are here?

The petī:

2. "I was your own mother formerly in other lives.[7] I have been reborn in the peta-world, afflicted with hunger and thirst.
3. "The discarded, the cast-out, saliva, nose-mucus, phlegm, the fat of burning bodies, and the blood of delivered women;
4. "And the blood both of the wounded and of those whose noses and heads are cut off, in short whatever (disgusting) is connected with men and women, I, half dead with hunger, eat.
5. "Pus and blood I eat of animals and of men; I am without refuge and without a home, lying upon the black bed.[8]
6. "Give, dear son, a gift for me, and when you have given it, assign to me the credit; thus indeed I may be freed from eating pus and blood."

The following day Sāriputta with the other three, seeking alms in Rājagaha arrived at the residence of King Bimbisāra. When the king asked: "Reverend sirs, why have you come hither?" the venerable Mahāmoggallāna told the king what had happened. Saying, "Reverend sirs, it is permitted," the king dismissed them, summoned his minister, and bade him: "Build in the grove the city four cabins provided with shade and water."

When the huts were finished, he gave them with all life-necessities to the elder Sāriputta. Then the latter presented it to the universal congregation of monks at whose head was the Buddha and assigned the credit to the petī. She deriving its benefits was reborn in the deva-world. Rich in all she wanted, she one day approached the venerable Mahāmoggallāna, and told him in detail both her peta and deva rebirth.

Wherefore it is said:

7. After he had heard his mother's speech, the compassionate Upatissa[9] summoned Moggallāna, Anuruddha, and Kappina.
8. Having made four huts,[10] he gave them to the Church of the four regions; he designated the huts, the food and the drink as a gift of his mother.
9. Immediately afterwards, when the credit for this was transferred to her, the result was produced; of the gift, this was the fruit: food, drink, and clothes.
10. Thereupon, pure, having clean garments, dressed in the best Benares cloth and ornaments, arrayed in various kinds of clothes and ornaments, she approached Kolita.[11]

Mahā-Moggallāna:

11. "Devī, you are of excellent appearance, you who are illuminating all the regions like the morning star.
12. "As a result of what do you have such an appearance?

On account of what is happiness your portion here, and why fall to your lot whatever pleasures are dear to the heart?

13. "This I ask of you, devī, very powerful one, you who have become human, what good deed have you done? Whence have you such radiant majesty, and why does your splendour illuminate all the regions? "

The petī:

14. "Through the gift of Sāriputta I am happy, having no fear from any quarter. Reverend sir, it is you, the merciful seer here in the world, that I have come hither to worship."

THE STORY OF MĀTTA

While the Teacher was sojourning at Jetavana, he told this story.

At Sāvatthī there was a certain landowner, believing and pious. His wife, however, named Mattā, was unbelieving, without faith, of an angry disposition and barren. Then this man, out of fear lest his lineage be cut off, married a young woman by the name of Tissā. She was believing, pious and pleasant to her husband. She bore a son, who was named Bhūta. As the mistress of the house, she respectfully served four monks. Unable to endure her rival, Mattā when she had swept the house, poured the rubbish upon the head of Tissā. At a subsequent time Mattā died, and being reborn as a petī, she endured five-fold misery through the power of her own *karma*. Her suffering is clear from the text.[12] Then one day that petī with memory of the past appeared unto Tissā, who was making her ablutions behind the house. When Tissā saw her, she asked her:

1. "Naked and of hideous appearance are you, emaciated and with prominent veins. You thin one, with your ribs standing out, now who are you, you who are here?"

Mattā:

2. "I am Mattā, you are Tissā; formerly I was your fellow-wife. In consequence of having done an evil deed, I went from here to the world of the petas."

Tissā:

3. "Now what evil deed was done with your body, speech, or mind? As a result of what act have you gone from here to the world of the petas?"

Mattā:

4. "Both wrathful and unkind was I, envious, niggardly, and deceitful. Since I used abusive language to you, I have gone from here to the world of the petas."

In the following stanzas the conversation is continued:

Tissā:

5. "I too, know it all, how violent you were; but there is something else now which I shall ask you. Why are you covered with dirt?"

Mattā:

6. "You had washed your head and were dressed in clean clothes; and I, forsooth, was still more so; I was more adorned than you.
7. "While I was thus bedight and was looking on, you were talking with our husband. On account of that, great jealousy and wrath arose in me.

8. "Then I took some dust, and you, forsooth, I bestrewed with dust. In consequence of that deed, I am covered with dust."

Tissā:

9. "I verily know it all; you sprinkled me with dust. But there is something else now which I shall ask you. Why are you eaten up with the itch?

Mattā:

10. "Both of us fetching simples, we went into the forest. You took the remedies, and I the fruits of the *kapikacchu*.
11. "Then without your knowledge, I scattered them over your bed. In consequence of this deed I am devoured with the itch."

Tissā:

12. "Verily I know it all; you bestrewed my bed. But there is something else now which I shall ask you. Why are you nude?"

Mattā:

13. "There was an assembly of friends; a gathering of kinsmen took place; and you were invited with our husband, while I was not.
14. "Then without your knowledge, I took away your garment. In consequence of this deed, I am naked."

Tissā:

15. "Verily, I know it all. You took away my clothes. But now something else I shall ask you. Why do you have an odour of ordure?"

Mattā:

16. "Your perfume and garland and new ointment I threw into the cesspool. This evil deed was committed by me. In consequence of this conduct, I give out a smell of ordure."

Tissā:

17. "Verily I know it all; that evil was done by you. But now something else I shall ask you. Why are you in distress?

Mattā:

18. "Whatever property was in our house belonged to both of us equally. Though deeds of charity are a duty, I did not provide for myself a refuge. As a result of that sin, I am in misery.
19. "These very words you told me: 'You are practising wicked deeds; for not with evil works will you easily obtain bliss.'"

Tissā:

20. "With a hostile attitude you approached me; and you also envied me. Behold of what nature is the punishment of evil deeds!
21. "You had maid-servants in the house; verily also those various ornaments of yours; these are now enjoyed by others. Pleasures are not eternal.
22. "Now the father of Bhūta will come home from market. Perhaps he will give you something. Go not hence till then."

Mattā:

23. "Naked and of ugly appearance am I, lean and with my veins standing out on the surface. Here is my loincloth; let not the father of Bhūta see me."

Tissā:

24. "Come, what shall I give you, or what shall I do for you that you may be happy and blest with all you desire?"

Mattā:

25. "Here are four monks from the congregation and four other men. Feed these eight and transfer to me the credit of the gift. Then I shall be happy, blest in the fulfilment of all I desire."

Narrative:

26. She assented, saying, "Very well," and fed the eight monks. She clothed them with garments and ascribed to her the virtue of the donation.
27. Immediately thereupon, when the credit for this was transferred to her, the result came to pass. This was the fruit of the gift: food, clothes, and drink.
28. Then pure, having clean clothes, wearing the best Benares cloth, dressed in various kinds of garments and ornaments, she approached her co-wife.

Tissa:

29. "O devī, you are of excellent appearance, you who are illuminating all the regions like the morning star.
30. "As a result of what do you have such a form? On account of what is happiness your portion here, and why fall to your lot whatever pleasures are dear to the heart?
31. "This I ask of you, devī, you very powerful one, who have become human[13]: What good have you done? Whence have you such radiant majesty, and why does your splendour illuminate all the regions?"

Mattā:

32. "I am Mattā, you are Tissā. Formerly I was your fellow-wife. In consequence of having done an evil deed, I went from here to the world of the petas. Through the gift presented by you I rejoice, having nothing to fear from any quarter.
33. "May you live long, sister, with all your kinsfolk! May you attain the abode free from sorrow and passion, the dwelling of those who have will-power.[14]
34. "Here living a religious life and giving gifts, beautiful one, remove the stain of selfishness together with its roots and enter heaven blameless."

ENDNOTES

1. Cf. above I, 6, 5[1].
2. = *devate*
3. *Osadhī tārakā*, literally, 'star of healing.'
4. = *devi in text also.*
5. *Upakaṇḍakiṃ.* Variant readings: M, D, and B, *uppaṇḍukiṃ*, 'showing jaundice,' 'having a jaundice colour'; C, *upaṇḍukiṃ*, 'suffering from itch.'
6. *sabbābhideyyam.* Read with B. *sabbapāteyyam* (sic Hardy).
7. Lit.: births *(jātīsu)*
8. Commentary: The funeral pyre
9. Upatissa, the personal name of Sāriputta (Sāri's son).
10. *Kuṭiyo kaivā:* a curious misstatement in the text.
11. Kolita, the proper name of Moggallāna. This stanza is only in the Burmese MS., Phayre Collection.
12. *Pālito.*
13. Cf. I, II, 2.
14. *Vasavattīnaṃ.* Commy.: *dibbena adhipateyyena attano vasaṃ vattentānam:* "(of those who) by deva-function carry out their own will." Is this a reference to the fifth group of the next world: *para-* and *nimmitavasivattentā*? (The word *vasa* comes nearest in Pali terms to our 'will,' but is rarely used.)—ED.

Chapter 22

Death, Kingship, and Royal Ancestors in Buganda

Benjamin Ray

Most early writers on the kingdom of Buganda portrayed Buganda's rulers in the light of Sir James G. Frazer's famous concept of "divine" kingship.[1] Later anthropologists showed this interpretation to be fundamentally mistaken and put forward the view that the kingship of Buganda was essentially a political—not a religious—institution; its mythology and ritual served primarily sociopolitical ends.[2] However, much of Buganda's royal ritual and symbolism remains little understood. Frazer's views were often mistaken, but a virtue of his "ritual" approach is its integration of rites and symbols of royal death and vitality into a coherent symbolic pattern. In rejecting this pattern, social anthropologists also turned their attention away from the symbolic dimension of Buganda's royal cosmology, thus leaving largely unexplained the complex of royal ritual constituting the ideological foundation of the kingship.[3] As will become clear, Ganda rites and myths of death and homicide as well as the shrines of the royal ancestors provide a unique perspective for understanding the symbolic dimension of the kingship and hence the ideology on which it was based.

RITES AND POLITICS OF THE ROYAL CORPSE

Unless the king (Kabaka) was killed in battle or died at the hands of a princely usurper, he was allowed to die a natural death. Unlike other African kingdoms, Buganda did not practice ritual regicide as a means of "saving" the divine soul of a dying or ailing monarch from the dangers of mortal decay.[4] In the past the Kabaka's death was, however, kept secret until his ministers could secure the safety of the capital (in the face of impending anarchy) and could choose his successor, who, in turn, frequently had to kill off rival princes for the throne. When all preparations had been

"Death, Kingship and Royal Ancestors in Buganda," by Benjamin C. Ray in *Religious Encounters with Death*, edited by Frank E. Reynolds and Earle H. Waugh, University Park, PA: The Pennsylvania State University Press, 1977, pp. 56-67.

made, the monarch's death was publicly signaled by the beating of the royal drums. The sacred fire, which burned at the palace and symbolized royal vitality, was put out and its official attendant was strangled. Officials announced the Kabaka's death by the expressions "the fire has gone out" or "the Kabaka is no longer able to fight." No one ever said the Kabaka had died. Instead, people referred to their deceased king as having "gone away" or as having "disappeared," both expressions being common Ganda euphemisms for death. In reference to the Kabaka, these expressions also recall the mythical tradition about the "disappearance" of Kintu, the sky-born founder of the kingship, who did not die but went away or disappeared into the forest at Magonga after establishing the kingdom. Indeed, Kintu's legendary disappearance became a symbolic paradigm for the death of his successors and for the architecture of their spirit shrines. Like Kintu, the Kabakas do not die; they disappear into the forest sanctuaries of their shrines.

In Buganda the purpose of the royal funerary-accession rituals was not the transference of the divine soul of the king to his successor (as Frazer's theory assumed)[5] but rather the transference of the political rights and duties of the kingship itself. In these ceremonies the body of the deceased Kabaka played a crucial role; royal accession rites followed the general Ganda funerary-inheritance ritual pattern in which the body of the deceased is an essential ingredient.[6] It is proof that the person has died, and without it the designated heir cannot perform the inheritance ceremonies that invest him (or her) with his (or her) predecessor's social role. In the royal context, the accession ceremonies require the king-elect together with his chief ministers to perform a leave-taking rite, which involves placing a new barkcloth over the royal corpse while gazing into its face and saying, "I cover it with barkcloth." Possession of the king's body was therefore a *sine qua non* for accession to the throne, especially in cases of disputed succession between rival princes. As Professor M.S.M. Kiwanuka observed, "the prince who had it [the body] would be the one who performed the funeral rites and then went through the accession ceremonies."[7]

That the royal corpse still had political as well as ritual meaning more recently is revealed by the Ganda response to the return of the body of the Kabaka Sir Edward Mutesa II from London in 1971. Mutesa had died in exile under the regime of Uganda's former Prime Minister Obote, who had abolished the kingship. When the army leader, General Idi Amin, overthrew Obote, one of his first acts was to call for the return of Mutesa's body and for a proper burial of Buganda's popular king. Although Amin was not himself a Muganda, he wished thereby to win all-important Ganda political support for his new government. When the body arrived, Ganda response was tumultuous and unrestrained. Thousands of mourning Baganda poured into Kampala, the capital, to greet the casket containing their beloved Kabaka. For five years the Baganda had lived without their Kabaka and although the kingship had been abolished, the exiled Kabaka still remained Buganda' s "symbol of ultimate concern."[8] In Ganda eyes, the return of the Kabaka's body meant nothing less than the return of their historic cultural identity.

Although the celebration of the return of Mutesa's body was primarily a Ganda event, Amin used the occasion to his own political advantage. Without forewarning the Baganda, he had the body taken by helicopter directly from the airport at Entebbe to Kololo Hill in Kampala, where Uganda's independence ceremonies had taken place just nine years before. By circumventing the twenty-mile road journey through the heart of Buganda, where thousands of Baganda were waiting to greet the Kabaka's casket, Amin quickly brought the body to a place of national rather than local Ganda significance. At Kololo, Amin made a major speech before Mutesa's body, reminding the Baganda that although Mutesa had been their king, he had also been the first president of "all" Uganda. In this way Amin tried to direct Ganda loyalty beyond their Kabaka to himself as the new president. Over the radio the Kabaka's brother also appealed to the Baganda not to kill members of political parties that had not supported the Kabaka, for some Baganda were reported to be saying, "I shall give my life [you shall slaughter me] if Mutesa really died." The next day, Amin went to Namirimbe Cathedral where, despite his Muslim faith, he attended services in order to receive the salutations of thousands of joyous Baganda, "You have saved us, Dada"; "Dada, you have redeemed us"; "Long life Dada."

For the Baganda, the return of Mutesa's body clearly raised hopes for the return of the kingship itself. Now Mutesa's successor could be ritually installed, thus achieving Buganda's political "redemption." But these hopes were quickly dispelled. Soon after the funeral ceremonies at the royal tombs at Kasubi, the new government was forced to clarify the situation. It had previously urged the Ganda chiefs not to allow the appointed successor, Prince Ronald Mutebi, to place the barkcloth over his father's body. In the government's view this "would signify his virtual enthronement." But the rite had been duly performed at Kasubi. Nevertheless, the government refused to recognize the existence of a new Kabaka, "the barkcloth act being only a rite."[9] As far as the government was concerned, the Kabakaship had been buried with the late Kabaka. While complying with the government's wishes against fully installing a new Kabaka, the Ganda chiefs had Prince Ronald perform the barkcloth rite in order to make him Mutesa's official heir and thus Buganda's prince regent. If the king was dead, the dynastic line still had a chance to survive.

CORONATION "CHARTER" OF CONQUEST AND REGICIDE

In the past, the royal corpse was removed after the performance of the barkcloth rite and was taken away for embalming and burial. This process lasted approximately six months; then the king went into mourning. In nonroyal contexts, the body is buried immediately after the family leave-taking ceremony, and mourning begins. In both instances, the mourning period is a time between the burial of the deceased and the installation of his successor when the descent group of the deceased lives in an anomalous situation without any jural or ritual authority. The significance of this period is appropriately expressed through symbols of reversal indicative of the "betwixt and between" status of the deceased's relatives. None of the relatives is allowed to work; their food is cooked and eaten charred and whole; they must wear old clothes; and they are prohibited from washing, cutting hair and nails, and from engaging in sexual relations.

In the royal context, the period of mourning was preceded by a series of "coronation" ceremonies at the royal shrines on Budo Hill.[10] As several authors have pointed out, the political purpose of these rites was to legitimize the chosen prince as the official successor to the throne. But, more important, their symbolic purpose was to link the princely successor to the origin traditions of the kingship in preparation for his accession. What these traditions recall is the precedent of royal succession by conquest and regicide.

The ceremonies began with a mock combat, called the "battle of reeds," between the advancing party of the Kabaka elect and the priestly guardians of the hill-top shrines. Both sides fought with elephant grass "spears" until the king's party "conquered" the defending priests and ascended the hill, thus capturing the kingship.[11] This battle reenacted previous conquests that had occurred at Budo, the last being Kintu's conquest of Bemba-Musota, the "snake" chief, who ruled the land before Kintu's arrival.[12] Kintu's victory marked the origin of the Ganda kingship and expressed its ideology of succession by conquest. Following this tradition, the "victory" of the new Kabaka's party demonstrated that the chosen prince has the right to obtain the supernatural resources of the kingship and to succeed to the throne in conformity with the precedent of conquest and killing. Although succession by election of the ministers of state frequently occurred, conquest by rival princes was, until recent times, the dominant pattern. As Kabaka Mawanga was told at his installation in 1884, "Fight your enemies and conquer Buganda." According to one Ganda author, this meant "a kingdom is always conquered, not succeeded to,"[13]

After the ritual battle the Kabaka-designate was taken by the priests to view the relics of the four shrines on the hill. These commemorated a succession of indigenous rulers who attained the throne by regicide. The most important shrine (and the only one now standing) is the House of Budo, which contains the jawbone of the legendary priest Budo. As if to put an end to the tradition of regicide associated with the kingship, Budo made a magic horn and gave it to prince Namugala and his brothers, saying, "If any of you becomes king and steps on the horn he will never be overthrown."[14] When Namugala succeeded to the kingship after killing his predecessor, he established Budo hill as the main "coronation" site because of the power of the horn he had implanted there in a mound, called Nakibuuka.[15] The mound is located on a promontory where Kintu slew Bemba, and it marks the grave where Bemba and his predecessors are buried. The climax of the ceremonies occurred when the Kabaka-elect and his queen sister crawled across the promontory toward the mound for their investiture. Stripped of their regal dress, the royal pair were pulled to their feet on top of the mound by Budo's chief priest and invested with new barkcloths signifying their accession. Then the chief priest gave the new king the royal spear and told him, "Go and conquer all your enemies." Grasping the spear, the Kabaka responded with the words, "I am the king to live longer than my ancestors, to rule the nations, and to put down rebellion." With this vow the king confirmed his authority to kill for the sake of his own longevity for the security of the kingship. A kingship that originated in regicide was thus to be sustained through homicide. This involved the authority not only to execute criminals and rebels but also to murder otherwise loyal subjects for ritual purposes.

THE "FOWL" AND THE ORIGINS OF DEATH

At the conclusion of the ceremonies at Budo, the king went into mourning for a period of about six months and lived secluded in a specially constructed hut in accordance with the symbolic restrictions described above. When the king was informed that his predecessor had been fully entombed and buried, he ordered the drums to be sounded and decreed the end of mourning. The next day the king "hunted" and killed a gazelle, and afterward he washed and shaved to remove all traces of mourning. The hunting ceremony was performed to commemorate the legendary return of King Kimera, the third Kabaka of Buganda, who was born in the foreign kingdom of Bunyoro and returned to Buganda to reclaim the throne, hunting as he came. In a symbolic sense, this rite also signaled the "return" of the Kabaka-elect from his secluded state of mourning ("outside" the sphere of the kingship) to the final ritual stage wherein he would acquire the full rights and duties of the throne and become fully incorporated into his kingdom.

When the "hunt" was over, two men were arbitrarily seized and brought before the king. The king wounded one of them slightly with his hunting spear. This man was called the "fowl," and he was then taken away and put to death. Another human "fowl" was wounded by the king and killed at the conclusion of the installation ceremonies. After taking his enthronement vows ("If I am the real king, I will conquer my enemies"), receiving the royal sword ("With it cut judgment in truth, and anyone who rebels against you, you shall kill with this sword"), and beating upon the Mujaguzo drums, two men were brought forward and the king wounded one of them with an arrow. This man was later taken to the border of the neighboring kingdom of Bunyoro (Buganda's traditional enemy) where he was killed, and his body was burned with a fire made from the center post taken from the deceased king's tomb. According to Kagwa, this man was called the "Fat Rooster killed during the king's ceremonies."

The killing and eating of a fowl is a customary feature in all Ganda funerary-inheritance ceremonies, and it precedes the installation of the heir. The fowl is cooked over a fire made from the center post of the house of the deceased and it is eaten by the members of the family. According to Roscoe and Gorju, this is done to remind the people of the origin of death.[16] In the beginning, death was unknown when Kintu and Nambi (here represented as the first couple) departed from heaven to live on earth.[17] As they were leaving, Nambi's father, Gulu ("Heaven"), told Kintu never to allow Nambi to return, even if she forgot something, because she would risk encountering her brother, Walumbe ("Death"), who would want to follow her to earth and "kill your children." But Nambi returned despite Kintu's warning because she had forgotten to bring along grain to feed her chickens. When Walumbe saw her return, he chided her for leaving and for no longer cooking for him, since this is an unmarried sister's customary responsibility. Walumbe's accusation is also the customary charge elder brothers make at their sister's betrothal ceremonies. Walumbe then went to Buganda with his sister and asked Kintu to give him one of his daughters as a cook, but Kintu refused. Whereupon Walumbe caused the girl to die, and in this way death became the fate of the rest of Kintu's children and descendants. Walumbe's claim to Kintu's children also follows Ganda social custom, since the mother's brother has first rights to his sister's offspring. Convention prescribes that a father must give his brother-in-law a token gift when his children come of age in order to "ransom" them, lest the mother's brother claim them for himself.[18] By thus portraying death as the "mother's brother," the Baganda explain why death has the ultimate claim on human lives. In the funerary context, the eating of the funeral fowl also serves as a reminder that death's claim stemmed from a chance misdeed at the beginning of time.

ROYAL HOMICIDE: ORDER AND VITALITY

Although no explanation for the substitution of men for birds in the royal installation ceremonies is explicitly given, it is apparent that these ritual murders are related to the theme of ritual homicide that dominates the concluding portion of the installation ceremonies.

These murders fall under the general rubric of *kukuza*—"strengthening," "maturing," and "protecting" the heir. In nonroyal contexts, the kukuza rite is performed by the heir by stepping over his ritual sister's legs, an act which, according to Mair, "symbolized sexual intercourse." On this and other occasions Mair reports that the purpose of the kukuza is "to produce a general beneficial effect on the process with which it is connected" and "the period which it inaugurates," in this case the accession of the new heir.[19] In the royal context, the killing of the second human "fowl" is followed by a series of subsequent kukuza murders, all of which are said to "invigorate" and "confirm" the king in his kingdom. The parallelism between the two forms of kukuza, sexual and homicidal, appears explicit: both are expressions of intrinsic power. The sexual form of kukuza is a display of intrinsic human power, while the homicidal form is a display of intrinsic royal power.

This connection between kingship and the act of homicide is confirmed by B. M. Zimbe in an interesting passage at the beginning of *Kabaka ne Buganda*. There he points out that "when an enemy was killed in battle, Baganda would say, 'I have killed you on behalf of the Kabaka' (because I have no power to kill, only the

Kabaka). God (Katonda) gave the power to kill exclusively to the Kabaka. Even when killing animals, one says *kulwa Kabaka*. All things lie under the power of the Kabaka, both men and animals."[20] Accordingly, the installation killings followed a definite sequence; first the king displayed his power over the animal world by a royal "hunt," and then he displayed his power over his human subjects by a similar act, thus extending his dominion over all living beings. As we have seen, the killing of the first human "fowl" was preceded by a "hunt" in which the king killed a gazelle, while the second "fowl" was killed after the king had wounded this victim with a hunter's arrow. Another murder committed several months after the king's accession (to "invigorate" the new king) followed the same pattern. First, the king killed a leopard, one of the most ferocious nocturnal killers, and then, with his spear, he wounded a man, who was taken away and strangled. The leopard skin was later stitched together with the skin of a lion, the "king" of the daylight predators, and made into a royal carpet, symbolic of the ultimacy of the king's power.[21]

Sometime after his installation at Budo, the new Kabaka went to Nankere where he inaugurated a final orgy of killing to mark his accession. First, according to Kagwa, "he went out of his way to Bukoto in Kyadondo for hunting."[22] Then Nankere presented him with one of his sons (or relatives), who was dressed as a prince, and thus as a potential challenger to the throne. This man was killed, and the muscles of his back were used to make royal anklets to add "vigor" to the king. A whip was also made from the skin of the victim's back and used to enforce order at the king's court. Later, at Busiro the king ordered a number of arbitrary executions among the ranks of his personal servants and pages. Those who responded obediently to a series of royal commands found themselves to be the unfortunate victims of royal anger; their dutiful behavior was interpreted in various ways as a failure to properly serve the king and thus implicitly as a form of rebellion.

Although these killings were said to strengthen (kukuza) the king, it is also clear that they were statements about the nature of royal authority. As one of Mair's informants put it, these murders were assertions that "the new king had entered on his reign and acquired the power of life and death over his people."[23] They may also have had an archetypal dimension, that is, to have been repetitions of an original mythical act, for homicide like the kingship originated from a primordial act of the founder, Kintu. In the beginning, murder did not exist until Kintu, in a fit of rage, speared and killed his faithful prime minister, Kisolo, for punishing a criminal at court without the king's knowledge. "Conscience-striken, Kintu ran away and vanished," never to return.[24] Homicide thus originated as an expression of royal anger against a suspected but otherwise dutiful palace servant, exactly as portrayed in the final sequence of ritual murders when the newly installed Kabaka "angrily" killed some of his most faithful servants on the pretext of failing to serve the king. What this showed, among other things, was that only the king could distinguish appearance from reality, that is, loyalty from rebellion. Thus he held the key to political order. Hence, when the king killed his subjects, even for what appeared to be perfectly arbitrary reasons, this was a display not only of royal authority but also of order in its purest form.

From time to time, and whenever the king fell ill, the priest of the war god, Kibuuka, also ordered arbitrary killings as a form of kukuza. As Mair points out, these murders were not performed as sacrifices to appease the gods nor were they occasions to execute convicted criminals as a display of royal power. Rather, like the installation murders, they were performed as ritual "purifications" (kukuza) to "protect" the king and to "set the land aright." This connection between taking human life and strengthening the king has been noticed by several authors, but it has not been satisfactorily explained. Drawing on Roscoe's account, Frazer regarded these murders as magical ways of transferring the victim's soul-vitality to the king, thus renewing his powers;[25] but Roscoe's informants never gave this or any other explanation. Mair was unable to discover any explicit formulation about the efficacy of such murders apart from their stated purpose of protecting (kukuza) the king, and setting the land in order.[26] Richards indicates that such killings were both magical rites and displays of royal power.[27] But why this kind of display, and how could it be thought to strengthen the king and to order the kingdom?

The explanation appears to lie in the myths and rituals of the kingship. As we have seen, the installation rites assert that the kingship originated in regicide and that it was to be sustained through homicide. Murder thus constituted the foundation and strength of the kingship. All royal symbols reinforce this point. The king is referred to as the lion and the leopard, predators whose power is manifested by killing. He is also a hunter, a killer among men; and he is likened to the "queen termite" who requires the supreme sacrifice of the members of her colony on her own behalf. Indicative of this attitude is one of the popular names that kings gave to their palaces, *kanyakasasa,* "Blacksmith's Forge." It derives from the proverb "Just as the blacksmith's shop has coal burning all the time, yet no ashes accumulate, so it is with the king who always kills his people, yet they go to him."[28]

To be sure, the practice of killing subjects could be carried too far, and kings who did so were said to be cruel and soon found themselves to be the object of revolt and the victims of regicide. But if not overdone, some public display of arbitrary death was an accepted phenomenon. Although appalling to European visitors, such as the nineteenth-century explorer John Hanning Speke, who suspected that Mutesa I used human beings for rifle practice, it was an accepted, indeed, expected mode of exhibiting royal power, especially when that power seemed most threatened by sickness in the palace or on the throne. The power thus displayed was the essence of the kingship; and display renewed that essence. This was not political murder but controlled symbolic killing that belonged to the "peace" of the incumbent's reign. It contrasted with the period of anarchical political killing of the chaotic interregnum when princes competed for the throne. At court, the occasional killing of palace officials for minor offenses was an analogous symbolic display. As a high form of entertainment, it provoked outbursts of mockery and nervous laughter from other officials in the competitive palace meritocracy. At most, the unfortunate victim could thank the Kabaka for "correcting" him and at least in this way achieve a measure of redemption by dying as a tribute to royal power and authority.

CYCLE OF THE MOON: DEATH AND LIFE

If arbitrary death by royal decree served as a constant symbol of royal order and vitality, the appearance of the new moon served a similar function on the celestial plane as a symbol of cosmic vitality and order. The appearance of the new moon signified a resurgence of life after a period of darkness when the lunar rhythm was momentarily interrupted.[29] According to one Luganda account, "On the day the new moon became visible, people rejoiced, took out their magic horns and requested that their lives might be prolonged and praised their gods for having enabled them to see the new moon. The following day was Bwerende. They did not do any work that day and congratulated one another upon having been able to see a new moon and wished one another to see it again."[30] These ritual days of rest were the principal occasions when the people visited the temples to honor the gods.

At this time also, members of the royal class visited the shrines of the dynastic ancestors. At the palace, the king's "Twin" (a vase-shaped container which held part of the royal placenta and personified the king) was taken from its temple and brought before the king who unwrapped and inspected it. Afterward the Twin was exposed to the moonlight and anointed with butter. Today this ceremony is no longer performed, but I have been told that on the night of the new moon the king did not sleep in the palace with his wives but went to another hut where he spent the night alone. The next day the king observed the prohibition against work and passed the day reviewing the relics of the national gods at his palace shrines "as a sign of respect and gratitude for having been tided over another month ['moon']."[31] These ritual prohibitions against work and sexual relations suggest that originally the moon may have been thought to "die" during its dark phase, since apart from the lunar days of Bwerende, such prohibitions are associated only with periods of mourning. In any case, at the time of the new moon the idea of passage through a period of darkness and a transition that reminded the people of death was explicitly expressed. When the moon became visible again, the kingdom celebrated a renewal of life and reestablished contact with the spiritual world of the ancestors and hero-gods, thus reforging the unity of the cosmos.

ROYAL SHRINES: HISTORY, DRAMA, AND PILGRIMAGE

As the preceding statement implies, Ganda cosmology is based on a division between the world of the living and the world of the dead. Since the spiritual realm is the world of the dead, the gods *(lubaale)* are regarded as the spirits of national heroes who became gods after they died. Similarly, the kings are revered as sacred beings only after they have died, when they become spirits in the service of the kingship. After the entombment of the royal corpse, the jawbone was removed and taken to a palace shrine where it was enthroned in the concealed forest portion of the shrine. This is where the spirit of the king also went to live. The spirit then chose a new "wife" to serve as a medium, and henceforth the spirit, called the Ssekabaka, appeared and spoke to the people of the Kabaka's court.

The divine aspect of the kingship thus belonged to the sphere of the dead Kabakas (Ssekabakas), not to the living kings, as early writers believed. To be sure, the Kabakas were surrounded by numerous taboos and were accorded an enormous degree of respect; their despotic authority inspired considerable awe.[32] But, unlike other African kings, they had no divine qualities or special mystical powers. They were entirely human figures within an institution whose political dimension was completely secular. What has been overlooked, however, is that the kingship as a whole included both political and spiritual dimensions, whose division and unity conformed to the dualistic living/dead character of Ganda cosmology. This is clearly marked in the spiritual geography of the kingdom. At the center lies the county of Busiro, which was set apart as the sphere of the royal ancestors. It was governed by a chief, called the Mugema, who had responsibility over the royal funerary ceremonies, and it is where most of the dynastic shrines *(masiro)* are located. The rest of Buganda is the sphere of the living denizens of the kingdom where the living monarchs reigned.

This spiritual division also involves an important temporal dimension. The ancestor shrines belong to the past, and the territory on which they are located is regarded as the ancient "center" of the kingdom, from which it later expanded as new territory was conquered and added on. Collectively and individually, the shrines thus constitute what Oliver has called the historical "charter" of Buganda.[33] Each is a miniature "palace," whose personnel and relics maintain an unbroken continuity between the past and the present. Living at or near the shrine are the descendants of the Kabaka's prime minister and his queen sister in addition to a small retinue of local princesses and other shrine attendants, including the resident medium. Within the shrine itself are displayed a number of spears, shields, and daggers. These stand together in an upright position before the *mwaliiro*, or "altar" platform, in front of the barkcloth curtain concealing the "forest" sanctuary, where the "lion" lives. This collection of relics is especially important as a mnemonic device for remembering the history of the Kabaka's reign. Each relic has a name associated with an important historical event in the Kabaka's life. The more sacred relics are hidden from view within the forest. They include the Kabaka's jawbone and his Twin, together with the Twins of his queen sister and other royal offspring.

As the foregoing description implies, the shrines are not merely museums of a long dead past, they are also living theaters where the past may be repeatedly revived and encountered anew in the present. They are palaces where royalty may go to "attend the court" of the dynastic spirits, hence the symbolic nature of the shrine's architecture. The forest portion of the shrine represents the "other" world of the spirits and it enables them to remain in close contact with their descendants in this world, and this world with them. Within the shrine the two worlds meet precisely at the center at the mwaliiro in front of the forest and the opened curtain. The mwaliiro lies directly under the main roofbeam or the dome (of the traditional conical shrines) and it is the point of juncture between the forest and the human world. This is where the mediums sit when they become possessed by the royal spirits. Since the curtain can be opened and closed, it both reveals and conceals the spirit world of the forest. When it is opened, the front portion of the shrine becomes a stage where the spirits manifest themselves "on the heads" of their "bearers" (mediums) as they dance and flourish their spears before the seated congregation.

Such ceremonies used to occur regularly at the time of the new moon. Now they are held less frequently because of the dispersal of some of the princesses in charge of the shrines. Even though the prime minister may still be living at or near the shrine (as most of them do), he has no jurisdiction over it. He acts primarily as a caretaker, subject to the authority of the head princess, who is the descendant of the Kabaka's queen sister. This situation represents a reversal of the prime minister's political role at the palace of the living monarch, where he is the chief official. But in the ritual sphere of the dead, the women are in charge. They lead and dominate the singing, dancing, and possession, in contrast to their minor role in the political sphere, which is dominated by men. Most mediums are, in fact, women, and even those who are men are still regarded as the "wives" of the royal spirit. In the absence of any royal clan, the kings belong to their mothers' clans, and the women of these clans are said to be the mothers of the shrine. On important ritual occasions, they bring food to feed the royal spirits. Today, when there is no kingship to provide money for the unkeep of the shrines, this responsibility has also been taken up by the members of the mothers' clans.

The primary attraction of the ceremonies at the shrines is the manifestation of the Kabaka's spirit. On these occasions people come to greet it with songs and to bask in the radiance of the king. At the beginning of the ceremonies the songs beseech the owner of the house (the Ssekabaka) to invade the assembly and settle down upon the heads of their mediums and greet the people. When the spirit arrives, the audience responds with the royal greeting, "You have conquered! You have conquered! You have conquered us, indeed!" The singing becomes more animated and lively as the mediums begin to dance, crouching and thrusting their royal spears toward the seated audience. "How have you been handsome son?/How have you been cowherd?" "Sing well, the 'lion' [the spirit] is 'roaring'/Eee, the iron [the spears] made him speak at [the shrine of] Nabulagala./Convey my message to Ssalongo [the spirit]," "Let me sing for those who will 'eat' [rule over] me." As the songs emphasize, this encounter with the spirits is an event not to be missed. Several songs refer to disappointed latecomers who arrive after the curtain has closed and the spirits have returned to the forest: "They are climbing [onto the mediums], the children of Golooba at

Mpinga./The elders are climbing, I shall come and see./I didn't see him. I found he had closed."

Some people also ask the royal spirits for blessings and money in the belief that they are like the lubaale gods and can materially help them. But members of the royal class who claim to know say this is a misguided (though popular) view and that the ceremonies are purely acts of commemoration, not divination, which is the purpose of the lubaale cult. In the past, however, living monarchs sometimes received advice from the royal spirits in dreams and visions, and as recently as 1954 it was said that the royal mediums sent messages of advice to Mutesa via telegram during his exile in London.

Today, in the absence of a ruling monarch the ceremonies appear to be primarily dramatic celebrations of the past by the royal class, which faces an uncertain political future. For this class, the shrines act as sacred centers, periodically drawing together groups of royalty which lack any clan or lineage unity of their own. Since the members of this class are numerous and tend to be scattered around urban areas, the shrines have acquired the character of pilgrimage sites. During most weeks there are small comings and goings of royalty, mainly princesses especially from nearby Kampala. They stay a few days near the shrine to which they are related, even when there are no ceremonies, simply to renew acquaintances and to spend some time in the country away from the city. The shrines are their country "estates," where there are vegetable and banana gardens, and where the graves of their relatives are located.

The shrines also serve as sacred centers on a broader scale, since they unite in themselves the cosmic, mythic, and historical foundations of the kingdom as a whole. The present ritual headquarters is at Kasubi, located a mile outside Kampala. This shrine, built in the traditional conical thatched-roof style, is where the last four Kabakas are buried, including Mutesa I (1854–84), who was Buganda's last and most powerful precolonial ruler. As a Muslim, Mutesa discouraged the practice of possession by forbidding anyone to become a medium of his spirit (after he died), unless he or she could show a reading knowledge of Arabic, in which Mutesa himself was literate, since he did not want to be "ridiculed." The Kasubi shrine has also become well-known to visitors from outside Uganda as one of Kampala's main tourist sights. During the busiest months of the tourist season, it draws more than two thousand visitors. Recently, the Lungfish clan of Mutesa I's father, Suna II (1824–54), completed a large new conical shrine at Wamala, a few miles north of Kasubi, with a view to its becoming the next ritual headquarters. At the inauguration of this shrine, a large number of Twins were brought in procession from their shrines in Busiro to pay their respects to Suna and his new palace. This was a rare event, unseen since the early years of this century when such processions of the dynastic Twins used to occur at each new moon. At this time the Twins were taken to the palace so that the Kabaka could greet them and thus restore his links to the sacred past as he looked forward to the future. Today, if the political dimension of the kingship no longer exists, its links to the past remain firmly established in the shrines of its dynastic ancestors, and hence its spiritual dimension still survives.

ENDNOTES

1. John Roscoe, *The Baganda* (London: MacMillan, 1911); R. A. Soxnoll, "The Coronation Ritual and Customs of Buganda," *Uganda Journal* 4 (1937): Tor Irstam, *The King of Ganda* (Stockholm: Ethnographical Museum, 1944); P. Hadfield, *Traits of Divine Kingship* (London: Watta, 1949).
2. Audrey I. Richards, "The Ganda", in Audrey I. Richards, ed., *East African Chiefs* (London: Faber & Faber, 1960); Audrey I. Richards, "Authority Patterns in Traditional Buganda," in L. A. Fallers, ed., *The King's Men* (London: Oxford University Press for the East African Institute of Social Research, 1964); Lucy Mair, *Primitive Government* (Harmondsworth: Penguin, 1964), chap. 9; Martin Southwold, "Was the Kingdom Sacred?," *Mawazo* I, no, 2 (December 1967).
3. The watershed of this social-functional approach to sacred kingship in Africa is Evans-Pritchard's Frazer Memorial Lecture, delivered in 1948, "The Divine Kingship of the Shilluk of the Nilotic Sudan," in E. E. Evans-Pritchard, *Social Anthropology and Other Essays* (New York: Free Press, (1962). Following this line is J. H. M. Beattie's interpretation of the royal rituals of Bunyoro, Buganda's powerful western neighbor, to whom Buganda is historically and culturally related. "Rituals of Nyoro Kingship," *Africa* 29, no. 2 (1959). Another essay by Max Gluckman, on Swazi royal rituals ("Rituals of Rebellion in South-east Africa," in Max Gluckman, ed., *Order and Rebellion in Tribal Africa* [New York: Free Press, 1960]) has touched off considerable criticism by advocates of a more "symbolic" approach. See T. O. Beidelman, "Swazi Royal Ritual," *Africa* 36 (1966). For a critical appraisal of Evans-Pritchard's original essay on the Shilluk, see Michael Young, "The Divine Kingship of the Jukun: A Re-evaluation of Some Theories," *Africa* 36 (1966). For further discussion see Benjamin C. Ray, *African Religions: Symbol, Ritual, and Community* (Englewood Cliffs, N. J.: Prentice-Hall, 1976), chap 4.
4. Traditions of this kind have been recorded in Bunyoro and in Nkore, Buganda's southern neighbor. Although Evans-Pritchard has doubted both the actual occurrence and religious motive of regicide among the Shilluk (emphasized by Frazer), regarding it as a political "fiction," what matters, as Beattie ("Rituals of Nyora Kingship," p. 138) has observed in connection with Bunyoro, "is not the question whether any kings died actually in this way, but rather the fact that this is how the kingship was thought about."
5. *The Golden Bough*, abridged ed. (New York: Macmillan, 1948), chap. 24.
6. On Ganda funerary-inheritance ceremonies, see Roscoe, *The Baganda*, chap. 4; and Lucy Mair, *An African Peoples in the Twentieth Century* (London: Routledge & Sons, 1934), chap. 8.
7. Ed., *The Kings of Buganda*, trans. of Apolo Kagwa, *Bassekabaka be Buganda* (Nairobi: East African Publishing House, 1971), p. 82.
8. F. B. Welbourn, *Religion and Politics in Uganda, 1952–1962* (Nairobi: East African Publishing House, 1965), p. 45.
9. *Uganda Argus*, 6 April 1971. Full reports of events surrounding the return of Mutesa's body were published in the *Uganda Argus* and in two Luganda newspapers, *Taifa* and *Munno*, 1–6 April 1971.
10. Accounts of the installation ceremonies vary in detail. I have drawn upon the following authors: Apolo Kagwa, *Ekitabo Kye Empisa za Baganda*, (London: MacMillan, 1952), chap. 3; Apolo Kagwa, *The Customs of the Baganda*, translations of *Ekitabo Kye Empisa za Baganda*, 1st ed., 1918, by E. B. Kalibala, ed. M. Mandelbaum Edel (New York: Columbia University Press, 1934), chaps. 3 and 6; Roscoe, *The Baganda*, chap. 7; B. M. Zimbe, *Baganda ne Kabaka* (Kampala: Gambuze Press, 1939); A. R. Cook, *Uganda Memories, 1847–1940*, (Kampala: Uganda Society, 1945); Audrey I. Richards, *The Changing Structure of a Ganda Village* (Nairobi: East African Publishing House, 1966), chap. 4.
11. The reverse occurs in the Shilluk installation "combat" in which the "kingship captures the king" (Evans-Pritchard, "The Divine Kingship of the Shilluk of the Upper Nile," p. 205).
12. Richards, *The Changing Structure of a Ganda Village*, pp. 36ff.; M. B. Nsimbi, *Waggumbulizi* (Kampala: Uganda Bookshop, 1952), chap. 1.

13. Zimbe, *Buganda ne Kabaka*, p. 81.
14. Apolo Kagwa, *The Kings of Buganda*, p. 75.
15. In 1969 one of the stately old acacia trees flanking the mound fell to the ground. This happened, I was told, when Mutesa died in exile—a fitting testimony to the loss of one of the main underpinnings of the kingship.
16. Roscoe, *The Baganda*, p. 121; Julien Gorju, *Entre le Victoria l'Albert et l'Edouard* (Rennes: Oberthür, 1920), p. 361, n.1.
17. Kagwa, *The Kings of Buganda*, p. 1; Roscoe, *The Baganda*, pp. 462–64.
18. On the Ganda concept of the mother's brother, see Mair, *An African People*, pp. 61, 80, passim.
19. Ibid., pp. 43, 248.
20. *Kabaka ne Buganda*, p. 6.
21. Together these animals represent the total animal world of herbivorous/carnivorous eaters and prey/predator beasts.
22. Kagwa, *Customs*, pp. 16–17; see also Roscoe, *The Baganda*, pp. 210–14.
23. *An African People*, p. 179.
24. Kagwa, *The Kings of Buganda*, p. 7.
25. James G. Frazer, *The Golden Bough, Part IV: Adonis Attis Osiris*, vol. 2, 3rd ed. (London: MacMillan, 1927), pp. 223–26.
26. *An African People*, p. 179.
27. "Authority Pattern," pp. 276–79.
28. Kagwa, *Customs*, p. 9.
29. This idea is found in the kingdom of Nkore and among the Swazi of southern Africa. See John Roscoe, *The Banyankole* (Cambridge: Cambridge University Press, 1923), pp. 110, 125; Hilda Kuper, *An African Aristocracy* (London: Oxford University Press for the International African Institute, 1961), pp. 76, 201–2, 208.
30. Zimbe, *Kabaka ne Buganda*, p. 13.
31. Kagwa, *Customs*, p. 9.
32. Roland Oliver, "The Royal Tombs of Buganda," *Uganda Journal*, vol. 23, pt. 2 (1959).
33. As Southwold points out, "ultimate authority tends to acquire sacredness" ("Was the Kingdom Sacred?," p. 21). However, Southwold sees the sacredness of the kingship exclusively in terms of its political power without recognizing its primary connection with the symbolic role of the king as the representative of the nation and with the rituals of the kingship and the shrines.

Chapter 23

Cults of the Dog

Howey M. Oldfield

THE DOG AS ORIGIN OF DEATH

The dog is closely associated in ancient religions and mythologies with death and the world beyond. "There is reason to suppose" wrote Harold Bayley, "that the Dog-headed Titanic Christopher, who is said to have ferried travellers pick-a-back across a river, was at one time an exquisite conception of Great Puck or Father Death carrying his children over the mystic river." But perhaps we should rather connect his strange, cynocephalous figure with that of Anubis, whose office it was to guide and protect the souls of the dead along the perilous path that led to Osiris.

Whatever its origin, the myth of the dog in the role of an Ambassador from men to the Lord of Life and Death who lived in the sky, but yet maintained close, personal contact with the dwellers on earth, was widely diffused in Africa. And, though the dog does not always figure in these fables of intercourse between gods and men, we frequently meet with the conception that its special mission is to act as intermediary between the denizens of the two worlds. Of this belief we have a typical example in the story of The Two Messengers, which finds a prominent place in the mythology of many African peoples. Whilst divers versions are extant, certain common features are readily recognisable and enable the student to realise that they emanate from a common source.

As might be anticipated, the dog, because of its close association with man, is often one of the messengers. Sometimes it conveys the message from God to man, whilst in other instances it carries the prayers of man to God. Let us look at some representative cases.

The Konde tribe aver that in ancient days death had not visited the earth, yet men had at least some conception of it, for they debated together whether it would be well

"The Dog as Origin of Death," "The Dog as Guide of the Dead," "Canine Funeral Observances," and "The Sagdad or Dog Gaze" from *The Cults of the Dog* by Mary Oldfield Howey, Rochford, England: The C. W. Daniel Company, 1972.

to pray God to grant them death, or no. Opinions were divided and those who considered death would be a boon chose a sheep as their emissary to persuade the deity to bestow it, but those who desired to continue their lives for ever sent a dog to put their case before God. It so happened that the sheep arrived in Heaven before the dog, and obtained the deity's dictum that death should come to earth, and when the dog arrived it could not be reversed. Therefore, ever since that fatal day, men and animals have been mortal.

A very similar fable concerning the origin of death is related in Calabar, on the west coast of the continent, and in it we meet with the same two messengers. According to this account, till long after the creation of the world, death was nonexistent. But the day came when a man fell ill and died. His distressed fellows sent a dog to God to ask him what they should do with the dead man; but the dog was so long returning that the people became weary of waiting, and dispatched a sheep to God with the same question. The sheep quickly came back and announced that God commanded that the dead man should be buried. So this was done. Later the dog also returned, but he brought word that God said, "Place warm ashes on the dead man's belly and he will rise again." But the people told the dog he was too late, for the dead man had already been buried as the sheep had instructed them. And this is why men are buried when they die. And for this cause the dog is driven from men and humiliated because it is through his fault that men are mortal.

In the interior of Togo, a province of the Slave Coast, live a tribe known as the Akposos. They worship the great sky deity Uwolowu, who is believed to be not only a good god, but the Supreme Being and Creator of all things including the lesser gods. Various myths are related concerning Uwolowu, but the one which concerns us here purports to explain the origin of death and is another variation of the Tale of Two Messengers.

In the far away past men sent a dog to bear a message to God to say that when they died they would like to return to earth again. And the dog trotted off on his mission. But on the road he began to feel hungry and he entered a house where a man was boiling some magic herbs, thinking to himself "He is preparing food." Meanwhile an officious frog had decided to take a message of his own composing to Uwolowu, though no one had asked him to do so, and he hopped off to tell the deity that when men died they would rather not return to life. On his way he passed the dog who still sat hopefully watching the hell-broth, and, when he saw Froggy, said to himself: "I'll soon overtake that fellow when I've had a bite of food." But Froggy reached the goal first, and told God that men did not want to live again after death. Soon after up trotted Doggy and said men wanted to continue life after they had died. Of course Uwolowu was very puzzled, and he said to the dog: "I really can't understand such different messages, but as I heard the frog's message first I will accede to it, and will not do what you have asked." This is the reason why when men die they do not return to life again. But frogs come to life again when the sky thunders at the beginning of the rainy season, though they have lain dead all the dry season whilst the Harmattan wind was blowing. And when the rain pours down and the thunder peals you may hear them croaking in the marshes.

So it would seem that Froggy had selfish motives in distorting the message, and gained for his own race the immortality of which he deprived mankind. (Fr. Muller)

Such are some of the legends that centre around the theme of the two messengers, but there are others which show more individuality that we must also consider.

To primitive peoples life and health appear as the natural and normal state of being, whilst death and illness are unnatural, and inexplicable except through violence, or sorcery, or the act of a supernatural artificer. The Louyi, a tribe of the Upper Zambesi, like many other Africans, attribute the origin of human death to their Sky deity, Nyambe, and relate the following legend to explain how the calamity arose. Nyambe owned a dog which, not sharing the immortality of the gods, died, and caused his master to cry: "Let my dog live." But his wife was unsympathetic and said "No, the dog is a thief and ought not to live." In vain Nyambe pleaded with her, saying: "For my part I love my dog." His wife was inexorable and peremptorily demanded that his dead pet should be cast out. Finally Nyambe yielded and together they threw the body outside. Sometime afterwards the god's mother-in-law departed from this vale of tears, and her daughter, Nyambe's wife, cried to her divine spouse: "Let her come to life again." But this time it was the deity's turn to be inexorable. "By no manner of means," he sternly replied. "Let her die and be done with it. I told you my dog ought to be brought to life again and you refused: well it is my will that your mother also die once for all."

This story, which is ostensibly told to account for *human* mortality, has a special interest because the persons and animal involved were so intimately associated with a deity and yet were not exempted from the common fate of death, though after they had suffered this, the god could at will restore them to life. Whether the new life was of a more permanent nature we are not informed. (Jacottet)

The following story illustrating another divergent trend of thought is told by the African tribe of Banyoro (or Bakitara) to account for the occurrence of death, which to them also appears as a strange, unnatural imposition on living beings. The tale relates how once, in the long ago, men rose again after dying and returned to their earthly friends, but animals were not resurrected once they had died.

At this period a certain brother and sister lived together and the woman had a dog to which she was devoted, but, to her great grief, it died. Now when human beings returned after death it was customary for all those living to don their best garments and turn out to welcome their risen friends. On one such occasion the brother and his comrades said to the sister, "Put on your finest clothes and come with us to meet the risen ones." But she, being sad at heart, refused their request, saying, "Why should I do so, since my loved dog has died and departed?" But the great God Ruhanga overheard her reply and was filled with anger because she would not pay respect to the resurrected persons. "So", he exclaimed, "the living do not care what befalls the dead! They shall arise no more, but their lives shall be terminated by death." And this is why when a man dies, he no longer returns to life. (J. Roscoe)

Another African legend which purports to explain the enigma of mortality is related by the Nandi tribe of Masai, a people of Negro stock inhabiting Uganda. This too, though it accords with the widely accepted tale setting out that the dog and not the deity is responsible for what they regard as the dire calamity of death, in other respects differs markedly from the stereotyped pattern of the two messengers. They tell that when men first inhabited the earth a dog appeared before them one day and solemnly announced: "All people will die like the moon, but unlike the moon you humans will not return to life again unless you give me some milk to drink out of your gourd and beer to drink through your straw. If you do this I will arrange for you to go to the river when you die, and to come to life again on the third day." But the people only laughed at the dog's warning and gave him milk and beer to drink off a stool. This made him feel deeply insulted, for he thought he should have been served in the same vessels as were used by his hosts, and although he sacrificed his pride to the point of drinking the milk and the beer, he was yet furious and on his departure proclaimed: "All people will die, and only the moon will return to life." This is why when men die they remain dead, but when the moon dies, she reappears after three days' absence. If only the dog (or the deity which had assumed canine form) had been more courteously treated, human beings would undoubtedly have risen from the dead on the third day, just as does the moon. (Hollis)

Some strange beliefs yet linger on in the islands of the Gambier, and the following which is recorded by Robert Casey in his interesting volume on Easter Island will serve to illustrate our theme.

"When a person is about to die in Manga Reva everybody knows it, for on such occasions the Old Man and His Dog come out of the lagoon. On a bright sunlit morning you can see their footprints coming up the beach of coral sand out of the water. They are clearly defined, these footprints, but not deep as would be those of a living man and dog. Several persons, including two Americans, who saw them state that the marks represent a pressure of not more than five pounds. And if this is taken to indicate that ghosts weigh five pounds it is undoubtedly an important scientific fact. The prints follow the beach to a point opposite the house of the person about to die. Then they turn inland and are lost in the shrubbery. After the expected death occurs the Old Man and His Dog return to the lagoon and resume whatever work is done by ghosts in lagoons. No more is heard of them until another death is imminent."

Such are some of the mythical—or should we say allegorical?—explanations of life's greatest mystery: the origin of Death, when viewed from the stand-point of primitive man. But whilst we smile at their infantile simplicity, let us not forget that our boasted modern science finds itself equally baffled by the same problem and has no acceptable alternative to offer, no solution to give. We live in a universe of impenetrable mystery, a mystery that deepens with our endeavours to discover its hidden meaning.

BIBLIOGRAPHY

Etudes sur les langues du Haut-Zamèze, Troisième Partie, Textes Louyi, pp. 116 et seq, by E. Jacottet. (Paris, 1901.)
Das deutsche Niassaund Ruwuma—Gebiet, Land und Leute, p. 266, by F. Füllerborn. (Berlin, 1906.)
Calabar Stories. (Journal of the African Society No. 18, p. 194, January 1906.)
Die Religionen Togos in Einzeldarstellungen, Anthropos II, by Fr. Muller. (1907.)
The Nandi, p. 98, by A. C. Hollis. (Oxford, 1909.)
The Bakitara, p. 337, by J. Roscoe.
Archaic England, p. 264, by Harold Bayley. (Chapman and Hall, London, 1919.)
Easter Island, p. 64, by Robert J. Casey. (Elkin, Matthews & Marrot, London, 1932.)

THE DOG AS GUIDE OF THE DEAD

It is claimed that in the Neolithic period the Orkneys were one of the most populous portions of the British Isles and that there are nearly as many collective tombs on Rousay as there are farms today (Childe). Of these burial mounds, which number over 2,000, the majority belong to the Pictish period, and there is much evidence that these people were the original inhabitants of the islands. But apart from such monuments scarcely any information regarding them is extant. Circular cairns cover chambers into which from three to fourteen cells open. In them human skeletons have been found, and in one are the skulls of twenty-four dogs and in another seven. It seems at least probable that these animals were sacrificed for, rather than to, the dead, not for the purpose of propitiating the departed, but offered in love to enable them to continue to help, guard and guide those who had been their owners on earth. For though primitive man has no clear conception of the nature of death, he usually regards it with a mystic terror as is inferable from his funeral customs.

The idea of a canine guide for the dead, who would lead them through the unknown and perilous paths of the Underworld, immediately summons the vision of Anubis before the eye of the mind, but, though it seems probable that the Egyptian deity was the prototype of the Old World fantasy that the Guardian of the Dead assumed the form of a dog, we cannot question the evidence that it originated spontaneously and independently in some of the countries that entertained it, since their widely separated situations admit of no other solution. Moreover, Anubis is so many faceted that to endeavour to identify him with any single aspect of his multiple personality is to violate his integrity, and I have found it necessary to devote a special chapter to the contemplation of certain of his attributes including his function as Guide of the Dead. Hence the most prominent example of the theme we are considering is here omitted. None the less we may assume that the adoption of this duty by Anubis explains why in Egypt human beings were so rarely sacrificed to enable their souls to attend their dead masters in the world beyond the tomb. But some few instances of human immolation are discoverable, the most salient examples of which were found in tombs of the First Dynasty grouped around the royal sepulchres. Though by far the greater number of burials were those of women, King Den

(Udymu) also had dwarfs and dogs to minister to his pleasure and safety in the Hereafter, and at least a hundred interments surrounded his tomb. Probably such colossal sacrifices were abandoned at a later date, at least we have no evidence of them.

Similar ideas of loyalty to the dead and a belief that the positions accorded to them on the Other Side were conditioned by the retinue of satellites they took along with them were very prevalent in Africa until quite recent times, and among the Ashantees, in the interior of the Gold Coast, human victims were often immolated in large numbers together with the dogs and other animals that had been co-dwellers with the departed in this world.

The same custom was followed in the northern territories of the Gold Coast and we have Cardinall's vivid description of the ritual practices of the Nankanni tribe in their funeral observances. These involve the slaying of a dog and other animals for the deceased's use in the next world. A fire is first lighted from the branches of the *Kase* tree and into this the dead man's quiver and other essential belongings are thrown, tobacco and salt being added. "A fowl, a sheep and a dog are then sacrificed, the dead man's walking stick is used to poke the fire; and lastly, when all is burnt and the food and beer distributed, the people go home. The deceased is finished with; the man's life is properly ended, and he can and should from now on dwell in the land of the departed and return no more from *tyiru dyega*."

But whether such ideas of African primitives had percolated to them from Egypt, or were spontaneously generated in their own minds, we need feel little hesitation in taking our stand with Herodotus, whose travels in Egypt had convinced him that the Grecian gods were of Egyptian origin. His theory is supported by the celebrated Greek poet and philosopher, Lucian, procurator of the province of Egypt during the reign of Marcus Aurelius, who voices the same opinion in his work on the Syrian goddess, Ashtar.

The Egyptian gods certainly attracted the Greeks, at least in certain circles, and, as we have seen, Anubis was highly venerated in the Greek city of Hebennu, so it is not surprising that in Greece, as in Egypt, the dog had a role of considerable importance in the burial rites of his master and usually accompanied him to continue his mission as guardian and guide when he departed this life. Homer, writing *c.* 850 B.C. mentions the sacrifice of household dogs at the pyre of Patroclus:

"Of nine large dogs domestic at his board,
Fall two, selected to attend their lord.:
Iliad XXIII, 212, Pope.

But though dogs were thus believed to continue their office as guards and even to become the guides of their earthly masters on the farther side of the tomb, an amusing anomaly, recorded by Frazer, is that "An ancient Greek robber or burglar thought he could silence and put to flight the fiercest watch-dog by carrying with him a brand plucked from a funeral pyre."

Did the dog see in the brand a portent of his own impending fate?

Etruscan thought and art appear to have been considerably influenced by that of Greece and evidence of the Etruscan belief in a future life for animals and the continuance of their association with man was discovered more than a century ago in the necropolis of the ancient city of Vulci which once stood on the right bank of the river Fiora. There, in two of the "warrior-tombs" (as also in other excavated sites) the bones of a horse and dog were found alongside those of the human occupants.

Later discoveries have amplified and confirmed this evidence and in the Spring of 1917 the existence of a large subterranean building near the Porta Maggiore at Rome was revealed, at a depth of some 50 feet below the railway that connects Rome with Naples and Pisa. Engineers who were probing the ground to discover the cause of a threatened displacement of an embankment came upon a circular shaft, and through it penetrated into a corridor and thence into a large hall measuring 12 × 9 metres, which proved to be an underground basilica, probably formerly dedicated to chthonian or underworld worship. In the apse they found two sacrificial pits and close to these the skeletons of a buried dog and pig. Because of their habits of digging or rooting in the ground both animals were sacred to the gods of the lower regions and it has been conjectured that the temple had been devoted to services for the dead and that the animals had been sacrificed over the pits on the day of its consecration as an offering to the spirits of the departed. But perhaps it is more probable that they were slain so that their souls might be freed to accompany the dead and together with them take part in the ritual worship of the ancient Etruscan goddess Mana, Mania or Manuana, queen of the Manes and Summanes, the deified souls of the blessed dead, sometimes erroneously identified with Hekate. Her cult was secret and dark with mystery but we know that young puppies as well as grown dogs were immolated on her altars, for Pliny says: "*Catulos lactentes adeo puros existimabant ad cibum, ut etiam placandis numinibus hostiarum uice uterentur his. Genitae Manae catulo res diuina sit, et in coenis deum etiamnum ponitur cotulira.*" (*Historia Naturalis* xxiv, xiv, 4.)

Yet when all the prescribed ritual had been accomplished, doubts as to the welfare of the dead still lingered and the goddess was entreated not to allow any of the sacrifant's family to become "a good one", meaning to die. The city of tombs rose menacingly above the huts of the living and their concentration on death made mortal life one long and painful preparation to escape its penalties and win the proffered pleasures in the world to come, which men would share with the faithful animals who had safely conducted them on the dark and perilous path that led to its golden gateway.

The same far-flung belief in animal immortality and the continuance of their faithful services to those they had loved on earth was clearly the inspiration of Brunhill, the heroine of the *Nibelungenlied,* who, when she threw herself on the funeral pyre that she might not survive Sigurd, had two dogs and two hawks immolated with her, so providing herself and him with trusty and far-seeing guardians and guides.

Among the Greenlanders too, the idea of the dog guide through the intricate labyrinth of the world immediately adjoining our own was strongly held some hundred years ago. The need for its services was especially emphasised where small children were concerned and Hans Egede, writing in 1818, says that when the little ones "die and are buried, they put the head of a dog near the grave, fancying that children having no understanding, they cannot by themselves find the way, but the dog must guide them to the world of souls." Other Greenlanders when they bury a child, kill and bury a dog to be his guide in the spirit world, because they say that "a dog can find its way anywhere."

The Lakhers have the same belief and when a child dies before it has learned to talk a dog must be killed so that the child's soul may hold on to its tail and thus be guided by it to Athiki, the land of the dead.

The Eskimos also sacrificed and buried a dog, in their case actually in the graves of young children, who could not, unaided, find their way to the spirit-land.

Amidst the Garo Hills of Assam we find another example of this widespread belief which seems to have arisen spontaneously in the minds of the aboriginal population, known as the Garos, a tribe of uncertain affinities who are addicted to many curious customs. When one of their number dies they sacrifice a dog and cremate its body together with that of the dead man so that it may accompany his soul and be his guide on his journey to Chikmang, the Spirit-land.

And in the Malay Archipelago, the same conception is to be found among the Tamos, a settled, agricultural people who inhabit the Astrolabe district of New Guinea and exist in perpetual dread of ghosts, whom they believe linger around their former homes long after the death of their bodies. When any of their community die, their great desire is to persuade his soul to depart to the next world, and to accomplish this they expose his corpse on a scaffold in front of his former dwelling, decorated with ornaments and surrounded by flowers, presumably to propitiate him. Then, if finances permit, a dog is hung on either side of the scaffold, so that their souls may guide him to the spirit land and he need no longer trouble his earthly friends because he cannot find his way thither.

When, early in the sixteenth century, the Conquistadors on a voyage of exploration, found their way through the West India Islands to the southern mainland of North America, there to discover a highly civilised nation whose very existence had previously been undreamt of, the remarkable fact forced itself upon their cognizance that despite all the inevitable divergencies of language, mental outlook, climate, race and religion that divided the peoples of the Old World from the inhabitants of Mexico, they yet cherished certain fundamental, foundation beliefs in common. Among these must be counted the idyllic conception that the dog, there, as in the Old World, "the rich man's guardian, the poor man's friend," when earthly life had ended, not only continued to be his guard, but was also his indispensable guide in the life that followed. We have evidence of this in the Mexican *Codex Maghabecchiano* (sheet 60) preserved in the *Biblioteca Nazionale* which is (or was) in Florence and contains a native painting representing the Mummy bundle of a dead warrior, and beside it the blue, hairless dog which preceded the warrior's soul to the Mexican Hades, and had been sacrificed for this mission when its master died.

We meet with the hairless dog again in a fine example of funerary pottery from Colima, which, along with nearly 400 examples of ancient Southern and Central American art, was exhibited at the Berkeley Galleries in London in 1947. These dogs were not only used as guides for the dead, but were also a favourite Aztec table delicacy, so it seems possible that the intention of the sacrificant was not always clear and that the object of this particular offering—whether the actual dog, or its pottery counterpart—may have been to provide the departed's soul with sustenance for his journey. And this would explain why, in New Guinea, two dogs are slain, when finances permit.

But these opinions were not shared by the famous Spanish Jesuit, Francisco Saverio Clavigero, who unsympathetically describing the spells and magical amulets, including the sacrifice of a dog, which Mexicans considered essential to secure the safety and welfare of their friends in the World Beyond, writes:

"One of the chief and most ridiculous ceremonies at funerals was the killing of a *techichi,* a domestic quadruped, resembling a little dog, to accompany the deceased in their journey to the other world. They fixed a string about its neck, believing that necessary to pass the deep river of Chiuhnahuapan or New Waters, they buried the *techichi,* or burned it along with the body of its master, according to the kind of death of which he died. While the masters of the ceremonies were lighting up the fire in which the body was to be burned, the other priests kept singing in a melancholy strain. After burning the body, they gathered the ashes in an earthen pot . . . (which they) buried in a deep ditch, and fourscore days after made oblations of bread and wine over it."

A "ridiculous ceremony"—yes, but both within and without the orthodox religions lurk dark fears and phantoms that make this earth a place of dread to timid souls who shudderingly tread its shadowed pathways which they know inevitably lead to the tomb, however fair their starting points appear. The Aztecs and the mound-builders of Tennessee, like many other peoples scattered all over the world, looked for comfort and support to enable them to face the hidden perils that so closely threatened them in the gloomy regions of death. And they found it in the thought that the canine protectors, who had so faithfully guarded them on earth, would still be true, and able to shield them from danger and guide their footsteps to the desired goal. Even the damned were not left entirely uncared for, but were provided with a dog to assist them in crossing the dark and terrible river that bounded the shore of Mictlampa, the first of the nine hells of the Aztec theologians whither the souls of those who had ingloriously died of disease or old age were doomed to find their way. There the god Mictlantecutli held awful sway. The Spanish historian, Bernadino de Sahagun, has preserved for us many vivid pictures of its gloomy terrors and of the dread spirits who rendered the hellward pilgrimage fearful even to contemplate.

To reach it involved a four years' journey and the unhappy traveller had to pass between two clashing mountains, to run the gauntlet of an enormous serpent and a monstrous lizard, to traverse eight deserts and as many hills, and to pass through a terrific wind that blew stone knives. But when at last the pilgrim arrived at the deep and wide river Chiconahuapan (Nine Waters), he was met by a friendly red dog, which had been reared in his home, and slain at his funeral by having an arrow thrust down its throat, that it might be there to assist his passage over the water. For some obscure reason it kept its vigil on the farther shore and had to swim across before it could contact its protégé. It is not clear either whether the red dog guided the man's soul to Mictlampa, or merely preceded him to the river, but only that it was there to convey him over the dread water. When the passage had been accomplished, his soul came before Mictlantecutli (Lord of Mictlampa) who directed him to which sphere he must go in the land so graphically described by the Aztec scribe as having neither "light nor window."

An interesting parallel to the Mexican belief that the dog is the guide of the dead is said by Joyce to be held in some districts of Peru. But this country was originally peopled by six distinct nations, and other still more primitive races, which appear to have been eventually absorbed, inhabited adjoining districts. From this medley of sources innumerable traditions, beliefs and customs were inherited, making it impossible to trace any early myth to its derivation; but we may note for our purpose that the Ynca or Quichua tribes excelled as shepherds because of their patience and kindness to animals. This calling would bring them into contact with dogs as guides and guardians of the flocks and may have suggested to them that their protective powers would be extended rather than ended by transition to the Next World. But it was to a black dog that Peruvians assigned the post of honour, and they bred animals of this colour in considerable numbers to ensure that no souls might be left to wander lost and lone in the trackless desert that divided mortals from that larger life which awaited them beyond the grave.

Volumes might be written concerning the beliefs of the American Indians as to the continuance of life on the Other Side. These people number many millions and are divided into a multiplicity of tribes speaking some 760 distinct languages and occupy millions of square miles, so that there can be little or no uniformity in their respective creeds. We have here no space to follow the variations and deviations such conditions entail, but must content ourselves with a single instance that illustrates our theme. This is afforded by the belief of the Catios Indians, in Columbia, that it is essential for the dead to be accompanied by a dog guide to the Spirit-land. They accordingly provide for the necessity, but whether any special variety is consecrated to the purpose, I do not know.

CANINE FUNERAL OBSERVANCES

Long prior to the commencement of the Christian era the dog had not only been domesticated, but its qualities of intelligence, devotion and courage had caused it to be highly valued in China and Tibet. A Tibetan M.S. which is believed to be a retranscription of a document dating from about 3,000 B.C., refers to dogs as having been employed to destroy wolves and herd sheep from the remotest times. Nor did these early Asiatics believe that the animal's mission to man was terminated by death. Not only beyond the grave, but even in this world it still had duties to perform as its master's faithful friend. This is evidenced by the large number of pottery models of dogs found in ancient Chinese tombs, that had been buried alongside the human bodies to enable the watch-dogs to find in them soul-habitations and thus have the means to remain beside their former owners and guard them, here or elsewhere, as they had ever been wont to do.

These images figure the smooth-haired variety of watch-dog which is still common in China today, and in no way resemble the sacred Lion-dog. But the latter also appears to be represented in sepulchres of a later date by certain, somewhat grotesque jade carvings that belong to the Han dynasty (B.C. 206–A.D. 221) though it is certain that the watchdogs date from a much earlier period. The age-old custom of depositing the guardian images of the latter in the tombs was abolished by the celebrated Emperor Yüan, famous for his great learning and enormous library of 140,000 books. Thrusting aside the time-honoured observances of his ancestors, he expressly commanded that the pottery images of dogs which were usually buried with the dead were not to be placed in his tomb. He did not question that the figures enshrined the souls of the animals they represented, yet he dogmatically asserted: "Dogs will not be able to guard my grave."

But his unorthodox opinion was not shared by the last of the Manchu monarchs, the great Dowager Empress Tzu Hsi, whose subjects reverently denominated her "The Venerable Buddha" *(Lao Fo-yeh)*, when she died in 1908, after a tempestuous reign of fifty years. With her there passed the last of a long line of Imperial autocrats who had dominated the destinies of the Celestial Empire for more than four thousand years and her funeral obsequies were performed with fitting ceremonial magnificence. Those who had been her faithful friends whilst she lived among them, built the semblance of an enormous boat and so surrounded it with the sacred flowers of the lotus that it seemed as if floating on a lake. On its deck they placed life-sized figures of her attendants robed in silk, and along with them her furniture, jewels and gowns, the works of art she had valued most highly and models of all she might wish for or hold dear. But, most precious of all, her beloved Lion Dogs were there, ready to accompany her soul when the boat that bore them should be kindled in flames to expedite its voyage to the Better Land. In the funeral procession her own coffin was preceded by her favourite Pekinese dog, led by her chief eunuch; so came to its tragic close the illustrious dynasty of the Imperial house of the Manchus and with it the great Empire of China.

No subject occupies so large a proportion of the Chinese "Classic of Ritual Observances" as the mourning rites of the Chinese. These embrace a variety of sacrifices, symbolic images and observances, which, to uninstructed Western eyes appear somewhat tedious, though each has its special significance for those in the know. Thus to indicate that a corpse is masculine, the statue of a dog is placed on the hearse, and when Li Hung Chang, the great viceroy and foreign counsellor of the Manchu court was buried in 1903, an enormous, and, to European eyes, grotesque image of a Lion Dog was carried in his funeral procession together with many other curious beasts evolved from the fertile imagination of the poetical and creative Chinese to whom symbolism was the normal mode of self-expression.

Many other peoples showing traces of Chinese influence or ancestry have connected the dog with their funeral observances, among whom we may instance the tribe of mountaineers known as the Meo, who dwell in Tongkin in the north-eastern portion of the Indo-Chinese peninsular bordering on China. They are said by Diguet to array the body of a dead man in his best clothes, but are careful to see that all fastenings are loosened lest these impede his soul in its flight. This done they tether a dog on the right-hand side of his corpse so that his spirit may find in it a guide to the unexplored world he has now entered. But according to Baudesson, what he describes as "an interesting variation" of this practice is sometimes followed, in which the image of a dog made of lacquer is provided; this, he ironically remarks, "doubtless serves the purpose as well as the other."

As noted in the chapter concerning the dog as totem, the Kalang aborigines of Java also used effigies of dogs in connexion with their funeral observances, a custom obviously derived from the Chinese who form a large proportion of the population of the island.

The strange hybrid people known as the Gilyaks who inhabit the northern portion of the island of Saghalien (or Sakhalin) lying close off the east coast of the Maritime Province of Siberia were subjects of China till the beginning of the nineteenth century, and inherit strong Mongolian characteristics and beliefs. Among the latter Reclus has recorded their conviction that the soul of a dead man takes refuge at his death in the body of his favourite dog. The animal is sacrificed near his master's corpse, which is burnt or suspended in a coffin, hung on a tree, or laid upon a platform, but Reclus offers no explanation as to why the dead man's soul should thus be deprived of its newly acquired place of refuge and we can only surmise that it may be to compel it to seek a more suitable dwelling, or with the intention of providing the deceased with a canine companion who has closely followed him to the Other World and whose faithful guardianship may be relied on.

BIBLIOGRAPHY

Primitive Folk, by Jean Jacques Elisée. (1890.)
Les Montagnards du Tonguin, p. 143, *et seq.*, by E. Diguet. (Paris, 1902.)
The Dog, Man's Best Friend, p. 26, by Captain A. H. Trapman. (Hutchinson, London, 1929.)

THE SAGDAD OR DOG GAZE

The doctrine most closely associated with the name of Pythagoras is that of metempsychosis, a conception which he probably adopted from the Orphic Mysteries, or, perhaps from Egypt, which he visited *c.* 520 B.C. Once he had accepted the theory he became a most enthusiastic propagandist and founded a new sect at Croton, in the south of Italy, where he taught that the human soul did not expire when its body perished, but entered into the forms of other animals. Nor did he leave this important transition to Karma, or the vagaries of chance when any of his favourite disciples were about to die; he would cause a dog to be held to the mouth of the expiring man to receive his departing soul, with the remark that no other animal was so capable of perpetuating his virtues as that creature. Perhaps some vision or memory of the dog-headed Anubis inspired his words. But, as we know, such ideas were by no means confined to Pythagoras and the philosophers of Egypt, but may be found in recognisable form all over the world and it is to this prototypical thought that we must trace the conception of the *Sagdad* or Dog Gaze which is the subject of this chapter.

The extraordinary veneration with which Parsees regard the dog is explained by them as having arisen from the tradition that their ancestors during their emigration from Persia to India, were nearly driven upon the shores of Guzerat—where their ship would certainly have been wrecked—during a night of inky blackness; but that they were roused from their slumbers and warned of their imminent peril by the timely barking of the dogs on board their ship. Ever since that fateful hour the dog has not only been esteemed by them as the most holy of all animals, but as invested with a special mission to man when man's soul is about to leave his body. The Parsee regards it as guardian and guide in the shadow of death, and considers it to be of the very greatest importance that a dog should be present when a member of their faith is likely to die, as they believe it has the power to drive away the evil spirits who are ever on the watch to seize upon the expiring man's departing soul, and, moreover, will guide him after death to the Heavenly Land. This precaution is known as the sagdad or dog-gaze.

Tavernier, the famous French traveller of the seventeenth century, was greatly shocked by the account given him by a Parsee of the custom, as practised by the Guebres of Surat. The following is his description of the weird rite:

"They have another strange custom—when a person is on the point of death, to take a little dog and place it upon his breast. When they perceive that he is at his last gasp, they apply the dog's muzzle to the dying man's mouth, and make it bark twice when in this position, as if they meant to make the person's soul enter into the dog which they pretend will deliver it unto the angel appointed to receive the same. Moreover if a dog happens to die, they carry it out of the town, and pray to God in behalf of that piece of carrion, as though the brute's soul could derive any advantage from their prayers after its death."

As remarked by Tavernier in his footnote, the custom was even at that date becoming modified, and a more recent account (1920) by the Ven. Godfrey Dale, informs us that whilst the body lies on the bier, a sermon on the brevity of human life and the necessity of virtue is preached by the priest, during which the face of the dead is three or four times exposed to the gaze of a dog. This dog is regarded as a sacred animal and is believed to guide and guard the soul of the deceased on the road to Paradise. But the practice is fast vanishing as modern thought invades the ancient citadels of faith.

Though not considered essential for the effectual performance of the rite, a special variety of dog known as the Four-eyed Dog ought properly to be employed. This animal has a yellow spot on the side of each eyelid, which is regarded as an additional eye. The dog has yellow ears, and his general colouring is yellow and white, which is probably considered as suggestive of the solar rays. The four eyes are said to exert a kind of magnetic influence, and are believed to annihilate the impurities arising from the decomposition of the dead body. The dog was taken three times to gaze at the corpse, and later led back three times along the road traversed by the corpse on its way to burial.

Confirmation of the solar significance of the Parsee ritual may be found in the Mithraic symbol wherein Mithras is portrayed piercing the bull's throat with his dagger, whilst the dog beside his feet licks up the blood that gushes from the wound. But though the obvious interpretation is, as King remarked, "The penetration of the solar ray into the bosom of the earth, by whose action all nature is nourished," yet, he suggests, that "we may also find in it an allusion to the Guebres' belief that the dog affords a vehicle in which the bereft soul may find a refuge."

The Persian Hell is populated by many strange and terrible demons: there are Divs, Drujes, Darvants, Peris, monsters and dragons, all of whom were created by The Evil One: Angra-Mainyu, or Ahriman, the Spirit of Pain, the Plotting Lie, the Rebellion, the Creator of Death, whose dwelling is eternal darkness. Among the Drujes is the Nasu, a female demon, who personifies the corruption of corpses, the most impure of things. To enable her to accomplish her fell purposes she assumes the shape of a fly, but the gaze of a dog will drive her from the dead body.

Dogs were widely recognised as the guardians of the entrance to the nether world and the guides of human souls who had to traverse its perilous pathways. And the importance of the ritual we have been considering is emphasised in the *Zendavesta*, which states that certain dogs possess the power to protect departed spirits from the cruel demons that lie in wait for them on the passage of the narrow bridge that is suspended over the abyss of Hell.

BIBLIOGRAPHY

Six Voyages de F. B. Tavernier, qu'il a faits en Turquie, en Perse, et aux Indes, pendant l'espace de quarante ans, Vol. I, p. 493. (1676–77.)

The Gnostics and their Remains, by C. W. King, M.A. (Nutt, London, 1887.)